MISSION FAILURE

Also by Michael Mandelbaum

The Road to Global Prosperity (2014)

That Used to Be Us: How America Fell Behind in the World It Invented and How We Can Come Back (with Thomas L. Friedman) (2011)

The Frugal Superpower: America's Global Leadership in a Cash-Strapped World (2010)

Democracy's Good Name: The Rise and the Risks of the World's Most Popular Form of Government (2007)

The Case for Goliath: How America Acts as the World's Government in the Twenty-First Century (2006)

The Meaning of Sports: Why Americans Watch Baseball, Football, and Basketball and What They See When They Do (2004)

The Ideas That Conquered the World: Peace, Democracy, and Free Markets in the Twenty-First Century (2002)

The Dawn of Peace in Europe (1996)

The Global Rivals (with Seweryn Bialer) (1988)

The Fate of Nations: The Search for National Security in the Nineteenth and Twentieth Centuries (1988)

Reagan and Gorbachev (with Strobe Talbott) (1987)

The Nuclear Future (1983)

The Nuclear Revolution: International Politics Before and After Hiroshima (1981)

The Nuclear Question: The United States and Nuclear Weapons, 1946–1976 (1979)

MISSION FAILURE

AMERICA AND THE WORLD IN THE POST-COLD WAR ERA

MICHAEL MANDELBAUM

OXFORD
UNIVERSITY PRESS

OXFORD

UNIVERSITY PRESS

Oxford University Press is a department of the University of Oxford. It furthers the
University's objective of excellence in research, scholarship, and education by
publishing worldwide. Oxford is a registered trade mark of Oxford University Press in
the UK and in certain other countries

Published in the United States of America by Oxford University Press
198 Madison Avenue, New York, NY 10016, United States of America.

© Oxford University Press 2016

Cataloging-in-Publication Data is on file with the Library of Congress.
ISBN 978–0–190–46947–4

3 5 7 9 8 6 4 2
Printed by Sheridan, USA

In memory of my brother,

Jonathan Edward Mandelbaum, MD,

1949–1976

. . . we do not think of ourselves as the potential masters, but as tutors of mankind in its pilgrimage to perfection.

— REINHOLD NIEBUHR, *The Irony of American History*

Of course he remains essentially American in believing all questions have answers, that there is an ideal life against which everyday life can be measured . . .

— ANTHONY POWELL, *Temporary Kings*

You Americans are so naive.

— STEVE MARTIN, *Saturday Night Live*

CONTENTS

ACKNOWLEDGMENTS

CONVERSATIONS WITH TWO SUPERB editors, Adam Garfinkle of *The American Interest* and Gideon Rose of *Foreign Affairs,* planted the seeds that grew into this book. I am grateful to them. I am grateful, as well, for advice, assistance, and inspiration of various kinds to the following: Anders Aslund, Steven A. Cook, Robert Danin, Thomas L. Friedman, Leslie H. Gelb, Richard N. Haass, James Klurfeld, David M. Lampton, Starr Lee, Robert J. Lieber, Charles H. Lipson, Robert S. Litwak, Rajan Menon, John Mueller, Michael B. Oren, Daniel Pipes, Robert Satloff, and Dan Schueftan. The usual caveat applies: I alone, and not any of them, am responsible for what follows. Indeed, more than the usual caveat applies: I am confident that most of those I have mentioned will disagree, in some cases strongly, with at least some of what I have written.

It is a pleasure to thank, for financial support in the writing of *Mission Failure*, Daniel Pipes and the Education Fund of the Middle East Forum and the Hertog Foundation. I have enjoyed working on its production with David McBride of Oxford University Press.

My most profound gratitude, and that of longest standing, is to my wife, Anne Mandelbaum, whose wisdom, editorial virtuosity, and love continue to sustain me.

MISSION FAILURE

Introduction

ON MARCH 3, 1991, a ceremony took place in southern Iraq that marked the beginning of a new era in the history of American foreign policy. At the Safwan airbase an American commander, Norman Schwarzkopf, acting for the administration of President George H. W. Bush and accompanied by British, French, and Saudi Arabian officers, agreed on the terms of a ceasefire with an Iraqi general. The war that Iraq's invasion and occupation of tiny, neighboring, oil-rich Kuwait had begun in August 1990 had ended in a decisive victory for the United States and its allies.

The Gulf War, in turn, marked the end of a longer, larger, far more important American conflict: the four-decades-long political, economic, and military struggle with the Soviet Union, its allies and clients, and its ideology, Marxism-Leninism. The end of that conflict, the Cold War, had set the course of the Gulf War. For the first time since 1945, the Soviet Union did not oppose a major American international initiative. The United States was therefore able to assemble a broad international coalition to attack the army of the Iraqi dictator Saddam Hussein and to evict Iraq from Kuwait without fear of interference from Soviet-backed countries. The coalition defeated the Iraqi army swiftly and at very low cost. Although Saddam's Iraq had been a Soviet client and although Soviet officials did attempt to mediate between the Iraqi and American governments, in the end, for the first time since World War II, Moscow sided with Washington.

The opening of the Berlin Wall on November 11, 1989, fifteen months before the Safwan ceremony, symbolized more vividly than any other event the end of the Cold War. The dissolution of the Soviet Union itself, nine months after that ceremony, in December 1991, rendered its ending irreversible. It was, however, the ceremony in the Iraqi desert that made clear the main consequence, for the United States and the world, of the conclusion of what had been, with World Wars I and II, one of the three great, all-encompassing, era-defining global conflicts of the twentieth century. In its wake the United States possessed enormous, perhaps historically unprecedented, and seemingly unchallengeable power. The succeeding era in American foreign policy would be defined by what the United States chose to do with that power.

It could have chosen not to make any particular use of it at all. It could have withdrawn from its far-flung international presence, as it had done after World War I and briefly after World War II. This did not happen. Withdrawal had exposed the country to danger after the two world wars, Americans had become accustomed to an expansive global role, and the burden of that role was not prohibitively heavy. In fact, in the wake of the Cold War the economic burden of America's international activities lightened. Its costliest feature, the military budget, fell from more than seven percent of national output in 1988 to less than four percent by 2000.

Inertia—the tendency of the status quo to continue as long as it is tolerable—is a powerful force in human affairs, and it shaped the American response to the end of the Cold War. The military deployments, the political commitments, the economic institutions that the Cold War had involved had become, by the time Iraq surrendered, familiar and routine. They imposed no particular hardship or even discomfort on the American public, which therefore felt no pressing need to end them. For one particular group of Americans, moreover—the government personnel, academics, journalists, and others professionally concerned with the conduct of the nation's foreign policy, as well as the larger number of citizens for whom foreign policy had become an abiding interest—*dis*continuity in the American role in the world would have caused disruption and imposed hardship. Unlike the rest of the country, the informal, loosely connected American foreign policy community cared deeply about relations with the rest of the world. The members of that community, although divided on specific issues, strongly favored sustaining an expansive international role.[1]

So the United States did not appreciably reduce its international presence when the conflict with the Soviet Union ended, and in the wake of that conflict American foreign policy exhibited considerable continuity. Or rather, the *forms* of foreign policy—the institutions engaged in carrying it out—continued. The *content* of that policy—the goals the United States pursued—did change. Indeed, they broke with the pattern of foreign policy of the preceding four decades and of the entire history of the country before the Cold War. In fact, in its main objectives, post-Cold War American foreign policy differed sharply from the foreign policies of most countries for most of recorded history. The United States used the formidable power with which it emerged from the conflict with the Soviet Union in a distinctive and unprecedented way.

————

THE NEW ERA IN American foreign policy began in the aftermath of the meeting at the Safwan airbase that ended the Gulf war of 1991. The Kurds of northern Iraq, ethnically separate from the Sunni Arabs who dominated the country and from whose ranks Saddam Hussein had come, rose up in rebellion against him and them. Although routed by the American-led coalition, the Sunni-dominated Iraqi army retained enough firepower to crush the Kurds. Thousands were killed and hundreds of thousands put to flight. By the end of April two million of them were crowded along the country's borders with Iran and Turkey.

Moved by the Kurds' suffering, feeling pressure from its ally Turkey to shield it from a flood of Kurdish refugees, and equipped with United Nations Security Resolution 688 that laid the basis for intervention by designating the Kurds' plight a threat to "the international peace and security of the region," the United States and its coalition partners moved to protect them. Several thousand American, British, and other troops established a safe haven in northern Iraq and provided food and shelter to the beleaguered Kurds. Allied military aircraft patrolled the skies above the region to prevent further attacks by the Iraqi armed forces, establishing a "no-fly zone" that was to endure for the next twelve years.[2]

Although it followed directly from the Gulf War, the establishment of the Kurdish protective zone departed sharply from the principles for which the winning coalition had fought that conflict, from American policy during the Cold War, and indeed from the foreign policies of almost every country throughout history. The war had been waged in response to Iraq's external behavior. Its aim was to reverse Iraqi aggression across an international border against another sovereign state. Since the Kurdish region was located within what all countries recognized as Iraq's legitimate borders, by setting up a safe haven there the United States and its allies inserted themselves into Iraqi internal politics.

Moreover, America had gone to war against Saddam's army of occupation in Kuwait on the assumption that if his aggression were allowed to stand he would be able to intimidate neighboring Saudi Arabia and exert control over the oil of the Persian Gulf, the unimpeded flow of which to oil-consuming countries was crucial for their economic welfare. By contrast, the United States intervened in the wake of that war to help an embattled people whose distress, while troubling, could have no effect on the well-being of American citizens.

The operation to rescue the Kurds thus represented a major change: Saddam's attack on Kuwait threatened American interests; his assault on the Kurds affronted American values. The Gulf War was an act of self-defense. The intervention, tellingly named "Operation Provide Comfort," was a good deed. As such, it established the dominant pattern of American foreign policy in the post-Cold War era. Without announcing it, without debating it, without even fully realizing it, the goals of American foreign policy changed fundamentally.

For two decades thereafter the principal international initiatives of the United States concerned the internal politics and economics rather than the external behavior of other countries. The main focus of American foreign policy shifted from war to governance, from what other governments did beyond their borders to what they did and how they were organized within them. Invariably, the United States sought to make the internal governance of the countries with which it became entangled more like its own democratic, constitutional order and those of its Western allies. In the Cold War the United States had aimed at containment; in the post-Cold War period the thrust of American foreign policy was transformation. The Cold War involved the defense of the West; post-Cold War foreign policy aspired to the political and ideological extension of the West.[3]

The United States had taken an interest in the internal affairs of other countries before 1991. American military intervention in its southern neighbor Mexico, and in the smaller, even weaker countries of Central America to Mexico's south, began in the nineteenth century and continued well into the twentieth. During the Vietnam War the United States tried, unsuccessfully, to reform the government of South Vietnam so that it could win the contest with the communist North for "the hearts and minds" of the Vietnamese people. But the American government undertook those initiatives as part of broader policies that had more traditional goals: it fought the war in Vietnam, for example, as part of the policy of protecting the United States from global communism. Only in the post-Cold War period did the internal affairs of other countries become the primary focus of American foreign policy. That is what made this period distinctive. What had been a hobby became a full-time job.

Nor had countries other than the United States steered entirely clear of the governance of foreign peoples. To the contrary, powerful states that controlled empires, the dominant form of political organization until the twentieth century, bore direct responsibility for governing them. The United States itself, although the child of a revolt against British imperial rule and generally opposed to empire throughout its history, did govern the Philippines directly from 1898 to 1946.[4] Most imperial powers, however, had minimal concern for the way their imperial possessions were organized politically, being interested simply in maintaining control of them. They regarded their empires for the most part as vehicles for expanding their own wealth and power, not for improving the welfare of those they governed.[5]

Furthermore, by 1991 the age of empire had ended. Governing others had acquired a moral taint and had, in any event, become too expensive to be worthwhile. Whatever Americans thought was the purpose of their post-Cold War foreign policies, they certainly did not consider themselves to be following in the footsteps of the British, the French, the Habsburgs, or the Ottomans in acquiring and managing a grand imperial domain.

The emphasis on the domestic arrangements of other countries was common to the foreign policies of the 42nd, 43rd, and 44th presidents: Bill Clinton, George W. Bush, and Barack Obama. To be sure, they and the foreign policy officials they employed did not think of themselves as pursuing the same foreign policy. To almost all observers of American foreign policy, moreover, and to the American public as well, the most important feature of the first two post-Cold War decades seemed to be the division of the period into two sharply different parts. The terrorist attacks on New York City and Washington, DC midway through that period, on September 11, 2001, changed everything, or so Americans believed.

The attacks did in fact change a great deal, profoundly affecting the course of the nation's foreign policy over the decade that followed. The principal initiatives of the George W. Bush administration would not have taken place but for the events of September 11. Yet those initiatives led to the same kind of effort to transform the domestic political structures of other countries that the Clinton administration had undertaken.

The Clinton and Bush foreign policies had another feature in common: neither administration deliberately set out on missions of transformation. They embarked on these missions for different, and varying, reasons. In its policies toward China and Russia, the Clinton administration was largely responding to domestic pressures in the United States. In conducting military operations in Somalia, Haiti, Bosnia, and Kosovo, the Clinton officials sought to protect the people living in those places from the depredations of the local authorities. The administration of George W. Bush launched two substantial wars, in Afghanistan and Iraq, for the most traditional of reasons: to defend American security in response to a direct attack on the United States. Those two administrations and the one that followed, that of Barack Obama, all devoted time, money, and political capital to another familiar international activity seemingly unrelated to the internal affairs of the parties involved: mediation between Israelis and Arabs.

Yet all three administrations ended in the same place. All their initiatives led the United States—despite the original aims and sometimes without the American government fully realizing what was happening—into efforts to transform the political institutions, the political practices, and the political values of China, Russia, Somalia, Haiti, Bosnia, Kosovo, Afghanistan, Iraq, and the wider Arab world. Post-Cold War American foreign policy produced a two-decades-long series of unintended consequences. Why did this happen?

The fundamental reason that the United States concentrated on trying to transform domestic political and economic practices in selected places around the world was that it could. No other country or coalition of countries was in a position to stop it. America's enormous power, the vast superiority in disposable resources over all other countries that the 1991 Gulf War demonstrated, is the pervasive underlying cause of the direction that post-Cold War American foreign policy took.

Historically, most political communities have lacked the strength even to aspire to remake the way others are governed. Those sovereign states that were not weak, the great powers, had to devote their resources to protecting themselves against other great powers, as the United States had to do against the Soviet Union from 1945 to 1991. After the Cold War, by contrast, America had no major adversary against which it had to defend itself. In 1796 the nation's first president, George Washington, foresaw a day when his infant country would "possess the strength of a Giant and there will be none who can make us afraid."[6] With the end of the Cold War, that day had come.

Power is to sovereign states in the international system what money is to individuals: the more they have, the wider is the range of uses to which they can put it. Most countries most of the time, like most people most of the time, live in a world of scarcity. They must husband their resources for the necessities: security in the case of nations, food and shelter for individuals. Some people, however, are skillful enough or fortunate enough (or both) to amass a great deal of money, which they can spend in many other ways. The United States after the Cold War found itself in an analogous position: it became the equivalent of a very wealthy person, the multibillionaire among nations. It left the realm of necessity that it had inhabited during the Cold War and entered the world of choice.[7] It chose to spend some of its vast reserves of power on the geopolitical equivalent of luxury items: the remaking of other countries. While its enormous post-Cold War strength gave it the *opportunity* to choose, however, that strength did not, by itself, determine the choice that America made. That choice had three additional causes.

First, restructuring the domestic affairs of the countries where the United States attempted to do this seemed necessary to consolidate other gains. China and Russia had become far less bellicose and much more friendly to the United States at the outset of the 1990s than when both were orthodox communist countries. Promoting respect for human rights by the Chinese government and working free markets in Russia, the Clinton administration calculated, would reinforce these positive post-Cold War trends. That administration sent American troops to Somalia, Haiti, Bosnia, and Kosovo to relieve hunger, combat oppression, and stop massacres, which led to efforts to construct stable, decent governments in order to ensure that such outrages would not recur. The George W. Bush administration, having removed regimes hostile to the United States and dangerous to their own people in Afghanistan and Iraq, found itself deeply engaged in the internal affairs of those two countries in order to prevent similar (or even more dangerous) governments from gaining power.

Second, in the wake of the Cold War, building Western-style political and economic institutions seemed—albeit erroneously—eminently feasible. The whole world appeared to be moving in that direction. Democracy was on the march: between 1970 and 2010, by one count, the number of democratic governments worldwide increased from 30 to 119.[8] Free markets as the form of economic organization were more popular still, embraced even by governments such as China's that disdained political democracy. In seeking to build these institutions where they did not yet exist, the United States had cause to believe that it was pushing on an already open door.

The third reason that successive post-Cold War American administrations chose to concentrate on trying to encourage and even implant Western institutions in a series of non-Western countries is that this came naturally to Americans. The impulse to do so is an old and deeply rooted one in the United States. It is part of the country's political and cultural DNA. It goes all the way back to the first European settlers in

North America, who crossed the Atlantic not only to escape religious persecution but also to found communities that would serve as models for others. They wanted these communities to become, to use the Old Testament idiom in which they were steeped, "a light unto the nations." In 1630, while still on shipboard sailing to Massachusetts Bay, the Puritan leader John Winthrop told his fellow passengers that their new settlement would be "a city upon a hill," to be observed, admired, and emulated by the rest of the world. Three hundred fifty years later the American president Ronald Reagan was fond of using those words to describe the United States, a fondness that testifies to the enduring resonance of the idea they expressed.

Americans, in short, have always believed that they have a vocation to improve the world and have always wished to carry it out by helping others become more like themselves. The enormous power with which their country emerged from the Cold War gave them an unprecedented opportunity to attempt to do just that. Post-Cold War American foreign policy consists of their government's responses to that opportunity.

The responses had a religious overtone, and not surprisingly: from the moment that the Puritans landed at Plymouth Rock in Massachusetts in 1620, religion has shaped America. Because it is a country, founded by religious people for religious reasons, in which religious belief has always been strong, religious ideas and practices have played a part in America's public life. The English writer G. K. Chesterton called the United States "a country with the soul of a church." Its post-Cold War foreign policy bears a resemblance to one particular feature of America's religious tradition: the dispatch of missionaries abroad to convert nonbelievers. In the nineteenth century many of the Americans who traveled and lived in other countries were Protestant missionaries. In the twentieth century the American government established a secular version of their missions, one designed to spread the values, skills, and institutions that Americans considered crucial for success— above all economic success—in the modern world. It was called the Peace Corps. The main international initiatives of the United States in the last decade of the twentieth century and the first decade of the twenty-first had the same purpose, but on a far larger scale: they aimed to convert not simply individuals but entire countries.

These missions had a common feature. They all failed.

―――――

THE UNITED STATES DID not succeed in getting China to protect human rights, or in constructing smoothly functioning free markets or genuinely representative political institutions in Russia. It did not succeed in installing well-run, widely accepted governments in Somalia, Haiti, Bosnia, or Kosovo. It did not transform Afghanistan or Iraq into tolerant, effectively administered countries. It did not bring democracy to the Middle East or harmony between Israelis and Arabs.

As is customary in American public life, the government's policies designed to do these things came in for vigorous criticism while they were under way, and in every case the critics had a point: the policies were not perfect. The undoubted flaws in the way the United States carried out its post-Cold War missions, however, do not bear the main responsibility for their failures.

Nor were those failures due chiefly to the investment of insufficient resources, although that shortcoming was present as well: in some cases the United States could have done more than it did. Here, American foreign policy suffered from a contradiction. The enormous power of the United States made it possible to undertake the tasks the United States attempted in the Balkans, Africa, East Asia, the Middle East, and the Western Hemisphere. On the other hand, Americans turn out to be willing to underwrite long, painful, expensive projects abroad only for the purpose of meeting what they deem major threats to their own well-being, which historically have come from powerful countries that oppose the United States. So the feature of the post-Cold War world that made the American government's principal international project possible—the absence of a serious challenge to American security—also limited the resources the American public was willing to authorize to carry it out. The most important limits on what the United States was able to do when it intervened after the Cold War came not from without but from within. They came less from the resistance of other countries than from the reluctance of Americans to support what their government was trying to do.

Still, the principal reason for the failure of American efforts to improve other countries lay elsewhere—specifically, in the nature of what the

United States was attempting. It did not achieve its goals because those goals were not achievable with the available tools. The tools of foreign policy are guns, money, and words implying that either or both will be used. These can and do affect what other countries do outside their own borders; they are far less effective in shaping what other countries are like within those borders. In making the domestic transformation of other countries the object of its foreign policy, the American government resembled someone trying to open a can with a sponge. It unwittingly embarked on variations on what was, to borrow a phrase, mission impossible.

What the United States was trying to do and failed to do was commonly labeled "nation-building." In fact, the failed American missions involved two tasks. One was building nations, that is fostering a sense of national community among people of different backgrounds. The other is more appropriately termed "state-building": the creation of working political institutions. America failed at both endeavors for the simple reason that neither was within its power to accomplish.

After World War I the victors decided that the borders of states should coincide with those of nations: groups with a common language, or ethnicity, or history, or some combination thereof should have a common government. The nation-state became, and remains, the most familiar and widely accepted large-scale political unit. Sometimes, however, the borders of states and the location of national groups do not match: nations are dispersed among more than one state; two or more national groups live in a single state. The desire of divided nations to live in the same jurisdiction, and the determination of one nation not to permit another to dominate the state in which they both dwell, can lead to violence. That is what happened in Bosnia, in Kosovo, in Afghanistan, and in Iraq.

The United States could and did compel Serbs to live with Muslims in Bosnia and Sunni and Shia Muslim Arabs and Kurds to remain within the framework of a single Iraq; but Washington could not and therefore did not get them to do so voluntarily or peacefully in the absence of a military presence from the outside. Enduring American success required the creation of a widely shared Bosnian, or Kosovar, or Afghan, or Iraqi identity to supplant the narrower allegiances that had provoked conflict; but the United States, although the most powerful country in the world, did not have the capacity to do this.

As for state-building, establishing the institutions of government—courts, legislatures, administrative agencies—as the United States attempted to do, or to help to do, in Russia, in Haiti, in the Balkans, and in Afghanistan and Iraq—is inherently difficult. It involves changes in the habits, the skills, and the beliefs of the many people who must operate these institutions and the many, many more who must support and accept them. This cannot be accomplished quickly. It is at least a generation-long project.

It is all the more difficult without a consensus on the location of borders. People will not cooperate in building and supporting the institutions of a state if they do not want to live in that state or believe that the institutions, once built, will be used to their detriment. State-building is even more difficult when the institutions being built are supposed to be transparent, accountable, and respectful of individual liberty, which was invariably the post-Cold War American goal.

Yet another difficulty hindered American state-building, the same kind of difficulty that obstructed nation-building: loyalties of narrower scope than the project required. To function properly modern institutions must command universal compliance with impersonal rules. This is especially important for the rule of law. The natural allegiance of human beings, by contrast, is neither universal nor impersonal: it is to other people either with whom they have ties of blood or to whom they are bound by a history of reciprocal assistance.[9] The world has many such societies, including in China, Russia, Somalia, Afghanistan, and Iraq.

American foreign policy after the Cold War did not consist entirely of failure. The United States achieved some successes as well. It did not persuade the Chinese government to respect human rights, or make Russia a stable democracy, but it did find, briefly, a workable post-Cold War relationship with China and see Russia establish rough-and-ready free markets out of the ruins of the Soviet planned economy. It did not bring peace to Israel and the Palestinians, but its efforts seemed to make the Middle East, temporarily in the 1990s, a somewhat more peaceful place. Moreover, American military operations succeeded everywhere. The threat of force ended a military dictatorship in Haiti. The American military twice defeated or helped to defeat Serb forces in the Balkans and dislodged the Taliban regime in Afghanistan and that of Saddam Hussein in Iraq. All these victories—against, it is true, very weak adversaries—came at relatively low cost to America. The *military* missions that the United States undertook succeeded. It was the *political* missions that followed, the efforts to transform the politics of the places where American arms had prevailed, that failed.

The successes as well as the failures of American policies toward Russia and China in the 1990s are the subjects of Chapter 1. Chapter 2 deals with the military operations, and their aftermaths, in Somalia, Haiti, Bosnia, and Kosovo—the "humanitarian" interventions of the Clinton years. The American experiences in Afghanistan and Iraq are the subjects of Chapters 3 and 4, respectively, and Chapter 5 addresses the American record in the Middle East beyond Iraq during the three post-Cold War presidential administrations.

In retrospect, the initiatives that seized the country's attention and claimed its resources did not concern the issues that mattered most for the long-term security and well-being of the United States and the rest of the world. What Americans considered urgent was not what was important. What *was* important was the American role as the chief custodian of the benign international order that had emerged from the end of the Cold War. Making particular countries better by American standards, which the main initiatives of American foreign policy aimed to do, mattered less than keeping the world as a whole from getting worse. Just how well the United States did on this score is the subject of Chapter 6.

Together the chapters tell the story of good, sometimes noble, and thoroughly American intentions coming up against the deeply embedded, often harsh, and profoundly un-American realities of places far from the United States. In this encounter the realities prevailed.

I

China, the Global Economy, and Russia

[The Chinese government] is on the wrong side of history.
— BILL CLINTON TO CHINESE LEADER JIANG ZEMIN ON CHINA'S
HUMAN RIGHTS POLICY[1]

. . . expanding NATO would be the most fateful error of American foreign policy in the entire post-Cold War era.
— GEORGE F. KENNAN[2]

A New Administration in a New World

In the 1992 campaign that made him the 42nd president of the United States, Bill Clinton frequently invoked the memory of the nation's 35th chief executive, John F. Kennedy. The campaign showed a video of the candidate as a 17-year-old high school student from Arkansas shaking Kennedy's hand at the White House in 1963. He visited Kennedy's gravesite at Arlington National Cemetery, across the Potomac River from Washington, DC, during the week of his inauguration. In his speech after taking the oath of office he sounded one of the themes of Kennedy's inaugural address 32 years earlier: generational change.[3]

Both new administrations marked a transition from one generation to the next. Kennedy's assumption of office passed the presidency from the supreme commander in Europe in World War II, Dwight Eisenhower, to a man who had served as a junior naval officer in the Pacific in that conflict and had been born in 1917, two years after Eisenhower graduated from West Point. Similarly, Clinton had been born in 1946, the year after World War II had ended, and was the same age as the eldest son of his predecessor, George H. W. Bush. Like John

Kennedy, the senior Bush had been a naval officer in the Pacific in that war and turned out to be the last of the seven American presidents to have served in it.

In another and more important way, however, the circumstances of Clinton's assumption of power could not have been more different than those surrounding the beginning of the Kennedy presidency. The world in Kennedy's thousand days in office was the same as Eisenhower's: both were dominated by the Cold War. The world that Clinton inherited, by contrast, differed dramatically from the one in which his predecessor had taken power a mere four years earlier. In that period a revolution in international affairs had taken place, brought about by the end of the Cold War.

In this way the 1992 American presidential election resembled the watershed 1945 general election in Great Britain, in which British voters replaced the government of Winston Churchill, the prime minister who had led them, with eloquence and determination, through World War II with one formed by the opposition Labour Party. The British electorate decided that it could dispense with the services of the man who came to be regarded as the greatest Englishman of his time, and perhaps of any time, because the war over which he had presided had ended in victory. The moment had come, the British concluded, to concentrate on domestic matters, especially issues of social welfare. For this, they believed, the Labourites were better suited. The 1992 American election turned on the same point: Bill Clinton was elected because the Cold War had come to an end.

A telling sign of the impact of that conflict's end on presidential politics was the fact that Clinton, unlike all nine chief executives who followed Franklin D. Roosevelt, had never served in the armed forces.[4] Because each of the nine had presided over the global struggle with the Soviet Union, all had been wartime presidents. The constitutionally mandated presidential role as commander-in-chief had seemed especially important to American voters, who had regarded service in the military as an important qualification for that role.

Indeed, Roosevelt's term of office had given rise to the dual responsibilities of the twentieth-century presidency. For the first part of his 12 years in the White House he had functioned as "Dr. New Deal," implementing a variety of measures designed to pull the United States out of the worldwide economic slump known as the Great Depression. After the Japanese attack on Pearl Harbor of December 7, 1941, he had become "Dr. Win-the-War," presiding over the conflict with Japan in Asia and Nazi Germany in Europe. Each of his successors, through George H. W. Bush, assumed responsibility for both the nation's economic well-being at home and its security abroad. Clinton, by contrast, was elected to deal only with the first.

He had emphasized economic concerns during his presidential campaign. The electorate displayed little interest in foreign policy issues, to the disadvantage of Clinton's principal opponent, the incumbent president, who had guided the country skillfully through the end of the Cold War. In foreign policy George H. W. Bush was the most consequential and most successful American president since Harry Truman. American voters rewarded him for his achievement with the lowest percentage of the popular vote any president had ever earned in seeking re-election. An unusual feature of that presidential year was the independent candidacy of the multimillionaire businessman H. Ross Perot, who won almost 19 percent of the popular vote. Perot's signature promise was to reduce the fiscal deficit of the federal government, and deficit reduction is quintessentially a peacetime issue. During wartime, governments spend whatever is necessary to win, or to avoid losing. Only when wars end does fiscal responsibility rise to the top of the public agenda, as it did in the United States in 1992. Despite its echoes of John F. Kennedy's theme of generational change, Bill Clinton's first inaugural address did not, like Kennedy's, concentrate on foreign policy; it emphasized instead the challenges America faced at home. Shortly after taking office he promised to "focus like a laser" on the American economy.

Since the United States did not withdraw from the global positions it had assumed and the international commitments it had made during the Cold War, the Clinton administration could not ignore the world entirely. It had to have a foreign policy, and here, as the first post-Cold War presidency,[5] it faced a problem that had not affected its Cold-War predecessors. Their foreign policies had had a straightforward purpose: the containment of communist power and influence around the world. No comparably clear and compelling goal presented itself in 1993. The Clinton administration had to decide, as its predecessors had not, what the United States should do in the world.

After nine months of criticism that the administration was failing to offer a new foreign policy appropriate for the new, post-Cold War era, its National Security Advisor, W. Anthony Lake, announced one in a speech on September 21, 1993. "The successor to a doctrine of containment," he said, "must be a strategy of enlargement—enlargement of the world's community of market democracies."

While the term enlargement was an awkward one—evoking a medical condition rather than a great, heroic, national enterprise— transforming the internal politics and economics of other countries by fostering democratic political systems and free-market economies turned out to be just what the administration for which Lake spoke, and its successor, tried to do. The United States did undertake the mission of enlargement.

Despite Lake's words, however, this was not what the Clinton administration or the George W. Bush administration that followed it deliberately set out to do when each embarked on the foreign policies that turned into missions of domestic transformation. Nor did expressing the goal in these general terms offer useful guidelines for achieving it. Enlargement, as set forth by the Clinton administration, was an aspiration, not a program, a slogan rather than a strategy.

Without the clear guidelines available to its predecessors, in choosing its foreign policies the new administration followed not so much a strategy as a procedure. Those policies emerged from a familiar process of governmental decision-making in the United States: the interplay of domestic political interests and pressures.

Such a process does not determine all American public policies and did not determine foreign policy during the Cold War. In the United States, political issues fall into one of two different categories. A handful of them rise to the level of national importance. They affect the whole country, often in profound ways. They are the subjects of major public debates. They decide elections. The policies the country follows on these first-order issues, that is, emerge from public deliberations and have the support of the majority of the country.

Most issues are not like that. They do not have major significance. Many in this second category involve the allocation of resources on what qualifies—although they can involve billions of dollars—as a small scale: subsidies for one economic interest or another, for example, or provisions of the tax code that affect very few of the 320 million Americans. Relatively few people care (or even know) about these issues, and some of the few who do care can often get their way, small though their numbers are. Minorities rather than majorities rule here in the sense that the vast majority of the public is disengaged and a well-organized, highly motivated, and often well-financed minority can get its preferences adopted by the executive branch, or enacted into law by the Congress, or both.

Questions of war and peace, in which American lives are at stake, fall into the first category. During the Cold War, most foreign policy issues were connected to the great central conflict with the Soviet Union and international communism and thus captured the attention of the country as a whole. Foreign policy debates, sometimes extensive and often acrimonious, had large audiences. The participants in those debates invariably argued that the course they were proposing would maximize American power and security and thereby serve the interest of the nation as a whole. The 1960 presidential election, for example, which made John F. Kennedy president, was dominated by a debate between him and his Republican opponent, then Vice President Richard M. Nixon, about which of them would more vigorously prosecute the conflict with the Soviet Union.

By 1993, when Bill Clinton took office, foreign policy issues had been relegated to the second and less important category. With the stakes far lower than in the past, such issues were of parochial not national concern. Domestic interests and pressures had greater scope for influence in deciding American foreign policy than had been the case for decades. Accordingly, it was such interests and pressures that determined the Clinton administration's major initiatives toward the two large, formerly orthodox communist countries, China and Russia.

China and Human Rights

The single consistent feature of the history of relations between the United States and China is inconsistency. The relationship has undergone a series of reversals, from friendship to antagonism and back again,[6] and one of these reversals set the stage for the Clinton China policy. The American encounter with the world's most populous country began in the nineteenth century, when missionaries first undertook to spread Christianity among the Chinese: the sense of mission that animated post-Cold War American foreign policy informed the country's relations with China, albeit in religious rather than secular form, from the very beginning.[7]

At the end of the nineteenth century the American government joined the European imperial powers in carving out special economic zones along the China coast. In the wake of World War I, however, the United States took the opposite position, trying, unsuccessfully, to defend China against imperial encroachment by Japan and siding with the Chinese government against the Japanese in World War II.

In the post-1945 Chinese civil war the United States supported the losing side, Chiang Kai-shek's Kuomintang, the members of which fled to the island of Taiwan after their defeat. In 1950 the winners, Mao Zedong's communists, intervened in the Korean War on the side of communist North Korea against the United States. There followed two decades of hostility between them during which their governments had virtually no official contact.

Yet another reversal took place in 1972. After secret diplomatic preparations President Richard Nixon made a visit to China in February of that year, inaugurating a period in which the two countries were militarily and politically aligned if not formally allied. Common opposition to America's primary Cold-War adversary the Soviet Union, initially the patron of but by the 1970s at odds with Mao's China (the two countries engaged in brief, small-scale border skirmishes in 1969), underlay their rapprochement. It followed one of the oldest of rules of geopolitics: the enemy of my enemy is my friend.

More than geopolitical calculations drew the two powers closer together. In 1979, three years after Mao's death, China began to introduce market practices into its economy, which triggered an extraordinary run of three decades of double-digit annual economic growth. The strict Maoist-era controls on all aspects of Chinese life loosened considerably. Foreigners began to visit China and Chinese to travel abroad, both in large numbers. The United States and other countries began to trade with and invest in China, a sea change from the Maoist era when the Chinese economy was largely cut off from the rest of the world.

These developments gave Americans the impression, an accurate one, that China was changing rapidly. From this many inferred—inaccurately, as events would show—that the country was shedding the political as well as the economic system the Communist Party had imposed on it after 1949. Returning from his visit to Beijing in 1984, President Ronald Reagan referred to "this so-called communist China." Because the impression that Reagan expressed had such wide currency in the United States, the events of June 3 and 4, 1989, in Tiananmen Square in the heart of Beijing, came as a rude shock and led to yet another reversal in Soviet-American relations, which the Clinton administration inherited.

On April 15 of that year Hu Yaobang, a reform-minded leader of the Chinese Communist Party who had been removed from office two years earlier, died in the Chinese capital. Mourners gathered in Tiananmen Square in a rare public display of sympathy. In the following days the crowd there grew larger and similar groups gathered in 341 cities across the country,[8] initially to show their respect for Mr. Hu but increasingly also to demonstrate their support for the reformist ideas with which he was associated, which the Communist Party had resisted implementing, and to protest government policies they disliked. In Tiananmen Square itself students declared a hunger strike on May 13 to press their agenda. Many residents of Beijing came out to support them: the number of people in the square ultimately reached an estimated one million.[9]

The government cracked down. It declared martial law and sent troops to disperse the crowd in Beijing, firing on unarmed civilians and killing hundreds of them.[10] In the aftermath of the assault the regime arrested thousands of Chinese it suspected of political dissidence. Many of them lost their jobs or were jailed, in some cases after televised show trials. Some who managed to escape arrest fled the country. The harsh, brutal communist government intolerant of any political opposition that Americans had thought had disappeared from China had returned with a vengeance—or rather, had never left. Accordingly, public opinion in America turned against that government. In a February 1989 national survey, 72 percent of the respondents registered a favorable view of China. Six months later opinion had reversed: 58 percent had an unfavorable view.[11] In these circumstances, politicians in the United

States sought ways to express the disapproval that their constituents (and they themselves) felt.

The expression came from the Congress, the branch of the American government most closely attuned to public opinion. Many of the 43,000 Chinese who were studying in the United States[12] in 1989 decided that they did not wish to return to China, as required by the visas they held. The Congress enacted a law permitting them to stay. It passed the House of Representatives by a margin of 403 to 0, and was approved by a voice vote in the Senate.[13]

In early 1990, the Congress went further both in expressing its displeasure with the Chinese government's conduct and in trying to change it. By the terms of the Jackson-Vanik amendment to the 1974 Trade Act, China, as a country with a non-market economy, could only receive Most Favored Nation (MFN) trade status from the United States, a status that made possible the expanding volume of Sino-American commerce, by the designation of the president. Jimmy Carter had supplied the required designation in 1979 and his successors had renewed it annually. In 1990 the House voted 384 to 30 in favor of a bill requiring that, before extending its MFN status for another year, the president certify that China's government had improved its performance on human rights. The Senate did not take up the bill, but trade privileges became the focal point of Sino-American relations.

President George H. W. Bush opposed the direction in which the Congress sought to take America's China policy. In the immediate aftermath of June 4 he froze the military relationship between the two countries, moved to cut off international loans to China, and suspended high-level contacts between the two governments. At the same time, however, he tried to insulate, as far as possible, the relationship between the two countries from the popular hostility toward the Chinese regime in the United States. In fact, at the end of June, contrary to the suspension of high-level contacts he had ordered, he sent his National Security Advisor, Brent Scowcroft, on a secret trip to Beijing to reassure the Chinese leadership of his commitment to good relations and dispatched him to China again in December. These trips, when they became known, generated considerable criticism in the United States. The critics, invoking the custom in the imperial Chinese court of compelling all visitors to prostrate themselves before the emperor, accused the Bush administration of "kowtowing" to China. Despite the criticism, in 1991, when a bill linking MFN to Chinese human rights policy passed both houses of Congress, Bush vetoed it.[14]

As a one-time American representative in Beijing as well as a former director of the Central Intelligence Agency and vice president, Bush believed strongly in the strategic importance of Sino-American military and political cooperation. As president, he believed that he, not the Congress, should control China policy. The public outrage in the United States at what the Chinese government had done in Tiananmen Square and afterward, however, tilted the balance of power within the American political system on relations with China against him, which changed Sino-American relations in two important ways.

First, in a break from the pattern established in 1972, in which that relationship had been handled, discreetly and often secretly, by a few senior officials on both sides, after June 4, 1989, it entered the hurly-burly of domestic American politics. In contrast to the past, the public and their elected representatives insisted on having a say in American policy toward China. Second, whereas since 1972 the relationship had involved only geopolitical considerations, above all the common threat from the Soviet Union, in the wake of Tiananmen, domestic issues in China became relevant. Once Sino-American relations had been concerned solely with matters of power—that is, with America's interests. After Tiananmen, by contrast, the political values and political practices of the two countries entered the picture. American policy toward China ceased to be based exclusively on the Chinese government's policies toward the Soviet Union and took into account that government's policies toward its own people.

This represented a departure from the practice of the late 1970s. At that time, President Jimmy Carter had made the protection of human rights around the world central to the foreign policy of his administration. He had not, however, included China on his list of major human-rights violators, even when pro-democracy activists in Beijing invoking his policies had been jailed.[15] George H. W. Bush sought to treat China as Carter had, but failed.

The Chinese government did not respect or protect human rights. The Communist Party's monopoly of power, with the prerogative of using that power however it chose, was the central, defining feature of the Chinese political system. If the government were obliged to respect the rights of individual Chinese, the country would have a fundamentally different political system. It would no longer be communist. The condition the Congress sought to require for the extension of MFN status amounted to a demand for a political revolution in China. This the leaders of the Communist Party were determined to prevent, for self-interested reasons as well as, no doubt, because at least some of them genuinely believed their rule to be essential for the country's welfare.

The crackdown of June 3 and 4, 1989, and the months thereafter certainly violated human rights, but this episode was far from the first, or the worst, such violation the Communist Party of China had committed. Mao and his henchmen had killed millions of people upon first taking power in China and hundreds of thousands of Chinese had died or were persecuted in the Mao-inspired upheaval of the late 1960s known as the Cultural Revolution. The Great Leap Forward of the late 1950s, a Maoist campaign designed to force the pace of industrialization in the country, caused a famine in which as many as 30 million Chinese perished. Measured by the scale of suffering they produced, the policies of the second half of 1989 are modest indeed compared with previous communist atrocities in China; yet Tiananmen and its aftermath aroused a stronger reaction in the United States.

The principal reason for the difference lies in the fact that the world outside China did not know of the earlier horrors. The country was closed to foreigners. By 1989, by contrast, the international press had established itself in Beijing. From April through June of that year journalists transmitted eyewitness accounts of the protests. Some of the events were televised, and commanded unusually large audiences.[16] One image in particular captured the world's imagination: a single Chinese man standing in front of a column of four tanks on Chang'an Avenue, one of Beijing's main thoroughfares. The picture crystallized the way Americans had come to see China: as the site of a clash between individual bravery in the quest for freedom, on the one hand, and a ruthless communist military juggernaut, on the other. The American public, not surprisingly, sided with the "tank man" against the Communist Party and its tanks.

Congress acted to try to compel the Chinese government to respect human rights out of a natural sympathy for the protester and other

Chinese men and women who lived under what the Tiananmen episode had revealed to be oppressive communist rule. At the same time, a change in the context of the Sino-American relationship weakened the contrary impulse, to protect the military and political ties between the two countries, the impulse that had motivated President Bush. The Tiananmen events also illustrated that change. In mid-May, with the demonstrations well under way, Mikhail Gorbachev, the leader of the Soviet Union, made the first official visit of the principal Soviet leader to China in 30 years. The welcoming ceremony was scheduled to take place in Tiananmen Square but had to be moved. The visit marked the end of the hostility between the two countries that had propelled China into alignment with the United States in 1972. Gorbachev symbolized, however, an even more important development: the end of the Cold War itself. His visit was part of the transformation of international politics that he himself had initiated and that culminated two and a half years later with the end of the Soviet Union.

Because the Cold War was clearly winding down in June 1989, the United States had less need than before of a partnership with China that required ignoring the communist government's systematic violation of individual rights. The public and the Congress no longer felt constrained by the need to oppose the Soviet Union. "What brings us together," Richard Nixon had told the Chinese leaders in Beijing in 1972, "is a recognition on our part that what is important is not a nation's internal philosophy."[17] The end of the Cold War overturned that recognition, clearing the way for the Congressional demand to change American policy. Mikhail Gorbachev had made the world safe for an American effort to transform the Chinese political system, which is what the Clinton administration ultimately attempted.

In the second half of 1989, bringing about such a transformation also came to seem entirely feasible. Between June and December the communist regimes of Eastern Europe collapsed one by one. Poland, Hungary, Czechoslovakia, East Germany, Bulgaria, and Romania all overthrew their communist governments—peacefully in every case except Romania—and began to build democratic political systems. Communism, it was plain to see, was on the way out in Europe, to be replaced by democracy. Why, it followed, should China, where spontaneous, peaceful demonstrations had also taken place, where demonstrators in Tiananmen Square had constructed a 33-foot statue of a woman holding aloft a torch that became known as the "Goddess of Democracy," be different?

The effort to make China's trade status contingent on its human rights record attracted broad support. The fact that a Republican president opposed it made it even more attractive to Democratic politicians, who were happy to be on the popular side of a political dispute with their chief political opponent. Even some conservative Republicans, who disdained communism even when practiced by a government aligned with the United States and against the Soviet Union, supported the effort.[18] Groups devoted to promoting human rights globally naturally endorsed it. So did organized labor, an important constituency within the Democratic Party whose grievances against China had at least as much to do with the jobs its members were losing to China-based firms, jobs that trade restrictions might protect, as with the Chinese government's abuse of the rights of the Chinese people. By the time of the 1992 election the wisdom of linking trade with China to the status of human rights there had become one of the issues that divided the nation's Democrats, who controlled the Congress, from the incumbent Republican president.

In his presidential campaign Bill Clinton simply adopted the Democratic position. He had no reason to do otherwise. It was popular in the country. Congressional Democratic leaders, with whom he had every incentive to get along, strongly favored it.[19] At the Democratic Party's nominating convention in New York in July 1992, two Chinese students who had been present in Tiananmen Square in June 1989 and had then fled China appeared on the stage and received an enthusiastic reception. The convention adopted a platform asserting that "one day [China] too will go the way of communist regimes in eastern Europe and the former Soviet Union. The United States must do what it can to encourage that process."[20] Clinton himself charged his opponent with "indifference to democracy" and having "coddled the dictators and pleaded for progress."[21] Demanding a better performance on human rights by the Chinese government enabled Clinton to adopt a firmer, more confrontational position on China than the Republican incumbent, a partisan advantage because Democrats had suffered politically during the Cold War for seeming weaker and more reticent in dealing with communist countries than had the Republicans. Clinton's stance reversed the two parties' Cold-War roles.

Clinton did not come to this position out of deep personal conviction. He had never been to China (he had visited Taiwan), had almost no record on any international political issue, and said very little about foreign policy during his campaign: he presented himself as the man who could revive the national economy, which in 1992 was passing through a mild recession. For him, linking the protection of human rights to the extension of trading privileges to China followed the logic of partisan and electoral politics. He took a particular position on an issue of secondary importance to the country because it made sense, in domestic political terms, to do so.

Once elected, he moved to put that position into practice. His administration persuaded the Democratic Congressional leaders not to pass a bill linking trade and human rights in 1993 but rather, while renewing MFN for China for a year, to put the demand for a change in China's domestic governance in an Executive Order. The order stipulated that for China to receive a further renewal the secretary of state would have to determine that it had made "significant overall progress" in releasing and accounting for political prisoners, permitting access to prisons, protecting Tibetan culture, and allowing Chinese people access to international broadcasting.[22] The American government thus formally linked the continuation of trade with China to changes in that country's domestic political practices. What George H. W. Bush had resisted, Bill Clinton adopted. A hundred years before, American missionaries had worked to transform the spiritual lives of individual Chinese. Now the American government sought to transform the political life of the entire country. Compelling change, indeed sweeping change, in China's internal governance became official American policy.

To implement that policy, the man Clinton appointed to be secretary of state, Warren Christopher, traveled to Beijing in March 1994, less than three months before the deadline for Chinese compliance. Christopher was a Los Angeles lawyer who had served as deputy to Cyrus Vance, Jimmy Carter's secretary of state.[23] After the 1992 election, Clinton chose him as head of the transition team charged with helping the president-elect select a cabinet. At that time Christopher had said that he "assumed in undertaking this role that I would not have a major responsibility in the future."[24] From the deliberations that he supervised, however, he emerged with the position of secretary of state for himself.

Christopher had taken no noticeable part in public debates about foreign policy in the 12 years since the Carter administration had ended, was not identified with any particular issue or position, and was, for someone assuming a role of public leadership, an unusually poor public speaker. Patient and methodical, with a background in corporate law, he was said to be an accomplished negotiator. He did spend a great deal of his time as secretary engaged in negotiations, in the Middle East, with America's European allies, and, most notably in March 1994, with China. None, including the last, came to a successful conclusion.

Christopher's attempt to persuade the Chinese government to comply with the terms of Clinton's Executive Order failed conspicuously, swiftly, and completely. To emphasize its adamant rejection of those terms, on the day the secretary left for Beijing the Chinese government arrested 13 democratic and labor activists. The three days he spent in the Chinese capital were filled with acrimony, in sharp contrast to the atmosphere of elaborate formal courtesy in which such meetings had been conducted in the past. The Chinese prime minister Li Peng, who had enthusiastically supported the Tiananmen Square crackdown, informed him that China "would never accept the United States's concept of human rights."[25] The foreign minister publicly denounced American policy toward China and pronounced himself disappointed with the visit.[26]

Having traveled to Beijing to obtain Chinese concessions, Christopher returned home empty-handed. The Clinton effort to link MFN with Chinese human rights compliance had failed.[27] The administration decided to cut its losses and abandon it. Clinton said so publicly on May 26: "We have reached the end of the usefulness of that policy," he admitted, "and it is time to take a new path."[28]

The policy failed because the United States did not have the power to enforce it. The Chinese, not the American government, controlled what happened in China. The American side had calculated that access to the American market held sufficient importance for China that the

Chinese government would pay the price of affording greater protection to human rights in order to secure it. The Chinese leaders certainly wanted to be able to continue to sell their products to American consumers; but as important as that may have been to them, it stood lower in their hierarchy of preferences than preserving the political system over which they presided, from which they benefitted, and that they believed—some of them, at least, some of the time—assured their country's power and prosperity. They were determined not to go the way of the European communists. Nor would China's leaders, whose claim to govern rested in no small part on protecting the country's sovereign independence—on which the Western powers and later the Japanese had encroached throughout the nineteenth century and the first half of the twentieth—permit foreigners to tell them how to manage their own internal affairs.[29]

The Chinese leaders had a powerful commitment to preserving what the United States was trying to change and were willing to pay a high price to preserve it. The commitment of the American president, his administration, and their country, to promoting that change was far weaker. Nor, as it turned out, was it a high priority of third countries, whose solidarity in making trade dependent on political change would be required for linkage to be effective. In Asia especially, imposing sanctions on China for its political practices either did not catch on or was not sustained. Even America's closest ally in the region, Japan, preferred maintaining its trade relations with China to making them conditional on Chinese human rights practices.[30] The asymmetry of the stakes was one reason the Clinton administration's initial China policy failed. There was a second reason: the domestic politics of the issue continued to determine American policy toward China, but the politics in the United States had shifted.

By 1994 the American business community had mobilized in opposition to using trade with China as leverage for the pursuit of political goals. Many firms had incorporated China into their operations either as a source of components or products used or sold in the United States or as a rapidly growing market for goods and services made in America—and in many cases as both. China's remarkable economic growth since the beginning of reforms in 1979 had created an American political constituency for preserving economic ties between the two countries. The voice of business had been muted in 1989. The shock of the Tiananmen Square massacre had made it seem callous, at best, to advocate good relations with the Chinese government. Moreover, economic growth had slowed in China and the crackdown that followed Tiananmen had enhanced the power of those in the Communist Party with reservations about the market reforms of the previous decade. A reversion to greater government control of the Chinese economy, with reduced opportunities for foreigners, had seemed distinctly possible.

Five years later, growth had resumed. In 1992 the supreme communist leader, Deng Xiaoping, had made a well-publicized and politically decisive trip to southern China in which he had extolled the country's market reforms, recommitting the regime to sustaining and expanding them. China once again appeared to be a land of vast economic opportunity. American business did not want to forfeit that opportunity by linking trade to human rights and made its view clear to the administration.[31]

The shift in policy from trying to change a country's domestic practices to taking advantage of the economic opportunities it offered went beyond China. Economic engagement—increasing cross-border trade and investment—became the keystone not only of the Clinton administration's approach to China but of its foreign policy in general. In dealing with its failure on China, the administration found a basis for engagement with the world that seemed suited to the new, post-Cold War circumstances. The approach also had a domestic political component: it brought political benefits to the president himself.

Trade and investment became the basis of American policy toward China once the United States abandoned the policy of linkage, and even as it had to cope with a feature of Sino-American relations that was not only more difficult, but more dangerous: the status of Taiwan. Whereas the disagreement over China's human rights policy provoked political conflict and had the potential to cause an economic rupture between the two countries, the dispute over Taiwan threatened war.

The island of Taiwan, lying 100 miles off the coast of China, was originally populated by aboriginal people. In the seventeenth century, émigrés from southern China began arriving there. The Qing dynasty conquered it in 1683 but it was officially proclaimed a province of China only in 1885. Ten years later Japan seized the island. It has never since been governed from the Chinese mainland.

The losing side in China's civil war, Chiang Kai-shek's Kuomintang, retreated to Taiwan in 1949 in order to use it as a base from which to relaunch its campaign to control the mainland. When the Korean War broke out in June 1950, the American president Harry Truman sent the American Seventh Fleet into the Taiwan Strait, between the island and the mainland. The Chinese military intervention in Korea against the United States in November of that year set the seal on two decades of Sino-American hostility, during which Taiwan became an American protectorate. The Kuomintang regime continued to present itself as the legitimate government of all of China rather than of a freestanding, independent Taiwan.

In effecting its rapprochement with Beijing in 1972, the Nixon administration signed a communique with the Chinese government that reflected this status. It said that "the United States acknowledges that all Chinese on either side of the Taiwan Strait maintain there is but one China and that Taiwan is part of China. The United States government does not challenge that position." Nixon appears not to have cared much about Taiwan's future, but other Americans did. When the Carter administration established full diplomatic relations with Beijing in 1979 and cut formal ties with Taiwan, the Congress passed, by a veto-proof majority, the Taiwan Relations Act. The Act committed the United States to maintaining quasi-official diplomatic relations with the island, to taking seriously (although not necessarily using military force to prevent) any attack on the island, and to supplying Taiwan with defensive weaponry.

Taiwan's status as an independent country in fact but not in law, which carried over into the post-Cold War period, came about through the combination of the outcome of the Chinese civil war of 1945 to 1950[32] and the course of the Cold War. Had the Kuomintang won the civil war the defeated communists would have retreated to the Soviet Union, not Taiwan. Had the Korean War not begun when it did, and had China not intervened in it, Taiwan would not have come under the protection of the United States, and the mainland government might well have managed to conquer it, as it intended in 1950.[33] Taiwan's status may also be seen as an accident of geography. The island is too far from the mainland (100 miles) to be easily conquered, as this would require an amphibious assault—a difficult military operation under any circumstances; but it is not so far into the Pacific as to be outside the reach of communist military power and thus in a position comfortably to proclaim itself independent in defiance of the wishes of the government in Beijing.

Taiwan's location makes it a base for controlling China's sea lanes, which have both economic and military importance for any government on the mainland. This is one reason the communist government insisted on its right to sovereignty over the island.[34] It had another, equally powerful political incentive. The Chinese Communist Party did not derive its claim to rule, and the public's acceptance of that claim as far as it went, as communist regimes everywhere initially had, from its fidelity to the principles of Marxism-Leninism, with Maoism added in the Chinese case. By the Cold War's end, it had substantially abandoned these principles. Rather, the political legitimacy it enjoyed stemmed in no small part from its defense of China's territorial integrity.[35] When he announced the establishment of the People's Republic in 1949, Mao Zedong said that "China has stood up." He meant that the country had stood up against the predatory outside powers that had assaulted and exploited it and carved out chunks of it for themselves over the previous century.

The Chinese Communist Party proclaimed its dedication to the restoration of Chinese rule over all parts of historic China, which it defined as the most extensive territorial control in the country's long history. This objective commanded broad support among the Chinese people, whatever they may have thought of the system of governance that Mao imposed on them. The regime counted Taiwan as a part of China that had been wrongly wrested away by foreigners—first the Japanese, then the Americans. The communist rulers were willing to defer possession of the island during the course of the Cold War and afterward (Mao said that this could be put off for a hundred years, his successor, Deng Xiaoping, for fifty): they lacked the military power to accomplish this and the requirements of China's defense against the Soviet Union dictated alignment with Taiwan's patron, the United States. Still, they were adamant about asserting their claim ultimately to do so. They emphasized that they would regard any Taiwanese initiative to separate itself formally and permanently from China as a provocation, one to which war would be a legitimate response.

The United States had less invested in Taiwan's status than did the communist regime on the mainland, but the American stakes were not negligible. History had created those stakes. When the Cold War ended, the United States had had close relations with Taiwan, to which it had provided military support, for four decades. Given that history, the forcible conquest of the island by the Chinese military would not only offend Americans, it would damage America's reputation as a reliable friend. That reputation had mattered a great deal during the Cold War, for the purpose of deterring communist attacks on American allies. It did not suddenly lose its significance with the end of that conflict. Moreover, the island had become an economic dynamo by adopting a free-market economic system and trading with the West, especially the United States.

Then, in the wake of the Cold War, Taiwan changed in a way that made its status more contentious, and more dangerous. It became a democracy.

Beginning in the mid-1980s the ruling Kuomintang lifted martial law, permitted the formation of opposition political parties, and held free elections. Lee Teng-hui, a native Taiwanese (rather than someone who came to the island with Chiang Kai-shek), who succeeded Chiang Kai-shek's son Chiang Ching-kuo as president in 1988, presided over many of these changes and at the same time began to fashion a distinctively Taiwanese identity for the island rather than portraying it as a province of a much larger country the Kuomintang aspired to govern.[36] In 1992 the Taiwanese government dropped its claim to control all of China, raising the possibility that Taiwan would declare itself an independent country. All this alarmed the ruling Communist Party on the mainland, which regarded both full-fledged democracy and Taiwanese independence as threatening its interests. By renouncing its claim on all of China the Taiwanese authorities were, in effect, finally accepting defeat in the Chinese civil war, which made what they did perhaps the only time in history when one side's surrender in a war was taken as a hostile act by its adversary.

While alarming Beijing, Taiwan's transition to democracy improved its image in the United States. It ceased to be an authoritarian ally for a conflict that had long ended and became instead a fellow member of the global community of democracies. While becoming less valuable for American strategic interests,[37] the island became more attractive on the basis of American political values. Partly for that reason, and also because of the ongoing commitment to supply defensive weapons to the island, in October 1992 the George H. W. Bush administration agreed to sell 150 F-16 fighter aircraft to Taiwan. The facts that the sale guaranteed jobs in the politically important state, Texas, where the plane was manufactured, and was announced during the final weeks of the presidential election campaign, were not unrelated to the Bush decision. It angered the mainland authorities, as did the more respectful treatment President Lee himself received from the American government.

On May 4, 1994, on a trip to Central America and then to the inauguration ceremony of President Nelson Mandela of South Africa, Lee's plane stopped at Hickam Air Force Base in Honolulu, Hawaii. The Clinton State Department had not given him permission to spend the night there, fearing a harsh Chinese reaction. In protest, Lee refused to get off the plane at all and told the single American official sent to greet him that he would not accept the second-class treatment that the United States was according him.[38] The American Congress reacted just as indignantly. The next month the Senate passed a resolution by a vote of 94–0 calling on the State Department to grant visas to Taiwanese officials.

The next year the Taiwanese government requested a visa for Lee to attend a reunion at Cornell University in upstate New York, where he had earned a doctorate in agricultural economics in 1968. Although not responsible for the ultimate decision, the Congress weighed in here, too: the House of Representatives voted 396 to 0 and the Senate 97 to 1 in favor of granting the request. Once again, domestic considerations had a major impact on American China policy. In the face of such overwhelming support, the Clinton administration issued the visa. Lee made a forceful case for Taiwan in a speech at Cornell and the mainland government was furious, suspecting the episode of being a step toward American endorsement of Taiwanese independence.

One of the purposes of Lee's assertive diplomacy was to win support in Taiwan for his own candidacy in the island's first free presidential election, which was scheduled for March 23, 1996. It was in fact the first such election in which people in greater China had ever voted, and Lee won it with 55 percent of the vote.[39] This, too, the communist authorities regarded as a provocation, and their response went beyond the harsh rhetoric that his visits to the United States had occasioned.

The regime's People's Liberation Army massed 150,000 troops along the coast opposite Taiwan in February. On March 8, 1996, Chinese forces fired missiles into waters off the island, landing closer to it than had been the case in similar exercises the previous year. The United States responded by sending two American aircraft carriers, along with other warships, to waters near Taiwan, although not into the Strait between the island and the mainland. The American secretary of defense, William Perry, the ablest of the seven senior foreign policy officials (two secretaries of state, two national security advisors, and three secretaries of defense) whom Bill Clinton appointed, said that "Beijing should know, and this fleet will remind them, that while they are a great military power, the strongest, the premier military power in the Western Pacific is the United States."[40]

The United States and China did not go to the very brink of war in the spring of 1996, as, in the retrospective judgment of officials of both countries, the United States and the Soviet Union had done over the status of Berlin in the summer of 1961 and the presence of Soviet missiles in Cuba in October of 1962.* Neither side expected armed conflict to occur in 1996. But each was signaling that if the other went too far—if Taiwan declared independence or if China attacked Taiwan directly—it was prepared to go to war to defend its interests.[41] What happened in the waters around Taiwan served as a reminder, and a

---

* While neither crisis of the 1960s ended in war, and while it is not possible to calculate precisely how close to war the two sides came, participants on both sides believed that they were close. The spring of 1996 was not the first time China and the United States had approached war over Taiwan. In the 1950s the communist regime shelled several islands in the Taiwan Strait that Taiwan claimed. The United States issued a veiled threat of nuclear retaliation to keep the regime at bay.

warning, that the end of the Cold War had not eliminated completely the possibility of a war, and in this case a war in which both potential combatants had nuclear weapons.

As with the Soviet-American crises of the Cold War, the March 1996 episode in the Western Pacific had a sobering effect on the two countries directly involved. China took no further military initiatives against the island and tolerated, while hardly welcoming, a freely elected president of a functionally although not formally independent Taiwan. As for the United States, having previously abandoned the policy of linking trade with human rights and privately assuring the Chinese government that it would not support Taiwanese independence, the creation of two Chinas, or Taiwan's admission to the United Nations, the Clinton administration proceeded to make economic engagement, which it had already decided to foster rather than prevent, the basis of its overall relationship not only with China but with other countries as well.

Economics as Foreign Policy

Having failed to promote political change in China, the Clinton administration reversed its policy. Thereafter it became a priority of the American government to improve relations with Beijing and in particular to expand Sino-American economic ties. George H. W. Bush had tried to do just that. Bill Clinton, who had entered office embracing a different approach to China, found himself adopting the one his predecessor had tried to preserve and that he had promised to change.

Official rhetoric shifted. In his 1993 speech setting out the American goal of "enlarging" the community of market democracies W. Anthony Lake had included China among the "backlash states" that actively opposed the most promising global trends. Now, administration officials emphasized China's international importance and the need to treat it with respect.[42] In 1997 the man Deng Xiaoping chose as China's leader after Tiananmen, the Shanghai politician Jiang Zemin, visited the United States. The next year President Clinton traveled to China. In 1998 the United States ended its sponsorship of a resolution that had been introduced annually at the United Nations condemning China for its human rights record. In 1996 negotiations, over which the United States exerted considerable influence, began for Chinese entry into the newly established World Trade Organization, the global association of free-market economies. In 1999 those negotiations came to a successful conclusion. In 2000 the Congress, at the urging of the administration, passed legislation granting China open-ended rather than one-year-at-a-time MFN status. The status was relabeled "PNTR"—Permanent Normal Trade Relations.

The Clinton administration retreated from its initial China policy because it discovered, to its embarrassment, that it lacked the power to enforce the linkage of human rights with economic ties. Finding itself outgunned, it gave up. Yet this is not how its officials described what they were doing. They presented the new approach as a mid-course correction, a change in tactics rather than strategy, the adoption of a different path to the original destination.

In his confirmation hearings in January 1993, Warren Christopher had said that the incoming administration would "seek to facilitate a peaceful evolution of China from communism to democracy by encouraging the forces of economic and political liberalization in that great country."[43] After the failure of linkage, the administration asserted that it would encourage China's internal forces of liberalization not by restricting but instead by expanding economic engagement with the Chinese. In the administration's version of events, the United States had not abandoned the mission of fostering change in communist-ruled China; it had simply exchanged sticks for carrots as the principal instrument for bringing it about. From attempting to alter the political practices they disliked by threatening to make the Chinese people poorer, the Clinton administration shifted its policy to one based on the calculation that the Chinese would become freer as they became richer. Lloyd Bentsen, Clinton's first secretary of the treasury, stated this position in expressing his opposition to linkage in 1994: "One of the ways to promote human rights is to encourage market reform and trade."[44] Just as Beijing deferred acting on its claim to govern Taiwan in the belief that it would eventually get what it wanted, so Washington gave up actively trying to transform internal Chinese politics on the grounds that this would ultimately come about without such direct efforts.

Of course, as China became richer by trading with and receiving investment from the United States, Americans would become richer too. Under the terms of the new policy the United States would both do good and do well. The new approach was nothing if not convenient for Clinton: it combined the means favored by the opponents of his initial policy with the ends desired by its supporters. It promised all the different constituencies interested in American China policy what they wanted. Because Clinton was a "consensus" rather than a "conviction" politician—that is, one more concerned with pleasing as many people as possible than with promoting a particular set of policies even in the face of substantial opposition, and who anyway lacked strong convictions about China—the new policy suited his political temperament.[†]

Yet the new approach was not entirely cynical or purely the product of domestic political calculation. Its underlying premise, that economic growth and increasing contact with the outside world would bring about political change in China, was not implausible. In fact, this process had already begun. The China of Jiang Zemin was a decidedly freer place than that of Mao Zedong, and a major cause of that change was surely the post-1979 economic reforms, which had given individual Chinese far more power over their economic circumstances and far greater exposure to the world beyond China than they had had in the three decades after 1949.

Economic growth, it was plain to see, was rapidly and radically changing the Chinese economy and Chinese society in ways that, it was not unreasonable to believe, would enhance both the demand for Western political practices among the Chinese people and the felt need to permit them on the part of the communist leaders.[45] The decisive impact of economics on politics was the central tenet of the Marxism-Leninism that China's rulers had all but abandoned. Now they found the self-same precept wielded against them by that ideology's greatest historical opponent.

[†] In contrast to Clinton, the American president Ronald Reagan and the British prime minister Margaret Thatcher were conviction politicians, who tend to be rarer than the "consensus" variety. Of course all office-holders in democracies are consensus politicians up to a point, since all must win the favor of at least a plurality of voters in elections: otherwise they would not hold office. Conviction politicians who lose their elections become "gadflies."

The Chinese leaders did not, of course, favor the outcome that their American counterparts sought. They considered "peaceful evolution" to be an insidious Western plot to remove them from power, which was indeed what the American government hoped would eventually happen. They nonetheless welcomed the policy of economic engagement that the Clinton administration adopted, but for the opposite reason. While they, too, believed that trading with the United States would make China richer—it had done just that for more than a decade—they also believed that economic growth would strengthen, not weaken, their grip on power.

Along with their defense of China's borders (as they defined them), the communists' claim to govern China had come to rest on delivering prosperity to the Chinese people.[46] Since 1979 they had delivered it on an impressive scale. Economic engagement with the West, especially with the United States—the destination of a large part of China's exports—had contributed to the country's economic success. The regime therefore welcomed its continuation and expansion. The collapse of communism in Europe, which had made Americans confident about the prospects for democracy, made the Chinese communist authorities nervous, and for the same reason: it cast doubt on the permanence of their system. This made enhancing the country's economic performance under their stewardship all the more important to them.

On economic engagement between their two countries the American and Chinese governments found themselves in the positions of investors on opposite sides of a common financial strategy, one of them going "long" on an asset, betting that its value will rise, while the other goes "short" in the belief that its value will fall. Under these circumstances one of the parties will gain and the other will lose: they cannot both be right. In the second half of the 1990s, however, the American policy of economic engagement seemed to give both governments what they wanted. On the one hand, the space for personal liberty for individual Chinese, having contracted in the wake of Tiananmen, resumed its slow, steady expansion. On the other, the Chinese Communist Party retained its monopoly of power and with it the capacity to prevent the exercise of individual rights by any person at any time. Meanwhile, the commerce between the two countries enriched both.

For the Clinton administration, the solution to the problem of finding a viable, defensible China policy turned out to provide as well the answer to a broader question: what was the appropriate goal of foreign policy in the new, post-Cold War world? The answer, which Bill Clinton did not bring with him to the presidency but at which he arrived over the course of his time in office, was that the central American purpose in the new world was to expand cross-border trade, investment, and the number of countries actively participating in them. The Clinton administration put the kind of economic engagement for which it opted with China at the center of its approach to the rest of the world.

To be sure, the global economy did not come to the attention of the American government for the first time after the Cold War ended. After World War II the United States had helped to organize an international economic order based on the relatively free movement of products and capital across sovereign borders and had done a great deal to maintain and expand it in the decades thereafter. One justification for doing so was the Cold War. Economic interdependence bound the members of the American-led anti-Soviet coalition more tightly together, fortifying the position of the United States in the global conflict with communism. The trade and investment that the United States did so much to foster, especially in Western Europe and East and Southeast Asia, also helped to produce historically high post-1945 economic growth in these regions. By surpassing what communist economic systems were able to accomplish, that achievement contributed to the collapse of communism in Europe and the Western victory in the Cold War.

During the Cold War years however, in the hierarchy of the American government's concerns, issues involving the international economy took second place to matters of national security. Survival, after all, trumps prosperity. During the Cold War, international economics had been a branch of foreign policy. The Clinton administration reversed the order: much of its foreign policy became a subset of its economic policy.

This was so partly by default. With the end of the Soviet Union the United States and its friends and allies faced no major military or political threat. The kind of great-power rivalry present for almost all international history, if it had not disappeared permanently, had at least gone into hibernation. Survival was no longer at stake, which enhanced the relative importance of prosperity.

Moreover, coinciding with, and related to, the demise of the Cold War was the acceleration of globalization—the process of worldwide economic integration. This came about through the combination of technology and politics. The advent of new technologies such as cheap satellite communication, cell phones, and the Internet made possible the movement of goods and money (and people) across long distances ever more rapidly and in ever greater volume. At the same time, more and more countries that had had little or nothing to do with the global-ized international economic order that the United States had taken the lead in reviving after World War II, notably India and China, made the political decision to join it.

They did so in pursuit of the economic growth that, as the economic history of the second half of the twentieth century demonstrated, comes from organizing economic life around free markets that are integrated with the markets of other countries. Economic prosperity became all the more important to governments the world over in the wake of the Cold War because in many countries, as in China, the delivery of prosperity became the basis for political legitimacy. The American government itself was scarcely indifferent to economic considerations. Promoting global trade and investment was one way of achieving the economic growth in the United States that Clinton promised, and on which his own political future heavily depended.

In practice, the primacy of economics in foreign policy meant that international economic matters occupied a larger share of the time and attention of senior figures of the administration, above all the president, than had been the case in the past. It meant that influence over policy toward major countries that had once belonged to officials with expertise in politics and security passed to their colleagues with responsibility for economic affairs. This occurred with policy toward China after the demise of efforts at linkage.[47] It happened as well with policy toward Indonesia during the East Asian financial crisis in 1998. Economic officials of the Clinton administration wanted to attach con-ditions to an international loan to that country that those involved in foreign policy thought unwise on the grounds that the conditions would offend a strategically important government that would in any case never accept them. The economic officials prevailed.[48]

The new hierarchy of issues in American foreign policy became apparent in yet another way. During the Cold War the major international initiatives of the United States, the ones in which the president invested the most time and political capital, concerned security—arms treaties with the Soviet Union, for example. So did the major crises the government had to face, the most dangerous being those involving the status of Berlin in 1961 and the emplacement of Soviet missiles in Cuba in 1962. In the Clinton administration the principal international initiatives and the major crises were economic in character. Instead of arms treaties the president lobbied to pass trade agreements. Rather than military crises, the administration had to cope with financial emergencies in Asia, Russia, Latin America, and in the United States itself.

Passing legislation approving trade agreements had become more difficult when Bill Clinton took office.[49] The politically potent argument that Cold-War presidents had had at their disposal in selling such agreements to Americans and their elected representatives—that it would strengthen the American position against the Soviet Union—had disappeared. Even before the end of the Cold War, more industries had come to seek protection from foreign competition, which meant that they opposed lowering trade barriers. Organized labor, a key part of the Democratic Party's coalition and once a stalwart champion of trade expansion, had turned against it. Labor had begun to urge the inclusion, in trade agreements, of provisions compelling all signatories to conform to American-style labor standards, something poorer countries found administratively onerous, economically disadvantageous, and politically objectionable. Another important Democratic constituency, the environmental movement, had also begun to weigh in on trade, insisting that agreements include measures to protect the environment.

Both groups became involved in the single most important trade battle the Clinton administration waged, over the North American Free Trade Agreement (NAFTA). The preceding Bush administration had negotiated and signed the agreement, which created a free-trade area encompassing Canada, the United States, and Mexico. NAFTA aroused opposition from both labor and environmentalists and, for that reason, from Democratic leaders in the Congress.

During his presidential campaign Clinton took an equivocal position on NAFTA. He endorsed it, but only on condition that it include suitable side agreements on environmental issues, labor standards, and import surges from the other two countries. Once in office he received conflicting counsel about it: his economic officials favored supporting ratification but his political advisors, on the whole, did not.[50] NAFTA's opponents included not only senior Democratic legislators and important Democratic interest groups but also the independent candidate in the 1992 presidential election, H. Ross Perot, who charged that NAFTA would lower employment in the United States. He warned that it would create "a giant sucking sound" as jobs and factories moved to Mexico because of the lower wages there.

Clinton decided to endorse, and work for, ratification. He pronounced the side agreements that his trade representative had negotiated with the other two countries to be satisfactory[51] and threw himself into the political struggle for Congressional approval. He spoke out and made public appearances on behalf of NAFTA. He lobbied members of Congress to vote for it, using the familiar tactic of rewarding some of them with measures favorable to their constituents in exchange for their votes. When he began this effort the prospects for passage seemed uncertain, but his investment of time, energy, and political capital paid off.[52] NAFTA passed the House of Representatives by a margin of 234–200 and the Senate by 61–38, receiving votes from both Democrats and Republicans in both chambers. Clinton signed it into law on December 8, 1993, and it took effect on the first day of 1994.

The NAFTA campaign marked a turning point for Bill Clinton's political fortunes, for American trade policy, and even for the global economy. As with his China policies, domestic political considerations affected Clinton's position on trade. Because the campaign he waged on its behalf ended in victory it enhanced his reputation, which his rocky first year in office had undercut, as an effective political leader. Because he defied important interest groups on whose support the Democratic Party relied, he reinforced the image he had cultivated as a governor and presidential candidate as a "new Democrat," one less beholden to such groups than other Democratic officeholders. His energetic efforts on behalf of NAFTA brought him an additional political benefit: the support of much of the American business community, which had not traditionally been aligned with Democratic politicians and had successfully opposed his initial China policy of linking trade with human rights.

By 1993 trade had become a more prominent and divisive political issue than had been the case for most of the Cold War, and Clinton's decision to support NAFTA tilted the political balance in the United States in favor of trade expansion. His support was decisive because the most consequential opposition to lower trade barriers came from groups aligned with his own party. He thus did for trade what one of his predecessors, Richard Nixon, had done for American policy toward China. When Nixon, the life-long anti-communist, effected a rapprochement with Maoist China in 1972, he gave that policy a broader, sturdier political base than a Democratic politician could have done. Similarly, when Clinton, much of whose party opposed measures to expand trade, nonetheless supported NAFTA, he gave trade expansion a wider political base and greater political legitimacy than a president from the other party, which dependably supported such measures, could have provided.

By putting the United States firmly on the side of freer trade, finally, Clinton strengthened the global trend toward ever-increasing cross-border commerce. The United States had taken the lead in promoting the removal of trade barriers since the end of World War II. Had the American president opposed NAFTA, or even simply declined to press for its Congressional ratification, he would have signaled that his country was abandoning this 50-year commitment. That, in turn, would have altered the global politics of trade in ways unfavorable to trade expansion in particular and globalization in general. Making support for further global economic integration the signature issue of his foreign policy had the opposite effect.

NAFTA was one of two pieces of unfinished business on trade that the Clinton administration inherited. The other was the agreement reached at the conclusion of the eighth series of post-1945 multilateral trade negotiations. This one involved 123 countries and was known as the Uruguay Round because its initial meeting, in 1986, had taken place in Punta del Este in that country. It reduced tariffs on a wide range of items, including services. It also established a new umbrella organization for trade, the World Trade Organization (WTO), with headquarters in Geneva, Switzerland. The WTO replaced the General Agreement on Tariffs and Trade, which had begun in 1947 as a temporary set of rules but had lasted for almost 50 years.

Although it had a larger impact on American trade policy and the global economy than did NAFTA, the Uruguay Round agreement proved less politically contentious, perhaps because ratification took place a year after the major battle over NAFTA. Still, the WTO also encountered opposition. The House of Representatives approved it on November 29, 1994, by a vote of 283–123. It passed the Senate two days later with bipartisan support, as in the case of NAFTA, by 76–24.

The year 1994 marked the high point of the Clinton administration's legislative achievements on trade. Thereafter it failed to secure "fast-track" negotiating authority, giving the president the power to submit trade agreements to Congress for an up-or-down vote without the possibility of adding amendments. No further major trade accords were passed, although a number of minor ones did take effect. Demonstrations that turned disorderly marred the 1999 meeting of the World Trade Organization in Seattle, which Clinton himself addressed. Nonetheless, the volume of global and American trade continued to increase throughout the 1990s. As it did, the administration's economic officials turned their attention to international finance.

Trade enhances economic growth: this is why nations engage in it. The trade agreements the Clinton administration shepherded through Congress thus had the aim of increasing the chief benefit countries derive from participating in the global economy: the creation of wealth. The other great concern of American international economic policy in the 1990s had, in effect, the opposite purpose. Senior officials, including the president, contributed advice, brought political pressure, and provided money to countries in the grip of financial crises in order to contain the major undesirable effect that the working of the global economy can have: the destruction of wealth.

Money is indispensable for market economies but also dangerous to them. It can move swiftly and in large volume; and large, sudden movements can inflict severe economic damage. Investors and even banks have a tendency to pour money into assets or institutions where it seems likely to earn good returns. Investors' psychology can change suddenly, however, causing them to withdraw money rapidly and on a large scale. This can sharply reduce the value of assets, putting borrowing institutions in financial jeopardy and generally destroying wealth. Free trade—the unfettered flow of goods and services across national borders—always and everywhere enhances total welfare, a point established by the English economist David Ricardo in 1817 that has weathered many intellectual challenges since then. The same categorical statement cannot be made about the cross-border flow of money. It usually confers economic benefits but not always. Sometimes it does harm.

Money that moves across borders is particularly susceptible to sudden, massive flight because investors and lenders tend to be particularly skittish about the safety of money placed in foreign countries, where the lack of familiarity breeds concern. In the 1990s, with technologically and politically driven globalization in full swing, cross-border financial flows increased.[53] The American government strongly encouraged this trend, which brought profitable business to American banks and other financial institutions.[54] As a consequence, sudden flights of capital, with the potential for causing deep economic damage, increased as well. The Clinton administration took it upon itself to attempt to limit such damage.

Financial crises occurred in a number of countries in the 1990s when capital fled their institutions and assets on a large scale. This not only imposed losses by reducing the value of such assets and putting the institutions at risk; it also imposed hardship by forcing the devaluation of the local currency, which made imports—often of food and fuel—more expensive and through the dampening effect on local economic activity of the increases in local interest rates necessary to stanch the outflow of capital. Crises often threatened entire local financial systems, as banks weakened and sometimes collapsed.

Financial crises occur when investors or lenders lose confidence that their money is safe and therefore rush to withdraw it. Successful crisis management—really, crisis termination—requires restoring that confidence by making sufficient resources available to the beleaguered institutions or governments to calm the fears of the owners of capital that they will suffer large losses. Economists call the provider of such confidence-restoring resources the "lender of last resort," and in most wealthy countries, most of the time, the government plays that role. The countries that fell victim to the financial crises of the 1990s, however, needed hard currency for this purpose, which their governments did not have in adequate quantity. It came from the United States, acting in concert with other countries and almost always through the offices of international financial institutions, above all the International Monetary Fund (IMF).

Although founded at the end of World War II to help countries adjust their exchange rates without undue economic disruption, the IMF had become, in the decades since, the world's de facto lender of last resort. As such its role was to reduce, as far as possible, the duration and severity of national financial crises by lending money to governments under stress. By keeping crises at bay, the IMF aimed to protect countries beyond those it was trying to rescue. In this way the service it rendered extended to people living outside the borders of the particular countries where it was active.

This service was not an act of charity. Recipient countries had to repay the loans they received, with interest, and most did so.[55] The IMF's funds came from contributions from the wealthiest countries, with the United States the largest donor. The American government therefore had considerable influence on when, where, and with what conditions it made loans. In this sense the IMF served, at times, as an instrument of American international economic policy. The Fund's critics certainly accused it of being exactly that.

As with trade, the Clinton administration's initial engagement with other countries' financial pathologies began in Mexico. The Mexican government obtained the hard currency needed to fund its current account deficit by selling dollar-denominated bonds, many to foreigners. It promised to repay the loans at a fixed rate of exchange between the country's currency, the peso, and the dollar. In 1994, concerned that Mexico would devalue the peso and thereby reduce the value of the bonds they held, investors began to sell them. This depleted the Mexican supply of dollars and increased the chance that the Mexican government would have to devalue, or even default outright on its obligations.

The United States was not bound by any international convention to rescue the peso, but the Clinton administration found compelling political and economic reasons to do so. A collapse of the Mexican currency would have sent prices soaring and increased unemployment there. This would lead, American officials feared, not only to a reduction in Mexican purchases of American exports, thus costing American jobs, but also to a surge in illegal Mexican immigration to the United States. It would tarnish the administration's leading international achievement, NAFTA, and discredit Mexico's embrace of the globalization that NAFTA embodied. Not the least serious concern was that economic distress in Mexico would jeopardize currencies and banking systems in other countries through the process known as contagion: seeing Mexico become unsafe for their money, international investors might well conclude that their funds were unsafe elsewhere as well and withdraw them.[56]

So the Clinton administration decided to come to Mexico's rescue, which involved lending billions of dollars to the Mexican government to back the peso in order to restore confidence in it. The IMF also participated in the rescue, but the United States took the lead. In return, the Mexican authorities promised to carry out economic reforms to make investment there more attractive. The Congress balked at voting for a Mexican loan. Mustering economic resources for fiscal crises abroad proved unpopular in the United States: a poll showed public opposition to helping Mexico by a margin of 71–24.[57] As with his decision to support NAFTA, Clinton, ordinarily a cautious politician, decided to defy public opinion. His administration bypassed Congress by making use of the federal government's Exchange Stabilization Fund, which could be disbursed at the discretion of the secretary of the treasury. Ultimately, the United States put up $20 billion for Mexico and the IMF contributed a sum just short of that.

The rescue succeeded. The peso, and the Mexican financial system, did not collapse. Over the course of a year the Mexican currency stabilized, and its supply of hard-currency reserves grew. It even paid back the money it had borrowed ahead of schedule. Mexico turned out to be the first in a series of countries that found themselves, in the second half of the 1990s, beset by financial difficulties. The United States, invariably acting with and through the IMF, sought to keep those difficulties from becoming even worse.

In Thailand banks had borrowed from the West in hard currency and then made loans to local businesses in the baht, the Thai currency. When market psychology turned against Thailand the banks had difficulty repaying what they had borrowed from abroad at the exchange rate to which they had committed themselves. In July 1997, the Thai government cut the baht's tie to the dollar, and it plunged in value. The IMF stepped in with a loan to brake the baht's descent in exchange for domestic reforms to make the country more credit-worthy in the long run. Unlike the Mexican crisis, the United States did not play the leading part in this rescue. As the Asian financial crisis spread to other, larger, economically more significant countries, however, the American role expanded.

The next country to encounter financial distress was Indonesia. Two months after the Thai rescue, an IMF delegation arrived in Jakarta, the Indonesian capital, to negotiate a substantial loan. As a condition for the loan, the Fund demanded internal reforms to deal with the features of the Indonesian economy that had, in its judgment, led to the crisis. It thereby entered politically sensitive territory: many of the targets of the proposed reforms were programs or practices that benefitted the family and friends of Indonesia's leader for three decades, Suharto. It was the United States that pushed hardest within the IMF for such reforms. When Suharto resisted, Clinton called him personally to urge that he accept the changes being demanded,[58] and many were ultimately implemented.

Next came South Korea, of all the countries to become ensnared in financial crisis the one with the greatest importance for the international economy. At the end of 1997 its currency, the won, plunged in value. An initial IMF loan in December of that year[59] did not arrest the fall, but a second loan early in the next year brought better results. To the Korean rescue effort the United States, acting again through the IMF, made two signal contributions. First, the Clinton administration insisted that, as a condition of receiving help, the Korean government open its financial sector to foreign participation, which was a boon to the large American financial institutions that engaged in international business. Second, the United States was instrumental in arranging, in early 1998, a "standstill" agreement—an agreement in which lenders stop demanding the immediate repayment of loans—among Korea's major creditors. This entailed more or less voluntary commitments to renew (roll over) the country's loans, extend their due dates, and convert short-term obligations to longer-term ones.[60] Voluntary as the commitments may have been, they did not come about spontaneously. American economic officials, led by Clinton's second secretary of the treasury, Robert Rubin, obtained them through the persuasiveness of their arguments in combination with the force of their arm-twisting. The American government's power, prestige, and network of contacts made it possible for the United States to orchestrate this unconventional undertaking, something that other governments, and even the IMF itself, could not have done. In the end, the arrangement did not hurt the creditors and the Korean economy righted itself.

American economic officials also put together a standstill agreement at home. In September 1998, the giant American hedge fund Long Term Capital Management (LTCM) teetered on the edge of bankruptcy. It had lost $4.6 billion in four months, in part because of the damaging effects on its portfolio of the various financial crises around the world. American officials feared LTCM's collapse would tear through the American financial system like a tornado, devastating the financial institutions with which it did business and touching off a severe economic downturn in the United States and perhaps in other countries.[61] They feared, that is, what did happen a decade later after the collapse of the investment bank Lehman Brothers. With the New York branch of the Federal Reserve Board taking the lead, the government organized a standstill agreement among LTCM's creditors that, while it ultimately did not keep the hedge fund in business, bought time for an orderly liquidation of its assets that the financial markets could safely absorb.

In late 1998, contagion spread from Asia back to Latin America, to that continent's largest and most important country, Brazil. The IMF intervened once again. The Brazilian government, to protect its long-term reputation as a reliable borrower,[62] at first rejected both a devaluation and a standstill agreement. Because the United States supported the Brazilians on this point, the IMF refrained from organizing one. In November the IMF assembled a $41.5 billion package of loans for Brazil, which agreed in return to cut spending and raise taxes. At the beginning of 1989 the Brazilian currency began to trend sharply downward, and this time a standstill among its creditors was arranged. By spring the country's currency, and its economy, began to recover. The financial crises of the 1990s had come to an end.

As they wound down, the singular importance of international economic policy in the Clinton administration, due in part, of course, to the crises with which it had to cope, found expression on the cover of the February 15, 1999, issue of *Time* magazine. It showed the three most powerful American economic officials—Treasury Secretary Robert Rubin, his deputy Lawrence Summers, and Federal Reserve Chairman Alan Greenspan—with a bright yellow headline calling them "The Committee to Save the World." The accompanying story described their efforts to contain the crises.

The attention they received broke with precedent. During the Cold War the media spotlight had shone on officials responsible for political and military affairs who spent their time negotiating alliances, peace treaties, and arms control agreements—men such as Dean Acheson, John Foster Dulles, Henry Kissinger, and James Baker. In the first post-Cold War administration, by contrast, officials responsible for dealing with the global economy took center stage. It was they who managed American policy where the international stakes were highest. Like the celebrated diplomats of the Cold War era, moreover, the members of the Clinton economic team could claim substantial success. They helped to prevent the financial crises of the 1990s from worsening and threatening the global economy as a whole. Thailand, Indonesia, South Korea, Brazil, and other countries touched by financial distress all emerged from their experiences with their economies battered and their citizens at least temporarily poorer; but other countries, including the United States, avoided major damage.

Unlike its linkage policy toward China and many of the policies it pursued elsewhere, the Clinton administration's principal purpose in joining and sometimes orchestrating the rescue of distressed economies was not to transform the domestic arrangements within the countries being rescued. The crises did, however, have the effect of transforming them.

The conditions for the loans they received were intended to improve their economic performance, but those conditions had political consequences as well. The IMF compelled governments to carry out their policies in public view rather than secretly and to cease directing resources to politically favored individuals, a practice known as "crony capitalism." The goal was to avoid further financial crises;[63] but transparency and the application of impersonal, merit-based standards in public life are features of political democracy as well as economic efficiency. In one country the conditions had even more profound consequences. The American-inspired changes that the IMF imposed on Indonesia touched off a series of events that led to the fall of the Suharto dictatorship, free elections, and the establishment of a shaky but genuine democracy.

Economic officials make unlikely missionaries, and the Americans and others charged with treating the economic ills of countries convulsed by financial upheaval did not see themselves as agents of democratic transformation; but that is what they turned out to be. Working with other countries and through the IMF, the Clinton administration unintentionally[‡] produced more Western-style change than either it or its successor in office did where their policies had this explicit purpose—in China, Somalia, Haiti, the Balkans, Afghanistan, Iraq, and the wider Arab world. The United States proved to be a more successful missionary for democratic change when it was not trying to be one than when it was.

Although the rescue efforts for almost all the countries afflicted with financial difficulties enjoyed at least a measure of success, in one country they failed. That country was Russia, which, in spite of IMF loans, defaulted on its debt on August 17, 1998. In the world view and the policies of the Clinton administration, Russia differed from the other distressed countries. It was more important. The administration became far more heavily engaged in its internal affairs and its foreign policies than in China's. The United States explicitly sought to foster a transformation of Russian politics and economics. Despite this intention, what the Clinton administration did in, with, and to Russia subverted rather than advanced its own aims and American interests. Its Russia policy made things worse.

[‡] The explicit American goals were avoiding contagion from the financial crises, stabilizing the economies of the distressed countries, and creating opportunities for American business.

Russia: The Good Deed

A remarkable series of events that centered on Russia created the new world in which the Clinton administration conducted its foreign policy. For the global scope and historic importance of their impact, these events bear comparison with the great wars and revolutions of the modern era; but unlike the other world-historical developments, miraculously little violence and bloodshed accompanied those of the 1980s and 1990s.

They began in 1985, when a new leader took charge of the Soviet Union. Determined to invigorate the slow-growing Soviet economy, Mikhail Gorbachev introduced a series of reforms that relaxed the Communist Party's iron grip on the society it governed. The reforms permitted, indeed encouraged, unprecedentedly free political expression across the country's 11 time zones and in the European countries to the west where the Soviet Union had imposed communist regimes, and tolerated independent political activity for the first time in six decades. As in the story of the sorcerer's apprentice, Gorbachev's measures had effects he did not anticipate. The reforms he implemented had, ultimately, revolutionary consequences: in 1989 the people of Eastern Europe overthrew their communist rulers, and at the end of 1991 the Soviet Union itself collapsed. When it did, each of its 15 constituent republics—which were spread across Europe, the Caucasus, and Central Asia, reaching from the Baltic to the Pacific and from the Arctic to the Black Sea—emerged as independent countries.

This put an end to the Cold War. When the countries of Eastern Europe ceased to be communist, the founding cause of that conflict—Moscow's domination of these countries and the Western fear that, if unchecked, it would impose the same fate on Western Europe—disappeared. The dissolution of the Soviet Union dramatically diminished the size, wealth, and military might of its successor states and so reduced the potential for any of them to pose a threat to the West. The largest and most powerful of them, the Russian Federation, abandoned the Soviet Union's communist politics and economics and began to install free-market economic institutions and a democratic political system.

The threat that had animated American foreign policy for four and a half decades thus vanished. This put the United States, in its relations with the rest of the world, in the position of a man who has gone to work every day for 45 years only to discover one morning that his job has suddenly disappeared and he has been forcibly retired—albeit with a generous pension.

The administration of George H. W. Bush adopted a cautious approach to the collapse of communism, taking care not to become directly involved in the remarkable sequence of events that led to its demise. Bush and his foreign policy officials, however, did not do nothing; and what they did do, they did skillfully. They concluded several arms control agreements with the Soviet Union before it expired and supported the merger of formerly communist East Germany into democratic, capitalist West Germany. This was something that almost all Germans wanted but about which America's and West Germany's allies Britain and France had, if anything, greater reservations than did Gorbachev himself.

The Bush administration carefully steered clear, however, of the internal drama of communism's downfall. It saw no way to intervene effectively and, because the trend of events was so favorable to the United States, saw no reason to try to do so. At the end of 1991 a new, independent, non-communist Russia came into existence led by the former communist turned democrat and rival of Gorbachev, Boris Yeltsin. The Bush administration refrained from involving the United States in the great transformation to free markets and democracy Yeltsin proclaimed it his goal to undertake. Bush officials did not fully trust him or feel certain they knew where he proposed to lead Russia. Nor were they confident that the United States could weigh in effectively on behalf of American interests.

Bill Clinton took a different approach. He embraced Yeltsin, to whom he privately (and presumably affectionately) referred as "Ol' Boris."[64] He gave the Russian president extensive and, for a time, unqualified support. Along with expanding and defending globalization, ensuring the success of Yeltsin's project of building free markets and democracy in Russia became one of the two foreign policies in which Clinton seemed genuinely to believe, that he considered important, and in which he invested time and political capital.[65] His administration's initial effort to transform China came about more or less by accident, the result of taking the path of least domestic political resistance. Its effort to transform Russia, by contrast, was deliberate and the result of conviction. In Russia, Bill Clinton was not a reluctant missionary.

The administration made the transformation of Russia a higher and more enduring priority than the transformation of China because the Russian government, unlike its Chinese counterpart, itself favored such a course. Active support for that course seemed eminently worthwhile, in addition, because the conversion of what had been the citadel of anti-Western political values and practices into a member in good standing of the camp of democratic, capitalist countries would represent a great historical accomplishment and geopolitical prize. Clinton therefore entered into what he called "a strategic alliance with Russian reform."[66]

Such an alliance seemed necessary to ensure that Russia did not fall back into the autocratic and aggressive habits of the Soviet Union and Imperial Russia before it. A country with as long a history of expansion abroad and repression at home as Russia's could not be considered immune to backsliding.[67] If a relapse occurred, it would erase at least some of the gains that the end of communism in Europe had brought to the United States and its allies. It would be particularly dangerous because Russia had inherited the Soviet Union's nuclear weapons. Supporting Yeltsin was a way of protecting the new, post-Cold War European political order, just as leading the rescue squad that fought the series of financial crises was a way of protecting the new, post-Cold War global economic order.

Clinton supported the Russian president, finally, because Boris Yeltsin, despite his alcohol-fueled tendency to behave erratically, was, from the point of view of Western values and Western interests, the best leader Russia had ever had as well as the person on whom the prospects for transformation depended. This gave the West, and in particular the United States, a large stake in his political and economic success.

Clinton offered Yeltsin political support by meeting with him frequently—17 times between 1992 and 1999—and praising him enthusiastically. American political support also came in the form of indulging or ignoring Yeltsin's violation of the democratic norms he was supposed to be nurturing in Russia. The administration justified these departures on the grounds that the Yeltsin presidency, whatever its imperfections, remained democracy's best hope in his country.

In the fall of 1993, Yeltsin announced the dissolution of the Russian parliament by presidential decree. Clinton supported him. His conflict with the parliament turned violent, with forces loyal to parliamentary leaders launching attacks on public facilities in Moscow. Yeltsin responded by authorizing the shelling of the parliament building, killing 147 people. Clinton reaffirmed his support for the Russian president.[68]

In December 1994, Yeltsin ordered an attack on the province of Chechnya in the Caucasus, where a violent, undemocratic secessionist movement was under way. The attack started a war that lasted for a year and a half and led to as many as 50,000 deaths, many of them civilians, most of them killed by Russian troops, tanks, artillery, and aircraft. While not happy about what Russia was doing, the administration did not publicly criticize it, and Clinton even compared Russia's late-twentieth-century war against a rebellious province with American's own Civil War.[69]

In 1996, presidential elections were due in Russia. At the beginning of the year Yeltsin was so unpopular—more because of Russia's economic troubles than for the assault on the parliament or the war in Chechnya—that he seemed certain to lose. His main opponent was Gennady Zyuganov, the leader of the Russian Communist Party, which operated legally but had not made a credible commitment to democracy or free markets. Clinton decided to do whatever he could to assure a Yeltsin victory. " . . . we've got to stop short of giving a nominating speech for the guy," he said privately, "but we've got to go all the way in helping in every other respect."[70] He stepped up his supportive rhetoric, organized a meeting of the Group of Seven, the club of rich democracies, that Yeltsin attended as a way of enhancing his prestige with Russian voters, and urged the IMF to provide funds for Russia, presuming that this would redound to Yeltsin's political advantage.

For a time, Yeltsin considered canceling the election rather than run the risk of losing it. The Clinton administration disapproved, but did not say so publicly. Nor did it express its reservations about a scheme Yeltsin implemented to raise money, the "loans for shares" program in which wealthy Russians loaned money to the government in return for the right to bid on valuable state-owned economic assets, which in many cases they ultimately managed to secure at prices far below their value.[71]

Yeltsin won the election and served as president until the end of 1999, when he resigned in favor of his prime minister, Vladimir Putin. Since it was a major goal of the Clinton administration that he remain in power, his longevity in office counts as a success for American policy toward Russia—although the administration's contribution to Yeltsin's political survival was probably not decisive.[72]

In his time in office Yeltsin did, on the whole and with some exceptions, keep faith with the principles of democracy. Russia held elections that were more or less free and fair. The country was home to a free press, free speech, and freedom of political activity. Yeltsin conducted a pro-Western, or at least not an anti-Western, foreign policy. In these ways, the investment that Bill Clinton made in Boris Yeltsin paid off; or, to the extent that these trends would have occurred without the Clinton Russia policies, it was an investment in a good cause.

The close American identification with independent Russia's first president had a downside, however. Over the course of his term in office, both before and after his re-election, Yeltsin became unpopular, largely due to the country's economic struggles but also because of the corruption he tolerated, which included the enriching of his political allies through the loans-for-shares program. Some of that unpopularity rubbed off on the United States.

The Russian government's most urgent business, upon assuming responsibility at the end of 1991 for the affairs of a sovereign state, was not political but economic. It had to build a working free-market economy on the ruins of the Soviet system of centralized economic management. The success of that project, it was widely believed both in Russia and in the West, would determine not only Boris Yeltsin's political future but also the fate of Russian democracy itself.

Making the transition from central planning to free markets was not a simple task. Communists had demolished existing free markets and imposed central planning in the Russian empire after taking power there after World War I, and had done the same in Eastern Europe after World War II. Reversing the process posed an immense challenge. As the Eastern European saying put it, we know how to make fish soup from an aquarium but we don't know how to make an aquarium from fish soup. As the observation implied, the transition from central planning to free markets had never been attempted before 1989, when

Poland and the countries of Eastern Europe, newly freed from communist control, embarked on it. When they did, they had no blueprint to follow. Prior to that year, because the collapse of communism came suddenly and as a surprise, such a transition had barely even been imagined.

The Russian transition began with the freeing of prices, which central planners had previously set. This led to inflation, which was all the worse because in their last months Soviet authorities had printed money recklessly. Russia also had to build the institutions a market needs to function, such as a financial system for allocating capital and a legal system to enforce contracts. Free markets required transferring property from the state to private owners. The new Russian regime had to carry out these complicated and often controversial measures more or less simultaneously.

When Yeltsin's government set out on the transition at the outset of 1992 the George H. W. Bush administration, while sympathetic to what it was trying to accomplish, did not offer help. To the contrary, the initial economic initiative of the United States toward the new Russia made the transition more difficult: the American government insisted that the debts the former Soviet regime had accumulated be paid. Russia agreed to assume responsibility for them.[73] More than skepticism about Yeltsin's character and competence determined the Bush policy: the political climate in the United States did not lend itself to offering economic assistance to the new Russia. The United States had fallen into a mild recession, Bush was running for re-election, and most Americans disapproved of foreign aid in any form to any country.[74]

Clinton's strategic alliance with Russian reform, by contrast, led to active engagement with the economic transition. It came in three varieties. The United States made direct grants to Russia on a modest scale.[75] Along with other countries it supplied technical assistance in the form of experts on one or another aspect of market economics who advised and worked with Russian officials who had economic responsibilities.[76]

Finally, Russia, like other countries in the 1990s, received loans from the IMF, and for the same reason: to bolster confidence in its currency. Whereas the vulnerable feature of the Thai, Indonesian, and South Korean economies was the debt of their private sector, Russia's financial difficulties stemmed from the deficits of its government. The Russian government, not unlike governments of other countries (including the United States), found it difficult, for political reasons, to keep its expenditures in balance with its income. Parts of the old Soviet economy remained intact and needed large government subsidies to survive. In the more democratic political system of the new Russia their managers could and did lobby effectively for government assistance.[77] Moreover, closing down these large loss-making enterprises would have made hundreds of thousands of people jobless, which was a recipe for serious social unrest, or so it was feared.

At first the Yeltsin government printed money to fund its budget and current account deficits, but that aggravated the country's already serious inflation. So it began to borrow for this purpose, in hard currency at a fixed exchange rate. Much of the money it borrowed came from the sale to private investors of "GKOs"[78]—bonds with very short maturities paying very high rates of interest. To support the exchange rate to which the Russian government was committed—which made the bonds attractive—and to help with the deficits, Russia received IMF loans.

Whereas with the financially distressed Asian countries the United States had taken the lead in insisting that demanding conditions accompany the loans, with Russia the Clinton administration became the leading voice for leniency, even generosity. As Russian deficits persisted and its government failed to raise taxes and cut spending to reduce them, the officials and member governments of the IMF became increasingly reluctant to lend the country more money. They saw in the indulgence granted to Russia a classic case of "moral hazard," which arises when bad economic behavior on the part of an individual, a firm, or in this case a country is encouraged by sparing it what are ordinarily the negative consequences of that behavior. In this case, the IMF was creating a moral hazard, and so encouraging Russian economic irresponsibility, by continuing to make loans to Russia's government despite that government's failure to fulfill the conditions on which previous loans were extended. The American government, however, insisted on continuing the lending of money to Moscow.

The American commitment to Russia encouraged, for a time, the flow of the private capital that the government in Moscow needed.

Investors remained confident not that Russia would get its financial house in order but rather that the United States would never allow Russia's finances to deteriorate to the point that Moscow could not repay all it owed. Because of its size, location, and the military infrastructure it had inherited from the Soviet Union, Russia was deemed "too nuclear to fail."

Fail, however, it did.[79] The year 1998 brought damaging economic developments. The example of the Asian financial crises reduced foreigners' appetite for GKOs. A drop in the price of oil, the result of the crisis-induced recessions in Asia, cut back on Russia's one reliable source of hard currency. In the summer of that year, in the face of a continuing deficit and increasing doubts about the government's capacity to sustain the exchange rate to which it was committed, the market for GKOs began to dry up and investors started to flee the ruble. In July, under pressure from the United States, the IMF made a loan of $22.5 billion, to be disbursed over a period of 18 months, in an effort to bolster investors' confidence. The loan came with the usual requirements to reduce the deficit by cutting spending and raising taxes. The Russian government did not implement these measures, the drain on the country's hard currency continued, and on August 17, 1998, Russia defaulted on its GKO debt and devalued the ruble, which fell by two-thirds.

In the aftermath of August 17 the performance of the Russian economy improved. The devaluation increased its exports, which became cheaper. The government took steps to reduce the budget deficit. Most importantly, as an energy-rich country Russia benefitted from the sharply rising price of oil in the first decade of the twenty-first century.

The default and devaluation in the summer of 1998 brought to an end, however, the "strategic alliance for Russian reform" between the United States and post-communist Russia. The economic reformers with whom American officials had worked closely left the government. The reforms for which they had been responsible lost political support in Russia. The events of August 17 also brought an effective end to the Yeltsin presidency. Although he held office until the end of the following year, he lacked the political standing—and by this time the physical stamina—to take major initiatives.

When it ended, the goals of the strategic alliance had been partly achieved. Much, although certainly not all, of what the Clinton administration had hoped would happen in Russia had in fact come to pass. The country's political system had important democratic features: free elections, free speech, and a free press. Major elements of a Western-style economy were in place: prices were being set by supply and demand rather than by central planners; banks and a stock market were operating, if not always smoothly; much of the property the Soviet state had controlled had been transferred, however unfairly, into private hands. Corruption was rampant and much of the country's wealth belonged to a few politically favored individuals, but for the first time since the 1920s Russia had a functioning market economy.

Moreover, and also very much in line with American interests, the military infrastructure—the personnel, the hardware, and the factories—that Russia had inherited from the Soviet Union had shrunk to a fraction of its former size. The return of communist rule based on the principles of Marxism-Leninism, with all power vested in the Communist Party and the government seeking to control every feature of economic, political, and even social life had become inconceivable by 1998, as it had not been in 1993.

Under different circumstances Russia might have gone further, faster, in the transition to democracy and free markets during the 1990s. Boris Yeltsin might have strengthened democratic governance by making major political changes—calling fresh elections and writing a new constitution—immediately after the Soviet Union ended.[80] Because he himself was so closely identified with democracy in Russia, Yeltsin would have improved democracy's reputation among Russians had he proven to be a more stable, reliable, sober president. A more restrained person, however, might not have had the audacity, the imagination, or the courage to do what Yeltsin did—which was a very great deal—first to challenge and then to destroy the communist system.

As for the economic transition, it might have proceeded more swiftly and smoothly had the United States and other Western countries offered more generous assistance, perhaps including debt relief, during the first year after the Soviet collapse. At that point dedicated reformers occupied the key positions in the Russian government, Boris Yeltsin's prestige stood at its height, and the resistance to the radical dislocations that the transition necessitated was at its weakest. Skeptical of Yeltsin and preoccupied by domestic concerns, the Bush administration never seriously considered launching such an initiative.[81]

Russian reform also fell victim to events elsewhere. Had the Asian financial crisis not occurred, shaking confidence in the ruble, and had the recession that crisis triggered not lowered the price of oil, depressing Russia's hard currency earnings, the country might have avoided the financial debacle of August 17, 1998.[82] In that case Russians would have thought better of Yeltsin, the new political system over which he presided, and the economic reforms implemented during his time in office.[83] Russia's post-Yeltsin political environment would have been friendlier to democracy and free markets, and Russian policies at home and abroad might have taken a different course.

All this is, of course, speculation, susceptible to neither proof nor disproof. As it happens, the criticism of Russian economic policy made most insistently at the time, and since, turns out not to be valid. The Yeltsin government and its American advisors, Russians and others charged, erred in too-rapidly imposing too-radical economic reforms. Imposing "shock therapy," according to this criticism, caused unnecessary suffering among the Russian people, turning them against reform in general. In fact, Russia did *not* undergo shock therapy: reform in several countries in Eastern Europe was both more intensive and more extensive. Moreover, genuine shock therapy, where it was put into practice, yielded results superior to those that the more modest, partial, drawn-out reform in Russia achieved.[84]

Furthermore, the Russian transition faced formidable obstacles that different personalities and even different policies could not, in and of themselves, have overcome. To function successfully, political democracy requires a distinct set of institutions, practices, and underlying values. Where democracy has flourished these have accumulated over time, often for generations.[85] Russia had none of them. It had to start from scratch.

Democracy in Russia also had to contend with a special handicap that had a particularly powerful impact during the first decade of the next century: the "resource curse." The country's endowment of energy reserves provided the incentive and the means for a self-selected elite to perpetuate itself in power, avoiding free elections and suppressing political freedom.[86]

To expect the construction of a smoothly running democratic order in Russia quickly and easily in the face of these obstacles was unrealistic, although American officials often did seem to harbor such an expectation. This was true as well of the institutions and practices of a free-market economy, with which Russia had not had direct experience for almost seven decades.[87]

The transition to both democracy and free markets in Russia encountered another difficulty, one that beset American efforts to foster these political and economic systems in other countries as well. Both require institutions of a particular kind, institutions that are universal in scope—they apply to everyone—and have impersonal rules—they treat everyone the same way. The rule of law is the prototypical, indeed essential, institution of this kind.

Although such institutions are taken for granted in the wealthy industrial democracies where they hold sway (and that are wealthy and democratic *because* they hold sway), they are historically unusual and perhaps even, in some sense, unnatural. The dominant, possibly even genetically determined, human propensity is to favor some people over others. In most societies for most of history members of the same family, tribe, nation, or cohort of close associates with histories of mutual obligation and reciprocal assistance have had a privileged status in public affairs. Setting such ties aside in making political decisions and distributing economic resources would have been unusual, if not unthinkable, and even considered immoral, almost everywhere.[88]

Social scientists use the term "patrimonial" to describe political and economic orders based on personal connections rather than impersonal rules, and patrimonialism in one form or another is widespread even in the twenty-first century, including in Russia. Soviet communism in practice, while officially governed by impersonal rules—those of Marxism-Leninism—actually operated in a patrimonial fashion: politics was organized through networks of personal ties and patronage.[89] Post-Soviet Russia inherited and continued this method of conducting public business and managing economic life[90]—the group of officials and favored businessmen connected with Yeltsin was sometimes called "the family"[91]—which obstructed its progress toward the Western-style politics and economics that the Clinton administration sought to help create.

What seems, in retrospect, the excessive optimism of the American and other Western governments about the prospects for democracy and free markets in Russia stemmed in part from what they regarded as a precedent: Germany and Japan a generation earlier, whose conversions to democracy transformed the geopolitics of Europe and Asia after 1945. America's two principal enemies in World War II had easier transitions, however, because their circumstances were more propitious. Both were decisively defeated on the battlefield and then occupied by Western forces, unlike Russia. With the onset of the Cold War, the mission of the occupying troops changed from suppressing a defeated foe to protecting a valued ally against a common threat, which made possible an ongoing American military presence. That presence helped guarantee democracy in these two countries without incurring the resentment that occupation inevitably brings. Nothing comparable occurred in Russia.

Nor, unlike Russia, did Germany and Japan have to construct a free-market economy without any recent experience in operating one. Both had had highly productive market economies before World War II. That war had devastated their economic infrastructure, but the people who had built and manned it, with their skills and experience, remained; and unlike Russia, Germany and Japan received large infusions of assistance from the United States—Germany from the Marshall Plan beginning in 1947, Japan from American purchases for the war in Korea that began in June 1950.

The formerly communist countries of Eastern Europe preceded Russia in the transition to democracy and free markets, and on the whole did better in establishing both. They had, however, a head start. They had had free markets, and in some cases democratic governments, before World War II. They were smaller and easier to manage than Russia and had fewer large, unprofitable industrial conglomerates to liquidate. They had another important advantage: their people considered themselves culturally part of the West who had been involuntarily separated from their natural home after 1945—kidnapped, in effect—by the presence of Soviet troops. Adopting free-market economics and democratic politics was not for them a journey into unexplored territory. It was a restoration of what was normal and desirable and had once been familiar. It was what they had wanted for decades but had been

forcibly denied. They were therefore more willing to endure temporary deprivation and dislocation to get it than were the Russians, who
lacked their passionate attachment to the ways of the West. All of the
major differences between Germany and Japan after 1945 and Eastern
Europe after 1989, on the one hand, and post-communist Russia, on
the other, lay far beyond the power of the United States to affect either
decisively or quickly.

All things considered, therefore, the Russian transition to democracy
and free markets, rocky and incomplete though it was during the 1990s,
went, perhaps, as well as could be expected.[92] In arguing for establishing free markets through sweeping, radical, "shock therapy" Eastern
Europeans sometimes invoked the adage that "you can't cross a chasm
in two small jumps." The Russian transition, however, resembled less
crossing a chasm than climbing a very high mountain; and no one has
ever sprinted to the peak of Mt. Everest. Such an ascent is invariably
protracted, arduous, and not always successful: mountaineers sometimes stop and turn back short of the summit.

As for the American effort, between 1993 and 1998, to support and
encourage this climb, while the Clinton administration sometimes
claimed credit for its successes and sought to avoid responsibility for
its failures, the impact of what the United States said and did, while
not negligible, was not large: Russia did not receive enough American
money to make a major difference in its public policies, nor was the
advice that Americans offered always followed. In some ways the
Clinton policy toward Russia brought the United States the worst of
both worlds: only modest influence over the policies Boris Yeltsin carried out but also unpopularity among Russians because these policies,
with which the United States was nonetheless closely associated, generated deep discontent.[93]

The old saying that no good deed goes unpunished is relevant
to American support for Russian reform but not entirely applicable
because that support was more than a good deed; it was self-interested
as well as altruistic. Russia had a great deal to gain from a successful
transition, but so too did the United States. Despite the benevolence
motivating its Russia policy, however, at the end of the Clinton administration the standing of the United States was lower in Russia, and

American interests were less secure from Russia, than had been the case when George H. W. Bush had left office. The reason for this development, however, had less to do with the program of American economic assistance than with the course of American policy on European security.

Russia: The Bad Deed

With its powerful military forces the Soviet Union had posed a mortal threat to the United States and its allies. Cold War American foreign policy revolved around coping with that threat. The Soviet collapse removed it, making America safer than it had been since before World War II. For the security of the West, the end of European communism represented an enormous windfall.

Some loose ends remained, however, in the form of the thousands of nuclear weapons on the territory of what had been the Soviet Union.[94] The fact that a government bent on expanding its power at the expense of the West and by the use of force if necessary no longer controlled them enhanced American and global security. On the other hand, the fact that, with the fragmentation of the great communist multinational empire that had originally built and deployed them, these nuclear weapons had come under the control of more than one government, along with the prospect that some of the weapons might escape the control of the new governments and fall into hands of individuals determined to wield them for anti-American, anti-Western purposes, created a new threat. During the years immediately following the Soviet collapse the United States successfully addressed it.

Since the beginning of the atomic age the spread of nuclear weapons to countries not already possessing them—nuclear proliferation—had concerned the American government, which assumed that the more widely distributed such armaments came to be, the greater would be the chances of a nuclear war. The Soviet Union shared this concern and together the two countries forged the nuclear Non-Proliferation Treaty (NPT) in 1968. The Treaty established two classes of signatories: countries that had nuclear weapons at the time of accession and were allowed to keep them; and those that did not have such weapons and promised not to acquire them. The breakup of the Soviet Union, by leaving Soviet nuclear weapons scattered among what became four independent countries—Russia, Ukraine, Kazakhstan, and Belarus—triggered a sudden, unexpected, accidental outburst of proliferation.

The Bush administration, with Secretary of State James A. Baker III taking the lead, reversed the dispersion of Soviet nuclear armaments. Through American efforts, an accord was signed in Lisbon, Portugal in May 1992, by the terms of which the three non-Russian countries agreed to transfer the nuclear weapons on their territories to Russia and to adhere to the NPT.[95]

While Soviet nuclear weapons had preoccupied the United States during the Cold War—not surprisingly, since so many of them were aimed at North America—American officials had not worried that these armaments would be lost, stolen, or captured by people not authorized to have them. Police states, and the Soviet Union was perhaps the most formidable police state ever created, do not permit such things. Whatever its many shortcomings, the Soviet government was adept at exercising control, including control over its nuclear weapons.

The new Russian regime was committed to exercising less control than its predecessors over the society it governed, which was a good thing from the American (not to mention Russian) point of view, except when applied to nuclear armaments. American officials feared that the weapons themselves, the fissionable (that is explosive) material they contained, and the expertise needed to make them in the form of experienced scientists and engineers, would fall into the wrong hands.

In response to this danger, Senators Sam Nunn and Richard Lugar, the first a Democrat from Georgia, the second an Indiana Republican, drafted and persuaded the Congress to pass a bill providing American funds to prevent such unauthorized, dangerous, nuclear "leakage."[96] The Nunn-Lugar initiative, or the Cooperative Threat Reduction (CTR) program as it was officially called, supplied the funding and expertise for decommissioning and then safeguarding nuclear armaments, as well as chemical and biological weapons, on the territory of the former Soviet Union. The scenarios that the CTR program was designed to avoid—lost, stolen, or clandestinely fabricated nuclear weapons—did not come to pass in the two decades following the Cold War.

The Clinton administration inherited the results of the Bush counter-proliferation diplomacy, the Nunn-Lugar program, and one other signal contribution to American security. In the last years of the Cold War the United States and the Soviet Union signed a series of accords limiting the military forces they deployed against each other: in 1987 a treaty covering intermediate-range nuclear forces (INF) in Europe that eliminated all weapons in that category; in 1990 the Treaty on Conventional Forces in Europe (CFE) substantially reducing non-nuclear weapons such as tanks, troops, artillery, and aircraft on both sides, also in Europe; and in 1991 the first Strategic Arms Reduction Treaty (START I), reducing American and Soviet long-range nuclear weapons. Together these agreements put into practice two principles that transformed European security, creating a new and unprecedented security order on the continent where many of history's most devastating wars had been waged.

One of the principles embodied in these treaties was transparency. For the first time in history, thanks to the satellite reconnaissance that both sides had developed during the Cold War but also due to provisions of the arms treaties opening military facilities to direct (known as "on-site") inspection, every country could know at all times just what armaments all other countries had and what the other countries were doing with their military forces. Transparency put an end to the fear of surprise attack, which governments had harbored throughout history and that had weighed on American military planners during the Cold War.

The arms agreements also implanted on the European continent the principle of defense dominance. The treaties reconfigured the military forces on both sides to make them useful for defending against attacks but not for launching them. When no country fears an attack by another, and no country has the military means to attack successfully, no attack at all from any quarter is likely to take place. The combination of transparency and defense dominance, the first reducing the fear of war, the second circumscribing the incentives for war, is a formula for peace; a military balance embedding the principles in Europe's military deployments, and a Russian government committed to them, created a new "common security" order in Europe, one more resistant to armed conflict than any previous arrangements.[97] The Clinton administration inherited this extraordinarily favorable situation from its predecessor and proceeded to undermine it.

The initiative that began the unraveling of the geopolitical gains the United States had made with the end of the Cold War was the eastward expansion of the West's Cold War-era military alliance, the North Atlantic Treaty Organization (NATO), to include the formerly communist countries of Eastern Europe and ultimately former parts of the Soviet Union itself. The circumstances surrounding the Clinton administration's decision to expand NATO were odd. For one thing, its predecessor had explicitly promised the Soviet leadership, during the discussions about German reunification, that the Atlantic alliance would *not* be expanded.[98] For another, at no point did a formal decision-making process within the executive branch of the American government assess the issue and arrive at a decision.[99] The secretary of defense, William Perry, whose department would be responsible for carrying out the initiative and whose own understanding of American strategic interests led him to oppose it, did not discover that Clinton had decided on expansion until after the president had already done so.[100]

With a broken promise and an irregular American decision-making process as the background, in a July 1997 meeting in Madrid NATO's member countries voted, at the behest of the United States, to extend invitations to three Eastern European countries: Poland, Hungary, and the Czech Republic. They officially joined the alliance in 1999, and in the next decade seven more countries were added: Estonia, Latvia, Lithuania, Slovenia, Slovakia, Bulgaria, and Romania.

From the very start of the process of expansion, Russia objected to it. The objections came from across the entire Russian political spectrum, from both the Yeltsin government and its opponents.[101] The Russians felt deceived, because of the discarded American promise not to expand. They felt excluded, because American officials made it clear that Russia would not receive an invitation to join. And they felt disrespected, because the only sensible basis for expanding NATO, which was indeed what motivated the new members, was distrust of the new Russia based on the assumption that it would resume the aggressive policies toward the world and especially toward its neighbors that the Soviet Union had carried out. In 1994 at a meeting in Budapest, Boris Yeltsin warned, ominously, that NATO expansion risked leading to a "cold peace" in Europe.[102] He turned out to be prescient. A strained and often hostile Western and American relationship with Russia replaced the Russian goodwill toward, sense of partnership with, and desire for integration into the West that the Clinton administration had inherited.

The administration tried to mollify the Russians. It produced a special NATO-Russia charter, known as the "Founding Act," spelling out the relationship between the two.§ As a reward for swallowing the bitter pill of expansion, as well as for withdrawing all its remaining troops from the three Baltic countries, Russia received an invitation to join the Group of Seven.[103] These American efforts at compensation failed to achieve their goal. Russia accepted NATO expansion because it had no choice. It lacked the political or economic leverage to stop it, and military resistance was out of the question. But the Russians never came to regard expansion as fair, legitimate, or indeed anything other than a betrayal of Western promises and an assault on Russian prerogatives and interests.

By alienating Russia, NATO expansion undercut Western and American goals in Europe. It turned Russia against the remarkably favorable post-Cold War settlement. It made the almost automatic Russian response to any and all American international initiatives one of opposition. It squandered, in short, much of the windfall that had come to the United States as a result of the way the Cold War had ended and led, eventually, to an aggressive Russian foreign policy that brought the post-Cold War era to an end.[104] It did this in return for no gain at all, making NATO expansion one of the greatest blunders in the history of American foreign policy.

§ Bill Clinton himself understood why the NATO-Russian charter would not transform Russian attitudes toward NATO expansion: "So let me get this straight. What the Russians get out of this great deal we're offering them is a chance to sit in the same room with NATO and join us whenever we all agree to something, but they don't have any ability to stop us from doing something that they don't agree with. They can register their disapproval by walking out of the room. And for their second big benefit, they get our promise that we're not going to put our military stuff into their former allies who are now going to be our allies, unless we happen to wake up one morning and decide to change our mind?" Quoted in James Goldgeier and Michael McFaul, *Power and Purpose: U.S. Policy toward Russia after the Cold War*, Washington, D.C.: The Brookings Institution, 2003, pp. 204–205.

If the decision to expand NATO was odd, so, too, was the way the Clinton administration justified it. The reasons administration officials and their political allies offered for moving the organization eastward, far into Eurasia, made no sense. In keeping with the missionary spirit of post-Cold War American foreign policy they declared NATO membership to be a vehicle for promoting democracy in Eastern Europe. They gave, however, no reason to believe that this or any military alliance could serve as a school for the protection of rights and the conduct of free elections. During the Cold War, as it happened, NATO membership had not guaranteed democracy in Portugal, Greece, and Turkey, each of which had had spells of authoritarian governance while belonging to the alliance.

Nor did the countries of Eastern Europe require the encouragement of missionaries to practice democracy. They were already converted to the Western democratic faith. With their deep identification with Western Europe and their determination to join the European Union, they were not going to abandon that faith, whether or not they joined NATO. The formerly communist country whose commitment to democracy was shakiest, whose future political course had the most serious implications for the West, and to which any democracy-promoting powers NATO possessed could most usefully have been applied, was Russia, which was not offered membership. NATO expansion in fact set back the cause of democracy in Russia by discrediting Russian democrats, who had argued in favor of a close relationship with the country that, Russians came to believe, had betrayed its commitments to them and disregarded their interests—the United States.[105]

The Clinton administration also asserted that bringing the countries of Eastern Europe into NATO prevented a reimposition of the Cold War division of the continent. Churchill had memorably described Europe as being divided by an "iron curtain," and the symbol of that division became the concrete and barbed wire barrier dividing the eastern and western sectors of the former German capital, the Berlin Wall. In fact, NATO expansion had precisely the opposite effect: it established a new, post-Cold War line of division between members and non-members. Russia was deliberately excluded and informed by American officials that it would not receive an invitation.[106] Because Russian hostility to NATO expansion became so intense, the alliance, for fear of triggering a conflict with Russia, did not dare to admit several countries on Russia's border, notably Georgia, which very much wanted to join, and Ukraine, where the issue of NATO membership aggravated the country's principal political cleavage, between the Ukrainian-speaking west and the Russian-speaking east.[107]

The rationales that the Clinton administration advanced for NATO expansion did not justify the measure,[108] and indeed were not the major reason that it took place. As in the case of the policy of linkage with China, domestic political considerations motivated the American decision to expand.[109]

Americans with ancestral roots in the prospective new member countries lobbied for their inclusion in the alliance. Republican politicians, seeking to reaffirm the reputation for assertiveness in foreign policy that had served them well during the Cold War, pressed for expansion. These efforts succeeded because of the new political context in which they took place. During the Cold War such an initiative would have received intense national scrutiny because the stakes would have been so high. Any major policy toward the Soviet Union affected the security of the United States. With the end of the Cold War, that was no longer true. The public gained the impression that NATO expansion was simply a friendly gesture toward deserving countries at no cost to the United States. The costs were destined to be considerable over the long run, but in the early 1990s nothing contradicted that impression. The end of the Cold War had demoted policy toward Russia from the always-small group of supremely important national concerns to the consistently much larger category of issues of, at best, secondary importance.

On such issues in American politics, with their lesser political salience and thus lower public visibility, determined minorities often prevail because they face no serious opposition. So it was with NATO expansion. The country as a whole took little notice of the issue. A few groups mobilized politically to support it. Much of the foreign policy community, including the most prominent former government expert on Russia, George F. Kennan, opposed the initiative but had no organized constituency on its side.[110] The opponents had the superior arguments but lacked the requisite political muscle; and on this occasion brawn trumped brains. The Senate ratified NATO expansion on the basis of the same kind of political calculation that governs the authorization of dams, post offices, and changes in the nation's tax code favorable to a particular industry or firm: some politically significant forces favored it while no one with political clout pressed the negative case.

Had the American business community seen Russia as a country as economically promising as China in the early 1990s it might have mobilized to resist NATO expansion as it rallied against the policy of linkage toward China, and for a similar reason: concern that the measure would jeopardize American access to the Russian market. In that case NATO expansion, and its consequences, might never have occurred. Russia did not, however, capture the imagination of American business as China did.

Had the opposition to expansion been more formidable politically, the administration might have been moved to adopt one of a number of policies that could have reassured the Eastern Europeans wary of their giant neighbor and former imperial overlord without at the same time offending and alienating Russia. It might have maintained and expanded its initial institutional response to the new, post-Cold War circumstances of European security, the Partnership for Peace, on which its Department of Defense looked kindly.[111] It could have given specific security guarantees to the only one of the first three additional NATO members, Poland, that actually had a border with Russia.[112] It could have found ways to include Russia itself in NATO, or devised a new, pan-European security organization to replace it. The Clinton administration did none of these things because it experienced no political pressure to do so. It expanded NATO because, politically, it could.

The Russian-American dispute over NATO expansion brought out the worst in officials on both sides: in the Russian case, suspicion of American motives sometimes verging on paranoia and a deep sense of grievance about the sharp decline in their country's status with the end of the Soviet Union; on the part of the Americans, the smug assumption that they knew what was best for Russia even if Russia's own leaders disagreed.[113]

In the dispute the United States got its way. Russia lacked the power to resist NATO expansion. As with the policy of linkage toward China, however, by acceding to pressures at home the Clinton administration reaped trouble abroad. Unlike with China, the administration did not correct itself and repair relations with Russia. NATO expansion became a festering sore. The resentment it caused would damage American interests for the next two decades and beyond.

The resentment and the damage were predictable—and predicted.[114] As opponents of expansion noted, by proceeding with expansion the Clinton administration was ignoring the major lesson of the two world wars of the twentieth century: the need to conciliate the losing power. After World War I the victors alienated Germany with a harsh peace settlement. This produced an aggressive German attempt to overturn the settlement, which led to World War II. After World War II the Western allies welcomed West Germany into their political, economic, and military ranks, with far better results. After the Cold War the Clinton administration followed the first precedent, with similar although fortunately not—at least through 2014—equally disastrous consequences.

The expansion of NATO over their objections taught Russians two lessons that it was not remotely in the American interest for them to learn: that American promises were not to be trusted; and that the West would take advantage of a weak and accommodating Russia. The Russian government under Boris Yeltsin's successor, Vladimir Putin, made progress in strengthening the country and became the opposite of accommodating in its relations with the United States. When Yeltsin assumed the presidency of independent Russia he made cooperation with the West the heart of his foreign policy. Under Putin, cooperation ceased. It sometimes seemed, over the next two decades, that Russia aimed, above all else, to thwart the United States.

To be sure, in the wake of NATO expansion, as before, the countries of Eastern Europe remained democracies, the purported goal of the initiative. But that would have happened anyway. The common security order in Europe that the Clinton administration had inherited did not disintegrate completely, at least not immediately; but insofar as it endured this was not because Russia accepted it, as was the case when it was first created, but because Russia lacked the means to overturn it. Peace in Europe came to rest not on Russian consent but on Russian weakness; and ultimately Russia felt strong enough to violate that peace.

As relations with Russia deteriorated at the end of the 1990s, critics of the Clinton administration began to raise a question that echoed one with which the Republicans had taunted the Democratic administration of President Harry S. Truman after the communist victory in the Chinese civil war in 1950: who lost Russia? If the question referred to the failure to establish a full-fledged democracy and a smoothly functioning free-market economy on the ruins of the Soviet Union, the correct answer was that no one could rightly be held responsible: it was simply not possible, whatever the United States did, to turn Russia into a large, Slavic facsimile of Sweden in a decade—if it is possible at all. If, however, the question asked who was responsible for turning Russian foreign policy from a pro-American to an anti-American orientation, the answer was clear: the Clinton administration.

NATO expansion was the first and most potent agent of that change but it was not the only one. In the 1990s the United States waged two wars in the Balkans that increased Russians' resentment of what they saw as America's reckless and arrogant international conduct. The wars arose from the Clinton administration's major innovation in American foreign policy, an innovation that, like its initial policies toward China and Russia, ultimately involved efforts, in the spirit of the missionary, to transform the internal arrangements of other countries. That policy was humanitarian intervention.

2

Humanitarian Intervention

The United States has an inescapable responsibility to build a peaceful world and terminate the abominable injustices and conditions that still plague civilization.

— MADELEINE ALBRIGHT[1]

"But what good came of it at last?"Quoth little Peterkin,
"Why that I cannot tell," said he,
"But 'twas a famous victory."

— ROBERT SOUTHEY, "The Battle of Blenheim"

The Innovation

Any president, even one with the minimal interest in foreign policy with which Bill Clinton entered office, would have had to devote some attention to relations with China and Russia and to the nation's trade policy. Each was too important to ignore. The Clinton administration invested even more time and political capital, however, in places that had no significance for global peace and American well-being.

It dispatched American military forces to four poor, obscure parts of the world that had rarely commanded any discernible attention from the United States: Somalia in East Africa, Haiti in the Caribbean,*

---

* Being much closer to North America, Haiti had had a larger role in American foreign policy than the other three. The successful slave rebellion against France that established a free Haitian republic in 1804 provoked a heated debate in the United States about the wisdom and propriety of extending diplomatic recognition to the new government. See Ronald Angelo Johnson, *Diplomacy in Black and White: John Adams, Toussaint Louverture and Their Atlantic World Alliance,*

and Bosnia-Herzegovina and Kosovo in the Balkans in southeastern Europe. In each of the four, the Clinton administration undertook something novel: military action for the purpose of rescuing distressed people. The practice, the administration's distinctive contribution to American foreign policy and an innovation in international affairs, came to be known as humanitarian intervention.

As with the initial Clinton policies toward China and Russia, the humanitarian interventions aimed not at protecting American interests, the traditional goal of foreign policy, but at vindicating American (and what the Clinton administration considered universal) values. As in the case of the proposed trade sanctions on China, the United States sought to protect the human rights of the people living in these four places, which were under assault from predatory governments.

As with Russia and China, moreover, the policies the administration adopted toward Somalia, Haiti, Bosnia, and Kosovo led to efforts to transform the economic and political arrangements of these places. The four of them also became the objects of American missions. As with China and Russia, these four missions failed. As well as similarities, however, the humanitarian interventions had major differences from the Clinton policies toward China and Russia, and it was these differences that made them an innovation in American foreign policy.

Somalia, Haiti, Bosnia, and Kosovo did not matter in anything like the way China and Russia did. When the United States intervened on behalf of its values in these four places, that was the only basis for intervention: there were no substantial strategic or economic American interests at stake in any of them. Moreover, the United States sent its armed forces to the four. Military intervention in China or Russia, two large, nuclear-armed countries, was unthinkable. It was not unthinkable in Somalia, where American troops went to prevent starvation, or in Haiti, where their initial mission was to secure the exit of a military junta and the restoration of an elected civilian president, or in Bosnia and Kosovo, where the United States intervened to protect Muslims against the depredations of neighboring Serbs.

Athens, Georgia: University of Georgia Press, 2014. From 1915 to 1934 American military forces occupied Haiti. During the Cold War, however, the United States paid little attention to the country.

Military intervention did not, of course, begin after the Cold War. The United States sent troops beyond its borders on a number of occasions—on a large scale to Korea and to Vietnam—during the course of its four-decades-long conflict with the Soviet Union. It had dispatched forces abroad, to Cuba and the Philippines in 1898, for example, before that. Indeed, the tendency of strong states to impose themselves on weaker ones has a very long history. It is a theme of Thucydides' classic account of the war between Athens and Sparta in fifth century B.C. Greece.[2] The defining difference between the military operations of the past, including the distant past, and those the United States undertook in the 1990s is one of motive.

Historically sovereign states went to war beyond their borders to capture territory, seize riches, or defeat hostile powers. The American military interventions of the 1990s had none of these purposes. They were not designed to bring wealth, power, or security to Americans and in fact achieved none of these things. They had instead purely disinterested aims: the intended beneficiaries did not live, work, or vote in the United States.[3]

In comparison with the Clinton policies toward China and Russia the four humanitarian interventions had, initially, more modest goals. They sought not to transform Somalia, Haiti, Bosnia, or Kosovo but merely to protect the people living there. The Clinton administration saw itself as the gallant knight rescuing people in distress, not the architect and builder of new political and economic orders in faraway places. Yet the United States ultimately found itself attempting a transformation in each place, attempts that proved more protracted and expensive, although no more successful, than the abortive efforts to induce the Chinese government to respect the rights of the Chinese people and to install democracy and free markets in Russia.

Because of this pattern, the humanitarian interventions of the Clinton years contributed two new terms to the American political lexicon. One was "mission creep," denoting the tendency for rescue missions to turn into far more ambitious projects. The other term was "nation-building," which referred to the project the United States undertook in Somalia, Haiti, Bosnia, and Kosovo. In fact, "nation-building" was not precisely what the United States mainly attempted in these places. A nation is a group of people bound together by language, or ethnicity, or religion, or some other common cultural feature and thus can only truly develop over time. The more accurate although less frequently used term is "state-building": what the United States tried, without success, to do was to build what each place conspicuously lacked: the institutions of a modern, efficient, democratic, prosperity-supporting state.

The transformations the United States attempted in the wake of its humanitarian interventions were more ambitious than those it tried to foster in China and Russia because the American government had far greater power to bring them about: it occupied Somalia, Haiti, Bosnia, and Kosovo. It not only had a greater opportunity to transform these places, it had an incentive to do so because building working institutions seemed the surest way to prevent a recurrence of the violence that had triggered the interventions in the first place. Despite the American investment of time and money, and despite the presence of American troops, however, neither the institutions of a modern state nor a well-run free-market economy were established in any of them.

The impetus for the humanitarian interventions of the 1990s came from the desire to promote American values as well as American interests in the world. The United States has seldom done anything beyond its borders without justifying it as helping make the world happier, freer, and more prosperous. Before the 1990s, however, the aim of improving the world had never served as the primary, let alone the only, justification for military action abroad. Woodrow Wilson said of American participation in World War I, "What we demand is nothing peculiar to ourselves. It is that the world be made fit and safe to live in."[4] Wilson no doubt genuinely believed in American disinterestedness, but the United States was also fighting for the classic geopolitical aim of preventing any single power—in this case imperial Germany—from dominating the European continent, and in fact entered the war only after Germany began sinking American ships. The United States was defending freedom in World War II but also, and in the first instance, defending itself after Japan attacked its territory in Hawaii and Germany declared war on America.

Foremost among the values that spurred humanitarian intervention was the relief of suffering. Like the wish to improve the world, compassion did not suddenly become a part of the American outlook when the Cold War ended. Improvement and compassion gained a greater purchase on American foreign policy in the 1990s than ever before, however, and produced military interventions far beyond the country's borders, because of America's unprecedented power in the post-Cold War world.

The United States sent troops to rescue endangered Somalis, Haitians, Bosnian Muslims, and Kosovar Albanians because it could. No other power had the means or the motive to stop these operations and although some did object to the American military initiatives— the Russians, in particular, criticized the two Balkan interventions— none tried actively to block or hinder them. The lopsided distribution of power in the international system of the 1990s, combined with the longstanding American wish to make other countries more like the United States and the compassion of Americans—which was not necessarily greater than that of other people but was surely not smaller, either—partially account for the Clinton administration's foreign-policy innovation of humanitarian intervention. That innovation had two additional causes: a major feature of the established norms of international politics that had come, by the 1990s, to seem to many, including many Americans, to be an acute flaw in need of repair; and the personal inclinations of the individuals Bill Clinton appointed to positions of responsibility for foreign policy.

International law rests on the concept, given formal expression as long ago as the seventeenth century,[5] of sovereignty—the unchallengeable authority of the government of a sovereign state within that state's borders. Any attempt by another government to impinge on that authority by military force violates international law. Without this norm no basis would exist for international order of any kind: any country would be legally entitled—or at least not legally forbidden—to attack any other at any time. Article 2 of the United Nations Charter affirms the principle of sovereignty.[6]

The concept of sovereignty means, however, that no external power is entitled to interfere with whatever governments choose to do to the people they govern. Governments have done terrible things, especially in the twentieth century; and over the course of that century the prohibition against intervening to stop them came to seem increasingly problematical.[7]

In the wake of the crimes and atrocities committed during World War II a number of non-binding conventions were established putting limits on what governments may legally do to those they govern. These conventions concerned the rights that inhere in individuals—human rights—on which no authority is entitled to infringe. The Preamble to the United Nations Charter of 1945 affirmed the existence of fundamental human rights even as its text endorsed sovereignty. The organization's General Assembly voted to ratify the Universal Declaration of Human Rights and the Convention on the Prevention and Punishment of the Crime of Genocide 1948. In 1950 the European Convention on Human Rights was opened for signing.[8]

The 1970s saw another surge in international attention to the protection of individuals from their governments.[9] One section of the Helsinki Final Act of 1975, which concluded a pan-European conference on peace and security, committed all its signatories, including the Soviet Union and its Eastern European satellites, to respect a series of individual rights. (The communist governments honored these commitments in the breach.) Non-governmental organizations devoted to calling attention to human rights violations, such as Amnesty International and Human Rights Watch, came to prominence. The Carter administration gave the protection of human rights greater importance in American foreign policy than ever before.

By the 1990s, most of the large-scale violence in the world was being caused not by one country invading another—not, that is, by clear violations of international law[10]—but rather by assaults within countries, often by governments against their own people. The convention of sovereignty forbade any rescue of such people originating beyond the borders of the country in question. This prohibition seemed increasingly unacceptable, untenable, and unnecessary. UN Secretary General Javier Perez de Cuellar spoke for many in a speech in France in April 1991. After citing Article 2 of the UN Charter he said,

> But one could—and I would even say, should—inquire whether certain other texts that were later adopted by the United Nations, in particular the Universal Declaration of Human rights, do not implicitly call into question this inviolable notion of sovereignty. Has not a balance been established between the right of States, as

confirmed by the Charter, and the rights of the individual, as confirmed by the Universal Declaration? We are clearly witnessing what is probably an irresistible shift in public attitudes towards the belief that the defence of the oppressed in the name of morality should prevail over frontiers and legal documents.[11]

If the protection of human rights were sometimes to supersede the prerogatives of sovereignty, as Perez de Cuellar said it should and would, two questions had to be answered. First, how and when should exceptions to the inviolability of sovereignty be made? Second, if military intervention to rescue beleaguered citizens were to take place, who would undertake it?

In the course of the 1990s, despite the rescue missions in Somalia, Haiti, Bosnia, and Kosovo, no consistent, widely accepted answer to the first question emerged. The practice of humanitarian intervention did not acquire a principled basis. To the second question, however, the Clinton administration did have an answer: it was the United States that undertook the defense of the oppressed. It did so because it had, in the wake of the Cold War, the power to do so and because some of its senior foreign policy officials believed that they and their country had the right and even the duty to use the country's armed forces to protect human rights.

The Clinton administration had broad leeway to set the course of the nation's foreign policy. Because foreign policy addresses complicated, unfamiliar issues involving trends and events far from the United States, the general public ordinarily pays little sustained attention to it.[12] Foreign policy is to public policy in general what foreign films are to Hollywood extravaganzas: a minority interest. The minority of Americans that does follow it closely—the foreign policy community, with the president at its head—has broad discretion to carry out initiatives toward other countries.

It does not, however, have unlimited discretion. Foreign policy has boundaries that it is politically dangerous to cross. During the Cold War those boundaries ruled out, at one end, abandoning the global struggle with the Soviet Union and, at the other, pushing the confrontation to the point of engaging in armed combat with America's nuclear-armed adversary. An administration that seemed to approach either extreme would meet political resistance from both the foreign policy establishment and the public. A presidential candidate who appeared not to understand or respect the parameters of responsible foreign policy conduct would not get the political support necessary to win the office.

With the end of the Cold War these particular limits became irrelevant. The foreign policy community had greater leeway to choose what the United States would do beyond its borders. The Clinton administration chose humanitarian intervention. It made this choice because, among other reasons, its upper ranks were populated by individuals who had had reservations about some features of America's Cold War foreign policy. They had, for example, opposed the Vietnam War, which they had come to see as not only strategically futile—and the United States did in the end lose the war—but also morally compromised. Their country, as they saw it, had defended a corrupt, undemocratic South Vietnamese government and had waged a war that had killed many civilians. Humanitarian intervention gave them the opportunity to wield American power for what they considered nobler purposes.

Many of these Clinton officials had served in the Carter administration, which had made the defense of human rights around the world a higher American priority than ever before. Humanitarian intervention accorded with the spirit of the Carter foreign policy. It accorded, as well, with the guiding purpose of the Democratic Party to which they all belonged, by employing the power of the government to assist people in need of help—in this case people living outside the United States rather than Americans and who were suffering from physical assault rather than, as in the case of Democratic-sponsored domestic programs, economic hardship.

Humanitarian intervention had another appeal to Clinton foreign policy officials. Like most people who manage to obtain the kinds of positions they held, they wanted to leave their mark. They wanted, that is, to make foreign policy achievements that their contemporaries would admire and that posterity would celebrate. They wanted, like all ambitious people (and people without ambition seldom rise to the top of competitive bureaucracies) to build a monument to themselves. Humanitarian intervention, both as the rescue of individual Somalis, Haitians, Bosnian Muslims, and Kosovar Albanians and as an innovation in international practice and American foreign policy, seemed a worthy monument to erect. In this way they functioned as a classic interest group in American politics, pressing for policies that were of great value to them but of no particular interest to the wider public, which, however, did not in principle object to them.

Not all members of the foreign policy community regarded humanitarian intervention as an appropriate departure for American foreign policy. The George H. W. Bush administration adopted more detached policies toward the places to which its successors chose to send American troops. Bush deliberately eschewed the nation-building in Somalia that Clinton adopted. He did not intervene to restore the deposed president of Haiti, as his successor did. He resisted calls to involve the United States in the fighting in Bosnia, which had begun in 1992, the last year of his presidency.

The Bush conduct of America's relations with other countries resembled the approach to foreign policy that students of international politics call "realism," according to which countries concentrate on defending their vital interests, above all their security. The Clinton foreign policy conformed more closely to a different and more expansive approach known as "idealism," in which a major goal is the promotion of the country's values abroad. Two widely reported comments about the war in Bosnia by senior foreign policy officials capture the difference between the two approaches, and the two administrations. Responding to those urging intervention in Bosnia the Bush Secretary of State James Baker said, "We got no dog in that fight." No major American interests, he meant, were at stake in the conflict there. Arguing for intervention to the chairman of the Joint Chiefs of Staff, Colin Powell, who opposed it (and whom Bush, not Clinton, had appointed), the Clinton ambassador to the United Nations, Madeleine Albright, said "What's the point of having this superb military you're always talking about if we can't use it?"[13] Powell believed that the armed forces should be used only to defend American interests: Albright wanted to use them to promote American values.

Powell retired after the first six months of the Clinton administration. Albright stayed for eight years. During that time her preference prevailed. Because it transferred power from an administration committed to the realist approach to America's role abroad to one that embraced a particular version of idealism, the 1992 presidential election, in which foreign policy issues played almost no part, turned out to have significant consequences for American foreign policy.

Humanitarian intervention divided Republicans, who generally opposed the Clinton initiatives, from Democrats, who on the whole supported them; but within the foreign policy community the division did not follow strictly partisan lines. The Republican leader in the Senate, Robert Dole, for example, advocated intervention in Bosnia. A prominent and vocal minority of those associated with the Republican Party endorsed the use of American force to rescue distressed people. Often known as "neoconservatives," they approved of the promotion of American values abroad, something they believed President Ronald Reagan had undertaken with great success. For them, humanitarian intervention continued to be one of the most compelling features of the Reagan foreign policy.[14]

While the government takes the initiative in conceiving and implementing the foreign policy of the United States, in order to be sustained over the long term these policies require public support. In foreign policy, as in other sectors of public life in the American democracy, the public has the final say. Humanitarian intervention did not arouse any particular enthusiasm among Americans. Public pressure did not push the Clinton administration into Somalia, Haiti, Bosnia, or Kosovo. To be sure, some asserted that the rise of all-news cable television created what they called "the CNN effect," whereby the instant transmission into the living rooms of American viewers of images of people suffering far away created a powerful public demand to send the nation's armed forces to relieve that suffering.[15] Depicting starvation in Somalia and mass killing in Bosnia surely had an impact on American foreign policy, by bringing these events to public attention. But opinion polls showed that in no case did a majority of Americans come to believe that the United States had an urgent responsibility to act to stop them.[16]

While not pressing for humanitarian intervention, neither did the public object in principle to the operations in Somalia, Haiti, Bosnia, and Kosovo. It judged them, as it is wont to judge foreign policy initiatives, on the basis of cost. The cost Americans are willing to pay for any particular foreign policy depends on how important they deem the object of that policy to be. Costs are measured in money but above all in American lives. In general, the more important the American interest that is at stake—with the security of the United States being the most important interest of all—the more the public will be willing to pay in blood and treasure to secure it. It is sometimes said that the American public will not support an international initiative unless it aims to achieve some goal beyond mere security and self-interest. In fact, something closer to the opposite turns out to be true. Americans are disposed to pay *only* to safeguard American interests.[†] They are realists, not idealists. They regard the vindication of American values abroad as a luxury, not a necessity.[17]

Americans are willing to tolerate their government carrying out value-based policies but only as long as those policies don't cost much. They were willing for the Clinton administration to undertake rescue efforts in Somalia, Haiti, Bosnia, and Kosovo, but not at the cost of many—or indeed any—American lives. American deaths, as the administration discovered in Somalia, would trigger a political backlash. The major constraint on American military operations to rescue distressed peoples came not from the opposition of other countries but rather from the reservations of the American public.

The humanitarian interventions that he authorized, therefore, put Bill Clinton in an awkward political position. He was caught between the foreign policy officials of his own administration, many of whom considered these interventions to be major contributions to global well-being and international justice, on the one hand, and the voting public, which had no fundamental objection to them but opposed the loss of American lives in carrying them out, on the other. He was like Dr. Proudie, the Bishop of Barchester in the 1857 novel *Barchester Towers* by the English writer Anthony Trollope, who finds himself constantly pulled in opposite directions by his overbearing wife and his scheming

---

[†] Clinton advisor Dick Morris "argues that 'it is only through a focus on the abuse of people—particularly children—that the American people are willing to rise above their essentially isolationist prejudices,' an observation, the record suggests, that is probably pretty close to being sanctimonious nonsense." John Mueller, "Public Opinion as a Constraint on U.S. Foreign Policy: Assessing the Perceived Value of American and Foreign Lives," Paper prepared for presentation at the National Convention of the International Studies Association, Los Angeles, California, March 14–18, 2000, p. 13.

chaplain. In the manner of the bishop, who had no interest in the matters over which his wife and his chaplain contended and whose chief desire was for a quiet, conflict-free life, Clinton displayed little enthusiasm for the interventions over which he presided. Like Bishop Proudie his principal aim was to satisfy, or at least to avoid offending, the two constituencies with which he had to deal, and in these terms he succeeded. He had the courage of his lack of conviction: after a fiasco in Somalia he scrupulously avoided putting American personnel in harm's way when he deployed them abroad. In this way his administration was able, on the whole, to carry out the military interventions without the popularity-sapping loss of American lives.

It stands as a minor irony that one of the 42nd president's two distinctive contributions to the history of American foreign policy[18] was not something in which he himself seemed personally invested. In a further irony, this quintessentially Clintonian idealist practice was actually begun by his realist predecessor, George H. W. Bush.

Somalia, Haiti, Rwanda

The Bush administration's initial foray into the rescue of distressed people through American military action took place in northern Iraq. Having seen Saddam Hussein's army evicted from Kuwait by an American-led coalition, the Kurds of that region rose up against his oppressive rule.[19] The Iraqi military cracked down on them brutally, and hundreds of thousands of Kurds fled their homes, gathering near the border with Turkey. Secretary of State James Baker visited the border area and reported to President Bush: "You have no idea of the human nightmare here. People are dying every day. We've got to do something and do it now. If we don't, literally thousands of people are going to die."

The United States put together a package of assistance for the Kurds and, to assure its delivery, declared Iraq north of the 36th parallel a "safe zone" protected initially by American troops and over the longer term by a "no-fly" zone patrolled by American warplanes to prevent Saddam's aircraft from attacking. The United Nations Security Council passed a resolution approving the effort, asserting, for the first time, that repression within a country posed a threat to international peace and security.[20]

While breaking with the established pattern of American foreign policy (and laying the groundwork for the ultimate creation, after the second war against Iraq 12 years later, of a Kurdish state independent in all but name), this intervention was not seen as, and was not intended to be, an innovation in international relations. It was, rather, a coda to a war fought for the most traditional and conventional of reasons: to repel cross-border aggression. It was the George H. W. Bush administration, however, despite its realist bent, that launched the first purely, unambiguously humanitarian military intervention of the post-Cold War era, in 1992 in Somalia.

Located on the horn of Africa, with a coastline on the Indian Ocean, Somalia was ruled by Great Britain and Italy, each occupying different areas, from the late nineteenth century until 1960,[21] when the two regions merged to become an independent country. A military officer, Mohamed Siad Barre, seized power in 1969 and exercised dictatorial authority until 1992, when he was driven from the country. Somalia fell into anarchy, consumed by an ongoing conflict among militias based on its dominant form of social organization, kinship networks known as clans. In the chaos, a humanitarian crisis similar to the one in northern Iraq developed: hundreds of thousands of Somalis fled their homes, many to neighboring Kenya and Ethiopia. They lacked easy access to food. The capital, Mogadishu, was dominated by clan leaders—warlords—who seized food supplies for themselves and their followers. Mass starvation loomed.

The United States had provided economic assistance to Somalia in the 1980s[22] but had no strategic or economic interests there. Still, to prevent famine President Bush decided to send armed forces to the country to assure that food reached those in need. A total of thirty-five thousand American troops arrived in Somalia in December 1992 for this purpose. By some estimates their presence saved tens, even hundreds of thousands of lives.[23]

The Somalia mission contradicted the guiding principles and established practices of the Bush foreign policy; but Bush had been defeated for re-election the month before and this last chapter in his stewardship of American foreign policy was meant to stand as a valedictory good deed. It was a good deed that its authors fully expected to be limited in scope, cost, and duration: once the American troops had established sufficient order for relief supplies to get through, they would, it was planned, be replaced by forces under the control of the United Nations.[24]

Bush may have authorized the Somali initiative out of sensitivity to the charge that he was conducting a callous, heartless policy toward the Balkans by refusing to intervene in the fighting in Bosnia and that his foreign policy lacked a moral compass.[25] He certainly faced no strong public demand to do anything in Somalia[26] nor did he intend to set a precedent for a series of humanitarian interventions in the last decade of the twentieth century. That, however, is what the Somali operation turned out to be. Like those to come in Haiti, Bosnia, and Kosovo, a mission to relieve suffering turned, inadvertently but seemingly unavoidably, into an exercise in nation-building. Unlike those to come, the American effort at nation-building in Somalia proved to be an abbreviated one. Like the others, it failed.

In the early months of the Clinton administration the purpose of the international presence in Somalia changed. Mission creep occurred. With the United Nations in charge of the operation, its secretary-general, Boutros Boutros-Ghali, initiated a policy of transforming the country for the not-unreasonable purpose of putting an end to the violence that plagued it and had led to widespread hunger. In late March of 1993 the UN Security Council passed a resolution calling for "the rehabilitation of the political institutions and economy of Somalia."[27] Madeleine Albright, then the American ambassador to the UN, strongly supported the resolution. It represented, she said, "an unprecedented enterprise aimed at nothing less than the restoration of an entire country."[28] Chaotic and destitute, Somalia was a classic example of what came to be known as a "failed state." Boutros-Ghali and Albright proposed to reverse the failure, and to begin by disarming the local militias.

This far deeper intrusion into Somali affairs than the Bush administration had contemplated placed the United Nations, and therefore the United States, at odds with the most powerful clan leader, Mohammed Farah Aidid. He had succeeded in overthrowing Siad Barre, he held a strong position in Mogadishu, and he aspired to dominate the country himself. On June 3, 1993, Aidid's forces attacked Pakistani UN peacekeepers in the capital, killing 26 of them. The American representative in Somalia, Admiral Jonathan Howe, issued a warrant for his arrest and offered a $25,000 reward for his capture.[29]

In August, the United States sent a battalion of specially trained commandos to assist in the fight against Aidid. On October 3 they launched a helicopter-borne assault on a hotel in downtown Mogadishu in an attempt to capture him. The operation went badly wrong. Two helicopters were shot down by ground fire from Aidid's militia. American troops found themselves trapped in a dense urban area surrounded by an angry armed mob. Eighteen Americans were killed and 74 were wounded. (The Somali dead numbered 500 among 1,000 total casualties.) Video clips of a dead American soldier being dragged through the streets while the local crowd cheered were broadcast on American television.[30]

The American public reacted with shock and anger. The Senate passed a resolution calling for the withdrawal of American troops from the country. One poll showed that two-thirds of the public believed that Somalia had the potential to become a military quagmire for the United States, in the manner of the still-unpopular Vietnam conflict.[31] Clinton himself was surprised and dismayed. He had been paying no attention to Somalia.[32] He ordered the dispatch of more troops to Somalia to stabilize the country but promised that all of them would leave within six months, and they did. In his speech announcing these measures he said that, "it is not our job to rebuild Somali society."[33] The American commitment to nation-building in the Horn of Africa had come to an abrupt halt.

The mission lost the Clinton administration's support because it lost the support of the American public. It lost the public's support because the firefight in Mogadishu changed the public understanding of what the United States was doing in Somalia. The operation had been presented as a rescue mission for endangered people, with American soldiers acting as a kind of emergency medical service team, and that is what it was at the ouset: the name of the mission, "Operation Restore Hope," had a therapeutic rather than a bellicose connotation. The battle in the Somali capital caused the members of the public to see it in a different way—as a war. It was a war they did not support.

Secretary of Defense Les Aspin became the scapegoat for the misadventure and was fired two months later.[34] The United Nations also came in for a share of the blame, especially in the American Congress. This was only partly justified. It had indeed been Boutros-Ghali who had broadened the narrow mission the Bush administration had initially undertaken in Somalia. But the American representatives both at the United Nations and in Mogadishu had supported him, and the fateful military operation had taken place entirely under American command.

Somalia did illustrate two important features of international politics and American foreign policy that proved relevant to the interventions to come in the 1990s, and in the following decade as well. The first was that humanitarian operations inevitably become entangled in politics. The people of Somalia were victims of a manmade disaster. The conflict that imperiled them came about because different groups had different goals and were willing to fight to achieve them. These conflicting goals, in Somalia and also in Haiti, in Bosnia, and in Kosovo, belonged to the realm of politics. Ending the threat to the lives and well-being of the people in jeopardy in each place required ending the political conflict causing it, which involved opposing one or more of the contending parties. It required Americans to act, in the end, not as Samaritans but as warriors.

That imperative, however, ran afoul of the second exemplary feature of Somalia. When the goal was saving others rather than protecting Americans, the American public was willing to spend very little on military intervention. Indeed, the maximum number of politically allowable American deaths in Somalia—and in Haiti, Bosnia, and Kosovo—turned out to be zero.[35] The Somali operation became instantly unpopular when it exceeded that number. Bill Clinton understood this and conducted his administration's subsequent humanitarian interventions accordingly, notably in a place far closer to the United States than the Horn of Africa and where America did have a history of involvement.

Haiti occupies the western part of the island of Hispaniola in the Caribbean, 681 miles from Miami. The people of Haiti won their independence from France through a successful slave revolt in 1804, but the country's nineteenth- and twentieth-century history was marked by poverty and oppression. From 1915 to 1934 it was occupied by the United States. The American sojourn did furnish Haiti with some infrastructure but did not alter its unhappy political and economic trajectory. From 1957 to 1971 Francois Duvalier, known for his nickname "Papa Doc" and his claim to be a voodoo priest, presided over a brutal tyranny. Upon his death his son Jean-Claude succeeded him. In 1986 the younger Duvalier was ousted by a military coup, and in 1990 Jean-Bertrand Aristide, a Catholic priest whom the Church had defrocked because of his radical theological views, was elected Haiti's president. After eight months in office, in September 1991, the military overthrew Aristide and seized power.

Motivated by the political harshness of the military junta, as well as by economic hardship, Haitians began setting out for the United States in makeshift boats. The Bush administration adopted a policy of returning those who managed to reach Florida. During the 1992 presidential campaign Bill Clinton criticized this practice, as he had criticized the Bush China policy, and promised a more welcoming approach to Haitian refugees. The Central Intelligence Agency (CIA) showed him aerial photographs of a new wave of boat building on the island and estimated that his more generous policy would attract 200,000 more people.[36] Fearing a political backlash in the United States, candidate Clinton retracted his promise; but upon taking office he felt the need to do something to improve conditions in Haiti. His administration launched a program of economic sanctions designed to apply pressure on the junta, and ultimately the ruling officers agreed to permit Aristide to return to power. The date set for his return was October 30, 1993.

In preparation for Aristide's return to power, a group of about 200 American soldiers and 25 Canadian engineers embarked on a ship, the USS *Harlan County*, for Haiti, where they were to train the police and participate in other projects. They arrived at the main port and capital, Port-au-Prince, on October 11. On the docks, 100 or so Haitians had gathered, undoubtedly at the behest of the ruling junta, which did not, despite its agreement, wish to relinquish power. The crowd jeered and shouted threats and anti-American slogans, including, just a week after the Battle of Mogadishu, "Somalia, Somalia." While the ship hovered offshore, a divided Clinton administration debated whether to order it to dock. On October 12, fearful of a repetition of the political disaster in Somalia, it decided to withdraw the *Harlan County* without unloading its passengers.[37] A small mob in the poorest country in the Western Hemisphere had intimidated and repulsed the government of the United States.

Embarrassed, the administration stiffened the economic sanctions on Haiti and searched for a way to restore Aristide to power. It settled on an invasion. In mid-September 1994, 25,000 troops were poised to take control of the country for the purpose of returning the deposed president to Port-au-Prince. Once more the United States was preparing to send troops into harm's way not to protect American interests but to assure the well-being of others, in this case Haitians suffering under a repressive military government.

As the moment to begin the assault approached, former president Jimmy Carter volunteered to travel to Haiti to try to negotiate a peaceful entry for the troops. He took with him Sam Nunn, the senior senator from Georgia and long-time chairman of the Senate Armed Services Committee, and Colin Powell, who had stepped down a year previously as chairman of the Joint Chiefs of Staff. As the news reached Port-au-Prince that the invasion was about to begin, the three of them succeeded in persuading the ruling junta to step aside without resisting the American forces.

Unlike in Somalia, in Haiti no Americans died. Partly for that reason, and again unlike in Somalia, American forces did not withdraw immediately; some remained until 1996. In the end, however, the longer effort at political and economic transformation in the Caribbean had no more success than the far briefer one on the Horn of Africa.[38] The next chapter in the Clinton experience with humanitarian intervention also took place in Africa. It made an impression on American policymakers not only because of what happened there, which was worse than the damage to the people of Somalia and Haiti, but also because, unlike in Somalia and Haiti, the United States did not intervene.

American ties to, history with, and interest in Rwanda, in the Great Lakes region of central Africa, had been even flimsier than they were in the case of Somalia. Before 1994 few Americans, it is safe to say—even those sophisticated about international affairs—could have found Rwanda on a map. A German possession from 1886 to 1916 and a Belgian colony from that date until 1962, the country's population consisted of two tribal groups, the Tutsi, who dominated it during the colonial period, and the more numerous Hutu. After independence the groups had fraught, periodically violent, relations with each other.

In the early 1990s Tutsis mounted an armed insurgency against the Hutu-dominated government. In 1993 the United Nations brokered an agreement between the two groups in the Tanzanian town of Arusha, which called for a greater Tutsi role in the government and the army. A small contingent of UN peacekeepers arrived in the country to oversee the accord.

On April 6, 1994, a private plane carrying the Hutu president of the country to its capital, Kigali, was shot down by a surface-to-air missile. Hutus blamed Tutsi rebels for the attack (responsibility was never definitively established) and began a massacre of Rwanda's Tutsi, as well as of moderate Hutu politicians. Over the course of 100 days at least 500,000 Tutis were killed, a total amounting to more than three-quarters of the group's population in the country.[39] Half of them died in the first two weeks of the slaughter. The Hutu rampage came to an end when Tutsi insurgents conquered the country in June and July 1994, making refugees of an estimated two million Hutu, who fled to neighboring countries, especially Zaire.

On the first day of the violence, 10 Belgian peacekeepers were executed. Western governments, led by the French, then launched an emergency evacuation of the several thousand Westerners in Rwanda. A week after the beginning of the massacres all of them had left.[40] France had supported the Hutu government and actually landed troops in the country to supervise the evacuation, but the French forces did not move to stop the killing. As for the Clinton administration, the slaughter provoked consternation in its ranks but, in the wake of Somalia, it did nothing.‡

Just what could feasibly have been done to save the Tutsis is a matter of debate. General Romeo Dallaire, the commander of the UN mission in the country, later said that 5,000 peacekeepers could have saved 500,000 lives.[41] There were half that many UN personnel in the

‡ The administration was careful not to apply the term "genocide" to what was happening in Rwanda, out of concern that this would create obligations it was not going to fulfill: " ... through the person of its then UN ambassador and future secretary of state Madeleine Albright, the Clinton administration made sure that the word 'genocide' was never applied [at the United Nations] to what

country when the killing began. Fewer than half of those were peace-keepers, who were in any event neither trained nor equipped to stop it.[42] This meant that intervention from abroad was the only way to protect the Tutsis. One careful study concluded that because the slaughter was not foreseen by foreigners and because so much of the killing occurred so rapidly, even if Western governments had chosen to act as quickly as possible once the massacre got under way most of those who died could not have been saved.[43]

The Rwandan massacres left the Clinton administration with a sense of guilt at not having acted on what its senior officials thought was, or should be, the basic American principle of preventing mass slaughter. The Rwandan Tutsi had been in dire need of protection and the United States had failed to provide it. In a brief visit to the country in 1998, Bill Clinton apologized for American inaction and later called the omission one of the greatest regrets of his presidency.[44] While the United States did not rescue the Tutsis, their fate did have an impact on American foreign policy. It increased the already vocal sentiment within the foreign policy community to use American armed forces to protect another beleaguered people, in the former Yugoslav province of Bosnia-Herzegovina.

Bosnia

Yugoslavia was formed after World War I as a union of southern Slavic peoples formally known as the Kingdom of the Slovenes, Croats, and Serbs. It was invaded by the Axis powers during World War II and after the war was reconstituted as a multinational state under communist rule consisting of six constituent socialist republics: Serbia, Slovenia, Montenegro (far smaller than the others), Macedonia, Croatia, and Bosnia-Herzegovina. Josip Broz Tito, who had led the communist

was taking place in Rwanda while the killing was actually going on ... Susan Rice, an Albright protegee who would go on to become assistant secretary of state for African affairs, demanded of her then colleagues on the National Security Council, 'If we use the word 'genocide' and are seen as doing nothing, what will be the effect on the November [Congressional] elections?'" David Rieff, *A Bed for the Night: Humanitarianism in Crisis*, New York: Simon & Schuster, 2002, pp. 161–162.

resistance to the invaders during the war, presided over it. Tito refused to subordinate his country to Russia and the Yugoslavia he ruled was less repressive than the Soviet Union and its satellite countries; but it was also a country in which all expressions of nationalism were firmly suppressed. Tito's Yugoslavia was founded on his version of Marxism-Leninism and on the Yugoslav patriotism he tried to foster.

Of all the communist countries Yugoslavia was the one with which the United States had the most cordial relationship prior to the rapprochement with China in 1972. Washington appreciated and, in modest ways, rewarded Yugoslavia's greater political independence from the Soviet Union than that of any other European communist government. Two senior foreign policy officials of the George H. W. Bush administration had served there: Lawrence S. Eagleburger, the secretary of state in the final months of the Bush presidency, as a foreign service officer and Brent Scowcroft, the national security advisor, as a military attache. None of the senior figures of the Clinton administration had direct experience with the country, which did not prevent them from bringing to office strong views about its fate.

Tito died in 1980 and a decade later, with the collapse of orthodox communism across Eurasia, the country he had re-created broke up: nationalism was the dynamite that blew it apart.[45] Nationalist sentiment proved more potent than belief in communism or loyalty to a united Yugoslavia. Nationalist politicians gained popularity and ultimately power in Slovenia, Croatia, and Serbia—the last of these the largest of the republics where an ambitious communist functionary named Slobodan Milosevic made himself the outspoken and aggressive champion of Serbs and Serb interests everywhere. In elections in 1990, nationalists took power in Slovenia and Croatia, putting independence for each of them at the top of the Yugoslav agenda.[46]

In the summer of 1991, as Croatia moved toward independence from Yugoslavia, its Serb-populated eastern parts seceded, with help from the Serb-dominated Yugoslav National Army (JNA). At the same time, in June, Slovenia declared its independence. A brief, 10-day war with the JNA followed, but the federal troops withdrew and Slovenia became a sovereign state. In both cases only limited fighting took place.

The Croatian and Slovene exits from Yugoslavia put pressure on Bosnia, which differed from them and from Serbia in a crucial respect:

no single nationality dominated it. Within its borders lived Croats, who in 1991 made up 17.3 percent of the population, Serbs, who constituted 31.4 percent, and Muslims, the descendants of inhabitants of the region who had converted to Islam during the long period of Ottoman rule from the fifteenth to the nineteenth centuries, who were numerically the largest group but a plurality, not a majority, at 43.7 percent.[47]

Bosnia had no history of independence. It had always been part of a larger unit: the Ottoman Empire from 1463 to 1878, the Habsburg Empire from 1878 to 1918, and Yugoslavia thereafter. Before Yugoslavia began breaking apart no one had ever lived, or had had any expectation of living, in an independent Bosnia. Its eligibility for independence, as a republic of Yugoslavia, was an accident of history. Tito had decided to designate it as such in 1943, in the midst of the Second World War, perhaps because alternative statuses more compatible with the national composition of its population seemed too complicated and certainly without any thought that it would some day become a sovereign state.[48] Its three communities had coexisted more or less peacefully for most of Bosnia's history. None had had to fear the domination of either of the other two because all were dominated by an outside power—Ottoman, Habsburg, and then communist. There had been little economic and social integration among the three.[49] During World War II, relations among them were not peaceful. A good deal of bloodshed occurred, the memory of which lingered through the communist period. It left a legacy of resentment and suspicion in much of the province's population, especially among Bosnia's Serbs, who had suffered the most.[50]

The breakup of the country in which it was lodged posed an acute problem for Bosnia because it was, in effect, the Yugoslavia of Yugoslavia. If the constituent nations of the country as a whole could not remain peacefully together, how could the same people be expected to do so in one of its provinces? If most of the people living in Yugoslavia did not think of themselves as Yugoslavs, it was hardly realistic to expect most of the people living in Bosnia to think of themselves as Bosnians, a national identity that had never existed.[51]

Yet with Croatia and Slovenia leaving that larger unit, without seceding itself Bosnia would become a minor province in a Serb-dominated Yugoslavia, something neither its Croats nor its Muslims wanted. The Muslims wanted an independent Bosnia in which, as a plurality of the population, they could expect to enjoy the largest share of power. The Croats and Serbs did not wish to remain in a free-standing, Muslim-dominated Bosnia and attempted, violently, to leave it: from their point of view, at best they would join Croatia and Serb-dominated Yugoslavia respectively; at the least they would avoid becoming a minority in the new, separate, Bosnian state. This was the cause of the war in Bosnia, in which the Clinton administration ultimately became entangled. The administration did not become involved in that war because of its views, such as they were, on the root cause of the conflict. The United States intervened in Bosnia for humanitarian reasons. Yet other principles were at stake.

Bosnia's Muslims, Serbs, and Croats could and did all base their preferences on a well-established international principles, but they were different principles. The one to which the Muslims appealed was the sanctity of existing borders, a concept firmly grounded in international law. Of course, the existing borders of Yugoslavia were not being preserved; but sovereignty was therefore, by this rule, being conferred upon the next largest units, the constituent republics, of which Bosnia was one. It was on the basis of this corollary to the principle of the sanctity of existing borders that the Soviet Union dissolved, at the end of 1991, into 15 independent countries, each of which had been a republic of the larger multinational state; and it was on this basis that Slovenia and Croatia declared independence.

Bosnia's Serbs and Croats, by contrast, could and did invoke the principle of national self-determination, which the American president Woodrow Wilson had placed at the center of international affairs at the Paris Peace Conference after World War I. The principle holds that distinctive nations—and the Serbs and Croats were certainly that—are entitled to their own sovereign states and, by implication, that sovereign states are most appropriately composed of a single, or at least a dominant, national group.[§]

[§] Yugoslavia's Serbs generally took the position that Yugoslavia, in which they were the largest group, should stay together but that, once it broke apart, so should Bosnia. They favored a united Yugoslavia, but, if that was not possible, they opposed a united Bosnia. The Bosnian Muslims took the opposite position: for the breakup of Yugoslavia but against the breakup of Bosnia.

Each principle has a claim to precedence. The absence of the presumption in favor of existing borders could encourage international chaos, as dissatisfied groups agitate and fight to secede from, or conquer all or part of, established states. On the other hand, spurning national self-determination can trap self-identified groups in political units to which they have not chosen to belong and do not wish to belong. The first principle assures order at the expense, potentially, of justice; the second reverses the priority.

In independent Slovenia and Croatia, where sovereign borders more or less coincided with national populations, the two principles for allocating sovereignty did not come into conflict. In Bosnia, because no single nationality dominated, they did. The conflict was settled not by legal proceedings or debates about the relative merits of the two approaches in this particular case. It was settled by war, a war that ultimately drew in the United States.

As Yugoslavia disintegrated, the European Community (EC)[52] stepped in to try to limit the violence involved. During the Cold War the Europeans had depended heavily on the United States for military protection against the Soviet Union and had allowed the Americans to take the lead in geopolitical issues. Now, with the Cold War over, they sought a more independent role in resolving conflicts, especially conflicts within Europe. In 1991, upon arriving at one of the many negotiations concerning Yugoslavia that were to take place in the next five years, the foreign minister of Luxembourg, Jacques Poos, declared, "The hour of Europe has dawned."

The Europeans had a source of leverage on the former Yugoslav republics seeking independence: the granting or withholding of formal diplomatic recognition. They agreed to act together to maximize their influence, but in December 1991, Germany broke ranks and accorded recognition to Slovenia and Croatia. The other European countries followed.** Attention then turned to Bosnia.

** With the Serbs already having seized the Serb-populated parts of Croatia, the Germans believed, or said they believed, that recognizing these former republics as independent would send a message that would deter them from taking similar steps in Bosnia. It had the opposite effect.

The EC convened talks about Bosnia in February 1992. Although it might seem to have offered a logical way to deal with the problems that Bosnia presented, neither then nor at any other time did the international community support a formal three-way partition, which would have left the Serbs and Croats free to join Yugoslavia and Croatia, respectively. For this omission there were, presumably, at least three reasons. First, the Europeans and Americans were reluctant to violate the principle of respecting existing borders. Second, such a partition would have left a small, vulnerable Muslim political entity. Third, and perhaps most important, the three nationalities were not concentrated in geographically distinct parts of Bosnia. They were intermingled, settled among each other, in a leopard-spot pattern. There was no easy way, before the war, to divide Bosnia into three ethnically homogeneous parts.

Instead, the European mediator, the Portuguese official Jose Cutileiro, offered a proposal calling for independence within the existing borders but with autonomy for the three national communities within the new country. The Cutileiro Plan represented perhaps the best chance to avoid large-scale bloodshed. Indeed, the settlement subsequently reached after three and a half years of war and tens of thousands of deaths resembled it in important ways.[53] But the three parties could not agree on the details of the plan. At the outset of 1992 the divisions between and among them, based on suspicion and hostility, were already deep. They soon became much deeper.

In early March the leader of the Bosnian Muslims, Alija Izetbegovic, declared the province to be independent. In April the EC and the United States recognized it. The Bosnian Serbs and Croats declared their own independence from the new Bosnia with its Muslim plurality, for which they had been preparing since the year before. Violence broke out across the new country and forces from Serbia crossed the border into eastern Bosnia. The war had begun.

It was a three-way conflict, with each group—Serbs, Croats, and Muslims, each of which had its own militias and criminal gangs[54]—battling the other two. Overall, an estimated 150,000 to 200,00 people died in Bosnia's war between 1992 and 1995. During that time 1.2 million people fled to other countries and between 1.3 and 1.5 million were displaced within Bosnia, few of whom returned to their original homes.[55]

Each side used its armed forces to remove people of the other two nationalities from the territory it controlled as a way of creating—inhumanely—ethnically homogeneous political units. This ugly tactic came to be called "ethnic cleansing." The term was new but the practice was not. After World War I, with the emergence of an independent Turkey on the ruins of the Ottoman Empire, about 1.5 million Greeks left Anatolia for Greece and 500,000 Turks fled to the new Turkish republic in Anatolia. After World War II an estimated 12 million ethnic Germans were expelled from the countries to Germany's east, which the Nazis had conquered before being evicted by the Red Army but where most of the refugees had roots going back decades, even centuries. An even larger population exchange, this one numbering 14.5 million people, took place, under violent conditions, between India and Pakistan after the partition of British India into those two sovereign countries.

If ethnic cleansing in the Balkans in the 1990s was neither a new development in international affairs nor, measured by the number of people displaced, the worst such episode of the twentieth century, it nonetheless shocked as well as appalled Western societies. The other three episodes had occurred in the aftermath of the mass bloodletting of the two world wars. The ethnic cleansing in Bosnia came after almost five decades of uninterrupted peace in Europe, at a time when the threat of major war on the continent had disappeared and the Europeans had come to regard large-scale violence as an ugly feature of their past that they had left behind permanently.

Much of the violence occurred in rural parts of Bosnia but some of it took place in Sarajevo, the capital city that had become internationally known by playing host to the Winter Olympic Games of 1984. Members of the European and American press gathered in the city to cover the war, and what they saw and reported turned public sympathy in the West decisively against the Serbs and in favor of the Muslims.[56]

Although each of the three communities engaged in violence and ethnic cleansing, the Serbs accounted for far more of both than the Croats or the Muslims.[57] They were the most powerful of the three because they had the support of the JNA, which became the army of the Serbs. By 1993, the Serbs controlled 70 percent of Bosnia's territory. They rounded up Muslim men, incarcerated them in camps fenced off by barbed wire, and denied them food. When journalists discovered the emaciated prisoners the images they described and broadcast to the world reminded some of the survivors of the World War II Nazi concentration camps.[58]

The Serbs were responsible—or were held responsible—for three striking and widely reported atrocities in Sarajevo, which had a pronounced effect on how the world understood the conflict. On May 27, 1992, Serb shells struck a line of people waiting to buy bread, killing at least 20 and injuring more than 100 others. On February 5, 1994, Serb ordnance landed in the Markale marketplace in the center of the city. The death toll was 68, with 144 wounded. The same marketplace was shelled again on August 28, 1995, killing 43 and injuring 75. In each case the dead and wounded were civilians. As much as any other events in the war, and in combination with the Serb siege of the city, the three attacks gave the Serbs a reputation, which was scarcely undeserved, for brutality. That reputation, in turn, shaped the official American attitude to the conflict during the Clinton administration and generated demands in Europe and in the United States for Western military intervention to protect the Muslims.

The United Nations did intervene at the beginning of the conflict. UN forces were deployed to Bosnia in 1992 to support humanitarian relief. They accomplished this initial mission: no one starved during the war. The UN also took control of the Sarajevo airport and helped ensure that supplies reached the city, to which the Serbs laid siege for much of the conflict. UN peacekeepers, mainly from Great Britain and France, were also sent to Bosnia. Their number grew from 1,500 in 1992 to 23,000 by the end of 1994. Among other duties, they patrolled designated "safe areas" for Muslims, which functioned as zones of protection against Serb assaults.[59]

Unlike its humanitarian relief, the UN's peacekeeping efforts failed. Peacekeepers can be effective when the parties to a conflict have agreed on a settlement and need a neutral force between them to provide mutual reassurance. That was not the case in Bosnia: there was no peace to keep. Worse, the peacekeepers became part of the conflict. In response to air attacks against Serb positions launched by NATO warplanes, Serb forces several times took UN personnel hostage.[60] The vulnerability of the UN-mandated forces stationed in Bosnia made the European countries reluctant to take the kind of military action against the Serbs that the American government (and many Europeans as well) came to favor.

The war in Bosnia, like all wars, had political causes and could not end without a political settlement. Recognizing this early on, the Europeans attempted to provide one. In August 1992, the EC and the UN convened the International Conference on the Former Yugoslavia. The conference appointed former American secretary of state Cyrus Vance and former British foreign secretary David Owen as its representatives to try to bring the war to a conclusion. In February 1993, after extensive consultations, the two of them presented a plan for the governance of Bosnia that they hoped the three national groups would be willing to accept and so stop fighting. Like the Cutileiro Plan that preceded it, it was designed to combine the maintenance of an independent country within its Yugoslav-era borders, which the Muslims demanded, with autonomy for the three communities, which the Serbs and Croats wanted. The Vance-Owen Plan divided Bosnia into 10 different regions, each with appreciable independent authority and in most of which one of the three nationalisms predominated. It was a blueprint for a highly decentralized state.

None of the parties involved in the conflict found the plan appealing. The Muslims and Serbs, in particular, considered it insufficiently generous to themselves. It had a provision for the enforcement of its terms by an international force and while the Europeans and ultimately the Americans agreed in principle to furnish the necessary manpower, none had much enthusiasm for the task and all suspected that the Plan would prove unworkable in practice. Negotiations about the Vance-Owen Plan among the various parties took place through the spring of 1993, but it never seemed close to acceptance. On May 15–16 the Bosnian Serbs rejected it in a referendum, thereby extinguishing what little hope had existed of implementing it.

During the first two years of the Yugoslav crisis the United States played an episodic and, in comparison with the Europeans, minor role in it. The Bush administration wanted as little to do with it as possible. The words of Secretary of State James Baker—"We got no dog in this fight"—expressed, pithily if inelegantly, its judgment that no important American interests were at stake in the Balkans.[61] In any event, the administration had more urgent priorities: in 1991 the war to evict Iraq from Kuwait and then the collapse of the Soviet Union; in 1992 the president's re-election campaign, which had to contend with a widespread feeling in the American electorate that during his term in office George H. W. Bush had spent too much time on foreign affairs and not enough on enhancing the welfare of the voters of the United States.

The Clinton administration brought to office a different approach to Bosnia. Its senior officials generally differed from their predecessors on two points. The Clinton people believed that what was happening in the Balkans was consequential for the United States and deserved more attention from the American government than the Bush administration had given it; and in the war itself they strongly supported the Muslim side. This new approach had three bases.

First, the Clinton officials regarded the war as the result of Serb aggression against a legally established and politically legitimate country. Without engaging in any public debate on the matter, they accepted the principle of sovereignty that the Muslims were defending—the sanctity of existing borders—and ignored the one on which the Serbs were acting—national self-determination.

Second, they believed that another principle, one particularly important to Americans, was under assault in Bosnia: the principle of pluralism. They conceived of Bosnia as a Balkan version of the United States, where people of different ethnic backgrounds had been living in harmony, or at least mutual toleration, until the Serb assault on their community. This description was accurate for some parts of Bosnia, especially the cosmopolitan city of Sarajevo—the only part of it of with which most Americans had had any experience—but not for all or even most of it.[62] Opinion polls and election results showed that the majority of those living in Bosnia did not embrace a multiethnic Bosnian identity. If they had, there would have been no war, or at least not a war that mobilized so many members of the three communities within Bosnia against each other. Instead, the inhabitants of Bosnia saw themselves, first and foremost, as members of one of the three national groups. This was the case even for the Muslims, although their leaders sometimes used the rhetoric of pluralism to describe their goals in order to attract Western and American support.[63]

Third, although the administration did not officially declare it to be such, the Clinton officials came to see what Serbs were doing to Muslims in Bosnia as an act of genocide. The term comes from the Nazi destruction of Europe's Jews during World War II. That assault was a minor feature of the war in the eyes of the world when it was being waged but came to loom ever larger after the war as the years passed. A 1948 international convention prohibited it. Just what, however, does that convention prohibit? The definition of genocide is a broad one,[64] but its crux is the intent to eliminate a people as such: that was what the Nazis attempted to do to the Jewish people. It is not what Serbs were attempting to do to Bosnia's Muslims. The Serb goal was to drive from their homes those who lived in territory the Serbs wished to control, not to kill all of them, let alone to kill all Muslims everywhere.[65]

The use of the term genocide carried political significance because it had come to be seen, in the decades following World War II, as the ultimate evil, the attempt to perpetrate which justifies, even requires, intervention to stop it.[66] On this account, if the Serbs were committing genocide against the Muslims the international community, emphatically including the United States, had a moral obligation to go the rescue of the intended victims.

Whether or not the Serb war against Bosnia's Muslims truly qualified as genocide, and whatever the virtues of the two competing principles of sovereignty in the Bosnian case, the Serbs did employ exceptionally brutal tactics in pursuing their political goals. That brutality turned the Clinton administration (and many others) against them and convinced its senior officials that the United States ought to employ its armed forces to oppose them.

As in the cases of China and Haiti, during his presidential campaign in 1992 Bill Clinton promised to change the Bush policy toward Bosnia, as much out of political calculation as personal conviction.[67] On August 5 he called for President Bush to "do whatever it takes to stop the slaughter of civilians" and suggested that "we may have to use military force."[68] When the Clinton administration took office, the European efforts to stop the fighting centered on the Vance-Owen Plan. The administration expressed reservations about this plan on the grounds that it conceded too much to the Serbs[69] and never had to make good on its promise to send Americans to Bosnia to enforce it.

When its probable failure became apparent, the administration began to work on a new policy for Bosnia, one more robust and more favorable to the Muslim side than its predecessor.

The Clinton administration devised a two-part scheme that came to be known as "lift and strike," which entailed relaxing the embargo against selling or giving weapons to the combatants in Bosnia that the UN had approved in September 1991 and that Western countries were generally observing.[70] The administration saw it as unfair to the Muslims because it affected them more than it did the Serbs, who had a ready supply of armaments from neighboring, Serb-dominated Yugoslavia that the embargo did not affect. As part of the new policy the United States would also conduct air strikes on Serb forces in Bosnia. The two measures combined would, the Clinton administration hoped, tilt the battlefield in favor of the Muslims.

Lift and strike had the virtue, from Bill Clinton's point of view, of not requiring American troops on the ground in Bosnia, where some might well have been killed, thereby triggering the kind of backlash that the administration suffered later that year as the result of combat in Somalia.[71] Because the Europeans were already involved in Bosnia, and because the war was taking place on their continent, the administration sent its secretary of state, Warren Christopher, to several European capitals to secure support for the new American policy.

He did not receive it. Although revulsed by the Serbs' conduct, the European governments were not as well disposed to the Muslim cause as the Americans were and did not regard Muslim military success, the aim of the Clinton policy, as being either as desirable or as feasible as Washington did. More importantly, the Europeans, unlike the United States, had troops on the ground in Bosnia and feared—rightly, as it turned out—that these troops would suffer Serb reprisals if the Western governments went to war on the side of the Muslims.[72] In the end, the administration abandoned lift and strike.

With the failure of the peace plan of which he was the co-author, Cyrus Vance retired from the UN- and EC-sponsored mediation effort in Bosnia, and Thorvald Stoltenberg, a former Norwegian foreign minister, replaced him. In August 1993 Owen and Stoltenberg proposed a less complex version of the Vance-Owen Plan, one that came closer than its predecessor to dividing Bosnia into three ethnically homogeneous sectors. Like Vance-Owen, the Owen-Stoltenberg plan did not gain the acceptance of the warring parties, but in 1994 two developments occurred that helped pave the way for ending the war the following year.

In March 1994, after intensive negotiations in which the United States played an active role, Bosnia's Croats and Muslims agreed to the basic framework of a federation encompassing them both and covering about half of Bosnia's territory.[††] This turned the war from a three-way to a two-sided contest and strengthened both the Croats and Muslims at the expense of the Serbs.

In April, the United States proposed the establishment of a Contact Group to serve as the vehicle for international efforts to stop the war. It included representatives of Great Britain, France, and Germany as well as the United States and Russia.

Still, the war continued throughout 1994, albeit at a reduced tempo in many parts of Bosnia. It came to an end the next year because of a change in the policy of the Clinton administration, a change in the balance of power on the ground in Bosnia, and a change in the diplomatic representation of Bosnia's Serbs and Croats.

Political calculation tied to an election determined the Clinton administration's initial policy toward Bosnia, and political calculation tied to the next election caused a change of course that helped make it possible to end the war. In December 1994, Clinton authorized American military participation in the withdrawal of the UN peacekeepers from Bosnia, were this to occur and American assistance be requested.[73] In the early months of 1995 such a request seemed increasingly likely. The

---

[††] Ivo Daalder, *Getting to Dayton: The Making of America's Bosnia Policy*, Washington, DC: The Brookings Institution, 2000, p. 27; Steven L. Burg and Paul S. Shoup, *The War in Bosnia-Herzegovina: Ethnic Conflict and International Intervention*, Armonk, New York: M.E. Sharpe, 1999, p. 409. The federation did not imply, nor did it create, solidarity between the two groups. The Croats entered it "because the fighting between Muslim and Croat forces had resolved a number of the military control issues concerning western Herzegovina in favor of the Croats; because the agreement provided extensive local control for ethnic minorities within cantons, thus delaying the inevitable confrontation between Croats and Muslims over control of the mixed cantons; and because by accepting the agreement Croatia would get the United States behind partition." *Ibid.*, p. 294.

administration feared that the American force sent to extricate the peacekeepers would become involved in combat and that the resulting casualties would trigger a political backlash in the United States. That backlash, Clinton and his political advisors worried, would be all the stronger because Americans would have died not while asserting American power or achieving the administration's goals in the Balkans but rather as part of an ignominious retreat. Such a scenario, they believed, would cloud his prospects for re-election in 1996.

Accordingly, the American approach to the conflict in Bosnia changed. The Clinton administration decided to become more actively involved in the search for a diplomatic end to the war. This required closer cooperation with the Europeans. Having kept its distance from the Contact Group's peace plan on the grounds that it conceded too much to the Serbs and amounted to a de facto partition, the administration reversed course. It accepted the need for some concessions to the Serbs, and for postwar arrangements that did not leave Bosnia with a strong central government, as the price for stopping the fighting and avoiding the threat of serious domestic political damage.

The change in the Clinton approach to Bosnia combined with a change in the control of territory there. The United States had indirectly helped the newly independent Croatia build its armed forces.[74] On August 4 the Croatian army launched an offensive against the Serb-occupied Croatian region of Krajina. The Serb forces did not resist and the Croatian army gained control of the region in a few days. The 200,000 Serb civilians living in the region fled. The offensive, indirectly aided and encouraged by the United States, triggered one of the largest episodes of ethnic cleansing of the entire war.[75]

The next month Croatian forces launched an offensive in western Bosnia in cooperation with the Bosnian Muslim army, with American bombardment of Serb positions supporting their ground operations.[‡‡]

[‡‡] The occasion for the bombing was the Serb massacre of 8,000 unarmed Muslims in what had been a UN-designated safe area in the town of Srebrenica. As well as being a reprisal for the massacre, the bombing campaign had a political purpose. "The importance of the air campaign was not so much to bomb the Bosnian Serbs to the negotiating table as to demonstrate to the Bosnian Moslems the limits of what the US was prepared to do." Carl Bildt, "The search for peace," *Financial Times*, July 2, 1998, p. 16.

The Croat-Muslim offensive succeeded in capturing a good deal of Serb-held territory. Before August the Serbs had held about two-thirds of Bosnia. Afterward they had less than half. The success of the offensive brought the lines of division on the ground between and among the national communities into closer alignment with the map for the settlement of the conflict that the Contact Group was proposing and that the American government had come around to supporting.

Also in August, the leader of Serb-dominated Yugoslavia, Slobodan Milosevic, assumed personal responsibility for the negotiations to end the war. The Bosnian Serbs had always depended heavily on Yugoslavia for economic and military support but had been able to act with considerable political independence. Milosevic had a stronger commitment to ending the war than did they because ending it was the condition for lifting the economic sanctions that Europe and the United States had imposed on his country.[76] The sanctions had the potential to create sufficient hardship to threaten his own power, which mattered more to him than the fate of Serbs in Bosnia, not to mention those in Krajina, whom he had abandoned in the face of the Croatian assault. At the same time the leader of Croatia Franjo Tudjman, with whom Milosevic had discussed partitioning Bosnia between their two countries as early as March 1991,[77] took over the representation of Bosnia's Croats. The conditions necessary for ending the fighting—an American commitment to do what was necessary for this purpose, a distribution of territory that all parties to the conflict found, if not optimal, at least not unbearable, and negotiators for two of the three sides in the war willing, indeed eager, to bring it to a conclusion—had at last fallen into place.

Accordingly, at the end of November 1995, the United States convened a conference on an American air base in Dayton, Ohio, that produced a settlement. The American delegation, which dominated the proceedings, was led by Assistant Secretary of State for European Affairs Richard Holbrooke. Ordinarily a higher-ranking figure would have played this role, but the two most important foreign policy officials of the Clinton administration, Secretary of State Warren Christopher and National Security Advisor W. Anthony Lake, were both reticent people who shunned the public limelight. When it came to seeking and basking in public attention, Holbrooke, by contrast, was situated as far at the opposite end of the spectrum as it is humanly possible to be. In the

wake of Dayton he was not shy about designating his own personal diplomatic virtuosity as crucial for the outcome of the conference. In fact,
he was well suited to the role he played, but not for the reasons he liked
to cite. Of the warring sides the one most resistant to the terms on the
table at Dayton was the Muslims. They insisted on a unitary and centralized Bosnian state. The major task at the conference was therefore to
cajole and bully them into modifying their position. Holbrooke's temperament qualified him for this exercise. He was also well positioned for
it politically because he had been among those Americans who insisted
that the Muslims were right to reject the kind of settlement that his
government was now trying to get them to accept.[78]

The terms agreed upon at Dayton kept Bosnia as a single political unit,
within the borders it had as a Yugoslav province, but left it with a singu-
larly weak central government. It was divided into two state-like units: the
Croat-Muslim federation and a Serb entity. Each was given wide-ranging
powers, which were sufficient for either one of them to prevent Bosnia
from functioning effectively as a single, integrated, coherent state.[79]

In the wake of Dayton the balance sheet for the Clinton administration's three-year policy toward the war in Bosnia did show some successes. The United States did, finally, help bring the war to an end. Bill
Clinton himself achieved his major goal: avoiding substantial political
damage from his administration's approach to the fighting. He was
re-elected in 1996, and while Bosnia did not turn out to be an electoral
asset for him it was not, as he had feared it would be, a liability either.

American leadership proved crucial to settling the conflict, illustrat-
ing the major role of the United States in post-Cold War international
affairs. This was a source of satisfaction to the administration's senior foreign policy officials, validating, as it seemed to do, their own importance.
"We are the indispensable nation," Madeleine Albright later said of the
United States.[§§] Indispensability was to prove a mixed blessing from the

§§ "We are the indispensable nation. We stand tall and we see farther than other
countries into the future." NBC's *Today* program, February 19, 1998. This charac-
terization of America's international status had a basis in the political and economic
realities of the last decade of the twentieth century. As for the assertion about
the country's special powers of discernment, the foreign policies of Mrs. Albright's
administration and its successors did not provide convincing evidence for it.

point of view of the American public, which would have preferred that other countries bear a larger share of the burdens and pay more of the costs of the international initiatives that presidents and their foreign policy officials chose to undertake in the 1990s and in the following decade.

On the other side of the ledger, the Clinton administration's Bosnia policies failed to achieve some of the goals with which it had begun its term in office. The policies did not produce a unified country with the three constituent national groups living peacefully together: instead they were living apart, although formally in a single country. The Bosnia that Dayton designed had something in common with a minimum-security prison: the inhabitants could do pretty much anything they liked: they just couldn't leave.

The United States presided over the creation of what it had previously opposed: the partition of Bosnia in all but name. The Dayton settlement included major concessions to the Serbs, the very people whom Clinton officials regarded as having committed crimes against humanity. The administration had not stopped the most visible of these crimes, ethnic cleansing, nor reversed its consequences by restoring unjustly evicted people to their homes. Indeed, the administration provided tacit support for ethnic cleansing when it was perpetrated by Croats against Serbs.[80]

The American public did not favor an American presence in Bosnia, even in peacetime. All the same, the administration sent 20,000 troops there as part of a 60,000-person post-Dayton multinational peacekeeping force. To mollify the public, Clinton promised that the American contingent would stay for only a year. The last of them left eight years later, in 2004. The continued presence of American military personnel incurred no significant public displeasure in the United States, however, because none was killed. After Dayton, unlike in 1991 when the UN had first dispatched forces for this purposes, there was a peace to keep in Bosnia.

With the war at an end and a political framework in place, the American government announced a commitment to a by-now familiar goal: nation-building. Bosnia was to become, under international tutelage, what the officials of the Clinton administration had wanted it to be all along: a prosperous, democratic, tolerant, unified, multiethnic country. It became no such thing; but before this particular failure became fully apparent, the administration got the United States militarily entangled in the Balkans again, this time in direct opposition to its indispensable partner at Dayton, Slobodan Milosevic.

Kosovo

In 1999 the United States, in conjunction with its NATO allies, undertook a military intervention on behalf of the people of Kosovo, a region of Serbia 90 percent of whose population was Albanian Muslim. The predominance of Islam was a legacy of Kosovo's long history as part of the Ottoman Empire, from 1455 to 1912. Between 1912 and 1941 it came under the control of Serbia, which for most of that period was one of the constituent provinces of the first Yugoslavia. From 1941 to 1945 much of Kosovo belonged to Italian-controlled Albania, and at the end of World War II it reverted to Serbia within the reconstituted Yugoslavia.

Although designated by the Yugoslav constitution a minority group rather than a full-fledged nation like Serbia, Croatia, and Slovenia, beginning in 1974 the Muslim Kosovars enjoyed considerable autonomy. In 1989, however, Slobodan Milosevic revoked it. He had gained power as an outspoken champion of the rights of Kosovo's Serb minority, which he claimed were being violated. This struck a chord not only among them but with the Serbs of Serbia as well because Kosovo had an important role in the Serbs' version of their own national history. According to that version, in 1389 a Serb prince refused to surrender to an Ottoman potentate, choosing instead to make a stand at a place in Kosovo called the Field of Blackbirds. The Serb force was defeated but the battle was remembered thereafter by the Serbs as a courageous and glorious chapter in their national narrative. A key moment in Milosevic's rise to dominance in Serbia was his speech at the site of the battle on June 28, 1989, commemorating its six hundredth anniversary.

Serb history meant nothing to the Albanian Kosovars who made up the vast majority of the territory's population. They resented Milosevic's reimposition of what they experienced as harsh Serb rule and sought to escape it. With Yugoslavia breaking up and its constituent republics striking out on their own, the Kosovars, too, wanted independence.

Because of its importance in their own history, Milosevic and the Serbs would not concede it. This made Kosovo, like Bosnia, a theater of conflict between Serbs and Muslims.

Indeed, when Yugoslavia began to unravel, the United States had considered Kosovo to be more explosive than Bosnia, and in late December 1992 then-President George H. W. Bush had warned Milosevic that a violent crackdown on the Kosovars would provoke an American military response.[81] Kosovo's status did not, however, find its way on to the agenda of the Dayton conference. While ultimately siding with the Muslims, at the end of 1995 the United States could not afford to be at odds with Slobodan Milosevic, whose cooperation was needed to end the fighting in Bosnia. Nor were the Europeans or Americans eager to inject themselves into another Balkan conflict, their engagement in the one finally ending having proven distinctly unrewarding. Moreover, by international law Kosovo was part of Serbia and other countries had no legal right to involve themselves in its internal affairs. The same principle that the Clinton administration had cited to justify its support for the Muslims of Bosnia—the defense of internationally recognized borders against aggression—prohibited supporting the Muslims of Kosovo in their struggle against the Serbs. The administration ultimately supported them anyway.

Because the experience in Bosnia had not been a happy one, and notwithstanding the Bush 1992 "Christmas warning," which Secretary of State Warren Christopher reiterated in early 1993, most of the members of the Clinton administration, including the president, would have preferred to have had nothing to do with the conflict in Kosovo. Yet the United States was drawn into that conflict, ultimately going to war against Serbia, and, as in Bosnia, found itself intervening on behalf of a position that neither of the warring parties favored. The American government advocated autonomy for the Kosovars within Yugoslavia. The Serbs were fighting to maintain the status quo—that is, Serb control of Kosovo—which meant that, for all their differences, the Americans and the Serbs did agree that Kosovo legally belonged to Yugslavia. The Kosovar Albanians disagreed. They were by far the weakest of the three parties, but they and not the other two achieved their goal. They were fighting for independence, and ultimately they got it.[82]

They achieved independence by resorting to violence. For most of the 1990s the leader of the Kosovar Albanians was Ibrahim Rugova, a man so devoted to nonviolent resistance to the Serbs in Kosovo that on the wall of his home hung pictures of that tactic's most celebrated practitioners: Martin Luther King, Mohandas Gandhi, and the Dalai Lama. The failure of the Dayton conference to address the Kosovars' grievances against the Serbs weakened support for him and for nonviolence.[83] The Kosovo Liberation Army (KLA), a guerrilla movement dedicated to the use of force to liberate the province from the Serbs, began to form in the wake of Dayton. By 1997 it had between 15,000 and 20,000 members. Arms flowed to the KLA from outside the country (especially from neighboring Albania), and it began to conduct hit-and-run attacks on Serbs in Kosovo.

The KLA had no hope of evicting the Serbs and winning independence on its own. It aimed, rather, to provoke a Serb reaction sufficiently visible and brutal to trigger intervention by the West, which did have the military means to force the Serbs out of the province.[84] That is exactly what happened. The KLA's tactics did incite a heavy-handed Serb response, which did draw NATO, led by the United States, into the conflict, to the ultimate benefit of the Kosovars. In this way the KLA became one of the most successful guerrilla organizations in history.[85]

Its chief ally, the person most responsible for its success, who pushed harder and more effectively for the United States to go to war in the Balkans than anyone else, was Bill Clinton's second secretary of state, Madeleine Albright. Albright was, in one sense, an unlikely choice for the position. She had outspokenly championed the policy of nation-building in Somalia that had ended disastrously for the administration. Her professed world view seemed out of touch with the realities of the post-Cold War era. "My mindset is Munich," she said of her outlook on foreign policy, referring to the German city where, in 1938, the British and French prime ministers made concessions to Hitler in the mistaken belief that they could satisfy his territorial ambitions in Europe and avoid war. Albright's bête noire, Slobodan Milosevic,[86] was a brutal and unscrupulous character but he presided over a small, weak, marginal country that bore no resemblance to Nazi Germany and had no prospect of dominating the Balkans, let alone all of Europe.[87] Insofar as the United States had interests in that part of the world, they were humanitarian and not, as Albright implied, geopolitical.

She was able to become America's chief diplomat because of two post-Cold War developments in the foreign policy and the politics of the United States. For much of the nineteenth century and into the twentieth presidents selected secretaries of state, like other members of their cabinets, on the basis of domestic political considerations. They sought to reward loyal constituencies. This did not necessarily produce officials with no aptitude for conducting the nation's external affairs. William Seward, whom Abraham Lincoln chose as secretary of state because he was the politically influential governor of New York, filled the post with distinction.

For most of the twentieth century, with foreign policy a more urgent and important matter than it had been for most of the nineteenth, demonstrated competence in dealing with other countries became the chief qualification for the American secretary of state. With the end of the Cold War and the consequent reduction in the importance of foreign policy in the life of the nation, the basis for selection reverted to the earlier pattern. Bill Clinton chose Madeleine Albright for the same reason his nineteenth-century predecessors had selected their secretaries of state, and indeed on the same basis that he made other foreign policy decisions: domestic politics. By the 1990s, however, American politics had changed. The principal constituencies to which national politicians had to appeal were not only states or regions, they were demographic categories as well; and Madeleine Albright belonged to one that was particularly important for Clinton. She had the support, as the journalist David Halberstam put it, "of a formidable new force within the Democratic Party, an important network of politically active women." For the president, therefore, "the temptation to name the first woman secretary of state was irresistible."[88]

Albright made Kosovo her highest priority and opposition to Milosevic and Serb domination there her major goal. Traditionally it is the president, not the secretary of state, who establishes the agenda for American foreign policy. During the months leading up to the initiation of war with Serbia, however, Clinton was preoccupied and, in

political terms, almost paralyzed by impeachment proceedings stemming from charges that he had committed perjury and obstruction
of justice in trying to hide his sexual relationship with a young White
House intern.

In late July 1998, with America's attention focused on the Clinton
scandal,[89] Serb forces launched an offensive against the KLA, which
had taken advantage of Serb restraint to exert control over much of
Kosovo. By way of retaliation, and following the precedent of their
compatriots in Bosnia, the Serbs practiced ethnic cleansing against the
Albanian Kosovars, driving them from their homes in large numbers.
From the beginning of the offensive to March 1999 a total of 350,000
fled.[90] On September 23, 1998, the UN Security Council passed a resolution demanding that the Serbs cease their assaults on the Albanians,
permit international monitors to enter Kosovo to confirm that they
had done so, and start a political dialogue with the majority in the
province.[91]

The next day, September 24, NATO issued an "activation warning"
threatening air strikes against the Serbs. Several European members of
the alliance believed that, because the Serbs had committed no act of
aggression against any of them, actual military intervention required
the explicit approval of the UN Security Council. Russia and China,
however, made it clear that they would veto any such resolution on
the grounds that the conflict in Kosovo was a purely internal Yugoslav
affair in which other countries had no right to intervene.[92] In the end,
therefore, the United States and NATO conducted their humanitarian
intervention without a UN mandate.

In October, the Clinton administration sent Richard Holbrooke to
the region to negotiate with Milosevic, and on October 13 he announced
an agreement under the terms of which Milosevic's Yugoslav forces
would abide by the Security Council resolution and the Organization
for Security and Cooperation in Europe (OSCE) would monitor Serb
compliance. As a result, most of the displaced Kosovars were able to
return to their homes. The agreement did not, however, bring peace to
the province. It had no provision for the enforcement of its terms and
the KLA took advantage of the retreat of Serb forces to recapture territory it had held before the Serb summer offensive and to resume its
guerrilla attacks on Serbs.[93]

The Serbs responded violently. In January 1999, troops and paramilitary forces killed 45 Kosovars, almost all of them civilians, in the village of Racak. That massacre convinced the Clinton administration's senior foreign policy officials that the Holbrooke-brokered arrangement had failed and that further steps were necessary.[94] The Contact Group, which had carried over from the conflict in Bosnia and included Russia, as NATO did not, issued a list of principles to govern a settlement in Kosovo and summoned the Serbs and Kosovars to a conference to ratify them and agree on ways to implement them. NATO, with the United States in the lead, expressed its readiness to act in Kosovo, which Albright made clear meant air strikes on the Serbs if they did not accept the Contact Group proposal.[95]

The conference convened in a fourteenth-century castle in Rambouillet, a French town 27.5 miles southwest of the center of Paris. The town was the home of France's Bergerie Nationale—its national sheep farm. The venue of the meeting notwithstanding, the Serbs and Kosovar Albanians refused to be herded. Both declined to accept the Contact Group's terms. Even though they depended on the Western countries, and even though the Clinton administration sided with them, the Kosovars were not, initially, willing to sign any agreement that did not guarantee them the opportunity to choose independence,[96] something that even their staunchest international champion, the United States, would not at that point accept. The conference adjourned, the Americans put pressure on the Kosovars, and three weeks later, on March 18, in Paris, they accepted the Contact Group's proposal.

The Serbs did not. Milosevic refused to permit NATO forces in Kosovo, as required by the Contact Group plan,[97] because he feared that they would never leave and that Serbia would lose Kosovo, which is what ultimately happened. While the Serb leader had been willing to give up the Serb-populated Krajina to Croatia, and to force Bosnia's Serbs to accept a settlement that did not give them full independence, Kosovo was different. Serbia had the right to govern it under international law and, for historical reasons, it had greater emotional and political importance for the Serbs than the Serb parts of Croatia or Bosnia. Milosevic could not afford, politically, to relinquish it voluntarily. He decided instead to fight for it.[98]

This decision did not surprise, and perhaps did not even trouble, American officials. According to one of Madeleine Albright's close aides, the purpose of Rambouillet had not been to resolve the conflict peacefully. Its aim, rather was "to get the war started with the Europeans locked in."[99] Accordingly, on March 24, 1999, with air strikes against Serbia, America's Kosovo war—a war fought for humanitarian rather than strategic goals, to vindicate American values rather than to protect American interests—duly began.

At first everything went wrong. NATO anticipated a short war, planning for three days of bombing.[100] Instead, the conflict lasted 78 days. In announcing the bombing, Bill Clinton said that its purpose was to "deter an even bloodier offensive against innocent civilians in Kosovo."[101] It had the opposite effect. It triggered a massive ethnic cleansing of Muslims from Kosovo. The Serbs' "Operation Horseshoe" displaced an estimated 1.3 million Kosovars (out of a total population of 1.8 million): 800,000 fled to neighboring countries and 500,000 abandoned their homes but remained within the province.[102]

In the days after March 24, therefore, two distinct wars took place in the Balkans. One was being waged by NATO, led by the United States, against the Serbs. This was a war of persuasion. Its aim was to inflict enough punishment on the Serbs—mainly in Serbia proper, not Kosovo—to persuade them to accept the Contact Group proposal, which was the condition for ending the bombing. The American government assumed that minimal punishment would bring Milosevic around. This assumption proved erroneous.[103] At the outset of the war, NATO's strategy failed.

The Serb strategy, by contrast, succeeded. The Serbs were waging a second war, against the Albanian Muslims of Kosovo. It was a war of expulsion, not a war of annihilation; thus it did not qualify as a genocide.[104] The NATO air strikes did not materially interfere with the Serb assault, nor did they, initially, dissuade the Serbs from continuing it.

The failure of NATO's bombing campaign recalled an earlier, similar failure, in the 1960s in Vietnam. The United States bombed North Vietnam with the aim of inflicting enough punishment to persuade the North Vietnamese communist government to desist in its support for the communist insurgency against the pro-American, non-communist government of South Vietnam. The North Vietnamese regime chose to absorb the punishment and continue the support. Similarly, the bombing of Serbia did not at first weaken the Serbs' resolve in Kosovo. Instead, the Serb people rallied around Milosevic.[105]

In Indochina, gaining control of South Vietnam mattered more to the North Vietnamese regime than keeping it free of communist rule did to the United States. The North Vietnamese were willing to pay a much higher price, in casualties and in destruction from bombing, to achieve their goal than the American side was willing to pay—in American lives—to secure its own aim. The American side reached the limits of its tolerance for casualties before the North Vietnamese reached theirs. The Americans withdrew from Indochina and North Vietnam won the war. Similarly, it was more important to the Serbs to hold on to Kosovo than it was to the NATO countries to take it away from them. The Serbs were willing to pay considerably more for their goal than the Americans and Europeans were to get what they wanted.

The NATO countries were, in fact, willing to pay almost nothing. President Clinton made this clear when he said, in his address to the nation announcing the start of the bombing, that he "did not intend to put our troops in Kosovo to fight a war."[106] The United States would wage the war from aircraft far above the contested territory so as to avoid American casualties. Clinton told the Serbs, in effect, that if they could weather the bombing, which was relatively restrained at the outset, they would be able to keep Kosovo. If they kept Kosovo they would win the war.

In the early weeks it looked as if they would win, which presented Clinton with a dilemma: if he kept to the initial strategy, NATO, the most successful alliance in history, the United States, the most powerful country in the world, and he himself, the leader of both, would suffer a humiliating defeat at the hands of a small, poor, weak country led by a small-time dictator. To ensure victory, however, would require sending troops into Kosovo to defeat the Serb forces. This the NATO forces would certainly accomplish, but not without casualties, which the precedent of Somalia and opinion polls taken at the time made clear the American public and the European allies did not want.[107] The nineteenth-century German leader Otto von Bismarck is said to have remarked of the geopolitical significance of the Balkans that the region wasn't "worth the bones of a single Pomeranian grenadier." The American people made the same assessment of Kosovo's late-twentieth-century value in American lives.

As in Somalia and Bosnia, the enthusiasts for humanitarian intervention whom he had appointed had led Clinton into a commitment that the American public was reluctant to vindicate. By deciding to bomb, and with the bombing not achieving the expected results, the president found himself caught between the prospect of an ignominious, legacy-defining defeat and a deeply unpopular victory. The NATO allies had made no fallback plan to be carried out if the initial bombing failed to achieve its goal.[108] Faced with the dilemma to which its failure gave rise, they managed to piece together a revised, four-part strategy that ultimately secured the goals for which they had gone to war.

In the first place, NATO escalated its attacks on the Serbs. At the outset of the war its planes struck air defense systems. When the Serbs did not submit, the alliance tripled the number of aircraft being used and expanded the target list to include infrastructure such as transportation routes, electrical grids, and water purification facilities, as well as Milosevic's party headquarters in Belgrade and factories belonging to his political allies. NATO also attacked, in cooperation with the KLA, the Serb military and paramilitary forces engaged in ethnic cleansing in Kosovo, although subsequent assessment suggested that these attacks did only limited damage.[109] The expanded bombing of Serbia itself, however, brought the war home to the people on whose support Milosevic depended in order to remain in power.[110]

Second, the European members of NATO maintained their support for the war. NATO solidarity blocked one path to success for Milosevic: enough discord within the ranks of the alliance to cause it to abandon its goals for Kosovo.[111] Among the Europeans, the British prime minister, Tony Blair, developed a particularly strong conviction that the war was both just and necessary.[112] More generally, the heads of the European governments involved, whatever their reservations about the way the war was being conducted (and in some cases about conducting it at all), decided that the damage NATO would suffer from failing to win the first real war in its 50-year history was unacceptably high; and so they resolved to see it through. While the war generated no substantial enthusiasm in any of their countries (and significant discontent in some), the scale of Serb ethnic cleansing in Kosovo did make an impression on the European publics, which helped to keep opposition to the war in check.[113]

Third, as the war continued the American government began suggesting that it was rethinking the initial Clinton commitment not to insert ground troops into Kosovo. Planning began for an invasion through Albania. NATO already had troops there, which had been sent to serve as peacekeepers in the event the Serbs accepted the Contact Group plan, and their numbers were increased.[114] The British favored making serious preparations for a land invasion and pressed the other NATO countries to agree to one.[115] On May 18, in response to a reporter's question, Clinton said that "NATO will not take any option off the table," reversing his statement at the beginning of the war that had explicitly ruled out the one option guaranteed to produce victory, the dispatch of American ground troops.

An invasion of Kosovo would have been logistically complicated and would have strained the political cohesion of the alliance. In addition, the Republican members of Congress had gone on record in opposition to such an operation.[116] Whether Clinton would ultimately have ordered it cannot be known.[117] In the end, he did not have to do so, in no small part because of the fourth element of NATO's revised strategy: the support of Russia.

The Russian government had opposed the NATO policy toward Kosovo from the beginning.[118] It supported the Serb claim to control the province without interference from other countries and condemned the attacks on Serb targets,[119] even introducing a resolution in the United Nations calling for them to stop. The Russians had an affinity for the Serbs, their fellow Orthodox Christian Slavs, they rejected in principle outside intervention in the affairs of sovereign states (perhaps with an eye on their own troubles in the rebellious Russian province of Chechnya), and they resented the fact that, because they did not belong to NATO, they had no say in the decision to conduct military operations in a place not far from their own borders. The war was unpopular among Russians and, because the Russian president Boris Yeltsin was so closely identified with the cultivation of good relations with the very Western countries that were waging it, as the conflict continued it weakened him politically at home.[120] He decided to help end it. He appointed former prime minister Viktor Chernomyrdin as his special representative,[121] and Chernomyrdin joined with the American deputy secretary of state Strobe Talbott and Martti Ahtisaari, the former president of Finland, to form a negotiating team for that purpose.

Chernomyrdin told Milosevic that NATO was prepared to invade Kosovo,[122] and that message, in combination with the toll that the NATO bombing campaign was taking on Serbia, the apparent resolve of the allied governments to continue to prosecute the war indefinitely, and the loss of the support of his Russian ally, finally persuaded Milosevic to give in. On June 2 he agreed to the Contact Group plan and the next day the Serb parliament ratified it. The war was over.

It ended with NATO and the United States achieving their immediate goals. Serb forces left Kosovo and a 50,000-person multinational peacekeeping force entered it. Control of the province and its future passed from Milosevic to the Western powers. The Kosovars whom Operation Horseshoe had put to flight, unlike almost all the earlier victims of ethnic cleansing in Bosnia, were able to return to their homes. Bill Clinton got what he wanted. He avoided both a humiliating defeat in the Balkans and a politically dangerous ground war involving American troops. As a bonus, Kosovars erected an 11-foot-high statue of him in Pristina, the capital, which he himself unveiled on November 1, 2009.

On the other hand, the United States and NATO had violated the fundamental principle of international law by intervening in the internal affairs of a state—Serb-dominated Yugoslavia—that had not attacked them or any other country. The Serbs were certainly guilty of criminal behavior within the borders of their own country[123] (although they could claim, rightly, that they were responding to an armed rebellion), but their crimes were not of a magnitude usually accepted as defining genocide and thereby justifying overriding the basic international norm of non-intervention. Nor did the international community as a whole, acting through the United Nations, authorize the war. NATO, a regional security organization to which most countries in the world (not to mention several in Europe, including Russia) did not belong, simply gave itself permission to attack Yugoslavia.

NATO went to war partly because of the ethnic cleansing of Albanian Kosovars that had taken place in 1998, but its bombing campaign triggered a far worse episode of it in March and April of the following year. That episode of ethnic cleansing was reversed, but, as in the Bosnian conflict when the United States had stood by while Croats expelled tens of thousands of Serbs from Croatian Krajina, after NATO's victory 100,000 Serbs fled from the southern part of Kosovo.[124] They went either to the Serb communities in northern Kosovo or to Serbia proper. NATO did little to reassure them or keep them in their homes.

In the matter of ethnic cleansing therefore, in the second Balkan war of the 1990s as in the first, America's hands were not entirely clean. To be sure, war almost never affords the opportunity for moral purity; its essence, after all, is killing people. The two Balkan wars, however, unlike other conflicts, were waged explicitly and exclusively for moral purposes.

Every war has a political outcome and this one's was perverse. The United States fought on behalf of the Albanian Kosovars and against the Serbs. Yet on the central political issue at stake—whether Kosovo should become independent, as the Kosovars wanted, or remain a part of Yugoslavia, as the Serbs insisted—NATO and the Americans sided with the Serbs. This put the victors in the odd position of having gone to war to vindicate the position of the country against which it was fighting. Victory, in turn, put the members of the winning coalition at odds, on this central issue, with the people it had fought to protect and whose territory it had come to occupy. NATO and the United States ultimately resolved the contradiction, after nine years of occupation, in 2008, by granting sovereign independence to Kosovo. This, however, vindicated the charge that the countries opposed to the war, notably Russia, had made and that the American government had denied: that the war was intended to violate a basic international norm by conquering territory legally governed by a sovereign state.

The conduct of the war emphasized the mixed blessing of American dominance within NATO. The United States was responsible for most of the bombing and virtually all of the high-tech operations.[125] The European members of the alliance supported the war effort in principle but lacked the military forces to contribute significantly to it.

The Clinton administration waged neither the Kosovo nor the Bosnia war on behalf of American interests because the United States had none in the Balkans, a place of no strategic or economic importance to anyone beyond those living there. Even with the Cold War in the past, however, the United States continued to have strategic and economic interests in other parts of the world and these interests were damaged by the military operations in Kosovo.

The war worsened relations with China, the rising power in the world and a country that Clinton's first-term foreign policy had attempted to placate.[126] In the middle of the war, on the night of May 7–8, 1999, an American bomb struck the Chinese embassy in Belgrade, killing three Chinese and injuring more than 20 others. The attack was inadvertent. The CIA had mistakenly identified the embassy building as holding Serb communication facilities.[127] The American government apologized and paid compensation to the Chinese. But the bombing aroused the Chinese public against the United States. Angry demonstrations took place outside the American embassy in Beijing and elsewhere throughout China.[128]

Relations with Russia suffered even more. The war deepened the alienation of Russia from the United States and the West that the Clinton policy of NATO expansion had begun. While the Russian government ultimately helped to end the war, on NATO's terms, it never accepted the necessity for, or the legitimacy of, the attacks on Serbia. The Russian prime minister, Yevgeny Primakov, was en route to Washington when he learned of the start of the NATO air campaign. He ordered his plane to turn around and return home in protest.

In the immediate aftermath of the war a confrontation took place between the United States and Russia that was reminiscent of the Cold War era. Two hundred Russian troops serving as peacekeepers in Bosnia entered Kosovo and headed for its main airport, perhaps the advance guard of a larger deployment intended to secure a Russian-dominated (and Serb-friendly) zone in the northern part of the province. The American NATO commander, General Wesley Clark, ordered a British general, Sir Mike Jackson, to seize the airfield and stop them. Jackson replied that he would not start World War III for Clark. In the end, no airlift of Russian forces to Kosovo took place (Eastern European countries denied Russia overflight rights) and

Russian troops were integrated into the multinational peacekeeping force in Kosovo, as in Bosnia.[129]

Even without a dangerous military confrontation, the war increased Russians' anger at their Cold-War adversaries; and while NATO expansion disturbed the Russian foreign policy community, the Kosovo war made a strongly negative impression on the Russian public as a whole. Polls taken in April 1999, showed that 90 percent of the Russian public regarded the NATO campaign as a mistake and 65 percent considered NATO the aggressor in the conflict.[130] It gave the lie to the assurances the Clinton administration had conveyed to the Russian government in an attempt to soften its opposition to extending the Atlantic alliance toward Russia's borders while excluding Russia itself from membership: that NATO was in the process of transforming itself from a military to a political organization; that insofar as it retained its military mission this was strictly a defensive one; and that, while not a NATO member, Russia would be a full participant in European security affairs. Instead, NATO had fought a war against a country, Yugoslavia, that had attacked none of its members, a war to which Russia objected but that Moscow had been unable to prevent.[131]

Finally, the outcome of the war in Kosovo left NATO, led by the United States, in possession of the province and therefore with responsibility for governing it. As in Somalia, Haiti, and Bosnia, American officials proclaimed their intention to transform Kosovo, to make it a tolerant, democratic, and prosperous place. As in the other places, this did not happen.

Famous Victories

Each of America's humanitarian interventions of the 1990s had three goals. They aimed, first, to end the killings and the oppression that had provoked the intervention in the first place. This goal the United States achieved.*** The use of American military power prevented mass starvation in Somalia, evicted a military junta from power in Haiti,

---

*** American policy in Bosnia and Kosovo, it could be argued, was guilty of fostering the political equivalent of what economists call "moral hazard"—that is, unintentionally encouraging reckless and destructive conduct. By staunchly supporting the Muslims' maximal demands in Bosnia, the Clinton administration complicated the European effort to broker a peace agreement there, which became

and stopped—belatedly but finally—wars in Bosnia and Kosovo. With the exception of the Battle of Mogadishu, moreover, the United States accomplished these goals without the loss of American lives. Whatever could be done in these places by military means, the armed forces of the United States were able to do. True, in none of them did the American military confront anything like formidable opposition. Still, in Somalia, Haiti, Bosnia, and Kosovo the American armed forces did their job.

The second goal, implicit in each of the military interventions, was to establish a precedent for intervening in the internal affairs of sovereign states for humanitarian purposes. Because each operation violated the basic international norm of nonintervention except in cases of cross-border aggression, the United States had to demonstrate how, in these particular cases, violating this norm was justified by other standards that deserved precedence. There is, after all, a good deal of suffering in the world. When do governments have the right—indeed the obligation—to invade other countries to relieve it? The Clinton administration never answered this question. It never articulated a justifying doctrine. In fact, it never seriously tried to do so.

The nearest thing to the public presentation of a doctrine of humanitarian intervention came not from Bill Clinton but from Tony Blair. In a speech in Chicago in April 1999, largely devoted to other matters, Blair offered vague and not particularly helpful guidelines for overriding the principle of non-intervention.[132] As for Clinton, at a meeting with Kosovar refugees he said, "We are proud of what we did because we think it's what America stands for, that no one ever, ever should be punished and discriminated against or killed and uprooted because of their religion or ethnic heritage."[133] These may have been laudable sentiments but they did not offer useful principles for deciding when and how to stop such things when they are taking place in other countries.

possible only when the administration ceased that support. Similarly, in Kosovo the KLA abandoned peaceful protests for violence against Serbs explicitly—and successfully—for the purpose of provoking Serb atrocities that would bring the United States into the conflict on the side of the Albanian Kosovars. There is, of course, no way of knowing whether different American policies would have reduced the violence in the two places.

Some in the administration scoffed at the idea of formulating a doctrine for humanitarian intervention.[134] Without one, however, there was no basis for persuading other countries that this practice did not simply amount to the United States intervening whenever it chose, for its own reasons, wherever it had the power to do so—which was more or less how the Russian and Chinese governments saw the policies of the Clinton administration. To establish humanitarian intervention as an acceptable feature of international conduct requires not only a definition of the circumstances in which it is justified but also a mechanism for determining when those circumstances have arisen and authorizing action to address them. Most discussions of the practice cite the United Nations, an organization with universal membership, as the appropriate body for this purpose.[135] The military operations in Bosnia and Kosovo did not have the approval of the UN.

Nor did the Clinton administration persuade the American public that humanitarian intervention should become a regular feature of American foreign policy. None of the operations was popular. Despite the retrospective regret about having done nothing to stop the killing in Rwanda that Clinton expressed, in the 2000 presidential election both major candidates—one of them Clinton's vice president, Al Gore—assured the public that they would not have intervened there.[136] American participation in the Balkan wars and its dispatch of troops to Haiti did not have Congressional authorization. Clinton did not seek it because he would not have received it. Finally, in those two wars the United States fought to implement diametrically opposed political goals: in Bosnia the goal was to keep a multinational state together; in Kosovo, NATO's victory led to breaking such a state apart. What the two conflicts had in common was American opposition to the Serbs, which, however justified in the particular cases, hardly furnished the basis for a universally applicable doctrine.

The third goal of the American humanitarian interventions of the 1990s was to transform the places in which the United States had intervened to make them more tolerant socially, better governed and more democratic politically, as well as more prosperous economically. In none of them did the American government initially undertake military operations with these objectives in mind. Each intervention, however, gave rise to mission creep. Its military successes gave the United

States control of Somalia, Haiti, Bosnia, and Kosovo, and therefore responsibility, at least temporarily, for governing them. Moreover, Americans had strongly held ideas about the political institutions, economic policies, and social practices that are desirable—and feasible—everywhere. For these reasons, and in order to prevent the recurrence of the problems originally responsible for bringing American troops to these places, the American government found itself undertaking the same fundamental mission—in radically different circumstances, to be sure—as it had proclaimed for China and Russia. As in those two cases, in Somalia, Haiti, Bosnia, and Kosovo the mission of internal transformation failed.

The United States occupied Somalia for a shorter time than was the case in the other three places. Once the Americans left,[137] the country reverted to the violence that they had arrived to stop. Somalia became the prototype of what the world came to call a failed state. It lacked a government capable of keeping order, let alone providing any other services. Militias based on the country's four major clans waged constant war for control of territory and resources. It was these clans, not any wider sense of Somali identity, that commanded the loyalty of the people living within Somalia's borders. The fierce rivalries among these clans and their culture of feuding[138] made the country a chaotic, dangerous place.

Amid the violence, the Islamist terrorist organization al Qaeda established a presence in Somalia and in 2008 a movement linked to it took over the southern part of the country. In 2006 Ethiopia intervened in Somalia and five years later Kenya also sent troops, in both cases to fight the Islamists. In 2011 a serious drought brought back hunger and even starvation, precisely what had drawn the United States to Somalia in 1992. In the two decades following the ouster of Siad Barre, an estimated 2 million people, out of a total population of 10 million, became refugees, half of them fleeing abroad.[139] With the economy in shambles and few opportunities for peaceful gainful employment, some Somalis took advantage of the country's coastline on the Indian Ocean—the longest in Africa—to raid unprotected commercial shipping passing near the coast. Somali piracy came to the world's attention through a Hollywood movie depicting it, *Captain Phillips*, starring the well-known American actor Tom Hanks. Ongoing violence, terrorism, famine, and piracy were presumably not what Madeleine Albright had had in mind with her 1993 promise of the "restoration of an entire country" in Somalia.

Haiti received considerably more sustained attention from the United States and other countries than did Somalia. American troops stayed there, in small numbers, until 2000. The United Nations set up a mission in the country. Swarms of non-governmental organizations (NGOs) sent representatives to the island with the goal of bettering the lot of the poorest people in the Western Hemisphere; between 3,000 and 10,000 of these organizations established a presence there.[140] Yet the political, economic, and social conditions in which Haitians lived did not improve.

Jean-Bertrand Aristide, the president whom the United States had restored to power in 1994, left office in 1996 but was elected again in 2000. Four years later a rebellion that had begun in northern Haiti forced him from office. A UN stabilization force entered the country, and the man who had succeeded Aristide in 1996, René Préval, won the presidency again in 2006 in an election that, like previous contests, brought with it popular demonstrations and charges of fraud. Préval's rule, like Aristide's, was marked by widespread corruption and regular violence. Throughout this period Haitians remained desperately poor, with many of them illiterate and living on one dollar a day or less. The mainstay of the economy continued to be an unproductive agricultural sector. Haiti had an external debt that was large in relation to the country's total output. In the wake of the American intervention the gap in wealth and power between a small elite and the mass of Haitians[141] did not narrow; if anything, it widened.

Even nature was cruel to Haiti. On January 21, 2010, the most severe earthquake in 200 years struck the island, leaving 316,000 people dead and 1.6 million homeless. It was followed by the worst outbreak of cholera in recent history. Once again, American attention turned to the country. American troops returned to assist in humanitarian relief. Bill Clinton, by now out of office for a nearly decade, was appointed UN special envoy for Haiti. His wife, now the secretary of state, said, "We want Haiti to succeed. What happens here has repercussions far beyond its borders."[142] The rhetoric was familiar but the renewed interest and the assistance it brought made no discernible impact on the country's pathologies.

The commitment of largely American-based NGOs and the periodic presence of American troops made Haiti a kind of informal international protectorate. In the wake of the American-led wars in the Balkans, Bosnia and Kosovo became protectorates of a formal kind. As in Somalia and Haiti, however, the mission to transform them that the Clinton administration had proclaimed did not succeed.

To be sure, after 1995 fighting ceased in Bosnia: Serbs, Croats, and Muslims stopped killing each other. They did not, however, come together to form a single, integrated, tolerant, multinational state. The Dayton settlement left the former province effectively partitioned among the three national groups. The constitutional structure that Dayton had created did not permit the functioning of a genuinely national government, as had been the American goal.[143] Once again, insufficiently broad loyalties prevented the creation of the kinds of institutions necessary to fulfill that goal. Efforts to reform the Dayton structure foundered on Bosnia's deep national divisions. It became "a delicate assemblage of ethnic statelets disguised as a state."[144] The mission to transform it failed.

It was Europe, not the United States, that assumed the principal responsibility for such a transformation soon after the war ended. The chief international official there, the head of the Office of the High Representative, was invariably a European national. The Europeans hoped that the lure of ultimate membership in the EU would induce the three peoples to put aside their differences and work together to build a coherent, democratic, economically vibrant political community. It did not.

Instead, the divisions that had caused the war in the first place persisted and nothing the Europeans or Americans did overcame them.[145] The Croats identified with Croatia, not Bosnia, and the Serbs with Serbia. The Bosnian Muslims became more Islamic in their politics and their international affinities. No robust, widespread sense of Bosnian identity developed, nor did the resentments and hatreds aggravated by the war disappear. In 2013, Momcilo Krajisnik, a former Speaker of the Bosnian Serb parliament, was released from a British jail where he had been incarcerated after being convicted of war crimes by the Hague tribunal and returned home. He received a hero's welcome.

Despite being showered with foreign aid and technical assistance,[146] Bosnia remained economically moribund. Two decades after Dayton the unemployment rate exceeded 40 percent, with youth unemployment even higher. In early 2014 discontent with economic conditions, as well as disgust with corruption among the political elite, boiled over into public protests around the country.[147] These did not, however, lead to political reforms or the erosion of the barriers among the three constituent communities.

In Kosovo, as in Bosnia, American military operations helped bring intercommunal killing and ethnic cleansing to an end. Kosovo, like Bosnia, became an international protectorate. Kosovo, like Bosnia, was partitioned along ethnic lines, although this was the result of the ethnic cleansing that took place after the entry of American forces and not, as in Bosnia, before. Serbs living in the southern part of the country fled to the north, next to the border between Kosovo and Serbia, to become part of a more or less homogeneous Serb community that resisted efforts to draw it into the affairs of the Albanian-dominated province as a whole.

In 2008 the United States and the EU countries granted the Kosovars what they had gone to war against the Serbs a decade before to achieve: independence. More than 100 countries recognized Kosovo's sovereignty but many, including China and Russia, did not. The Serbs clustered in the north of the country had little to do with the national government in Pristina, the capital: their political, economic, and social connections were with Serbia.[148]

The new, independent Kosovo, while not a failed state, was scarcely a model of democratic governance or economic dynamism. The government was riddled with corruption. It was suspected of ties to organized crime and even accused of trafficking in human organs. Fifteen years after the end of the war, official unemployment stood at 40 percent, although some estimates put it higher. Kosovars depended heavily on remittances from countrymen working abroad. The enduring achievement of NATO's first-ever war, which Madeleine Albright called "the most important thing we have done in the world," was to transform Kosovo from the poorest province in Yugoslavia into the second-poorest country in Europe.

The United States failed to turn Somalia, Haiti, Bosnia, and Kosovo into better places because, first of all, it did not try very hard to do so. The Clinton administration was not willing to invest substantial resources or significant political capital for that purpose in any of them. The president himself had not set out to transform them. He had presided over American entanglement in their affairs for reasons he could not or did not control. He made his highest goal for each place getting it off the national agenda of the United States so that it no longer had the potential to cause him personal embarrassment and political harm. Once American troops left Somalia, the military junta lost power in Haiti, and the killing of Muslims stopped in Bosnia and Kosovo, that goal was accomplished.

Clinton showed no sign of caring what came next in each place.[†††] More importantly, neither did the American public, which had not favored military operations in any of them and did not demand successful state-building as the sequel to these operations. Perhaps the most generous way to describe the American role is that the United States acted as the surgeon, dealing with pressing emergencies, and left the laborious, protracted work of rehabilitation to others.[149]

Transformation failed in each place, as well, because making Somalia, Haiti, Bosnia, and Kosovo more orderly, better-governed, democratic, and prosperous would have proved formidably difficult even in the face of a more serious American commitment to doing so. Unlike the American experience in Germany and Japan after World War II, the gold standard for state-building, Somalia, Haiti, Bosnia, and Kosovo were not generously endowed with the human resources needed to build them from scratch.[150]

Moreover, Germany and Japan had something crucial that the four others lacked: sufficient demographic homogeneity that their institutions commanded broad loyalty throughout the country. The people living in them considered themselves Germans and Japanese and

---

[†††] During the American war in Indochina the economist John Kenneth Galbraith looked forward to the day when Vietnam would "return to the obscurity it so richly deserves." Clinton's actions suggested that he had something like the same attitude to Somalia, Haiti, Bosnia, and Kosovo. In any event, all four did eventually, from the American point of view, return to obscurity—whether merited or not.

behaved accordingly. Such was not the case for Somalia, Haiti, Bosnia, and Kosovo. Divided as they were by clan, tribe, religion, ethnicity, and nationality, they did not have the political, social, and psychological basis for all-encompassing impersonal institutions, above all democracy and the rule of law, without which modern states cannot exist. Unlike the United States, Germany, Japan, and the other modern countries that Americans wanted them to emulate, they had not escaped the great and fundamental obstacle to modernity—the tyranny of kinship.[151] So deeply embedded in the culture of each place were these primary and in some cases primordial loyalties that an outside military presence could not remove them. Foreign troops could keep the people there from killing each other but could not coax, coerce, or otherwise induce them to trust and cooperate with each other.

The Clinton administration ended in 2001. Its successor entered office critical of the nation-building of the 1990s, only to find itself engaged in the same enterprise, and engaged in it as well in two places far from the traditional centers of American foreign-policy interest. Unlike the Clinton administration, its successor did invest a great deal of blood and treasure in trying to transform the countries in which it intervened. Like its predecessor, however, in these missions the administration of George W. Bush also failed.

3

The War on Terror and Afghanistan

We are at war with terror. From this day forward, this is the new priority
of our administration.

— GEORGE W. BUSH, September 11, 2001[1]

. . . [Afghanistan] is one of the poorest countries on earth, a slice of sub-
Saharan-style deprivation set down in Asia. A land broken by war, and
drought, and extreme poverty, and neglect. Every journey, every meeting,
is a reminder that most Afghans have somehow to exist on less than a
dollar a day.

— SIR SHERARD COWPER-COLES, British Ambassador to Afghanistan,
June 25, 2007[2]

To the World Trade Center

During his campaign for re-election in 1996 one of his political aides
advised Bill Clinton that the 42nd president was destined not to join
the company of presidents considered to have attained greatness in
office.[3] For this, history was to blame. It had not furnished Clinton
in his first term, and would not present him in his second, with the
occasion for greatness: war. The four of his predecessors whose faces
appear on Mount Rushmore in South Dakota—George Washington,
Thomas Jefferson, Abraham Lincoln, and Theodore Roosevelt—had
all taken part in one or another of the nation's important wars.[4]
The most celebrated Democratic president of the twentieth century,
Franklin D. Roosevelt, presided over the greatest of all American
armed conflicts between 1941 and 1945 and Ronald Reagan, the

Republican equivalent of the second Roosevelt, held office during the latter stages of the Cold War.*

Nothing comparable occurred during Bill Clinton's presidency. It unfolded in a world safer for the United States than it had been for any president since Herbert Hoover. The absence of major military threats or crises provided the context for his foreign policy. The military operations over which he presided in Somalia, Haiti, Bosnia, and Kosovo were triggered by affronts to America's values rather than threats to its interests; and conflicts in which a major goal is to avoid American casualties, as was the case for all four, barely qualify, at least for the United States, as wars at all.

Indeed, the decade of the 1990s was free of major national challenges of any kind, a fortunate circumstance for the country as a whole if not for Clinton's historical aspirations. In this way it resembled the post-Civil War era, when the most enduringly important figures were business tycoons, not political leaders. A century later, the lives and works of Cornelius Vanderbilt, John D. Rockefeller, Andrew Carnegie, and J. P. Morgan commanded far more interest than those of Grover Cleveland, Chester A. Arthur, or William McKinley. So it will surely be for the early years of the post-Cold War period: in the eyes of posterity, Bill Gates, Steve Jobs, Mark Zuckerberg, and Sergey Brin and Larry Page will eclipse William Jefferson Clinton.

Still, Clinton did conduct a foreign policy, which had three major elements. His administration made humanitarian intervention a major feature of the American role in the world. The Balkan operations did finally put an end to fighting and ethnic cleansing, and the interventions that preceded them, in Somalia and Haiti, did relieve starvation in the first case and remove a military dictatorship (though without replacing it with stable or democratic rule) in the second. The Clinton administration did not, however, succeed in establishing humanitarian intervention as a widely accepted international practice or in persuading

---

* The two most skillful foreign policy presidents during the Cold War were the Republicans Dwight D. Eisenhower and George H. W. Bush. Their common principal achievement was to avoid pitfalls, a major contribution to the national well-being for which, however, monuments are not raised nor celebratory poems composed.

the American Congress to endorse it or the American public to support it. Despite its officials' promises to do so, the administration did not make the places where it intervened politically cohesive or economically prosperous.

In the two areas of foreign policy that, unlike humanitarian intervention, Clinton did approach willingly and with something approaching enthusiasm, he achieved mixed results. He recognized the importance of the global economy, the need for presidential leadership in promoting trade, and the role of American leadership in coping with the financial crises of the 1990s. He took some political risk in providing both.

He recognized, as well, the desirability of encouraging the creation of a democracy in post-communist Russia and forging a good working relationship between the new Russia and the West. He decided that the key to achieving both lay in assisting the Russian economy to make the transition from central planning to free markets. That transition proved to be a rocky one, as it would have been whatever the United States did. The difficulties it involved helped to discredit the government of Boris Yeltsin, in which the Clinton administration invested considerable political capital and a limited amount of money.

The responsibility for the deterioration of Russia's relations with the United States and the West, however, rests with Clinton. The American insistence on the eastward expansion of NATO turned the Russian political elite against the United States and fostered a constituency among the Russian people for a reflexively anti-American foreign policy, which the Russian government proceeded to carry out in the twenty-first century. With this checkered record in the management of the country's role beyond its borders, Clinton turned the office over to his successor, the Republican former governor of Texas and son of the man he himself had defeated to win the presidency in 1992, George W. Bush.

Born within six weeks of each other in 1946,[5] on the leading edge of the post-World War II baby boom in the United States (between that year and 1964, 76 million Americans were born), the 42nd and 43rd presidents came from different backgrounds. Bush was a product of the political aristocracy, his father a president, his grandfather a senator. Clinton, by contrast, rose from the middle class. He was raised in Hot Springs, Arkansas, by a mother who was a nurse and a stepfather who sold cars. Bush and Clinton's lives also had, however, two politically significant features in common.

Both came to maturity during the Vietnam War, graduating from college (Bush from Yale, Clinton from Georgetown) in 1968, the most turbulent year of that conflict. Both were eligible to serve in Vietnam, neither did so, and this became controversial when each first ran for the presidency. Clinton avoided military service altogether. Bush enrolled in the Texas Air National Guard instead of going to fight overseas, as he could have, and his diligence in carrying out his duties as a reservist came into question during the 2000 campaign.

For much of American history military service was all but mandatory for anyone seeking the presidency. For four decades after the Civil War, and again after World War II, veterans of those conflicts enjoyed decided political advantages. That pattern came to an end with Vietnam.

First Clinton's and then Bush's electoral success demonstrated that a stalwart military credential was no longer necessary to become commander-in-chief, which was the result of the unusually peaceful circumstances of the years following the Cold War.

In 1992 and 1996 Clinton defeated two decorated veterans of World War II—the senior George Bush and former Senator Robert Dole of Kansas. In 2000 and 2004 the younger Bush defeated two Democratic candidates who had served in Vietnam—Vice President Al Gore and Senator John Kerry. (In 2012 Barack Obama, 12 years old when the American combat role in Vietnam ended, defeated Senator John McCain, a naval aviator who had been a valiant prisoner of war in North Vietnam for six years.) For two decades after the American military withdrawal from Vietnam that war's shadow had hung over American electoral politics. The careers of Bill Clinton and George W. Bush showed that, with the end of the Cold War, that era had come to a close: the divisions the war had opened, if they had not disappeared entirely, had at least lost much of their political salience. Moreover, without the Cold War the world had come to seem less dangerous and serious military experience therefore a less-valued credential for the American presidency.

Bill Clinton and George W. Bush had a character trait in common as well, one that profoundly affected their presidencies. Both behaved in a reckless fashion. Clinton's recklessness was personal. He conducted a sexual relationship with a young intern, denied what he had done under oath, and was impeached by the House of Representatives— only the third American president to suffer this fate in 200 years—for perjury and obstruction of justice. His impeachment trial in the Senate ended in acquittal, not because the senators believed he had not committed the misdeeds of which he was accused but because they decided, following the majority opinion in the country, that what Clinton had undoubtedly done did not justify removing him from office.

Although it dominated the final stage of his presidency as the most memorable event in the eight years of an otherwise not particularly eventful presidency, Clinton's scandal had at best a modest impact on public policy and virtually none on America's relations with the rest of the world.[6]

George W. Bush, in contrast to Clinton, comported himself as president with impeccable probity. Unlike his predecessor, moreover, the younger Bush conducted his life in disciplined fashion: his meetings in the Oval Office, unlike Clinton's, began and ended on time, the result, by many accounts, of a life-changing decision at the age of 40 to give up alcohol.[7] Bush's recklessness manifested itself in his policy decisions, in particular his decision to invade Iraq without a well-considered plan for the aftermath of that invasion.[8] Like Clinton's recklessness, that of George W. Bush came to define his presidency; but Bush's did affect his policies. It had a broad and ultimately negative impact on America's standing in the world.

The two presidents displayed another similarity. Issues of foreign policy played almost no role in their initial presidential campaigns.

Bush presented himself to the country as a plausible steward of the nation's foreign policy by virtue of the advisors with whom he surrounded himself as a candidate. They had almost all worked in the administration of his father, which had helped bring the Cold War to a peaceful conclusion and evicted Saddam Hussein's army from Kuwait at low cost. The experience and the record of success of the foreign policy team he would appoint and that of his vice presidential running mate, Richard B. (Dick) Cheney, who had served as his father's secretary of defense, the Bush campaign conveyed to the electorate, would compensate for the presidential nominee's lack of both.

In the tradition of presidential candidates seeking to win the office when the other party holds it, Bush proposed to conduct foreign policy differently from the way in which the incumbent Democrats, whose sitting vice president, Al Gore, he was opposing, had managed it. In particular, he criticized the efforts at political and economic transformations in other countries on which the Clinton administration had embarked. "The vice president and I have a disagreement about the use of troops," he said during one of his debates with Gore. "He believes in nation-building. I would be very careful about using our troops as nation builders. I believe the role of the military is to fight and win war."[9]

After an election that ended in a virtual tie, a protracted and contentious recount of the votes in the state of Florida, and a Supreme Court decision in his favor, George W. Bush became the nation's 43rd president. The first eight months of his presidency were, by the foreign policy standards of the previous century, relatively quiet ones. The secretary of state, retired general Colin Powell who had been the Chairman of the Joint Chiefs of Staff during the Gulf War of 1991, attended to one of the State Department's preoccupations, the Arab-Israeli peace process.[10] The secretary of defense, Donald Rumsfeld, who had served in that capacity in 1975 and 1976 in the administration of Gerald Ford and who thus became the oldest as well as the youngest person to hold the office, began to reconfigure the American armed forces to make them lighter and more mobile in order to meet what he anticipated would be the needs of the post-Cold War world. On April 1, an American spy plane operating off the coast of China collided with a Chinese fighter jet and was forced to make an emergency landing on the Chinese island of Hainan. After 10 days of diplomatic activity and the dispatch of a letter from the American government expressing regret for the incident,[11] the crew and—three months later—the disassembled aircraft were returned to the United States.

Then came September 11. The terrorist attacks on New York and Washington on that day seemed to change everything for the Bush administration and for American foreign policy. They did, in fact, change a great deal. They made foreign policy important again. Bush devoted more of his time and his political capital to it than had Clinton. Because of the renewed importance of issues of foreign policy, Bush did not decide his policies on the basis of domestic political considerations, as Clinton had. Instead, as during the Cold War, Bush made his decisions according to his view of America's interests, foremost of which was the nation's safety. Still, the foreign policy of George W. Bush did exhibit a fundamental continuity with that of Bill Clinton. The Bush initiatives propelled the United States into missions similar to those that the Clinton administration had undertaken. Like the missions of the 1990s in Somalia, Haiti, Bosnia, and Kosovo, those of the first decade of the twenty-first century also failed. Those missions began with the events of September 11.

On that morning two hijacked American commercial airliners crashed into the two towers of the World Trade Center, at the southern tip of Manhattan. Shortly afterward a third commercial aircraft, also hijacked, struck the Pentagon, the headquarters of the Department of Defense in Washington. A fourth plane failed to reach its hijackers' target, the Capitol building in Washington, when passengers overpowered the men who had commandeered it. That plane crashed in a field near Shanksville, Pennsylvania, killing all on board.

The attacks caused death and destruction on a large scale. The twin towers crumbled into a smoldering ruin. The Pentagon was seriously damaged. Almost 3,000 people died, most of whom had worked in offices in the World Trade Center.[12] What happened in the American capital and in its financial and cultural capital that morning also caused shock—around the world but especially in the United States, the mainland of which had not suffered a serious foreign attack since 1812. The shock was all the greater because the attacks were broadcast on live television. Millions of people saw the twin towers fall. Within hours the American intelligence community had identified the perpetrators: an Islamic terrorist organization called al Qaeda.[13]

Al Qaeda was founded, led, and partly financed by Osama bin Laden. He was the son of a Yemeni immigrant to Saudi Arabia who became a wealthy construction magnate there—Osama was the 17th son among his more than 50 children. Bin Laden was educated in the Kingdom of Saudi Arabia and in 1979, at the age of 22, went to Afghanistan to join the Islamic resistance to the Soviet occupation there. He established al Qaeda in 1988, was banished from Saudi Arabia in 1992, and set up a base of operations in Sudan. When forced to leave that country in

1996, he went back to Afghanistan, joined forces with the Egyptian Islamic fundamentalist Ayman al-Zawahari, who become his second-in-command and close associate,[14] and built training camps for terrorists in the cause of his version of Islam. By authorizing the attacks on New York and Washington and then going into hiding he became the most widely and intensively sought person in the world. He earned a place for himself, along with Saddam Hussein, Adolf Hitler, and other murderous tyrants, in the American pantheon of evildoers.

Bin Laden was an Islamist: he aspired to impose what he considered authentically Islamic social and political norms as well as rules of personal conduct on all Muslims. By this he meant the original, uncorrupted faith at the time of its origins on the Arabian peninsula in the seventh century. His vision of a properly governed Islamic order encompassing all Muslims was imprecise at best—the details of early Islam are not a matter of unchallenged record, and in any event he himself had little actual knowledge of Islamic history—and his ideas were scarcely realistic given the many political jurisdictions in which contemporary Muslims live and the wide variety of their religious beliefs and practices. He did, however, have a strategy for implementing his vision. What he deemed the heretical governments of Muslim countries, above all in his native Saudi Arabia, stood in the way of the pure Islam that he believed the faithful required. These governments, which he called "the near enemy," depended, in turn, on the support of the "far enemy," the United States. He therefore declared war on the United States on August 23, 1996.[15] He considered America to be as weak and ripe for destruction as had been its rival superpower during the Cold War, the Soviet Union, which had collapsed in 1991 as a result, as he saw it, of its defeat in Afghanistan by pious Muslims such as himself.[16]

Bin Laden's grievance against the government of his native country and its American ally dated from 1991. In that year, in response to Saddam Hussein's invasion and occupation of neighboring Kuwait, the Saudi royal family invited American troops into the kingdom. In bin Laden's eyes their presence desecrated holy Muslim soil.[17] The roots of his hostility, and the Muslim anger at the West on which he drew to assemble al Qaeda, however, extended farther back in history. They sprang ultimately from the centuries of Islamic inferiority to the West in wealth and power and the sense of humiliation this fostered among people whose faith taught them that they were, as God's elect, destined to dominate others, as indeed they had in the religion's early years.[18] The defeat of the Turks at the gates of Vienna in 1638, which marked the beginning of the long decline of Islamic power in the world, has as good a claim to being the event that caused the attacks of September 11 as the Soviet invasion of Afghanistan in 1979 or the arrival, at the invitation of the Saudi government, of American troops in bin Laden's native land in 1990.

Having declared war on the United States, bin Laden and al Qaeda proceeded to wage it. The organization carried out almost simultaneous truck bombings of the American embassies in Nairobi, Kenya, and in Dar es Salaam, Tanzania, on August 7, 1998, which killed over 200 people, 12 of them Americans. It also attacked the American destroyer the USS *Cole* with a bomb-bearing small boat in Aden Harbor, at the tip of the Arabian peninsula, on October 12, 2000, costing 17 members of the United States Navy their lives.[19]

These operations ensured that the American government became aware of al Qaeda. More than merely aware, in fact, the United States treated bin Laden and his organization with considerable seriousness. The CIA established a special cell devoted to tracking his activities. In response to the African embassy bombings the Clinton administration launched cruise missiles at a suspected terrorist training camp in Afghanistan and a pharmaceutical factory in Sudan that allegedly manufactured chemical weapons. Richard Clarke, the chief counterterrorism official on the National Security Council staff in the Clinton administration who carried over into the Bush presidency, issued a series of increasingly urgent warnings about the threat from al Qaeda in 2001. The headline of one of the items in the President's daily intelligence briefing memo of August 6 read, "Bin Laden determined to strike in U.S."

Despite those warnings, the September 11 attacks succeeded. The 19 hijackers managed to enter the United States, board and take over four airplanes, and fly three of them into their targets. The Clinton administration, while acutely aware of the danger of an al Qaeda attack, did not go beyond the isolated cruise missile attack it launched. It never mounted a sustained military campaign against the organization. In

2001 information that, if properly analyzed, would have alerted the government to the September 11 plot was buried in the vast American intelligence bureaucracy.[20] The Bush administration did not make dealing with terrorism a high priority in its initial months in office.

While one administration did not persist militarily against al Qaeda and its successor did not devote sufficient high-level attention to it, the failure to anticipate, discover, and prevent the attacks of September 11 came ultimately from a failure of strategic imagination.[21] The use of hijacked commercial airliners as instruments of mass murder by religious fanatics willing to kill themselves in order to kill others fell too far outside the normal experience of American officials and the historical experience of the United States. These officials did not conceive of such an event as being likely enough to warrant decisive preventive measures. The American view of the world, and how it worked, did not have room for such attacks.

When the attacks did take place, that view changed. September 11 had a powerful impact on the nation's foreign policy. It seemed a great historical dividing line, and in some ways it was. It wrenched the nation's foreign policy out of the course on which it was proceeding. The attacks on New York and Washington gave rise to three wars that the United States would not otherwise have waged. Yet two of those wars led the country, unintentionally, into precisely the kinds of missions into which the Clinton administration had stumbled, and with similar results.

In their consequences the September 11 attacks followed a familiar pattern. In the past, attacks on American territory, or on Americans, had triggered war: that is, in fact, the way most American wars have begun. The skirmish with British troops in Lexington and Concord, Massachusetts, in 1775 proved to be the opening shot of the Revolutionary War. The Confederate bombardment of Fort Sumter, South Carolina, in 1861 started the Civil War. The explosion on the American battleship USS *Maine* in Havana harbor in 1898, widely blamed on Spain at the time,[22] led to the Spanish-American War. The German attack on American ships in 1917 brought the United States into World War I, and the Japanese bombing of the American fleet at Pearl Harbor, Hawaii, triggered American participation in World War II.

One close historical parallel to September 11 was not an attack and did not lead to a shooting war. This was the Soviet launch of the first earth-orbiting satellite, Sputnik, on October 4, 1957. While Americans had long since come to regard the Soviet Union as an adversary, Sputnik, like the attacks on the Pentagon and the World Trade Center, shocked them: it was unexpected, a feat of which the adversary had not been thought capable. Like the September 11 attacks it seemed to come out of the blue, without warning. Sputnik presented a new kind of threat to the United States: the unprecedented danger of an attack from space; 44 years later September 11 revealed the menace of large-scale terrorist attacks originating abroad. Both events seemed particularly ominous because each showed the continental United States to be vulnerable to direct foreign assault after long decades of immunity.

While Sputnik caused Americans to worry, the attacks the American colonists experienced in 1775 and the United States suffered in 1861, 1898, 1917, and 1941 made them angry. So did those of September 11, which created a bellicose national mood out of which emerged an impulse to retaliate against those responsible.

Like Sputnik, the events of September 11 also engendered fear, based on the expectation that what had happened was a harbinger of more, and perhaps even worse, attacks to come. The Bush administration worried that al Qaeda would strike again, frequently. It worried that terrorists had or would acquire weapons of mass destruction—chemical munitions and even crude nuclear devices[23]—that would kill many more people than the airplane hijackers had managed.[24] These fears were reinforced when, only a week after the attacks, envelopes containing the deadly toxin anthrax arrived at the offices of several media outlets and two United States senators. Five people died and 17 more were infected. The September 11 attacks, in the eyes of some, had inaugurated a conflict on the scale of the three large, all-encompassing ones the United States had waged in the twentieth century. There was talk of "World War IV"[25] and of terrorism presenting an "existential" threat that could destroy the United States as a functioning, independent, political community.[26]

Among all the 300 million people in the United States, with the exception of the people killed on September 11 and their families, no lives changed more drastically, in ways that promoted an outsized fear

of terrorism, than those of the two people responsible for determining the American response to the attacks: the president and the vice
president. Security for both was enhanced: uniformed men with rifles
began to patrol the White House.[27] To avoid a circumstance in which
both nationally elected officials could be killed or disabled simultaneously, the vice president spent much of his time outside his office, at a
"secure, undisclosed location."[28] With the exception of the officials with
direct responsibility for it, the national security bureaucracy had largely
ignored terrorism before September 11. Afterward, it shifted decisively
in the opposite direction: virtually every piece of evidence, rumor, or
suspicion of another attack that the vast American intelligence-gather-
ing apparatus picked up was funneled to the White House.[29] If the
government's imagination had failed it before September 11, afterward
its imagination ran wild.

The world that George W. Bush and Dick Cheney inhabited on
September 12 and thereafter seemed to them—could not help but
seem—a grim, forbidding, perilous place. Bearing the responsibility for
protecting the United States in such a world, they responded aggres-
sively. Their countrymen, almost all of whom shared their outlook in
the wake of the attacks, approved. The attacks, like a sudden torrential
downpour, enlarged the reservoir of public support for American military action abroad, which the end of the Cold War had drained. The
Bush administration considered each of the three wars it initiated to
be necessary for the safety of the United States. It went to war, shortly
after September 11, in Afghanistan, the place from which the attacks
had come. Eighteen months later, in the spring of 2003, still under the
influence of those attacks, the administration also took the country to
war in Iraq, from which the attacks had not come.[30] These two conflicts entangled the United States, once again, in unsuccessful efforts
at nation-building. The Bush administration also embarked on a third
and more amorphous conflict: a war against terror itself.

The War on Terror

"We are at war with terror," Bush told his senior advisors a few hours
after the planes had struck the World Trade Center and the Pentagon.
Three days later Congress authorized the president to use "all necessary

and appropriate force" against those responsible for the attacks. It also recognized presidential authority "to take action to deter and prevent acts of international terrorism against the United States."[31] The war on terror—sometimes called the global war on terror, with the acronym "GWOT"—became the umbrella term for American efforts to prevent additional attacks like those of September 11.

The term's first word had a certain logic: it signaled that the United States would no longer regard terrorism, as it had before September 11, as simply a crime, with the responsibility for dealing with it resting with the police and the courts.[32] By using the word "war," the administration made counterterrorism the highest national priority, to be pursued apart from the procedural restrictions of the criminal justice system.

The third word of the phrase, however, has an odd ring to it in this context. Terrorism is a tactic. Declaring a twenty-first-century war against terror was akin to pronouncing World War II a war against tanks or the blitzkrieg. One reason for this awkward construction was surely the wish to avoid naming the enemy—radical Islam—for fear of offending the hundreds of millions of Muslims around the world who were not radical.[†] Another was the American tendency, born of the domestic experience of pluralism and, unfortunately, irrelevant to most of the rest of the world (including Muslim-majority countries), to see religions—all religions—as essentially benign. "Islam is peace," Bush, not previously known as an authority on that particular faith, told Americans on September 17.

Beyond the imprecision with which the term identified the enemy, prosecuting a war on terror had another drawback: defined in this way it could never be won. Terrorism—attacks by irregular forces on civilian targets for political purposes—has a very long history, dating back at least to ancient Rome.[33] It is a weapon of the weak, employed by individuals and groups without the power or the numbers to assemble organized military forces on behalf of their causes.[34] Some people and groups will always be less powerful than others, and a few will be desperate or fanatical enough (or both) to attempt to compensate for

---

† It was also a way to avoid offending governments with which the United States had friendly relations, such as that of Saudi Arabia, whose governing principles were not all that distant from the ones al Qaeda professed.

their weakness with the tactics of terror. Since terrorists seek to pub-
licize their cause in order to win adherents to it—terrorism has been
called "propaganda by deed"—the modern era, with its mass media,
has made it a more plausible and therefore more frequently employed
tactic than in the past.

While terrorism has recurred throughout history and became particularly common from the middle of the second half of the nineteenth
century to World War I,[35] al Qaeda's version differed from its historical
ancestors in one particular way. Previous terrorists generally chose as
their targets officials with some responsibility for the policies to which
they objected—the Russian tsar, for example, whom Russian radicals
assassinated in 1881. Al Qaeda, by contrast, sought to kill as many people as possible, as long as they were living in the United States. In this
way Osama bin Laden followed in the footsteps not of the assassins of
Tsar Alexander II but of Hitler and Stalin, who had people killed not
for anything they had done but rather for who they were: members of
the wrong social group in the first case and of the wrong economic class
in the second.

Because they aimed at mass slaughter, twenty-first-century terrorists such as al Qaeda did pose a genuine threat rather than simply
being a nuisance to the countries they targeted. These targets included
countries around the world, including in Europe and the Pacific Rim,
as well as the United States. While the Europeans suffered terrorist
attacks both before and after September 11, however, they did not commit themselves to a full-scale war against the perpetrators. Their com-
parative restraint no doubt had something to do with the fact that none
of the attacks in Europe did remotely as much damage as did those that
toppled the towers of the World Trade Center and blasted a hole in
the Pentagon. The difference in approach also stemmed from a different view of the threat. The Europeans regarded terrorism as a chronic
problem to be controlled rather than a fearsome enemy against which
their countries had to mobilize.[36]

Like wars waged by soldiers on battlefields, the American war on
terror had a defensive component: the government took steps to protect the country against further attacks and to limit the effects of such
attacks if they did occur. The United States went on the offensive as
well, seeking out and killing people around the world identified as

anti-American terrorists. In the decade and a half following September 11 nothing like the attacks of that day took place in the United States. In this sense, and although its contributions to this outcome can never be precisely determined, the war on terror can be seen as a success. Like other wars in American history, however, it became controversial in the United States because the government, in waging it, infringed on traditional American liberties.

The institutions on which the United States relied to protect its territory and its citizens from further terrorist assaults already existed on September 11, 2001. The defensive aspect of the war on terror that Bush declared consisted of reorganizing them and giving them more money.

Historically, the American federal government has signaled its assumption of a role in a new area of national life by establishing a cabinet office devoted to it. The twentieth century saw the creation of the Department of Labor, the Department of Health, Education, and Welfare (later Health and Human Services), and the Department of Housing and Urban Development. In this spirit, in 2002 the Department of Homeland Security (DHS) came into existence.[37] Of course, protecting the homeland was not a new responsibility for the federal government—it is the basic task of all governments everywhere—but rather a newly urgent one. The new department brought together under a single administrative roof a variety of federal agencies, including the Coast Guard, the Border Patrol, and the Federal Emergency Management Agency. The federal government also established a National Counterterrorism Center and removed some of the institutional and legal barriers to the sharing of information among various agencies concerned with terrorism, especially the Federal Bureau of Investigation (FBI) and the CIA,[38] both of which remained outside the DHS.

If one characteristic American response to a new, or newly pressing, national problem is to create a federal department to deal with it, another is to provide money for it. This the United States did with terrorism in the wake of September 11. By one estimate it spent more than $1 trillion over the next decade:[39] 46 percent of it on protecting property and infrastructure in the United States, 44 percent on preventing and disrupting attacks, and the rest on "mitigation and resilience"—that is, reducing the costs of attacks should they occur.[40] While the surprise attack on Pearl Harbor on December 7, 1941, rearranged the lives of millions of Americans, the surprise attacks of September 11, 2001, did not. Their most direct impact on Americans' lives came in the form of the screening through which passengers had to move at airports before boarding their flights. The government also took to issuing color-coded alerts about the level of terrorist threat, which the American population soon came to ignore.

In the decade and a half after September 11, foreign-based terrorists did not manage to kill a single American in the United States.[41] This was not because none tried to do so. In the 10 years following the September 11 attacks at least 50 instances of Islamic terrorism aimed at the United States came to light. In almost none, however, did the prospective attacker come close to achieving his aim.[42]

Up to a point, the generosity of American spending on homeland security had a certain logic. Tracking terrorists is a major undertaking: they do not identify themselves and almost anyone could, in theory, carry out a terrorist attack. Moreover, almost any place in the United States could become, again in theory, the target of a terrorist attack. In this sense the United States allocated resources to protect the country on the principle of the corporate executive who said of his advertising budget, "I know half of it is wasted, but I don't know which half."

Still, whatever the contribution to keeping the country safe of the trillion-dollar defensive measures the American government undertook in response to terrorism, it is difficult to conclude that they met the test of cost-effectiveness. It seems likely that the country could have purchased the same amount of safety at lower cost.[43] In no small part because of its affluence, the United States has tended to spend lavishly on its wars, as on other things.[44] In the case of protecting American lives and property from terrorist attack, moreover, the political incentives worked in favor of overspending and against frugality. No public official was going to be criticized for doing too much. The Bush administration had come in for considerable criticism after the attacks on New York and Washington, by contrast, for having done too little.

The effectiveness of the countermeasures the United States undertook is one plausible reason for the more or less perfect record on terrorism the country compiled after September 11. Another equally plausible explanation is the modesty of the threat. On September 11, and in the days thereafter, Bush and Cheney feared, not unreasonably, that al Qaeda would mount many more lethal assaults on the United States. In fact it did not, nor did any like-minded groups, which supports the hypothesis that the threat that terrorist groups posed to the United States was never as great as the events of September 11 all but inevitably suggested that it was. In the wake of the attacks, the American government and the American public may have suffered, as the political scientist John Mueller put it, from "a false sense of insecurity."

Historically, terrorists have seldom become strong enough to achieve the political goals on behalf of which they have employed the tactic. The September 11 attacks succeeded through the kind of guile, resourcefulness, and discipline that the would-be perpetrators of the subsequent, unsuccessful plots, conspicuously lacked,[45] suggesting that terrorists in general may not be drawn from the most competent segments of the population. James Bond was not working for al Qaeda after all.

In historical perspective, the attacks on the World Trade Center and the Pentagon appear not as the beginning of an era of mass terror but rather as a horrible but isolated episode in American history. They succeeded, above all, because Americans were not expecting them. Al Qaeda's success depended ultimately on the failure of the American imagination and that success was self-liquidating: it removed the condition that made it possible. The approach of the American government to terrorism shifted, beginning in the late morning of September 11, from indifference to hypervigilance. In its overpayment for protection from terrorism the United States was, metaphorically, using a sledgehammer to swat a fly. While it is not the most efficient instrument for the purpose, a sledgehammer will kill a fly. Moreover, beginning shortly after September 11, to the defensive measures it took to ward off terrorist attacks and the new attitude it adopted toward terrorism the American government added a third response: it tracked and killed would-be terrorists outside the United States.

As the chief instrument for hunting and eliminating terrorists abroad the American government deployed the CIA. While the agency had devoted most of its resources, since its establishment in 1947 as the successor to the Office of Strategic Services of World War II, to collecting and analyzing intelligence, it had also engaged in secret, small-scale military operations.[46] On September 17, 2001, President Bush signed an order giving the CIA expanded authority to conduct covert operations and to use deadly force.[47] For the offensive phase of the war on terror, the United States also made extensive use of the army's Joint Special Operations Command (JSOC), which had been founded in the wake of the failed 1980 effort to rescue Americans held hostage in Iran and which specialized in swift, targeted, clandestine operations. JSOC became active in Afghanistan and Iraq but also in such places as Somalia, Yemen, Syria, the Philippines, and even Iran.[48]

The terrorist whom the United States devoted the most time, attention, and resources to killing was Osama bin Laden himself. He escaped from Afghanistan after September 11 and evaded detection for a decade thereafter, occasionally issuing videotapes broadcasting his message of war against the West. Finally, in 2011, the American intelligence community concluded, with high but not absolute confidence, that he was living in a modest villa in Abbotabad, a Pakistani town 30 miles from the capital city Islamabad, that was home to one of Pakistan's principal advanced military training academies. The man who had succeeded George W. Bush as president, Barack Obama, ordered a commando raid on the villa, which was launched from a base across the border in Afghanistan. The raid ran the risk that the Pakistani government, to which it was not disclosed in advance, would take it for an enemy attack and respond accordingly. On May 2, 27 men,[49] ferried to the site by helicopters, invaded the villa, found and killed bin Laden, and flew out of Pakistan without the Pakistani authorities discovering what was happening. The American military buried the al Qaeda leader at sea.[50]

The dramatic killing of the man responsible for the September 11 attacks, who had come to personify the terrorist threat and had eluded capture for a decade, provided a sense of momentary satisfaction to the American public: 10 years after the crime, rough justice had finally been done. It also enhanced Obama's credentials as a fighter against terrorism, which assisted his successful re-election campaign the following year.[51] On the actual terrorist threat to the United States, however, the operation had, at best, a modest impact. The organization that bin Laden had built had fragmented—in part, to be sure, because of the American elimination of some of its leading figures. While disintegrating, however, al Qaeda had also morphed into a kind of franchise

operation, with terrorist groups in different countries sharing its outlook, drawing inspiration from its example, and sometimes appropriat-
ing its name. The al Qaeda that had flourished in Afghanistan begat
al Qaeda in Iraq, al Qaeda in the Arabian peninsula, and al Qaeda in
the Islamic Maghreb, for example, none of which took orders from al
Qaeda's founder. According to one intelligence official, at the time of
his death "Bin Laden wasn't really the CEO of a multinational corporation. He was the slightly out-of-touch coordinator of a broad, dysfunctional family who were frankly operating more on their own agendas
than on his agenda."[52]

To cope with these and other terrorist organizations and cells that
aspired to harm Americans, the American government increasingly
relied on the most important military innovation of the war on terror: the unmanned aerial vehicle (UAV), or drone.‡ These are small,
pilotless aircraft operated by remote control—often from tens of thousands of miles away—originally used for battlefield surveillance and
then armed with missiles that the controller can fire at targets over
which the vehicle is hovering.[53]

Like other wartime military innovations, the drone emerged from
the confluence of technology and strategy. It provided the United
States with a way to kill individual terrorists from high altitudes with
powerful munitions, without the extensive collateral damage wrought
by conventional bombing campaigns—although not without any collateral damage at all—and also without putting American troops in
harm's way, as searching for terrorists on the ground would entail.
Drones offered the United States a metaphorical scalpel instead of a
sledgehammer with which to eliminate terrorists, and a scalpel that
could be wielded at long distance.[54]

---

‡ Officially named "Predator," the term by which these vehicles became commonly known is, given their purpose, an odd one. A drone is a male bee, which
lacks a sting as UAVs, when armed, do not. In literature the term is associated
with P. G. Wodehouse's lovable but dimwitted member of the English upper
class, Bertie Wooster, who whiles away some of his free time (and all his time
is free time) with other upper-class wastrels at the Drones Club in London. The
name presumably comes from the low hum, the "droning" sound that the vehicle
makes when hovering over its target.

Perhaps the closest strategic parallel to the drone in recent American military history relied, ironically, on the most indiscriminate of armaments, the most powerful sledgehammer ever invented—nuclear weapons. In 1953 the Eisenhower administration proclaimed the "New Look." Frustrated with the casualties exacted by the grinding, inconclusive war in Korea and committed to defending American interests against communist challenges around the world, the administration declared that, rather than attempting to block every communist initiative when and where it occurred, the United States would respond, at a time and place of its choosing, with "massive retaliation," including the use of nuclear weapons. By raising the possibility that communist attacks, even modest ones, would evoke a devastating nuclear response, the administration hoped to deter such attacks. Radically different though it was in the magnitude of the force it proposed to employ, the New Look had the same general aim as the use of drones: to protect American interests without putting tens of thousands of American troops in harm's way.

Because drone strikes fit America's military and political needs so well, their number increased sharply after the first one was used in 2002.[55] By 2013 the Obama administration had conducted nine times as many drone strikes in four years—in Pakistan, Yemen, and Somalia—as the Bush administration had in eight.[56] Their effectiveness depended on accurate and timely intelligence: killing terrorists required correctly identifying them and knowing their whereabouts precisely enough for drones to find them. Neither was easy to accomplish because anti-American terrorists took pains to conceal both their identities and their movements. Because of the difficulty of getting the relevant information in time to act on it, the United States sometimes used drones for "signature strikes," targeting people not positively identified as terrorists but whose patterns of behavior strongly suggested terrorist activity. This amounted to execution without conclusive evidence of guilt, which caused unease in the United States, a country committed, in its domestic legal culture, to strict standards of due process.[57]

Because those whom the American government sought to kill seldom lived and traveled alone, moreover, attacks aimed at terrorists often killed others. This, too, caused unease among Americans, whose legal system is designed to prevent the punishment of the innocent. It also frequently provoked outrage where the attacks took place.[58] The drone campaigns against anti-American terrorists certainly generated anti-American sentiment.

By eliminating individual terrorists the American government surely reduced the terrorist threat to the American homeland; and however great or small the contribution of the campaign against its would-be attackers, the homeland did remain safe after September 11. In this sense, the war on terror succeeded. It did not, and could not, however, eliminate all threats to the United States, let alone all terrorism everywhere. Terrorism has its roots in political conditions, religious beliefs, and the vagaries of human psychology that lie outside the power of any government to control. In that sense, the war on terror was destined from the outset never to reach a fully satisfactory conclusion.

Like all wars, this one had costs: costs in American treasure; costs in ill will generated by the deaths of innocent people killed by drones;[59] and costs of a third kind, costs paid by Americans rather than foreigners, counted in the damage, at least in the eyes of some Americans, the war on terror did to fundamental, constitutionally protected liberties in the United States.

The tension between waging war and protecting liberty has a long history. In one of America's founding documents, *The Federalist Papers*, Alexander Hamilton wrote: "Safety from external danger is the most powerful director of national conduct. Even the ardent love of liberty will, after a time, give way to its dictates."[60] Individual liberty requires restraining the power of the government. In time of war, however, citizens want the government to do whatever is necessary to protect them and thus its power expands. In American wars that expansion has sometimes violated the boundaries that the American Constitution and American governmental practice have set to safeguard liberty.

In 1798, with the wars of the French Revolution raging and an undeclared naval war with France under way, Congress passed, and President John Adams signed, the Alien and Sedition Acts, which permitted the president to imprison or deport aliens "considered dangerous to the peace and safety of the United States." During the Civil War, President Abraham Lincoln suspended the writ of habeas corpus, the traditional Anglo-American requirement that an arrested person be brought before a judge or into court rather than be held indefinitely.

In 1942, after the Japanese attack on Pearl Harbor of December 7, 1941, the federal government ordered the interning of 110,000 American citizens of Japanese descent in "War Relocation Camps," in clear violation of their basic rights as American citizens. During the early 1950s, under the influence of the Cold War with the Soviet Union and its offshoot, the Korean War, thousands of Americans suspected of being communists or communist sympathizers were subjected to FBI investigations and sometimes dismissed from their jobs on questionable grounds.

In each case the widely perceived need to cope with a dangerous threat led to measures that encroached on civil liberties, measures that would not have been enacted in peacetime. Invariably, when the threat eased, the measures were modified or retracted entirely and in historical perspective came to seem regrettable, sometimes even shameful.[61]

The pattern repeated itself after September 11, and for the same reason: the world suddenly seemed a more dangerous place, obliging the government to exercise more extensive powers to protect Americans. The war on terror had two particular features that lent themselves to the expansion of government authority in ways that seemed to some to violate the principles of liberty. First, the secrecy in which terrorists operated created an extraordinary need for information about them. Identifying and locating them was by far the best defense against their attacks; and the best sources of information about terrorists who were at large were terrorists who had been captured by the United States. Second, terrorists did not fit easily into existing legal or political categories with well-established protocols governing the treatment of captives. They were neither ordinary criminals, subject to American or other countries' systems of justice, nor uniform-wearing soldiers entitled, when apprehended, to the protections of the Geneva Conventions. Because the suspected terrorists lacked the status of either ordinary lawbreakers or prisoners of war, and because of the pressing need for information that might save lives, American government lawyers deemed it acceptable to treat them more harshly than either criminals or captured soldiers.

With some suspected terrorists, therefore, the American government practiced "extraordinary rendition"—seizing them outside American territory and dispatching them to prisons in third countries that, it was widely supposed, permitted methods of interrogation forbidden in the United States that were employed to obtain valuable intelligence.[62] The American government did not voluntarily disclose the existence or the locations of some of the prisons, known as "black sites," to which it sent some of the terrorists it captured, and these prisons remained secret for several years after September 11.[63] One destination for captured terrorists that was known from the start was the prison at the American naval base at Guantanamo, Cuba. The American government sent them there on the theory that, because it was located outside the country, the rights prisoners enjoy and the procedural safeguards designed to protect them in the United States did not have to be scrupulously respected. (In 2004 the American Supreme Court ruled that, to the contrary, Guantanamo was not beyond the reach of American law.)[64] To try some of the suspected terrorists at Guantanamo, the Bush administration resorted to a practice from World War II—military commissions before which defendants had fewer protections than in the criminal courts.[65]

Americans tend to be sensitive about their own liberties but not necessarily about those of non-Americans suspected of plotting to blow up their buildings and kill them. Outside the small (albeit vocal) community of lawyers and others particularly concerned about civil liberties, therefore, the way that the government treated people it apprehended for terrorist activity did not trouble most American citizens, with one exception. Unlike extraordinary rendition, secret foreign prisons, and military courts, allegations that some suspected terrorists had been tortured aroused a strong, and strongly negative, reaction. The deliberate infliction of severe pain or suffering, whether physical or mental, which is the definition of torture, is forbidden by international law, including the 1984 Convention Against Torture and Other Cruel, Inhuman, or Degrading Treatment or Punishment, which the United States took the lead in drafting and ratifying.[66]

To extract information from suspected terrorists in the aftermath of September 11, the United States employed what the government called "enhanced interrogation techniques." According to the standards the Bush administration adopted, these did not qualify as torture and were therefore permissible; but the standards became the subject of controversy,[67] and one in particular proved especially controversial.

"Waterboarding" involves pouring water over a cloth covering the face and breathing passages, causing the sensation of drowning. Khalid Sheikh Mohammed, the mastermind of the September 11 attacks who was captured in Pakistan and spirited to Guantanamo, underwent waterboarding a reported 183 times.[68] The Bush administration asserted that waterboarding was not a form of torture. When its use came to light, however, many disagreed. The revelation that the government had used this interrogation technique triggered three debates in the United States and elsewhere: over whether it fit the definition of torture; over whether its use had yielded information that had helped to prevent future attacks, a matter on which government officials themselves differed;[69] and a more general debate about whether any circumstances could ever justify the use of torture.[70]

As time passed after September 11 without a subsequent serious attack on American territory, the national sense of urgency about terrorism declined. The government banned the practice of waterboarding during interrogations, imposed rules on extraordinary rendition intended to prevent the torture of the prisoners involved, and transferred prisoners from black sites to Guantanamo. That prison remained open, despite President Obama's promise to close it, for lack of an acceptable facility to which to transfer the men held there. The pattern occasioned by previous American wars of expanding then retracting government power in ways affecting liberty recurred during the war on terror. As Americans felt safer, the marked solicitousness for civil liberties that is a feature of American political life in normal times reasserted itself.

One encroachment undertaken to prevent terrorist attacks did persist on an appreciable scale, however. This was a practice that, unlike the other violations (or alleged violations) of liberty, directly affected millions of Americans, which would have seemed likely to make it the most unpopular of all of them and thus the one likeliest to be terminated entirely. Like the other post-September 11 measures, it was designed to obtain information about possible terrorist attacks. Like the others, the Bush administration kept it secret, and when it was revealed, a political backlash ensued. The backlash did not, however, end it entirely.

Immediately after September 11 the National Security Agency (NSA)[71] began to collect the telephone and email communications of millions of Americans and non-Americans. It flagged and followed up on those that seemed connected to terrorist activity. The giant communications companies that handled the traffic in which the government was interested cooperated with the NSA.[72]

Surveillance of this kind did not, of course, begin in 2001. Governments have always interested themselves in the communications of those they consider threatening and have sought to intercept messages they suspected of being pertinent to their countries' security. As the technologies of communication have changed, so, too, have the technologies of intercepting communications. Before the digital age, in the era of the telephone, the government collected information through wiretaps.

The revelation of extensive wiretapping in the Nixon administration led to laws placing limits on the practice. The Federal Intelligence Surveillance Act (FISA) of 1978 required judicial authorization for surveillance within the United States. It established courts that, operating in secret, entertained requests and issued warrants for such surveillance. After September 11, the Bush administration, acting on the advice of some of its lawyers, circumvented the FISA requirements[73] and cast a very broad net for data on telephone calls and email messages. The information the NSA collected included the identities of the senders and recipients of the calls and messages, known as metadata,[74] but not, in almost every case, the content of the messages.

When the program came to light it provoked objections. They came, first, in 2004, from within the Bush administration. Senior officials of the Justice Department insisted that the administration use the FISA courts rather than ignoring them, as it had been doing. In 2005 articles describing part of the program appeared in *The New York Times*, despite the administration's request that they not be published, and triggered widespread public criticism. The biggest backlash in public opinion against the post-September 11 NSA program came with the publication, in 2013, of data stolen by a former NSA contractor, Edward Snowden, which revealed the surveillance to be broader than had been previously known and to have included tapping the personal telephones of foreign leaders, even friendly ones such as German Chancellor Angela Merkel.[75] Despite the outcry both in the United States and abroad, the program of surveillance, albeit under somewhat stricter monitoring, continued.[76] It would no doubt continue as long as terrorism remained a threat to the American homeland, which, since the tactic can never be fully and finally eradicated, would be a very long time indeed.

A decade and a half after September 11, if the threat of terrorist attacks on the United States had not ended, terrorism had ceased to be the object of a war. Without announcing it publicly, the American government and the American public had come to regard it as the Europeans did: not a mortal peril but rather a chronic problem that could be controlled without mobilizing the country, spending enormous sums of money, or rewriting the American Constitution. A concrete—literally—symbol of this change in the national attitude toward terrorism was the building intended to house the Department of Homeland Security, the agency created to fight it. On May 21, 2014, *The Washington Post* reported that the building, in southwest Washington, was running more than $1.5 billion over budget, was a full 11 years behind schedule, and might never be completed.[77]

The fate of the war on terror was to evolve into something else, something less alarming and less taxing. The two other conflicts that the attacks of September 11 triggered followed different trajectories. The first, in Afghanistan, became the longest war the United States had ever waged.

Afghanistan: Success

The place from which the orders for the September 11 attacks came and to which the United States therefore sent troops was a poor, landlocked country in southwest Asia. Afghanistan is situated at the crossroads of three major geographic and cultural regions: the Indian sub continent to the southwest, Central Asia to the north, Iran and the Middle East to the west. A little smaller in area than the state of Texas,[78] its almost entirely Muslim population consists of several major ethnic groups that are concentrated, for the most part, in one of the country's four major regions. Pashtuns, who live on both sides of the border with Pakistan, are the principal group in the south, the major city of which is Kandahar. They make up about 40 percent of the country's population. Tajiks, in the north, where the main city is Mazar-e-Sharif, comprise about 30 percent of all Afghans. This group also lives in Tajikistan, one of Afghanistan's northern neighbors, which was once a constituent republic of the Soviet Union. Uzbeks and Turkmen also inhabit the north of the country and number about 10 percent of the population. Hazaras, in the west, where the largest city is Herat, are, like the people of neighboring Iran, Shia Muslims, and speak a dialect of the Iranian language, Farsi. They make up about 15 percent of all Afghans. All these groups are present in Kabul, the capital, which dominates the eastern part of the country.

Afghanistan is a largely rural and traditional society in which, for virtually all of its history, kinship ties have mattered more than ethnicity and ethnicity has trumped any sense of national identity, although unlike Bosnia and Kosovo it did have a history as a loosely unified political entity. From 1747 until 1978 one member or another of the Durrani tribe of Pashtuns ruled the country, for most of that period as the king.[79] The social conditions prevailing in Afghanistan turned out to affect the American experience there in the first decade and a half of the twenty-first century as profoundly as had the ethnic divisions in the Balkans in the 1990s. In contrast to most of the places where the Clinton administration conducted its humanitarian interventions, serious American involvement with Afghanistan did not begin in the post-Cold War era. The Cold War first drew the United States into Afghan affairs in 1979, when the Soviet Union invaded and occupied the country.

In April 1978 a radical Marxist group, the People's Democratic Party of Afghanistan (PDPA), overthrew the government, seized power, proclaimed its loyalty to the international communist movement and to the Soviet Union—then a neighboring country—and began a sweeping social, political, and economic transformation along communist lines.[80] The vast majority of Afghans found the PDPA program alien and unacceptable, and resisted it. The upheaval that followed placed the new regime in jeopardy. Unwilling to see what had become a client government fall, the Soviet Union sent troops to Kabul in December 1979, installed a new ruler whom the Soviet leaders considered loyal to them, and remained to pacify the country.[81]

As in the past,[82] Afghans opposed foreign occupation. Their traditions of tribal feuding and the country's topography, with its mountain ranges suitable for sheltering guerrilla forces, enabled the badly outgunned Afghans to wage an effective war against the world's second superpower. They had yet another asset in their battle against the Soviet Union: assistance from third countries. Saudi Arabia provided financial support to groups identifying themselves as Islamic and fighting for religious reasons in addition to national or anticommunist ones. Many non-Afghans, including Osama bin Laden, joined the fight under the banner of radical Islam. On the basis of motives having nothing to do with Islam and everything to do with the Cold War, the United States shipped arms to the Afghans through Pakistan.

The 10-year-long Soviet occupation, and the resistance to it, devastated the country. Out of a population of 30 million, one million people died and three million became refugees, many in Pakistan. The country's agricultural economy suffered disruption that necessitated the importing of food.[83] In 1989 the Soviet leader Mikhail Gorbachev, as part of his program of reform (a program that led, unintentionally, to the collapse of the Soviet Union two years later), withdrew Soviet troops from Afghanistan.[84] The government it left behind managed to survive until 1992: the government's leader, who as a Soviet client had called himself Dr. Najib, changed his name to the more Islamic Najibullah. When his regime fell in 1992, a multi-sided civil war followed that was almost as destructive as the Soviet occupation,[85] in which leaders from different ethnic groups commanding militias loyal to them—warlords—dominated various parts of the country.[86]

Few countries were as poor as Afghanistan in 1979 and none suffered more destruction over the next quarter century. By the mid-1990s it fit the definition of failed state. Its economy had collapsed, and it had no working institutions. Out of these miserable conditions emerged the Taliban, an Islamist movement committed to restoring order based on what its members considered an uncorrupted version of the faith. It consisted of young Pashtuns—"taliban" is the Arabic word for student—many of whom had been educated in Saudi-supported fundamentalist Islamic religious schools in Pakistan after their families had fled or been driven out of Afghanistan during the Soviet war. With logistical support from the Pakistani intelligence service and money from Saudi Arabia, the Taliban managed to conquer most of the country, including the capital. They then proceeded to govern in as radical a manner as had the PDPA, attempting to enforce their own version of

Islam, which prohibited, among other things, music, kite flying, dog races, and education for women.[87]

With the Soviet exit from the country in 1989, the world in general and the United States in particular lost interest in Afghanistan. Only three countries—Pakistan, Saudi Arabia, and the United Arab Emirates—formally recognized the Taliban government. Insofar as other countries took note of that government at all, they regarded it as extreme to the point of derangement but not a danger to anyone except the Afghans themselves. An episode in March 2001 fortified this impression: the Taliban government destroyed one of the country's cultural treasures, two monumental sixth-century statues of the Buddha, carved into the side of a cliff in the Hazara region of the country, on the grounds that the statues were un-Islamic idols. Contrary to the prevailing view, however, the Taliban did prove dangerous to Americans. Their regime permitted Osama bin Laden to settle in Afghanistan and to operate his terrorist training camps there. Afghanistan was the base from which al Qaeda launched the September 11 attacks, which made it, for the United States, enemy territory.

In Brussels on the day after the attacks, the representatives of the 19 countries belonging to NATO invoked, for the first time in the alliance's 52-year history, Article 5 of its treaty, which commits all members to respond militarily to protect any one of them that has been attacked. Thus, for the first time, they voted for war. In an address to Congress on September 20, 2001, President Bush demanded that the Taliban turn over al Qaeda to the United States and shut down its training camps. The Afghan leaders, he said, "will hand over the terrorists or they will share their fate."[88] The Taliban refused to hand over al Qaeda or close its camps.[89] The United States went to war to secure both objectives.

That war proved, in the short term, to be one of the easiest, cheapest, and most successful campaigns in American military history. The American government made common cause with the Northern Alliance, a largely Tajik group based in the northern part of the country that had fought against the Soviet Union and that opposed the Taliban.[90] Two weeks after the September 11 attacks a handful of CIA operatives arrived in Afghanistan carrying cash for their new allies. JSOC personnel also arrived in small numbers to identify Taliban military and political targets for American planes to strike. Altogether, only about 400 Americans set foot in the country in the final months of 2001. In the war against the Taliban it was the Northern Alliance that supplied the ground forces; the United States provided the air-power. [91] Together they routed the Taliban in five weeks, capturing first the northern city of Mazar-e-Sharif, then Kabul, then the main southern city of Kandahar. The tribes that had accepted Taliban rule, sometimes grudgingly, because there had seemed to be no alternative, now deserted them.[92]

The Taliban had conquered most of Afghanistan with religious fervor combined with arms supplied by Pakistan, but these were no match for the punishing American air assault. B-52 bombers and A-130 gunships made short work of the ground forces that opposed the United States.[93] For a minimal investment in manpower America achieved its objectives in Afghanistan: al Qaeda lost both its home base and many of its cadres.

The Taliban leaders who were not killed or captured escaped over the border to Pakistan, as did Osama bin Laden and some of his confederates, including Ayman al-Zawahiri. This was not the outcome bin Laden had expected on September 11. His vision of an American collapse after the attacks he had planned had not come to pass. Instead, the United States had smashed its attacker.

The removal of what had passed for a government in Afghanistan created the need for a replacement. On November 27, in Bonn, the former capital of the former West Germany, the United Nations convened a meeting of the various Afghan groups to select an interim government.[94] As the head of the new government the conference chose Hamid Karzai, a Pashtun from Kandahar born into the clan from which the country's rulers traditionally came, the Durrani, who had spent the years from 1994 to 2001 in Pakistan. All the factions represented at the meeting found Karzai acceptable, and he had an additional advantage. Because Afghanistan has always been a poor, loosely organized, and weak country surrounded by stronger ones, the country's leaders have invariably had to deal with powerful foreigners who took an interest in its affairs. Karzai was suited to this task: with his effective command of English, brothers who owned restaurants in Boston and Baltimore,[95] and his good relations with Americans, especially the CIA, he was well positioned to deal with the country likely to be most important in the wake of Taliban rule, the United States. On December 7, 2001, Karzai entered Kabul as the country's new leader.

In June 2002 a meeting was held in the capital to select a government for a two-year term. One thousand elected representatives and 500 additional delegates chosen by the organizers attended.[96] They confirmed Karzai's position. In December 2003, a similar meeting convened to ratify a new constitution. This led to a presidential election in October 2004, a relatively free and fair one, in which Karzai won a majority of the votes, avoiding the need for a runoff. After a terrible 25 years not only peace but also democracy had, it seemed, come to Afghanistan.

The people of Afghanistan, even the Pashtuns from whose ranks the Taliban came, did not oppose the new regime. After the political radicalism of the PDPA, the brutality of the Soviet occupation, the chaos and violence of the civil war, and the religious radicalism of the Taliban, almost any kind of government could not help but seem an improvement. Nor did Afghans, despite their history of hostility to the presence of foreign armed forces on their territory, resist the small—5,000-strong—American military contingent that entered the country and became the core of the multinational International Security Assistance Force (ISAF) charged with keeping order. It seemed a bulwark against the return of the disorder and violence of the first half of the 1990s.[97] The next year, by one estimate, as many as three million refugees returned to Afghanistan.[98] Economic activity, stifled under the Taliban, resumed and expanded. Between 2003 and 2012 the economy grew, admittedly from a very low base, by an average of over 9 percent annually. Schools opened and girls flocked to them. Access to health care became available, with the number taking advantage of this access expanding tenfold over the next decade. By 2014 life expectancy had increased by 20 years, to 62.[99] In the years following the ouster of the Taliban, 20 million people acquired mobile phones. Newspapers and radio and television stations, all banned before 2001, proliferated.[100]

The high point of political success for the new, American-sponsored dispensation in the country came in 2005. In that year 83 percent of all Afghans polled approved of Karzai, and the same percentage had favorable attitudes to the United States.[101] Things were then going well enough in the country that the American government decided to cut its aid budget request for Afghanistan by 38 percent and the Department of Defense announced plans to reduce the number of American troops by 3,000.[102]

The American engagement with Afghanistan, for its first three years, differed in important ways from the Clinton experience with humanitarian intervention. The United States went to Afghanistan on the basis of interests, not ideals. It intervened not because others were being killed but because more than 3,000 American citizens and residents had been murdered. American military operations had the goal of preventing further attacks not on the people of other countries but on the citizens of the United States.

The Bush administration had strong backing in the United States and virtually unanimous support from the international community[103] for its war in Afghanistan, neither of which the Clinton administration had enjoyed for its wars in the Balkans. In Afghanistan, Bush acted swiftly and decisively, in contrast to Clinton's hesitations over Bosnia and Kosovo. In the Balkans, and in Somalia and Haiti as well, the Clinton administration achieved, at best, a qualified success. In Afghanistan, the United States scored, at first, an unqualified triumph, and at a very low cost. The apparently decisive character of the policies there helped to foster the confidence in American capabilities that contributed to the decision to invade Iraq in 2003.

The Afghan operation and the humanitarian interventions of the 1990s did have a central feature in common: although none was undertaken for the purpose of transforming the politics and economics of the countries American forces came to occupy, that is what the United States found itself doing—unintentionally, unwillingly, and ultimately unsuccessfully—both before and after September 11. The attacks of that day, which seemed at the time a great dividing line in the history of American foreign policy, in fact produced a fundamental continuity: afterward, as before, the United States found itself undertaking, without success, missions of transformation.

The Bush intervention in Afghanistan and the Clinton humanitarian interventions had one more dissimilarity, and a crucial one. In the Balkans, the war was over when the American forces arrived. The

United States failed to make Bosnia and Kosovo united, tolerant, and democratic countries, but it did not have to conduct serious military operations in either place after 1995 and 1999 respectively. Afghanistan turned out differently. At the moment when the policy of the United States there seemed most resoundingly successful, the real American war was just beginning.

Afghanistan: Failure

In 2005 the Taliban returned. They mounted an insurrection in southern and eastern Afghanistan in conjunction with other fundamentalist Islamic groups.[104] Violence against government, military, and civilian targets mounted. The insurgents conducted raids and ambushes, attacked convoys, captured and held government facilities for brief periods, assassinated local government officials, and destroyed Western-funded development projects.[105] They launched suicide attacks against Afghan and foreign personnel: 17 in 2005, spiking to 123 the next year.[106] While the troops of ISAF could defeat the Taliban fighters when they encountered them—and they fought some fierce battles in 2006 and 2007—these troops were not numerous enough to patrol all the territory that the insurgents infiltrated.[107] By 2009 the Taliban and their allies controlled or threatened an estimated 40 percent of Afghan territory.[108]

The insurgency jeopardized what the United States had accomplished in Afghanistan in the wake of September 11. It threatened, in the worst case, to make the country once again a base for groups with the political and religious outlook that had motived the attackers. It threatened, that is, the goal for which the United States had gone to war in Afghanistan and had at first seemed to have achieved there.

Insurgencies succeed to the extent that the governments they seek to displace fail.[109] The resurgence of the Taliban testified to the failure of the Karzai government to secure the allegiance of Pashtun Afghans because, among other things, of its failure to provide services, in particular the most basic service of all, security. In some parts of the south and east, in fact, by 2009 it was the Taliban that provided such government as was available, including courts to adjudicate disputes.[110] The insurgency testified more broadly to a failure of the state-building

project that the defeat of the Taliban had made both possible and necessary. The international community in general, and the United States
above all, had established, sponsored, and supported Hamid Karzai
and his government. His failure was also theirs. It was, that is, another
failure of the kind of mission on which the United States had embarked
in Somalia, Haiti, Bosnia, and Kosovo.

One reason that the United States failed to build an Afghan state
strong enough to prevent the Taliban from returning was that it did
not try very hard to do so. In his speech announcing American military
operations in that country President Bush said, "the oppressed people
of Afghanistan will know the generosity of America and our allies. As
we strike military targets, we will also drop food, medicine and supplies to the starving and suffering men and women of Afghanistan."[111]
He promised humanitarian relief but said nothing about rebuilding the
country.[112] The Department of Defense pressed for confining military
deployments to Kabul rather than sending more troops to keep order
outside the capital. Its preference was to train an Afghan army for that
task, but in the years immediately after the fall of the Taliban it trained
very few.[113] The troops the United States did send to the country, moreover, had as their mission hunting the remnants of al Qaeda.[114] The
aversion to nation-building that Bush had expressed in his presidential campaign carried over to his administration's initial approach to
Afghanistan.[115]

In April 2002, Bush seemed to change his mind. Speaking at the
Virginia Military Institute, the alma mater of George C. Marshall,
secretary of state in the Truman administration, he invoked, in the
Afghan context, the 1947 program of economic assistance to the
countries of Europe to help them recover from the ravages of World
War II that Marshall had announced and to which his name became
attached.[116] The United States did not, however, provide a Marshall
Plan to Afghanistan, or at least not a generous one. Per capita financial
assistance to the country was lower than for almost any comparable
effort since World War II. Similarly, the ratio of foreign troops to the
overall Afghan population—such troops were crucial for maintaining
order in the absence of effective police forces—was historically low.[117]
Within the American government, aid to Afghanistan never had a high
priority.[118]

Furthermore, even if the United States had desired to make a greater effort at state-building, it lacked the expertise necessary to have a clear idea of what to do and how to do it. Very few Americans had any knowledge at all of the history, the culture, the society, and the customs of a country as different from the United States as any in the world. Almost none could communicate with Afghans in their native languages, Pashto and Dari. In Afghanistan, therefore, the conditions for effective American tutelage, or partnership, in building the institutions of a government strong enough to resist the challenge of an insurgency were, to say the least, unfavorable.[119]

Another condition, external to Afghanistan, limited the American state-building enterprise there: the war in Iraq. Beginning even before the United States invaded that country in April 2003, the time and attention of the highest officials in Washington, two important and scarce resources for any government initiative, shifted from southwest Asia to Mesopotamia. Once the Iraq war began it had first claim not only on their attention but also on American money and troops. From at least mid-2002 until 2009, Afghanistan had a lower place in the hierarchy of American national priorities than did Iraq.[120]

Still, Afghanistan did command some attention and did receive some resources from the United States.[121] ISAF troops were eventually sent to cities beyond Kabul, although those from the European members of NATO often operated under such tight restrictions that they contributed little to the fight against the Taliban.[122] The United States did spend money on infrastructure and on training Afghans for both civilian and military employment.[123] The American mission did not fail only because of inattention. It failed as well because the material at hand for the task was inadequate.

President Hamid Karzai proved to be a flawed leader, mercurial in temperament, and an ineffective executive. Over time his relations with his American patrons deteriorated, and many Western officials and observers assigned the responsibility for the lack of working institutions and the rise of a virulent insurgency to his personal and political shortcomings. He became the latest in a long line of foreign leaders, from Chiang Kai-shek in wartime China, to Ngo Dinh Diem of South Vietnam, to the Shah of Iran, to Jean-Bertrand Aristide of Haiti, on whom the United States had counted for the effective leadership of a beleaguered client state and who had failed to provide it. The failure of the American mission in Afghanistan certainly had something to do with Karzai's inadequacies, but its causes went deeper.

Of all the countries in the world, Afghanistan offered perhaps the weakest basis for building and sustaining a modern state. On every international ranking of the national properties that determine successful modern countries, Afghanistan was to be found at or near the bottom. Even before the horrible two decades between the Soviet invasion and the American invasion it had had, compared to other countries, a low per capita income, a low literacy rate, low life expectancy, and sparse and decrepit infrastructure. A high percentage of its population lived in villages without electricity and engaged in subsistence agriculture. It was a country that, before the term became politically incorrect, would have been labeled "backward."[124] The great historical developments that had created the modern part of the modern world—the Enlightenment, secularism, the French and the Industrial Revolutions—had all bypassed Afghanistan.

Then came the Soviet occupation, the civil war, and the Taliban regime, the combined effect of which was to pulverize what little economic and social capital Afghanistan had. The country had had relatively few people with modern educations, for example, and lost most of them during those two decades through flight or death.[125] The quality of any product depends in part on the quality of the materials from which it is made. The post-Taliban Afghan state had to be made from very poor materials indeed.[126]

To compound the difficulty of state-building there, Afghan society was deeply traditional in nature.[127] Kinship ties dominated social and political life.[128] Such societies find the bedrock of modern states—the rule of law and impersonal, rule-governed institutions—to be alien, unacceptable, even threatening. The idea of gearing behavior to abstract rules and allocating resources on this basis rather than favoring relatives provokes, in traditional societies, incredulity, ridicule, and resistance.[129] Unlike in Bosnia and Kosovo, the various Afghan ethnic groups did not object to living in a single state. But many of them did object to the kind of state that well-meaning outsiders were trying to help them build. The American version of a modern society struck many Afghans as being, although less violent and oppressive, akin to the Marxism-Leninism of the PDPA and fundamentalist Islam of the Taliban in being based on principles they did not share.[130] In all human endeavors culture matters, and the indigenous culture of Afghanistan did not lend itself to the project that the United States undertook—fitfully and halfheartedly, to be sure—in that country.

If the United States made only a comparatively modest commitment and the features of the local society were poorly suited to it, state-building in Afghanistan suffered from yet a third problem: the manner in which it was carried out. The international community designed a centralized system of government that gave Afghanistan the worst of both worlds.[131] On the one hand, it contradicted the native Afghan tradition of decentralization. The country's ethnic groups had been willing to remain under a single political roof for several centuries because the central authority in Kabul did not intrude on their day-to-day affairs. Hamid Karzai, by contrast, was vested, on paper, with considerable power. He had, most importantly, the power to appoint local officials. On the other hand, Karzai lacked the resources to exercise effectively the powers he theoretically possessed. Beyond appointing people, he himself could do little outside Kabul, and so he came to rely on local leaders who had functioned, in the previous decade, as warlords. These were the men who had dominated the country's political affairs after the collapse of the Soviet-imposed PDPA government in 1992. Their venality and brutality had made them deeply unpopular, which had helped to pave the way for the ascendance of the Taliban in 1996. His association with them tarnished the reputation among Afghans of the president who had appointed them.[132]

While they were hardly desirable allies and surrogates, Karzai had no good alternative to relying on them.[133] Moreover, the United States was willing to cooperate with them in the pursuit of the al Qaeda cadres remaining in Afghanistan,[134] the capture or killing of whom rather than the construction of a viable, decent Afghan state was the highest American priority in the country immediately following the fall of the Taliban. His association with regional warlords undercut Karzai's standing in the eyes of Afghans, making his government vulnerable to insurgents, as did another conspicuous feature of his regime: massive corruption.

Western assessments of the sources of the Karzai government's weakness and of the basis for the success of the resurgent Taliban invariably emphasized the corruption that pervaded that government.[135] Insurgencies fail when the population they are trying to win over remains loyal to the government, which its soldiers are willing to fight to defend. The corruption he permitted—some would say fostered—was an important reason that Karzai did not inspire such loyalty. His immediate family enriched itself on an impressive scale during his presidency. Most notoriously, a half-brother, Ahmed Wali Karzai, became the political overlord of Kandahar and accumulated enormous wealth, partly through his connections to the American government, before being assassinated in 2011.[136] It also did not help the president's standing with the sometimes-xenophobic Afghans that he depended so heavily on foreigners.[137]

Corruption in Afghanistan did not arise simply from the greed of the Karzai family. It was, in a sense, built into the country's tribal culture, in which assisting relatives and loyalists rather than obedience to impersonal rules had for centuries been the approved form of conduct. In the Afghan context, an official who did not help his family and his friends would have counted as unusual and, among those friends and relatives, immoral. Corruption in the Karzai era rose to levels unprecedented for Afghanistan, moreover, because the influx of foreigners, and foreign assistance, while modest—even miserly—in comparison with other state-building efforts, was very high by Afghan standards. By one estimate American aid accounted for 75 percent of the country's gross domestic product.[138] Officials stole more than ever before for the simple reason that there was more to steal than ever before. The presence, for the first time in the country's history, of modern forms of communication made corruption more visible to the people of Afghanistan than in the past. The all-too-accurate perception that the president, his cronies, and his political allies were taking for themselves funds intended for other purposes made Afghans less willing to support the American-sponsored regime that these people dominated, and more sympathetic to its Taliban adversaries.

Students of political development and state-building sometimes refer to the goal of these undertakings as "getting to Denmark."[139] That small Scandinavian country represents the ideal that others hope, in the long run, in the best of circumstances, to reproduce. Twenty-first-century Afghanistan stood as far from Denmark in social, economic, political, and cultural terms as it was possible to be and remain on the same planet. The American efforts at building an Afghan state, even with more resources devoted to the project, even with a better-designed political system, and even with a more honest and politically skillful leader, was bound, given the realities of the country, to be arduous, slow, and frustrating. Afghanistan was not going to approach Denmark for decades, if ever, no matter what Hamid Karzai or the American government did or did not do.[140] The inherent difficulties of state-building did not, however, make inevitable the virulent, powerful insurgency that pummeled the country beginning in 2005, which would not have taken place without the support the Taliban received from neighboring Pakistan. Afghanistan therefore became a source of contention in relations between the United States and Pakistan, a relationship dating back more than five decades that had seldom lacked for sources of conflict.

The former rulers of Afghanistan received shelter across the border. Their leadership lived and worked in the Pakistani city of Quetta. Their fighters received weaponry and training from Pakistan's intelligence agency, the Inter-Service Intelligence (ISI).[141] These fighters used the mountainous parts of Pakistan along the Afghan border—northern Balochistan Province, the Northwest Frontier Province, and the Federally Administered Tribal Area (FATA)—as the base from which they moved into Afghanistan to launch attacks and to which they repaired in the face of Afghan and American military pressure.[142] When fighting the Taliban, therefore, the United States was effectively at war as well with the country that sponsored the insurgency and that was also nominally, and in some ways actually, an American ally. This was the latest chapter in a decades-long relationship that was consistently fraught, complicated, and ambivalent.

The United States and Pakistan became allies in the early stages of the Cold War, but in their wars with India in 1965 and 1971 the Pakistanis believed they had received less American help than was their due.[143] With the Soviet invasion of Afghanistan in 1979, the United States found a new reason for close relations with Pakistan, which served as a sanctuary for anti-Soviet guerrillas and a staging area for

American-supplied weapons being sent to the Afghan resistance. With the Soviet evacuation of Afghanistan in 1989, and the end of the Cold War shortly thereafter, Pakistan lost its strategic importance for the United States. America began to take a greater interest in Pakistan's arch-rival India, a fellow democracy and, after its economic reforms of 1991, an increasingly attractive commercial partner. On this as on previous occasions, the Pakistanis felt that they had been used and then abandoned by their erstwhile superpower patron; but the partnership resumed after September 11.

The dramatic American military operation that killed Osama bin Laden in 2011 epitomized, and worsened, an already toxic relationship. The United States infuriated Pakistani officials by effectively invading their country without notifying them in advance, and humiliated them, as they saw it, by carrying out the incursion without being detected. The American government, for its part, chose not to alert the Pakistani authorities out of concern that they, in turn, would warn bin Laden, who would then escape. His presence in a town filled with military personnel strongly suggested that Pakistan had been protecting the man responsible for murdering almost 3,000 people in the United States.

The chronic difficulty of the Pakistani-American relationship stemmed from the fact that the two countries brought to it different and sometimes incompatible agendas. The American goals varied over time: opposition to the Soviet Union and Maoist China in the 1950s and 1960s; opposition to nuclear proliferation in the 1970s, 1980s, and 1990s; and opposition to terrorism in the twenty-first century. None had priority for Pakistan, which as often as not in fact supported what the United States opposed—befriending communist China, acquiring nuclear weapons of its own, and harboring fundamentalist Islamic groups that routinely committed acts of terrorism in India and Afghanistan. The overriding feature of Pakistan's foreign policy remained constant from independence to the second decade of the new century: hostility to India,§ a sentiment the United States never

§ "Popular animosity toward India flows from Pakistan's violent birthing process; from the country's national identity as a Muslim (read: not Hindu) state; from the Indo-Pakistani wars of 1947, 1965, and 1971; and from continuing

shared.[144] From the Pakistani point of view the on-again off-again relationship with the United States had the goal of strengthening its hand in its ongoing conflict with its larger, more powerful neighbor, a conflict in which America was usually neutral and sometimes sympathized with India.

The rivalry with India helped to determine Pakistan's policy toward Afghanistan. It counted on a friendly government in Kabul to provide it with what Pakistani officials called "strategic depth" against its large neighbor.[145] Pakistani officials also conducted their policy toward Afghanistan on the basis of their fears about their own country's unity. Pashtuns lived on both sides of the border between the two countries and no Afghan government had ever recognized the legitimacy or permanence of that border, known as the Durand Line, which the British had drawn in 1893.[146] Although more Pashtuns lived on the Pakistani than on the Afghan side of the line,[147] the Pakistani government feared that their country's Pashtuns would try to secede from Pakistan to join Afghanistan, or become part of an independent "Pashtunistan."[148]

The Taliban therefore served two Pakistani purposes: as a client of the Pakistani government they could be counted on to side with Pakistan rather than India; and as fanatical Muslims they could be counted on not only to disdain Hindu India but also to resist Pashtun nationalism in favor of Muslim solidarity, including solidarity with Pakistan.

In the immediate aftermath of September 11 the American government demanded that Pakistan support its efforts in Afghanistan, and the Pakistani government complied—up to a point.[149] It permitted the United States to ship troops and supplies to Afghanistan through

territorial disputes, most notably over Kashmir." Daniel Markey, *No Exit from Pakistan: America's Tortured Relationship with Islamabad*, New York: Cambridge University Press, 2013, p. 39. The Pakistani military has been content to keep the conflict with India alive in order to justify its own outsized role in the country's public affairs. India's view of Pakistan is not the mirror image of Pakistan's of India. "Indians in positions of power view neither military conquest nor the breakup of Pakistan as realistic or even desirable, despite having suffered from so many Pakistan-based terrorist attacks. Most Indian strategists see Pakistan as a huge mess, not one India would want to inherit even if it had the military tools to sweep across the border unobstructed," p. 47.

its territory. It helped gather intelligence about terrorists and secretly authorized American drone strikes against them in Pakistan. It captured and turned over to the Americans high-ranking al Qaeda personnel. It did not, however, cooperate with the American campaign, from 2005 onward, against the resurgent Taliban.

Because the insurgents were concentrated in border regions that the Pakistani government—and the British raj before it—had never successfully controlled, it would have been difficult for the Pakistani authorities to rein in the insurgents even if they had wished to do so;[150] but they did not wish to do so. They retained the interests in Afghanistan that support for the Taliban served. They assumed that the United States would ultimately leave the country, at which point they would need a friendly government in place in Kabul, one sympathetic to them, unsympathetic to India (with which the Karzai's government seemed to Pakistanis entirely too friendly),[151] and with no intention of luring the Pashtuns living east of the Durand Line away from Pakistan. These were central, vital interests, not marginal ones. The Pakistani government was not about to abandon the pursuit of them in order to please the United States.[152]

The American government recognized, as the Taliban insurgency metastasized, that Pakistan's policy was working against American goals in Afghanistan. American officials privately complained to, and ultimately publicly denounced, their Pakistani counterparts. In September 2011, Admiral Mike Mullen, chairman of the Joint Chiefs of Staff, told a Senate hearing that the Taliban-affiliated Haqqani network was a "virtual arm" of Pakistani intelligence.[153] Yet American interests in the region, as Washington defined them, kept the United States from making a complete break: American economic and military assistance continued. Pakistan was a troublesome and duplicitous partner but also, in the judgment of the American government, ultimately an indispensable one.

As long as the United States maintained a sizable contingent of troops in Afghanistan they would have to be supplied, and access to them through Pakistan was necessary for this purpose. The United States had another, different concern that argued against a rupture. In 1998 Pakistan had detonated its first nuclear explosion, and in the ensuing 15 years had built up a stockpile estimated at well over 100

nuclear weapons. With an increasingly formidable Islamic fundamentalist campaign on its territory that was aimed at the Pakistani government itself, American officials worried that that government would one
day be overthrown and its nuclear weapons fall into the hands of terrorists like those who had attacked New York and Washington, DC.[154]
That contingency, however remote, persuaded the United States to
continue its cooperation with and support for Pakistan[155] even as that
country was sponsoring the insurgency American troops were fighting
across the Afghan border.

Despite American protests, therefore, Pakistan continued its patronage of the Taliban. The Taliban insurgency grew in strength and the
United States sent more troops to try to control it. The price in resources
and casualties of the war in Afghanistan, which the Bush administration and the American public had believed had ended in December
2001, increased after 2005 without clear prospects of concluding it on
terms favorable to the United States. That is where matters stood at
the beginning of 2009, when the second and final presidential term
of George W. Bush came to an end and a Democrat, former Illinois
Senator Barack Obama, succeeded him.

Afghanistan: The Long Goodbye

Barack Hussein Obama first came to national attention with a speech
at the 2004 Democratic National Convention in Boston.[156] The speech
emphasized the basic unity of the American people beneath their political differences, a striking and evidently welcome message in a time of
increasing political polarization between the two major parties and a
particularly powerful one coming from a person who, as the son of a
Muslim father (hence his middle name) from Kenya and a white
American mother with roots in Kansas, embodied the oldest, deepest,
and most painful national division of all. Obama was born and raised
in Hawaii. He received his undergraduate education in two different
geographic and educational settings: first at Occidental, a small college in Los Angeles, then at Columbia, a major research university in
New York City. He did a stint as a community organizer in Chicago,
attended law school at Harvard, then returned to Chicago and entered
politics.

With only limited political experience, which included less than four years in the United States Senate and seven in the Illinois State Senate before that, and with no major legislative accomplishments to his credit in either body, Obama was an unlikely presidential nominee in 2008. Despite his modest credentials (and partly because of them: the Democratic Party and the country as a whole, as so often in American history, were looking for a fresh face), he managed to wrest the nomination away from the heavily favored candidate, Senator Hillary Rodham Clinton of New York, the wife of the 42nd president.

Obama won the nomination by becoming the preferred alternative to Hillary Clinton for Democrats who did not want the Clintons returned to the White House: in the Democratic primary elections he did particularly well in the states of Maryland and Virginia, where those with first-hand experience with Senator Clinton and her husband were concentrated. He won, as well, because he captured the votes of the overwhelming majority of African-Americans, a large constituency within the Democratic Party. As ethnic groups in American politics have often done, they voted for him out of ethnic solidarity, but not that alone. The Clintons were popular among African-Americans and to win their allegiance Obama had to demonstrate that he was a viable contender for the nomination and the presidency, as previous African-American aspirants, notably the Reverend Jesse Jackson, had proven not to be.[157] This he accomplished by winning the first real test of the candidates' strength, the Iowa caucuses, in January 2008. He owed his victory there to foreign policy.

Iowa Democrats, particularly the most politically active who dominated the caucuses, vehemently opposed the American war in Iraq, which was about to enter its sixth expensive, frustrating, bloody year. Of all the Democratic candidates, Obama had the strongest antiwar credentials, which gave him a major advantage over the others.[158] He acquired this valuable political asset through, among other things, that persistent and elusive determinant of political success, fortunate timing. In late 2002 the United States Senate had to vote on the prospective attack on Iraq. The Democrats who were to become presidential candidates six years later—Mrs. Clinton and her fellow senators Joseph Biden of Delaware, Chris Dodd of Connecticut, and John Edwards of North Caroline—mindful of the smashing success of the previous war against Saddam Hussein in 1991 and under the influence of the bellicose mood in the country that September 11 had created, voted in favor of the war.

At that time Obama, then a little-known state senator from the south side of Chicago, was beginning a campaign for the Democratic nomination in the 2004 election for a seat in the United States Senate. To secure the nomination, he sought to forge a coalition of African-Americans and liberals from Chicago. Those liberals, in contrast to most of the rest of the country at the time, already had serious reservations about the coming invasion of Iraq. Obama had, therefore, a political interest in speaking out strongly against the invasion, and he did so. In the fall of 2002, in a speech at an antiwar demonstration in Chicago held in advance of the Congressional vote, he called the proposed military intervention "a dumb war. A rash war. A war based not on reason, but on passion, not on principle, but on politics. I know that an invasion of Iraq, without a clear rationale and without strong international support, will only fan the flames of the Middle East . . . "[159] Ultimately all the other Democratic candidates came to oppose the war; but Obama got there first and, six years after getting there, reaped the political rewards. On the basis of his stance on the war, as well as for other reasons, he won the Senate nomination and then the Senate seat in 2004,[160] which became a steppingstone to the Democratic presidential candidacy in 2008.

By that time not only the entire Democratic Party but a majority of the American public considered the Iraq war to have been a mistake.[161] While reiterating his opposition to it during both the primaries and the general election campaign against his Republican opponent Senator John McCain of Arizona—a consistent champion of that war—Obama made it clear that he did support the ongoing military effort in Afghanistan. If Iraq was a bad war, Afghanistan was a good one. "For years," he said on August 19, "I have called for more resources and more troops to finish the fight in Afghanistan."[162] For this, as had been the case with his position on Iraq in 2002, he had good political reasons. The war in Afghanistan continued to command support among Americans. It was costing less in lives and treasure than the Iraq war, and unlike in Iraq, America had gone to war in Afghanistan for the most compelling and legitimate of reasons—in response to an unprovoked attack on the United States.

Moreover, if he had proposed withdrawing American troops from Afghanistan as well as from Iraq, Obama would have run the risk of appearing to the American public to stand well outside the national mainstream in matters of foreign policy. He would have risked being labeled a pacifist and therefore unqualified to be the commander-in-chief of the world's sole surviving superpower. Even in his 2002 address opposing war in Iraq he had been careful to say that he was "not opposed to all wars" and to endorse the post-September 11 campaign against al Qaeda.[163]

His position on Afghanistan was designed not so much to win the 2008 election as to avoid losing it. He won the presidency because he was a Democrat and the country was tired of Republicans after eight turbulent years of Bush and Cheney, and because the worst financial crisis in 75 years occurred in the middle of the fall campaign and Obama seemed to voters to be better prepared than McCain to deal with its aftermath.

Obama's highest priority after his January 20, 2009, inauguration was coping with the deep recession that the financial crisis of the previous fall had triggered. Foreign policy had a distinctly secondary importance, but among the foreign policy issues he had to confront the most urgent was Afghanistan. There, Obama inherited a war that was going badly.[164] In 2008, the American commander in the country, General David McKiernan, had requested 30,000 additional troops. President Bush had deferred a decision, leaving it to his successor.[165]

Once in office, Obama reaffirmed the commitment to persevering and prevailing in Afghanistan that he had announced in his campaign.[166] Just two days after his inauguration he said that Afghanistan, along with Pakistan, was the "central front in our enduring struggle against terrorism and extremism."[167] Two months later he repeated that commitment and announced an increase in American civilian workers in the country—"agricultural specialists and educators, engineers and lawyers"—to promote better governance and economic growth.[168] Obama was embracing, or at least appeared to be embracing, full-scale nation-building in Afghanistan, something that Bush had never explicitly done. He also sent more soldiers. The American troop strength in the country stood at 38,000 when he became president. In his first months in office he almost doubled that number, to 68,000.[169] He acted, in part, to help ensure that the Afghan presidential election, scheduled for August 2009, was not disrupted. (The election did go forward and Karzai won a second term, but not without widespread and credible charges of fraud.)[170]

Even as he was authorizing an increase in the American military presence in the country, Obama ordered a review of American policy in Afghanistan.[171] The review took place in the wake of what appeared to be a successful American military and political "surge" in Iraq. Under the leadership of General David Petraeus, the commander of American forces there, the United States had sent more troops to the rebellious western part of the country, where the local affiliate of al Qaeda was flourishing. Practicing the Petraeus-inspired doctrine of counterinsurgency (COIN), the troops made common cause with local tribal militias, helped provide security to the people living in the region, drove out the terrorist interlopers, and brought a semblance of peace to what had been the most violent part of the country.[172]

Impressed by what COIN had accomplished, the committee charged with the Afghan review recommended that it be repeated in Afghanistan. They advocated a "fully resourced counterinsurgency strategy."[173] The recommendation was consistent with the importance that candidate Obama had placed on the country. President Obama accepted the recommendation. His acceptance suggested that if Iraq had been Bush's war, Afghanistan was going to be Obama's. Secretary of Defense Robert Gates, who had replaced Donald Rumsfeld in that position in 2007 and whom Obama had retained in office, decided that a new American commander was needed in Afghanistan to implement the new strategy. He replaced McKiernan with General Stanley McChrystal, who had overseen special operations in Iraq. McChrystal arrived in the country in June and immediately set about calculating how many troops he would need to carry out the new policy on which the president had decided.

McChrystal concluded that he would need a larger force to stabilize Afghanistan. He told his military superiors, Admiral Mullen and General Petraeus, who was by then the American commander for the Middle East as a whole, that with 80,000 troops he could conduct a robust, countrywide counterinsurgency campaign and with 40,000 he could concentrate on the Taliban strongholds.

A much lower total, in the 10,000 to 15,000 range, would confine the American military effort to training the Afghan army.[174] The three choices he proposed, it was noted at the time, fit the classic bureaucratic pattern of submitting to policymakers a preferred option sandwiched between two unacceptable ones,[175] a construction sometimes sardonically described as "Armageddon, capitulation, or my option."

Even the middle choice caused the political equivalent, in the White House, of what a consumer experiences when asked to pay far more than expected for a desired item: "sticker shock."[176] The administration's deliberations until then had concentrated on the question of what course in Afghanistan would be desirable. McChrystal's request forced it to think seriously about the cost of the president's answer to that question. As such it touched off a debate within the administration that continued for two months, from the beginning of October to the beginning of December 2009.

In that debate most senior officials, including Gates and Hillary Clinton, Obama's defeated rival for the Democratic presidential nomination whom he had appointed secretary of state, favored proceeding with a counterinsurgency strategy and dispatching a substantial contingent of troops to the country. As conceived by Petraeus, COIN had a large political component: success demanded a functioning government that commanded the active allegiance of the Afghan people, which in turn required that the government be relatively honest, provide services to the population, and preside over economic growth. This meant that its proponents favored, in effect, a full-fledged American mission of transformation in Afghanistan.

Vice President Joseph Biden (another of Obama's rivals in the contest for the Democratic presidential nomination in 2008), along with more junior White House officials, dissented. A long-time electoral politician who had seen presidencies wrecked by wars in Vietnam and Iraq, Biden believed that the American public would not support a full-scale counterinsurgency effort, which would take time, consume resources, and cost lives.[177] He and others of his persuasion were skeptical that even a sustained American effort could succeed in creating a decent, effective, honest, popular government in Kabul.[178]

Nor did they believe that such a government, even if it could be established at a price the American public was willing to pay, was necessary to secure the most important American interests there. Afghanistan did not have to travel down the road to Denmark to prevent terrorists from using it as a base from which to strike the United States. Indeed, al Qaeda, such as it still was, was largely absent from Afghanistan. The Taliban, who were very much present, had a strictly local agenda: they sought to control their country, not to wage a global jihad against the West. Rejecting COIN as too expensive at best and hopelessly utopian at worst, Biden and his allies favored a more narrowly focused counterterrorism strategy for Afghanistan,[179] one that could rely ultimately on drones and cruise missiles rather than nation-building. Counterterrorism was, as it happened, what the Bush administration had undertaken after ousting the Taliban.

When Obama announced his verdict on the internal debate in a speech at the United States Military Academy at West Point on December 1, 2009, what he had decided seemed to be a compromise between the two contending positions. On the one hand, he authorized an increase in the American military presence in the country of 30,000 troops, close to the number that the American commanders had hoped to get. On the other hand, however, he set a specific timetable for beginning to bring the troops home—July 2011, only 18 months later.

The new policy did represent a political compromise in the short term, giving each side something of what it wanted. It vindicated the commitment to doing more in Afghanistan that Obama had made during his presidential campaign while at the same time placing limits on the duration of the Afghan enterprise and the price Americans would pay for it. From a longer-term perspective, however, Obama had sided with Biden and against Gates and Clinton. He had reversed the course he had set upon entering office. He had decided against nation-building, with all that it implied. He made clear that the political and economic transformation of the country was not something he was willing to attempt.[180] "Some call for a more dramatic and open-ended escalation of our war effort," he said at West Point, "one that would commit us to a nation-building project of up to a decade. I reject this course because it sets goals that are beyond what can be achieved at a reasonable cost, and what we need to achieve to secure our interests."[181] Having initially embraced it, he now rejected for Afghanistan the kind of mission on which his predecessors had embarked—for the most part halfheartedly and never successfully—for China and Russia and in Somalia, Haiti, Bosnia, Kosovo, and most recently, expensively, and controversially in Iraq. With his December 1 speech Obama set a direction for the United States in Afghanistan, and that direction was out.[182]

A generation before the 44th president arrived at the White House two of his predecessors had had to make similar choices about another obscure but, as it seemed at the time, strategically important country. Obama liked to say that he was the first president since the war in Vietnam not to have had his view of the world shaped by that conflict, but during the initial year of his presidency he and his colleagues read some of the literature on that war,[183] which may have affected the policy he ultimately chose for Afghanistan. Whatever the case, in the course of that year he shifted from the approach of one Vietnam-era president to that of another.

Initially he followed in the footsteps of Lyndon Johnson, whose priorities as president, like Obama's, were domestic. Just as Obama threw his energies first into a "stimulus" program to counteract the ongoing recession and then into ambitious legislation to extend health care coverage to the uninsured, so Johnson's proudest achievement was the series of programs he passed that were designed to uplift the poor, programs that were known collectively as "The Great Society." Despite misgivings about doing so, Johnson expanded—"escalated"—the American role in Vietnam, ultimately deploying 450,000 troops there. As the war dragged on inconclusively and the number of American deaths rose, both the conflict and the man presiding over it became increasingly unpopular in the United States, so unpopular that Johnson decided not to run for re-election in 1968.

On December 1, however, Obama assumed the mantle, where Afghanistan was concerned, of Johnson's successor, Richard Nixon. Nixon entered office in 1969 with a mandate to end American involvement in Vietnam, or at least to end American casualties there. This he did, gradually and in ways that provoked strong dissent in the United States; but by 1972, when he won re-election, all American ground troops had left. Nixon had implemented a policy of "Vietnamization," gradually turning combat responsibilities over to the South Vietnamese army in the hope that, with American training and assistance, it could protect its own country from communist North Vietnam. Obama had a similar aspiration for Afghanistan, hoping that an American-trained (and American-paid) Afghan army could secure the country against the Taliban without the active assistance of American combat troops.

Obama's December 1 speech did not end the political jockeying within his administration over Afghanistan policy. As the July 2011 deadline for beginning to reverse the troop increase approached, the military leaders sought to limit the number of troops to be sent home.[184] They wanted, not unnaturally, to field the strongest force possible to fight the Taliban. They and critics of the Obama Afghanistan policy contended, reasonably enough, that by setting deadlines for the withdrawal of American forces the administration was giving the Taliban a powerful incentive simply to wait until the troops had left and then resume their insurgency against far weaker opposition.[185] General Petraeus recommended a cutback of no more than 3,000 to 4,000. Obama rejected this recommendation and announced in June 2011[186] that 10,000 would be coming home and that the additional 20,000 that he had authorized in 2009 would be withdrawn by September 2012. The downward trajectory of American troop strength in Afghanistan continued after 2012. The president designated 2014 as the year when American combat operations in the country would end.[187] In May of that year he said that 9,800 soldiers would remain in non-combat roles after that, but only briefly. Half that number would leave in 2015, with all but a token number gone by the end of 2016.[188] After that, the responsibility for controlling the insurgency would fall entirely on the Afghan army.[189] That army had not, by the time Obama announced the endgame for the United States in Afghanistan, become a cohesive, professional, reliable force.[190] Without American support it was not guaranteed to keep the Taliban from regaining control of the country; but a continuing American combat role, along with a vigorous state-building effort, which important figures in his administration favored, was not acceptable to the president.

After 13 years, hundreds of billions of dollars spent, and more than 2,000 American lives lost the United States had certainly improved, by Western standards, the lives of many Afghans; but it had not transformed Afghanistan.[191] It was leaving the country closer to Denmark than it had been before September 11, 2001, but not so much closer as to inspire confidence that Afghanistan would continue on that journey by itself.

Obama's rejection of counterinsurgency in Afghanistan, and the efforts at social, economic, and political transformation that it entailed and that his two predecessors had undertaken in Europe, Asia, Central America, and Africa marked the end of an era in American foreign policy. It was an era in which the missionary impulse for spreading American values and American institutions with which the United States began life as a sovereign state and that had been a part of its national life for more than two centuries came, for the first time, to dominate the nation's relations with the rest of the world. In the case of Afghanistan, Obama decided, against the advice of most of the senior foreign policy officials he had appointed, that that mission was, if not impossible, then certainly too expensive to be worth pursuing.

This conclusion did not sit well with all members of the foreign policy establishment, including some in his own party; but he encountered little opposition to his decision from the general public.[192] Americans had become leery of paying for nation-building in Afghanistan because what they had already invested for this purpose had not brought satisfactory results, because, in the midst of the deepest recession in eight decades they did not want to pay anything for projects beyond their borders—strongly preferring that public monies be spent at home—and above all because they had already spent far more, in blood and treasure, in yet another distant country than they had expected or wanted to pay. That country was Iraq.

4

Iraq

I will not wait on events while dangers gather. I will not stand by as peril draws closer and closer. The United States of America will not permit the world's most dangerous regimes to threaten us with the world's most dangerous weapons.

— GEORGE W. BUSH, State of the Union Address, January 29, 2002

Saddam Hussein must be understood less as the cause of Iraq's violent political culture—or even of Iraq's role as a source of regional instability—and more as the symptom, albeit an extremely consequential one, of deeper long-term dynamics within Iraq's political sociology.

— TOBY DODGE[1]

From War to War

The most important, most sustained, most expensive and most controversial post-Cold War American mission to transform the internal political structure of another country took place in Iraq between 2003 and 2011. Like the missions in Somalia, Haiti, the Balkans, and Afghanistan, in Iraq military intervention undertaken for other reasons turned into an effort to rearrange the country's politics and economics to make them more like America's. As in the other places, the American mission in Iraq failed.

The country where it failed had come into existence only after World War I when Great Britain, a victorious power in that conflict, assembled three provinces of the defeated and collapsed Ottoman Empire to create a single sovereign state. Even the British official most responsible for creating Iraq, Sir Arnold Wilson, doubted the viability of his own creation from the beginning, a doubt that the country's subsequent history showed to be well founded.[2] The three provinces differed significantly from one another: Basra, to the south, was populated principally by Arabs belonging to the minority, Shia, branch of Islam; the province centered on Baghdad, the city that became the country's capital, was dominated by adherents to the rival, majority branch of the faith, the Sunni.[3] To the north, Mosul province contained a large number of Kurds, Sunni Muslims but not Arabs who spoke their own Indo-European language rather than Arabic.[4] The British chose as king of the new country a member of a Sunni family from the Arabian peninsula that had sided with them against the Turks in World War I and Sunni Arabs, although a minority of Iraq's total population, ruled it for the next eight decades.

A series of violent coups eventually brought to power the Baath Party, a secular, Sunni-dominated organization that aspired to the kind of total political control exercised by the ruling Communist Parties of Europe and Asia. A Sunni from the city of Tikrit, Saddam Hussein, an admirer of the bloodthirsty Soviet dictator Joseph Stalin, acquired supreme power in the Baath Party and dominated Iraq from the end of the 1970s until 2003. He ruled in a particularly brutal manner, fortified by the revenues generated by the sale of the country's oil.

In other parts of the world in the nineteenth and twentieth centuries, a strong state apparatus succeeded in forging a nation: a sense of community and common destiny grew among the people living within what were often arbitrarily designated borders. This is how the nation-states of Europe developed.[5] It did not happen in Iraq, where Sunnis, Shias, and Kurds never forged a shared sense of nationhood. After the unification of Italy in the 1860s, an aristocrat from the north of the country remarked, "We have made Italy. We must now make Italians." The British made Iraq, but neither they, nor Saddam, nor those who ruled in the years between them, succeeded in making Iraqis.[6] The failure to establish a sense of national identity in the three Ottoman provinces the British welded together had a greater impact on the outcome of the American mission in Iraq than anything the United States did or did not do during the more than eight years of its intense engagement with that country.

Oil wealth enabled Saddam to build an army and to use it to attack two neighboring countries. In his war with Iran, which had fallen under the control of Shia Islamic radicals in 1979, a war that lasted from 1980 to 1988 and ended in a stalemate, the United States remained officially neutral and supported an arms embargo on both countries while providing modest assistance to Saddam's regime.[7] Two years later Saddam's army invaded and occupied tiny Kuwait. This time the United States opposed Iraq because the occupation posed a threat to Saudi Arabia, the Middle East's largest producer and exporter of the oil on which the Western world depended and, for that reason, an American client.[8] The administration of George H. W. Bush was able to assemble an extraordinarily broad international coalition to eject the Iraqi army because the attack on Kuwait represented a clear and egregious violation of international law and because, with the ending of the Cold War, the Soviet Union, which had opposed whatever the United States wanted to do in the Middle East during Cold War, instead, under the reformist leader Mikhail Gorbachev, actually joined the coalition.

Led by the United States, a multinational force swept the Iraqi army out of Kuwait. The first Bush administration declined to pursue the fight into Iraq and depose Saddam because the UN resolutions under which the coalition had been formed did not authorize a change of regime in Baghdad and because the senior officials of the administration were leery of occupying an Arab country. The administration did establish "no-fly" zones in the north, to protect the Kurds,[9] and in the south, to shelter the Shia, both of whom had risen against the Sunni-dominated Baath regime and had been savagely repressed.

The United Nations, under whose auspices the coalition had officially fought, passed a series of resolutions requiring Iraq to disarm and providing for UN-sponsored inspections to ensure compliance. The American forces that remained in the region had the additional purpose of containing the Iraqi army within the country's borders. As part of the policy of containment the Clinton administration maintained an economic embargo on Iraq. It also took military action against Saddam's regime in 1998. From December 16 to December 19, in retaliation for the Iraqi government's refusal to comply with several UN resolutions as well as its interference with UN inspectors, the United States conducted Operation Desert Fox, a bombing campaign against military targets. Also in 1998, at the end of October, Clinton signed the Republican-inspired Iraq Liberation Act. It provided support to groups seeking to oust Saddam from power. It did not, however, commit the United States to go to war to do this and the Democratic president clearly had no intention of doing so.

The administration of George W. Bush entered office regarding the removal of Saddam Hussein from power as a piece of unfinished business—a number of foreign policy officials had served in George H. W. Bush's government—but not necessarily as one of the highest priorities of American foreign policy. The attacks of September 11 changed their view of the world and led directly to the second American war against Iraq. In the wake of the attacks, ending Saddam Hussein's rule seemed not only desirable but a matter of some urgency. On September 12 the president took aside Richard Clarke, the National Security Council's counterterrorism expert, and asked him to check to see whether Saddam had been involved in any way with what had taken place the day before.[10] At a meeting of senior foreign policy officials at the presidential retreat at Camp David, Maryland on September 16, Paul Wolfowitz, the deputy secretary of defense, argued in favor of striking Iraq. Bush rejected the idea of doing so immediately, choosing to concentrate first on Afghanistan; but 10 days later he instructed his secretary of defense, Donald Rumsfeld, to begin working on a plan for invading Iraq.[11]

The Department of Defense had a contingency plan that had been drafted under a previous American commander for the Middle East, which called for an invasion force similar in size to the one that had liberated Kuwait: on that occasion more than 500,000 troops had been sent to the theater of war. Rumsfeld was determined to use a far smaller contingent. Over the months leading up to the American attack he and the uniformed officers engaged in a protracted bureaucratic tug-of-war over how large an army was needed.[12] Ultimately the United States mustered 150,000 troops for the invasion,[13] more than Rumsfeld had initially wanted but considerably fewer than 12 years earlier.

Meanwhile, the president began making the case for war. He referred, in his 2002 State of the Union speech, to North Korea, Iran, and Iraq as forming an "axis of evil" and asserted that Saddam presented a "grave and growing danger."[14] There followed a drumbeat of warnings about Iraq, which escalated in the summer of 2002, from the president and other administration officials, particularly the vice president, Richard B. (Dick) Cheney.

Cheney earned a reputation, during the course of the Bush presidency, as perhaps the most influential vice president in all of American history. He came to the office with deep experience at the highest levels of the federal government, having served as chief of staff to President Gerald R. Ford, deputy leader of the Republicans in the House of Representatives during the Reagan administration, and secretary of defense in the cabinet of George H. W. Bush. He had opposed sending the American army to Baghdad in 1991 to overthrow Saddam but changed his mind after September 11 and became a strong proponent of ousting the Iraqi dictator.[15] He also became the administration's leading champion of anti-terrorism policies that, in the eyes of many (including some in the administration itself) wrongly encroached on civil liberties.

Cheney was the rare vice president who did not aspire to win the presidency himself, which enhanced his power since no one suspected him of putting his own political interests above those of the president. Cheney's lack of interest in a higher office than the one he held also freed him from the need, common to most office-seekers in a democracy, to project an emollient, conciliatory, cheerful personality to the country and the world. For that reason, and because his stance on the war in Iraq and the war on terror grew increasingly controversial, Cheney became unpopular with the American public, a status that he gave no outward sign of finding troubling. Especially in the administration's first term, the vice president was sometimes portrayed as manipulating the callow, younger president it was his role to serve. The charge was more an indictment of Bush than of Cheney, and it happened not to be true. Bush followed Cheney's advice, when he followed it, because he agreed with it. When he did not agree with Cheney's policy preferences, as was more frequently the case during his second term, he did not adopt them.[16]

In March 2002, Cheney made a 10-day, 12-country trip around the Middle East to enlist support for an American war against Iraq. He gave a speech to the annual convention of the Veterans of Foreign Wars in Nashville on August 26, making the strongest case yet that Saddam Hussein posed a serious threat to the United States.[17] Bush followed with an address to the nation on October 7, warning of the danger Saddam represented and making it clear that he was prepared to go to war to remove him.[18]

In seeking to persuade the American public of the merits of war against Iraq, Bush and Cheney were pushing on an open door. From the end of the first Gulf War public support for invading Iraq had remained consistently high. Immediately after the attacks of September 11, 2001, polls showed that supporters of such a course made up fully three-quarters of the American people.[19] The administration's efforts at persuasion did little to increase that support as measured by the polls, but they did not have to: Americans were already persuaded. Accordingly, when Bush asked the Congress to authorize him to take the country to war he received strong majorities in both houses. On October 10, 2002, the House of Representatives voted 296 to 133 in his favor. The next day the Senate approved the authorization by 77 to 23.

Bush received more Congressional support from Democrats than his father had for the 1991 war. On the earlier occasion the Vietnam War, which had gone badly for the United States, had ended barely a decade and a half previously and lawmakers were wary of involving the United States in what they feared would be a similar conflict in the Middle East. That concern turned out to be groundless: American troops won a relatively quick, cheap, easy victory. The memory of that victory influenced Congressional attitudes in 2002. Many members believed that the war for which they were voting would replicate the experience of 1991. That belief, too, proved to be incorrect. The second Iraq war had, in the end, more in common with the Vietnam War than with the first one.

Like his father before him, George W. Bush attempted to rally international support for his war against Saddam Hussein, but with considerably less success. The second Bush administration assumed that it could exercise the kind of leadership, at least with America's European allies, that had been the norm during the Cold War: during that era, once the United States decided on a course of action other countries generally fell in line.[20] This did not happen in 2003. With the Cold War a decade in the past, the allies were not inclined to join, or in some cases even endorse, the American war effort.

Turkey, a member of NATO that had played an important role in the 1991 war, refused the use of its territory as a staging area for an assault on neighboring Iraq.[21] American military planners had hoped to attack from the north, through Turkey, as well as from Kuwait in the south, but in the end launched the operation only from Kuwait.[22] As for the countries of Europe, America's oldest and closest allies, with whom the United States shared not only a history of cooperation but common values as well and who were the leading candidates to bear some of the burdens of combat and of whatever postwar costs had to be paid, they proved to be divided.

Two of the most important Western European countries, Germany and France, opposed going to war. A number of their leaders believed— correctly as it turned out—that the campaign would not proceed as quickly or as easily as the Bush administration assumed.[23] Their publics, as well as those of other European countries that did ultimately provide at least rhetorical support for America's Iraq policy, were far less favorably disposed than were Americans to the idea of evicting Saddam from power by military force.[24] Unlike the Americans, the Europeans had not been primed to attack a Middle Eastern tyranny by the trauma of September 11. Over the postwar decades, moreover, Europeans had developed a far more pronounced aversion to going to war under any circumstances than was to be found in the United States. Furthermore, many Europeans regarded the Bush administration with suspicion because of its governing philosophy, a brand of political conservatism that had little appeal on the other side of the Atlantic Ocean.[25]

The prospective American war in Iraq was sufficiently unpopular among Germans that the chancellor, the Social Democrat Gerhard Schroeder, made significant political gains by opposing it, and this in a country that had been a particularly faithful American ally during the Cold War because it depended so heavily on American military protection. French President Jacques Chirac's opposition had deeper roots in his country's history. It continued the 50-year tradition known as Gaullism, begun by the first president of the Fifth Republic, Charles de Gaulle, which involved staking out positions on foreign policy distinct from, and sometimes contrary to, those of the United States.[26]

As the transatlantic dispute over Iraq policy unfolded in the early months of 2003, neither side chose to dwell on a pertinent fact: European support, although hardly worthless, had limited value for the United States because the Europeans had very little military force to contribute to the war. The charge of "unilateralism" that some Europeans (and some Americans as well) flung at the Bush administration had only modest relevance because a more "multilateral" effort would not have substantially increased the combat power that could be brought to bear against Saddam Hussein's army. Had the French and Germans been in a position to provide a large number of troops, the American government would have taken their objections more seriously; but they weren't and it didn't.

The dispute over the wisdom of going to war became acrimonious and at the time seemed to mark a decisive rupture in the alliance that had held together during, and emerged victorious from, the Cold War. The breach proved, contrary to such expectations, to be shallow and temporary. American anger at Europe subsided as it became clear that the Europeans had been right about the difficulties of occupying Iraq. European anger at the United States abated as the governments there realized that an America distracted and weakened by Iraq did not serve their interests.

The George W. Bush administration also sought authorization for war from the United Nations Security Council, something that the George H. W. Bush administration had received for the first Gulf War. The decision to seek it occasioned controversy at the administration's senior level. Vice President Cheney believed previous UN resolutions concerning Iraq gave the United States all the authority it needed. The president decided, however, to follow the advice of his secretary of state, Colin Powell, and go to the UN; and on November 8, 2002, another Iraq resolution won approval, one that strongly criticized Saddam Hussein for his failure to comply fully with the resolutions already on record. The new resolution did not explicitly authorize the enforcement of the previous ones by war, however, and the administration returned to the Security Council in February in search of a mandate to that effect.

To sway the members of the Council, and global public opinion as a whole, Powell made a dramatic presentation at the UN on February 5, 2003. Relying on evidence supplied by the CIA, he set out a case that the Iraqi government had, contrary to what the UN had decreed in

1991 and reaffirmed periodically thereafter, retained a stockpile of weapons of mass destruction. The case turned out to be false: a thorough postwar search of Iraq revealed that Saddam's regime had had no such weapons. Powell's UN presentation became the low point in what was in most other respects an extraordinarily successful career.

Most of that career was spent in the military. Colin Powell rose to its highest position, serving as chairman of the Joint Chiefs of Staff at the time of the first Gulf War and becoming the most popular American military figure since Dwight D. Eisenhower.[27] The high esteem in which the American public held him made the endorsement he gave to George W. Bush's presidential campaign in 2000 a particularly valuable one.[28]

Like Eisenhower, Powell owed his popularity originally to his leading role in a victorious war, the first Gulf War being for Powell what the allied victory in Europe in World War II was for Eisenhower. Powell had, however, been skeptical about going to war in 1991 and harbored even stronger reservations 12 years later. Those reservations came from personal experience. While all the senior foreign policy officials of the George W. Bush administration had served in the Department of Defense—Cheney and Rumsfeld as secretary, National Security Advisor Condoleezza Rice at a lower level—only Powell had seen action in a war. His war was the one in Vietnam and the costly national failure there set him against putting American troops in harm's way without clear objectives and a plausible strategy for withdrawal, conditions that came to be known as the "Powell Doctrine."[29] He doubted that the prospective war against Iraq fulfilled either requirement. Although skeptical, however, Powell did not become a full-fledged dissident. While his doubts became well known, he never explicitly opposed going to war. His efforts to persuade the Security Council to support an American attack on Iraq failed. The French government made it plain that it would veto a measure approving war, and the Bush administration abandoned its effort to secure a second resolution.

Despite this failure, the United States did not lack support from other countries when the war began in March 2003. Middle Eastern countries provided assistance of various kinds: the overall commander, Army General Tommy Franks, was based in Qatar; the air war was directed from a facility in Saudi Arabia and the maritime campaign from Dubai; the base for ground operations was Kuwait. A total of 49 countries, most of them in Europe, announced support for the American effort. Of these by far the most important was Great Britain, which contributed 45,000 troops, many more than any other ally. Close cooperation with the United States, sometimes called the "special relationship," had been a central feature of British foreign policy since Prime Minster Winston Churchill and President Franklin D. Roosevelt had forged a partnership during World War II. Even more relevant for the British role was the fact that Prime Minister Tony Blair, who had thrown his political weight behind the American interventions in the Balkans, particularly in Kosovo, during the 1990s, shared the Bush administration's conviction that Saddam Hussein posed a serious threat to global well-being.[30] With strong British support, therefore, and with the approval of several dozen other countries although not the official endorsement of the United Nations, the United States went to war with Iraq.

The origins of that war raise two questions. The first, and lesser of them, is how the United States decided to go to war. There was apparently no single point between the beginning of the Bush administration and the beginning of the fighting at which the decision for war was made.[31] According to the vice president, the president "decided to go in" shortly after September 11;[32] but if so he did not communicate his decision to anyone else. A memorandum from the chief of British intelligence to Tony Blair on July 23, 2002, reported that in Washington "military action [against Iraq] was now seen as inevitable,"[33] but no public announcement to that effect was made. In mid-August a top-secret document, prepared for the president's signature, laid out the goals for which the United States would wage war,[34] but it was apparently not widely circulated even within the government. In the summer of 2002 Richard Haass, a top aide to Powell, met with National Security Advisor Rice to express his own reservations about a war with Iraq. She informed him that it was too late for such representations: the decision for war had already been made.[35]

Just how and when Bush made what turned out to be the fateful decision for war remains unclear; what is clear is that he did not make it in the way that is normal (or at least desirable) in democracies: at no point did a meeting of the president and his senior officials take place to explore and debate the arguments for and against attacking Iraq.[36] As Haass put it, "it's not a decision that was made so much as it 'happened.' "[37]

The larger question is why the United States went to war against Iraq at all. It was not responding to a direct attack on America, as it had on entering World War II in 1941 and in removing the Taliban regime from power in Afghanistan in 2001. Nor was it responding to an attack on a third party, as was the case in Korea in 1950 and in the previous Gulf War in 1991. It did not intervene to rescue people under assault from their government, as it did in Kosovo in 1998 and as it had in establishing the no-fly zones over Iraq in 1991.

In a very limited sense the United States was already at war with Iraq when the Bush administration took office. The United States Air Force was flying combat air patrols over the northern and southern parts of the country to enforce the no-fly zones and Iraqi forces occasionally shot at them. The American military launched two bombing salvos against Iraqi targets in the dozen years between the two wars with Iraq: Operation Desert Fox in 1998 and a raid on February 16, 2001, provoked by what American commanders considered an escalated threat to American patrols.[38] Over the course of the 12 years of enforcement, however, the United States did not lose a single aircraft. Its military relationship with Iraq during that period was one of deterrence, and deterrence was working well: Saddam's military, it became clear after he had been unseated, had been severely weakened during the 1990s and this, combined with the continuing American military presence in the region, meant that Iraq posed no immediate threat to its neighbors.

Like the humanitarian interventions of the 1990s, the 2003 Iraq war was, in the first instance, the product of the conditions of the post-Cold War world: the enormous superiority in military power over any other country that the United States enjoyed and the absence of a powerful rival to contest whatever military operations it chose to undertake. America had unparalleled freedom of action and used that freedom to attack Iraq. Like the Clinton administration's interventions of the previous decade, moreover, the Bush administration expected the war in Iraq to promote American values, if only by removing a regime that routinely violated them. The protection of human rights and the construction of democracy did not, however, drive the Bush administration's decision to go to war against Saddam Hussein. Indeed, it was not Saddam, but rather Osama bin Laden, who bore the primary responsibility for triggering the American attack. The United States went to war in the Middle East in 2003, first and foremost, because of the terrorist attacks on New York and Washington of September 11.

Administration officials hinted that Saddam was directly linked to the attacks. They suggested that he had been in contact with the hijackers and more generally had cooperated with al Qaeda.[39] Moreover, they were certain that he possessed weapons of mass destruction.[40] Since he had already used such weapons to attack Iraq's Kurdish population in 1988, the events of September 11, along with his presumed connection to them, suggested that he would be prepared to use them, either directly or through terrorist proxies, against American targets as well. The plausibility of such a scenario in the wake of the attacks on New York and Washington contributed to the high level of popular support in the United States for war with Iraq.[41]

The assertions about Saddam turned out to be untrue. No connection between him and the plotters and perpetrators of the September 11 attacks was ever confirmed.[42] Nor were any weapons of mass destruction found in Iraq once the United States had occupied the country and was thus in a position to conduct an unobstructed search for them.[43] The absence of such weapons, the presumed presence of which the administration had frequently invoked as a major reason for war, became the focal point of much of the discontent that American policy in Iraq aroused, especially as that policy became unexpectedly costly. Their absence called into question the administration's good faith and basic honesty. As American casualties mounted, "Bush lied, people died" became an antiwar slogan.

In fact, he did not lie. The assertion by senior officials that Saddam harbored weapons that a series of UN resolutions had prohibited his regime from having was not a deliberate falsehood: it was an honest mistake. The president and his colleagues genuinely believed that Iraq had retained and hidden the forbidden armaments. The governments and intelligence services of other countries, even some that opposed the American war, also believed this.[44] They believed it because Saddam had had such weapons before the 1991 war, because his government went out of its way to obstruct the UN-sponsored inspections designed to ensure that he no longer had them, and because once he evicted the inspectors in 1998, the world had no good way of verifying their absence.[45]

Since the mistaken conviction that he was hiding a stockpile of prohibited armaments helped to trigger the war that deposed him, Saddam might be thought to have had a strong interest in doing all he could to persuade the world, and especially the American government, that he was concealing nothing. He did not do so because he had higher priorities, which required perpetuating the impression that he retained the weapons. He considered that impression necessary to keep in check Iraq's restive Shia population, which had risen against him in 1991, as well as to deter the Islamic Republic of Iran, against which his regime had waged a long, bloody, grinding war in the 1980s. He evidently regarded an American attack to remove him from power as a more remote contingency, and thus not one worth revealing the truth about his military resources to forestall.[46]

The heated controversy surrounding the missing weapons was, in a sense, beside the point. What the Iraqi regime was erroneously believed to possess were chemical weapons, which get lumped together with nuclear (as well as biological) weapons under the rubric "weapons of mass destruction" but are in fact far less destructive. Like nuclear weapons they are unconventional armaments, seldom used and generally regarded as outside the boundaries of acceptable conduct, even in war;[47] but while chemical weapons are certainly lethal, unlike nuclear explosives they cannot readily cause massive destruction and have never in fact caused destruction on anything like the scale that the use of nuclear weapons did in August 1945 and would surely do in the future. Many countries, some of them hostile to the United States and the West, have chemical weapons or could easily obtain them but have not, simply for that reason, been proposed as the objects of an American attack.

The Bush administration emphasized Iraq's presumed stockpile of chemical munitions as a major justification for war partly as a matter of political convenience. The charge that it had such weapons evoked a strong reaction in the American public, it tied into a series of UN resolutions, and it was a cause of war on which different parts of the

American government could agree.[48] It was not, however, the only cause of war or even, for the people managing American foreign policy, the most important one.

The events of September 11 did set the Bush administration on the path to war with Iraq but not only, or even mainly, because of the erroneous imputation of a direct connection between Saddam Hussein and the attacks on New York and Washington. The Iraqi leader and the terrorist assaults were, in the minds of the president and his senior officials, connected *indirectly*, in ways that made the removal of Saddam from power seem urgently necessary.

They considered the September 11 attacks such a serious affront and challenge to the United States that a major response was in order. Simply overturning the government of poor, backward, isolated Afghanistan would not, in their view, suffice.[49] A bigger operation was needed. The United States, they believed, faced a large global threat from Islamist terrorism, a threat that would become all the more deadly if and as terrorists acquired weapons of mass destruction.[50] To neutralize that threat required making clear to all potential perpetrators and sponsors of attacks on the United States like those of September 11 that any such assault would incur severe punishment.[51] Uprooting the Baathist regime in Baghdad served that purpose in a way that ousting the Taliban did not. The administration envisaged the war on terror as a global conflict that had to be waged on a global scale, not only in Afghanistan and not only by taking steps to protect the continental United States.

Moreover, even though Saddam turned out neither to have aided al Qaeda nor to have kept a store of forbidden armaments, he was surely the kind of leader who *would* do such things if the opportunity arose and if doing them served his interests. In the wake of the September 11 attacks, and because of the September 11 attacks, not only what Saddam had done but also what he might do seemed to the Bush administration a pressing consideration.

While aware of the threat of terrorism and the aspirations of al Qaeda before September 11, the administration had underestimated their urgency. As a result, the United States had suffered serious damage and a traumatic national shock. Thereafter, the president and his senior colleagues not unnaturally reviewed the portfolio of outstanding potential dangers to the United States: which ones, they could not help asking themselves, were they now underrating? Which ones might catch them unaware, as al Qaeda had done?[52] Everything they knew about Saddam Hussein made him a plausible answer to those questions.[53]

The September 11 attacks increased the already robust disposition of the American public to support a war to remove him from power. It was all too easy to imagine what might happen if he remained in control of Iraq. The economic sanctions that had weakened the regime might well collapse: the French and Russian governments had already called for lifting them.[54] Free of the internationally imposed economic and political constraints that had weakened his regime, Saddam would be likely to pursue nuclear weapons.[55] After the 1991 war Iraq had been discovered to be much closer to acquiring them than Western intelligence agencies had previously estimated. A nuclear-armed Iraq would pose a grave threat to Iraq's oil-rich neighbors and, through terrorist proxies, to the United States.

None of this was, of course, certain to happen if Saddam remained in power, but it might happen: it could happen. After September 11 the Bush administration decided that the United States could not afford to risk letting it happen. One important reason for war was to prevent it from happening; in this sense the United States waged a preventive war against Iraq in 2003. A preventive war differs from a preemptive attack, which involves striking when the enemy is itself on the verge of attacking and war is inevitable. A preventive war, by contrast, is launched before an attack is imminent in order to forestall a danger that is anticipated to develop at some point in the future.[56] In his speech to the nation just two days before the attack on Iraq began Bush said, "We are now acting because the risks of inaction would be far greater. In one year, or five years, the power of Iraq to inflict harm on all free nations would be multiplied many times over."[57]

If the administration placed less public emphasis on the requirements of prevention than on the presence of weapons of mass destruction, this was no doubt at least partly because preventive war is difficult to defend.[58] It violates the common-sense idea that people (and presumably therefore countries as well) should be punished for what they have done, not for what someone else believes they might someday do. It also violates international law, in which war is ordinarily permitted only for self-defense or in response to cross-border aggression.

Preventive war carries what turned out to be another political disadvantage for the Bush administration: a self-canceling quality. When
successful, it removes the threat that, if it were to persist and grow,
would clearly justify military action.[59] When the operation in Iraq
went badly, the administration could not defend it by comparing the
costs the American public had to pay for it with the costs that it would
have had to pay if Saddam had remained in power. Just how high the
costs of what Bush decided to prevent from happening would have
been could never be known.

Yet another reason for the second American war against Iraq stemmed
from the attacks of September 11. Although based in Afghanistan, al
Qaeda had its roots in the Arab world. It emerged from what the Bush
officials, and not they alone, came to see as a toxic political culture.
Oppressive, unrepresentative governments presiding over failing economies created the conditions, the Americans concluded, in which young
Arab men, such as the hijackers of September 11, turned to terrorism.
The elimination of terrorism required changing these conditions. Iraq
seemed a good place to start. The uprooting of the Baath regime and
its replacement with a more open, tolerant, decent form of government
would serve as a powerful example for all Arabs of a different, and better, way of organizing and wielding political power.[*]

George W. Bush and his colleagues were not wrong to believe that
invading Iraq, unseating its government, and fostering a radically
different form of rule in the three former Ottoman provinces would

---

[*] Thomas E. Ricks, *Fiasco: The American Military Adventure in Iraq*, New York:
Penguin Press, 2006, p. 11. This was a major reason for war among those who
came to be known as neoconservatives, who were later accused in some quarters of exercising undue influence to push the United States into the war. The
neoconservatives certainly supported the war on this basis: a belief in the use of
American power to promote American values was one of their defining principles.
They were not, however, responsible for the decision to invade Iraq. None of the
senior foreign policy officials numbered him- or herself among their ranks, and
at least one of them, Secretary of Defense Rumsfeld, did not consider democracy-
promotion a major war aim. Douglas J. Feith, *War and Decision: Inside the
Pentagon at the Dawn of the War on Terrorism*, New York: Harper, 2008, pp.
286, 319, 392, 541. Nor were neoconservatives the only proponents of war for
this reason. "Believers on both the right and left were proposing one of the most
audacious turns in the history of American foreign policy: to establish, by force

serve America's interests. Their fatal mistake was to assume what virtually everyone else with any knowledge of the country, the region, or the kind of project the United States was undertaking believed to be false: that doing this would be easy.

The administration's plan for post-combat Iraq was not to have a plan. American military terminology calls the stage of a war after the fighting has ended "Phase IV." The military had no comprehensive plan for Phase IV.[60] The commanders expected to bring all but 30,000 of the troops home within a few months of the war's end. Nor did the civilians in overall charge of the operation have such a plan. Instead, they made a series of assumptions about what would happen in the country after Saddam Hussein was gone, assumptions so optimistic that in retrospect they seemed to border on fantasy.[61]

The Iraqis would, the senior Bush officials assumed, welcome American troops with enthusiasm.[62] The country's institutions—its armed forces and its bureaucracy—would remain intact and function according to American direction.[63] Economic assistance from abroad, normal for the reconstruction of war-damaged countries, would not be needed: Iraq's oil revenues would pay for whatever reconstruction it required.[64] Iraq would move to adopt Western political and economic institutions and practices. The whole operation would resemble the Allied liberation of France in World War II or the indigenous revolutions in communist Eastern Europe in 1989.[65] Like the Nazi occupation in the first case and Moscow-imposed communist rule in the second, only Saddam stood in the way of a bright future in Iraq, and the United States would remove Saddam. Making possible such a future was not the principal reason for war but it was, as senior officials saw it, sure to be one of its consequences. The campaign was therefore given the name "Operation Iraqi Freedom."

Events did not bear out any of these assumptions; and what is genuinely puzzling about the American experience in Iraq is that the otherwise sober and highly experienced officials at the top of the American government held them in the first place. It is puzzling because the

of arms, 'a beachhead of Arab democracy in the Middle East,' as Paul Berman called it." George Packer, *The Assassins' Gate: America in Iraq*, New York: Farrar, Straus and Giroux, 2005, p. 58.

origins of the Bush Iraq policy lie in a strange combination of extreme pessimism about what would happen if the United States did not invade Iraq and extreme optimism about what would happen if it did. It is puzzling as well because the optimism flew in the face of many cautionary warnings from both within and outside the government.

Position papers, reports, studies, and expert testimony from government agencies, think tanks, journalists, and specialists in both the Middle East and post-conflict governance conveyed the message that controlling Iraq after the end of Baathist rule, let alone turning it into an oasis of tolerance, good government, and prosperity in a region lacking, with the conspicuous exception of the state of Israel, all of these would be, at best, extremely difficult. It would take considerable time and money—if it could be done at all.[66] In discussing with the president the prospect of war, Secretary Powell invoked a rule the retail chain of home furnishing stores Pottery Barn was said to have applied to its customers: if you break it, you own it.[67] The prospect of owning Iraq apparently did not faze President George W. Bush.

The recent experience with Afghanistan undoubtedly had something to do with this complacency. At the time of the invasion of Iraq, Afghanistan looked very much like an American success story. After September 11 a brief, relatively inexpensive attack had removed the Taliban and an international conference had chosen what seemed to be a capable successor, refugees had returned, economic activity had picked up, and the country was generally peaceful. It was easy to assume that events in Iraq would follow a similar course.

Ignorance of Iraq surely also had something to do with what came to seem, in retrospect, the administration's insouciance about invading and occupying the country. None of its senior officials was a specialist in the politics and culture of the Middle East, or had ever lived there, or, with the exception of the first Iraq war, had had extensive experience with the region.

Indeed, ignorance about the Iraq of 2003 extended well beyond the upper echelons of the American government. The country had been more or less cut off in the 12 years after the 1991 war. During that time the population had become poorer, more religious, and more polarized along sectarian and ethnic lines and the government had, in some ways and in some places, effectively ceased to function. While

Saddam remained in power in Baghdad, however, the world outside Iraq was largely unaware of these changes.

In addition, as people are wont to do in response to information that contradicts strongly held beliefs or powerful wishes, members of the administration simply denied the validity of the warnings they received. Asked at a Congressional hearing how many troops would be needed in Iraq, the Army's chief of staff, General Eric Shinseki, gave an estimate of "several hundred thousand." Deputy Secretary of Defense Paul Wolfowitz retorted that such an estimate was "wildly off the mark,"[68] although it was based on widely used formulas for the desirable ratio of peacekeepers to total population after wars have ended.[69] It was "hard to imagine," he said, "that it would take more forces to provide stability in post-Saddam Iraq than it would take to conduct the war itself and secure the surrender of Saddam's security forces and his army,"[70] although the idea required no imagination, merely a familiarity with the aftermath of wars in other countries.

Perhaps most importantly in explaining the administration's fatally optimistic and casual approach to Iraq, behind the conviction that it would blossom without Saddam lay the missionary spirit that had animated the initial policies of the Clinton administration toward China and Russia, the humanitarian interventions of the 1990s, and the nation-building in Afghanistan. The Bush administration believed what Americans had believed since before the founding of the republic. While they had no direct experience with the people of Iraq, the president and most of his senior colleagues were confident that what those people wanted for themselves was what all people wanted, which was more or less what Americans wanted. Once American power removed the malevolent obstacle to fulfilling their aspirations, they would proceed, unaided, to fulfill them. In Iraq, however, as in China, Russia, Somalia, Bosnia, Kosovo, and Afghanistan, things did not work out as the American government expected.

From Success to Failure

The American war against Iraq began two days earlier than planned.[71] On March 17, President Bush gave Saddam Hussein an ultimatum to leave the country in 48 hours, with the expectation that he would not do so and that the attack would begin two days later, on March 21. Before the deadline, however, the United States received information about Saddam's whereabouts, in a part of greater Baghdad. Hoping that decapitating the regime would shorten the war, or even avoid it— an example of the extent to which the Bush administration presumed that Iraq's political pathologies were the work of one man and would disappear when he did—the president approved bombing the suspected hideout on March 19. Saddam, however, was not there.[72]

Starting in Kuwait and accompanied by air strikes on Iraqi military targets, American ground forces from the Army and the Marine Corps, with a contingent from the British Army and troops from Poland and Australia as well, pushed northward toward Baghdad, their ultimate destination. The campaign proceeded rapidly and with relatively few casualties,[73] and at the beginning of April, American troops reached the outskirts of the Iraqi capital. The American commanders had planned to besiege the city and gradually wear down its defenses.[74] Several probes by mobile American units into its center, however, met relatively light resistance, which the Americans overcame. The commanders decided that American troops should enter Baghdad in force. By April 10 it was clear that the capital had fallen. Saddam Hussein and his sons fled and the Baath regime collapsed. The war, at least the war that the administration had planned to fight, was over.

The campaign brought some pleasant surprises for the American side. Although the outcome of a war between the United States and Iraq was never in doubt—American military power dwarfed that of its adversary—as in Afghanistan the victory came more swiftly and cheaply than it might have.[75] American commanders had fully expected to encounter chemical weapon attacks and had made elaborate preparations to cope with them,[76] a clear indication that the Bush administration truly believed that Saddam possessed such weapons. Because he did not, their preparations proved unnecessary, which was another unexpected and welcome aspect of the campaign.

Nor did the American forces have to engage in what planners feared would be protracted and bloody street-to-street, house-to-house combat in Baghdad and other cities.[77] Nor, finally, did the Iraqi forces expected to mount the stiffest fight, Saddam's own militia known as the Revolutionary

Guards, play a major role in the conflict. All in all, the worst case scenarios the American commanders anticipated did not come to pass.[78]

That is not to say, however, that the 2003 war with Iraq lacked unpleasant surprises. Military planners had expected, or at least hoped, that units of the Iraqi army would surrender en masse. This did not happen. Instead, the soldiers put down their arms, took off their uniforms, and joined the civilian population.[79] The most important unanticipated and unwelcome development turned out to be an omen for the eight-year American military presence in the country. Irregular forces conducted hit-and-run raids on the advancing American forces. Some were non-Iraqi Muslims, drawn to the country to resist those they considered to be infidel invaders.[80] The irregulars drew on caches of weapons Saddam's regime had left, originally for the purpose of helping loyalists hold off uprisings by Shias in the south until the regime's organized forces could arrive to fight them. Such attacks complicated, but did not stop, the march to Baghdad.[81] After the capital fell, however, they would come to plague the American occupation, becoming the central problem with which American policy in Iraq had to contend.

In Iraq, as in Haiti, Bosnia, Kosovo, and Afghanistan, the American armed forces carried out the task assigned to them—precisely the kind of task for which they had been trained and equipped—with dispatch and efficiency. As in the other places, the strictly military mission of the United States succeeded. It succeeded, moreover, on the terms of the secretary of defense. A much smaller army than the one deployed in 1991 had, as he had envisioned, driven Saddam Hussein from power quickly and at a gratifyingly low cost in casualties.

If the people of Iraq did not give the American troops the ecstatic welcome that some proponents of the war had predicted—and the Sunni inhabitants of the west did not greet them at all, since the invasion did not pass through that part of the country—the end of the Baathist regime did occasion a sense of relief in the south and in the capital. The iconic, symbolic end of the campaign came on April 9 in Firdos Square in Baghdad, where a crowd gathered in front of a giant statue of Saddam. After unsuccessful efforts by Iraqis to topple it, the driver of an American tank retriever hooked a cable to it and pulled it down from its pedestal, an event captured on video and broadcast around the world.[82]

The comparable moment for the American public occurred on May 1, 2003, when President Bush landed in a fighter jet on the aircraft carrier *Abraham Lincoln* off the coast of San Diego and declared an end to major combat operations in in Iraq. He spoke on the flight deck in front of a banner that read, "mission accomplished."[83] In fact, the American mission in Iraq was just beginning.

With the end of the Baath regime Iraq had no government. The American military had no plan for providing one: its troops even lacked instructions on keeping order.[84] As a result, disorder broke out across the country. Massive looting took place in the cities. In Baghdad, the buildings of 17 of the 23 central government ministries were destroyed.[85] By one estimate, the postwar looting caused far more economic damage than the American bombing campaign.[86]

Asked about the wave of unrest across the country the secretary of defense, whose department had responsibility for the country,[87] dismissed it. "Freedom is untidy," he said.[88] But what followed the defeat of Saddam was not freedom; it was anarchy. The looting, and the outburst of robberies and other criminal activities that ensued,[89] gave the people of Iraq an unfavorable introduction to American tutelage; and the days following the fall of Baghdad saw the establishment of a pattern of violence that never fully ended.

To supervise American efforts in Iraq after the end of the Baath regime the administration initially dispatched retired Army General Jay Garner. He had been in charge of Operation Provide Comfort, in which the United States had furnished humanitarian assistance and military protection to the Kurds of northern Iraq after the 1991 war.[90] Before the 2003 war began, caring for refugees was one of the tasks the administration anticipated having to carry out in its wake.[91] Garner's appointment came very late, in early January 2003, just eight weeks before the conflict started. He had little time to prepare. He did gather a staff and arrived in Baghdad on April 18. Only three weeks later, however, the administration replaced him.[92]

His replacement was L. Paul (Jerry) Bremer, a retired diplomat who had served as ambassador to the Netherlands and had headed the State Department's counterterrorism office. He shared Bush's conservative politics and free-market economics, which commended him to the president. Bremer arrived in Baghdad with wider powers and higher ambitions than Garner had had, and while Garner had expected his stay in Iraq to be brief (although not as brief as it turned out to be), Bremer was prepared for an extended term as the country's overlord. He intended to act as an all-powerful proconsul for the country, as General Douglas MacArthur had done in Japan after World War II.[93] (Like MacArthur, with his communications written in the green ink that he alone in Japan was allowed to use, Bremer had a trademark feature: the tan combat boots he wore with his blue pin-striped suits.)

To govern Iraq, Bremer established the Coalition Provisional Authority (CPA), which had responsibility for the country from May 2003 to the end of June 2004, when the United States handed sovereignty back to the Iraqis. The CPA was in nominal charge of all aspects of Iraqi affairs: governing it, establishing political and legal systems, writing a constitution, rebuilding its infrastructure, and reforming its economy.[94] One CPA staffer even rewrote its traffic laws.

Bremer aimed to transform Iraq from a Baathist police state with an economy under heavy government control to a vibrant, free-market democracy. The goal, in short, was nation-building, in this case from the ground up. In the two-decades-long period in which nation-building stood at the center of American foreign policy, the CPA embodied that project in its purest and most ambitious form. More deliberately, explicitly, seriously, and at greater expense than in China, Russia, Somalia, Haiti, Bosnia, Kosovo, and Afghanistan, in Iraq during the life of the CPA the United States undertook the mission of transforming the domestic institutions and practices of another country.

As elsewhere, the mission failed. Iraq did not acquire a democratic political system or a prosperous free-market economy. Under American tutelage, both during the formal life-span of the CPA and in the years afterward when the United States maintained a large military presence and exercised considerable political influence in the country, Iraq made little discernible progress on the road to Denmark.

The CPA failed to transform Iraq because the task, assuming it could be accomplished at all, would have required a great deal of time and money; and Bremer and his colleagues were given, in the end, relatively little of both.[95] Nor did they make good use of the time and money that they did have.[96] The CPA's personnel were chosen for the most part not for their expertise on the Middle East, or even, in many cases, on the particular issue on which they were supposed to be working, but rather on the basis of political loyalty to the Bush administration and agreement with its political positions. Two people who did go to Iraq recalled being asked, in interviews for CPA positions, about their views of the Supreme Court's landmark abortion decision *Roe vs. Wade*,[97] the relevance of which to creating a democracy in the Middle East was not readily apparent.

Almost none of the Americans engaged in remaking Iraq could communicate directly with the people of the country, since they spoke no Arabic.[98] A few people attached to the CPA did have both a working knowledge of the local language and extensive experience living in the region. Rather than working closely with them, however, Bremer preferred to rely on younger, inexperienced aides distinguished by their loyalty to him.

Most of the members of the CPA not only could not speak directly to the people of Iraq, they rarely met any. The Americans lived, worked, and seldom ventured outside a heavily fortified, four-square-mile area in central Baghdad known as the Green Zone. It had served as Saddam's administrative center, and when the fighting ended, the United States took it over for the same purpose. The Green Zone became a slice of America—indeed, the America that leaned to the right politically; televisions were tuned to the Fox News Channel—set down in, but sealed off from, the Arab Middle East.[99] It was not, perhaps, the ideal base from which to bring about the sweeping transformation to which, with Bremer's arrival, the United States was committed. Most of the CPA personnel arrived in Iraq knowing virtually nothing about the country and left, in many cases, having learned little more.[100]

As the CPA began its work, administration officials drew a parallel between what was under way in Iraq and the reconstruction and rehabilitation after World War II of two other countries the United States had defeated and occupied: Germany and Japan,[101] both of which had changed from aggressive dictatorships waging vicious wars to peaceful democracies. The Bush administration aimed to bring about a similar transformation in post-Saddam Iraq, which, however, differed from America's two World War II adversaries in ways that made the hoped-for transformation impossible.

Germany and Japan had each had experience, short-lived though it was, with democratic governance and longer experience with the rule of law. Iraq had had no experience with either. Both Germany and Japan had had a well-functioning state apparatus before the war: Iraq had had nothing comparable.

Unlike Germany and Japan after 1945, moreover, Iraq had never had anything approaching a modern industrial economy. It had depended heavily on the export of oil, with the government dominating the country's small and backward industrial and commercial sectors. The CPA wanted to put these sectors into private hands but the policy of privatization turned out not to be viable: Iraqis did not have the money to buy the country's factories and firms; foreigners, who did have the money, would not buy them because they were, in free-market conditions, worthless; and the CPA had no way of taking physical control of the assets it hoped to sell.[102]

Perhaps the most important difference between the defeated Axis powers of World War II and Iraq lay in the strength of national feeling. It was powerful in Germany and Japan but not in Iraq, which complicated the American project: nation-building is difficult where no coherent nation exists. The inhabitants of the three Ottoman provinces that the British had stitched together after World War I had a narrower focus of loyalty.

Like the Somalis and Afghans but unlike the Germans and Japanese, not to mention the Americans, tribal ties played a major role in the social and political life of the people of Iraq.[103] Saddam's rule had relied heavily on his fellow tribesmen from Tikrit and the surrounding area.[104] Moreover, rather than considering themselves all to be citizens of Iraq, the people of the country gravitated to sectarian identities. They thought of themselves as Sunni or Shia Muslims or as Kurds.[†]

[†] "It was the fashion among progressive Arabs to say that those old sectarian schisms were over with, that a newer political world had emerged out of the modernisms and the new ideological movements. No such thing had happened: in Syria, Iraq, and Lebanon, the ideological movements were only containers for darker, deeper sectarian attachments. Indeed, more recent history had only sharpened the old sectarian differences. There had never been a reconciliation between the Sunnis and the Shia anywhere in the lands of Islam . . . " Fouad Ajami, *The Foreigner's Gift: The Americans, the Arabs, and the Iraqis in Iraq*, New York: The Free Press, 2006, p. 179.

These identities went back centuries. They had bound together, and separated, the people living in what had once been called Mesopotamia long before the British created Iraq.

Ultimately, the realities of the society they were occupying overwhelmed the American efforts to recast it in the image of the democratic West. The United States failed to build a modern, democratic, prosperous state in Iraq because, as in Afghanistan, the appropriate materials were lacking. The American effort was akin to trying to construct a modern skyscraper without steel and in the case of Iraq, with a construction crew lacking experience in putting up tall buildings. There was yet another problem: nation-building in Iraq after the American conquest of the country in 2003 was like trying to construct the building while some of the people who should be working inside are instead shooting at the builders.

Rather than forging a modern government and economy in Iraq, the United States found itself presiding over violence that began with the fall of the regime and escalated in the weeks and months thereafter, much of it directed at American military and civilian personnel. Coping with that violence, not transforming the country, became the highest priority of the Bush administration. It decided that a political process that returned control over the country to the people who lived there would pacify Iraq.[105]

On July 13, Bremer appointed what he called a Governing Council, composed of 25 Iraqis.[106] Despite its title it did no governing: it had a strictly advisory role and even in that limited capacity did not function smoothly.[107] On September 8, he published an article in *The Washington Post* outlining a seven-step plan for the transition from American occupation to full Iraqi sovereignty, which seemed likely to stretch into 2005.[108]

The plan changed for two reasons. The Bush administration became increasingly alarmed at the mounting violence, with its toll of American deaths and injuries, and concluded that transferring sovereignty to Iraq more quickly would calm the country.[109] In addition, the most influential Shia clergyman, Ayatollah Ali Sistani, denounced the Bremer plan from his headquarters in the city of Najaf, south of Baghdad, objecting to its provision for writing a constitution before an elected Iraqi government was in place.[110] On November 15, therefore, the Americans announced a new, foreshortened timetable.

Iraq would regain official control of its own affairs on June 30, 2004. The transfer of power in fact took place two days earlier, on June 28.[111] The CPA ceased to exist and Bremer left the country. The most intensive chapter of American nation-building in the post-Cold War era came to end. An interim government, chosen by the United States in conjunction with a United Nations official, Lakhdar Brahimi, took office. As prime minister they selected Ayad Allawi, a Shia who had lived in the West for many years and had good relations with influential Sunnis. In January 2005, the first free election in the country's history took place. People flocked to the polls and pictures of voters proudly displaying the purple mark on their thumbs that proved that they had cast their ballots were broadcast around the world. It seemed a triumph for democracy.

Two features of the election portended problems that would plague Iraq until the departure of American forces in 2011 and beyond. First, Sunnis did not participate on a large scale: turnout in the Sunni-dominated parts of Iraq was sparse.[112] Although democratically chosen, the resulting government did not command the allegiance of all the people of the country. Second, instead of electing representatives from specific, geographically-defined districts, as is the case with the American Congress and the British House of Commons, the entire country was designated a single district. Parties gained seats in the new parliament in proportion to their shares of the overall vote. This conferred an advantage on the best-organized parties, which turned out to be those based on Kurdish nationalism and Shia Islam. It ensured that the results of the election would express the principal social cleavages in Iraq rather than any sense of common nationality. It was remarked at the time that the election was tantamount to a census.

Shia religious parties won the largest number of seats. From one of them, the Dawa, came the country's first elected prime minister, Ibrahim al-Jaafari. His government presided over the drafting of a constitution, which received 78 percent approval, largely from Shia and Kurds, in a referendum held on October 15.

A second national election took place in December 2005. More Sunnis participated than had voted in January but again the Shia—numerically the country's largest group—dominated the results. Forming a government after this election took almost five months.

Jaafari had won few admirers as prime minister, but finding a successor proved contentious. Finally, in May, in part because of the influence of the United States, Nouri al-Maliki, a member of Jaafari's Dawa Party, emerged as the choice.[113] Maliki had joined the opposition to the Baath regime at an early age, had worked against it secretly within the country before fleeing first to Syria and then to Iran, and had returned only after the American victory in 2003. His career in the anti-Saddam underground had instilled in him a deep suspicion of anyone not close or beholden to him, which became a hallmark of his style of governance.[114] He would serve as prime minister for eight years. In that time he would do more than any other individual, certainly more than Bremer or any American, to shape the post-Saddam government and political system. Neither turned out to be what the Bush administration had originally envisioned.

The United States did succeed in establishing the principle of selecting the government of Iraq by voting, a marked departure from the series of coups by which new governments had come to power in the past. Regularly scheduled and more or less free elections took place not only twice in 2005 but also thereafter in 2010 and 2014. Yet the elections, in particular the first two, did not accomplish what the United States had hoped they would. They did not end the violence, which in fact increased in 2006 and 2007. While the elimination of the Baathist regime did bring voting to Iraq, it did not give the country genuine, stable democracy. Instead, it brought first anarchy and then a vicious and prolonged insurgency.

The gap between what the Bush administration expected to happen when the United States invaded Iraq and what actually did happen gave rise to several criticisms of the conduct of the invasion and especially of its aftermath. Beginning shortly after the fall of the regime and the start of the violence its downfall triggered, critics cited mistakes of policy that, they believed, had caused, or at least contributed to and worsened, that violence.

It became evident soon after the capture of Baghdad that the United States did not have enough troops in Iraq.[115] The American troop strength was inadequate to prevent the widespread looting that took place in the capital and elsewhere. It was inadequate to control the country's borders, across which reinforcements for the insurgency flowed. It was inadequate to pacify the country once the insurgency began. To achieve the ratio of troops to the total Iraqi population that was necessary to keep order, based on other post-conflict experiences—and even subtracting the Kurds, who welcomed the Americans, remained generally peaceful, and did not require pacification—the United States would have had to have sent at least twice as many soldiers to Iraq as it did.[116]

The shortage of troops contributed to the major scandal of the occupation. As the insurgency expanded, the Americans took into custody more and more suspected insurgents. Many were sent to the Saddam-era prison at Abu Ghraib, west of Baghdad.[117] It was run by American reservists who had no relevant training for the jobs to which they were assigned but were pressed into service in Iraq because regular forces were not available. In 2004, photographs of a number of them abusing prisoners were broadcast around the world. Evidence that the American armed forces, which had gone to the country to save the people of Iraq, were mistreating some of them embarrassed the Bush administration both in the United States and in other countries, as well as in Iraq.[118]

Despite all this, the secretary of defense refused to send more troops. Before the first of his two stints in that capacity in 1975 and 1976, Donald Rumsfeld had served as a member of Congress from Illinois, ambassador to NATO, and President Ford's chief of staff. In between his two terms at the Pentagon he had had a successful career as the chief executive officer of G. D. Searle, a large pharmaceutical firm, and of two other companies.[119]

He came to his second tour of duty with a particular agenda: to adapt the nation's armed forces to the strategic requirements, as he saw them, of the post-Cold War era. That meant smaller, lighter, more flexible forces that relied more on speed and high technology and less on manpower than they had during the decades of confrontation with the Soviet Union.[120] He saw the Iraqi operation as an opportunity to put his program into practice; and with a smaller army than the one that had won the 1991 war, the United States did succeed in toppling Saddam.

With that victory the mission changed. Coping with the insurgency required more troops than defeating the Iraqi army but Rumsfeld did not send them.[121] He was slow to recognize the new circumstances.

His resistance to increasing troop levels in the country came as well from his disdain for the Clinton-era efforts at nation-building, which required keeping forces on the ground after the fighting had ended. He wanted to avoid this in Iraq because he regarded it as being at best unnecessary and at worst counterproductive in that it perpetuated, he believed, dependence on foreign assistance.[122] Even when, with the establishment of the CPA, the administration embraced nation-building in Iraq, he maintained his opposition to dispatching additional forces.

Beyond Rumsfeld's personal preferences, however, stood another, more formidable (although seldom mentioned) obstacle to sending more American troops to Iraq: the United States did not have more troops to send.[123] The Department of Defense would have been hard pressed to find soldiers in large numbers to add to the contingent already there. At best, many would have had to be taken from other missions that were at least as important for national security, if not more so. Without conscription the government lacked the means to expand the army quickly; and no one, least of all the military leadership, wanted to bring back the draft. Fielding more American troops was surely necessary to contend with the most serious problem the United States encountered in post-Saddam Iraq; but the logistical, strategic, and domestic political constraints were such that dispatching them was just as surely not feasible.

Before the war, American officials had hoped that other countries would supply some of whatever forces were needed in post-Saddam Iraq[124] and assumed that, even if they did not, the Iraqi army would remain more or less intact and could be put to postwar use. No sooner had Bremer taken charge of the occupation, however, than he issued a decree—Order Number 2, on May 23, 2003—disbanding the Iraqi army. The order contradicted what President Bush had decided only a few weeks earlier.[125] It appeared especially damaging in retrospect because it seemed to have fed the insurgency by leaving several hundred thousand militarily trained Iraqis[126] without a source of income and thus with grievances against the Americans.

The American official in charge of military affairs in the CPA, Walter Slocombe, who had worked in the Department of Defense in the Clinton administration, later justified Bremer's order on the grounds that the army had already disbanded itself: its troops had discarded their uniforms and returned home. Critics replied that they could have been recalled or at least offered modest, temporary stipends that might have purchased higher tolerance of the American presence.

While disbanding the army (or ratifying its spontaneous disintegration) certainly made the American role in Iraq more difficult and dangerous, retaining it or trying to reassemble it would have posed risks as well. As with all institutions in Saddam's Iraq, Sunni Muslims dominated the army; and along with his Republican Guard and the secret police, Saddam had used the army as an instrument to repress the Shia. Difficult as it was, the American presence in Iraq proved sustainable for eight years only because neither the Kurdish minority nor, for the most part, the Shia majority actively opposed it. (Both had good reason for their forbearance: the electoral system the United States installed delivered power to the Shia and the American presence helped assure the Kurds a large measure of autonomy.) Maintaining or recreating the army would have risked forfeiting Kurdish and Shia goodwill.[127] It might have sent them into far more widespread and active opposition to the CPA and the American troops, with calamitous consequences for the United States.

The same cost-benefit calculus applied to another Bremer démarche, CPA Order Number 1, of May 16, 2003, which barred members of the top four echelons of the Baath Party, 30,000 people in all, from serving in the government.[128] Once again, the order deprived the United States of trained personnel who might, in theory, have made valuable contributions to post-Saddam Iraq, in this case by operating the government bureaucracies. Here, too, the order made into enemies of the American presence large numbers of people who, without it, might at least have remained neutral.

As in the case of the army, however, restricting the scope of what came to be known as de-Baathification might also have had adverse consequences for the United States by alienating the Shia majority in the country, for whom the Baath Party had served as an instrument of exclusion and oppression. Moreover, the Iraqi government bureaucracies that Baathists filled, unlike the German and Japanese bureaucracies after World War II, had not functioned as apolitical agencies that the Americans could use to run the country. To the contrary, they were part and parcel of the Baathist apparatus. Even if more officials had stayed in place, they would have been of limited use in administering Iraq.

A final Bremer initiative in Baghdad came in for criticism, and in this case not just from outside the government: civilian officials at the Pentagon strongly disagreed with it.[129] This was his decision not to put an Iraqi government in place immediately but to govern the country himself. Bremer made the decision because he found the Iraqi politicians he encountered, both the exiles who returned and those who had remained in the country throughout Saddam's rule, to be dismayingly inept: querulous, irresponsible, self-seeking, and scarcely models of probity.[‡] Yet the interim government that was formed in June 2004, his critics noted, consisted of precisely the people he had deemed unsuitable 11 months earlier.[130]

This suggests that nothing would have been lost by restoring Iraqi sovereignty sooner rather than later. There is no reason to believe, however, that much would have been gained either—that Iraq would have been appreciably more peaceful, better-governed, coherent, or pro-American—by establishing an indigenous government immediately after the fall of Saddam. The problems that afflicted Iraq and that

‡ Rajiv Chandrasekara, *Imperial Life in the Emerald City: Inside Iraq's Green Zone*, New York: Alfred A. Knopf, 2006, pp. 53, 78; Michael Gordon and General Bernard E. Trainor, *Cobra II: The Inside Story of the Invasion and Occupation of Iraq*, New York: Pantheon Books, 2006, p. 470. The exile politician who aroused by far the most controversy was Ahmad Chalabi. From a prominent Baghdad Shia family, he had been educated in the United States, had established a bank in Jordan that had failed in disputed circumstances (see Ali A. Allawi, *The Occupation of Iraq: Winning the War, Losing the Peace*, New Haven, Connecticut: Yale University Press, 2007, p. 464, note 9), and had founded an anti-Saddam exile group, the Iraqi National Congress, which succeeded in winning modest financial and political support from the United States. He had admirers in American political circles and in the Bush administration, particularly the Department of Defense, who saw him as the potential George Washington of his country. He also had opponents, especially in the State Department and the intelligence community, who considered him a dangerous charlatan. (Peter Baker, *Days of Fire: Bush and Cheney in the White House*, New York: Doubleday, 2013, p. 224.) He did not achieve his ambition of leading Iraq, but did remain on the fringes of power throughout the eight years of the American occupation and afterward. On Chalabi see also Fouad Ajami, *The Foreigner's Gift: The Americans, the Arabs, and the Iraqis in Iraq*, New York: The Free Press, 2006, pp. 227–234.

frustrated the American mission there had deep roots. The mutual suspicion and hostility among Sunnis, Shias, and Kurds, the winner-take-all approach to politics, and the view of public office as a mechanism for rewarding family and friends rather than serving the public interest all emerged from decades of experience and were bound to afflict whatever regime succeeded Saddam's no matter when it was formed and who formed it.

Because of its history, the Iraqi body politic rejected the Western institutions the Bush administration tried to implant in it. What came naturally to the people of the country, given that history, was not democracy or free markets but violence. While a larger American army would have done better in suppressing that violence, it is hard to see how keeping Saddam's army in being, or keeping more Baathist officials in their jobs, or handing power quickly to Iraqis, would have prevented it.

The United States could have bypassed the difficulty, the frustration, and the cost in lives and money in one particular way: by leaving the country, as initially planned, after removing Saddam from power.[131] This would not have avoided large-scale violence in the country, which almost certainly would have been worse in the absence of American troops, but that violence would not have been directed at Americans. Prompt withdrawal would also have left open the possibility of the return to power of Saddam or someone like him.[132] For that reason, when it became clear that the postwar disorder in Iraq would not abate by itself, the administration did not seriously consider the option of a rapid departure. It was not prepared to abandon the American mission.[133]

A measure of the failure of that mission is that the United States not only did not install democracy and free markets in Iraq, it did not provide the country with something almost as important and, in theory, easier to supply: infrastructure. Like all countries, Iraq needed reliable supplies of power and clean water. Under Saddam's rule, especially after the 1991 war, the systems for supplying them had deteriorated badly.[134] Unlike democracy and free markets, a country's receptivity to power plants and sewage treatment facilities does not depend on its political culture. Iraq's three major ethnic and sectarian groups may have had serious reservations about living together in a single political unit, but none opposed indoor plumbing or regular access to electricity. Yet the United States did not succeed in building infrastructure on a large scale despite a commitment to do so.[135] The ongoing violence prevented the building of the facilities the country needed. Construction projects became targets of the insurgency. The insecurity the insurgents created thwarted even the part of the American mission that was independent of the history of Iraq and the beliefs of Iraqis. Security in the public sphere, it is said, is like oxygen for individuals. In Iraq the United States found itself, because of the insurgency, perpetually short of breath.

The Wars After the War

Contrary to the Bush administration's expectation, the disappearance of Saddam's regime did not bring an end to armed conflict in Iraq. Instead, with the end of Baathist rule three different wars erupted.

In the western part of the country, as well as in Baghdad, the country's Sunnis, whom the American victory over Saddam had deprived of the power they had enjoyed since the British had created Iraq, attacked American soldiers and American civilians. The Sunni insurgency accounted for most of the more than 32,000 injuries and the more than 4,400 deaths the United States suffered in Iraq. Also in Baghdad and in some southern cities as well, Shia militias on occasion came into conflict with the Americans. The Shia population as a whole, which accounted for about 60 percent of Iraqis, although not necessarily favorably disposed toward the Americans let alone grateful to them, did not generate the kind of insurgency the Sunnis mounted, no doubt largely because the occupation had transferred power from the Sunnis to them. These two conflicts affected the duration of the American stay in Iraq: the toll of American casualties eroded public support for the war in the United States.[136] For the people of Iraq, the stakes in the third of the three conflicts were much higher: the ultimate control of the country itself.

As the Shia assumed command of the government through the American-sponsored elections, Sunni insurgents attacked them as well. The Shia retaliated, using not only the militias they formed but also the instruments of government they increasingly controlled, including the army, the police, and a number of ministries. This sectarian conflict proved to be the most destructive of the three, killing hundreds of thousands of people and displacing millions more. The United States tried, with limited success, to mitigate it.

The Sunni insurgency against the Americans, the chief concern of American commanders throughout the eight years of the American military presence in Iraq, had two sources. Al Qaeda set up shop in the country.[137] It recruited Sunni Muslims locally, from the wider Middle East, and from other parts of the world including Europe to come to Iraq to fight the infidel invaders. The American presence offered Al Qaeda the opportunity to continue its campaign against the United States but with more Americans within easier reach. Al Qaeda in Iraq mounted some spectacular and damaging attacks against American and other Western targets.

The insurgency also drew on veterans of the Baath regime, including some with military skills, who could count on a network of supporters in Sunni neighborhoods in Baghdad and throughout western Iraq and who had access to caches of weapons and explosives left over from their days in power.[138] They fought the Americans not, as did al Qaeda, for the glory of jihad, but as revenge for, and in the hope of ultimately reversing, the dispossession the American invasion imposed on them.

Although numerically a minority in Iraq—some of them denied this fact, mathematically indisputable though it was—Sunnis had dominated the country since the British had created it, monopolizing power and wealth and relegating the far larger Shia population to an inferior status. When the Shia rose up against Saddam's regime after its eviction from Kuwait in 1991, his forces had put them down savagely in an act of sectarian repression. The arrival of the Americans reversed the long-standing and, in the Sunni view, natural, even divinely ordained and certainly morally appropriate order in Iraq.[139] It turned their world upside down. They attacked American troops and American civilians for the purpose, eventually, of putting it right side up again. Like the al Qaeda jihadis, therefore, although for different reasons, they had powerful motives for making war on the Americans.

The Sunni insurgency fought the Americans with guerrilla tactics. Its fighters, who did not wear uniforms, operated in small, loosely organized bands. They engaged in hit and run attacks, striking and then disappearing into the larger Sunni population. In addition, and following the pattern of September 11, 2001, al Qaeda in Iraq made extensive use of suicide attacks. Recruits would approach their victims wearing civilian clothing that concealed explosives they then detonated, killing themselves but also killing or injuring others. In addition, they mounted explosives on cars and trucks, drove them into crowded urban areas, and blew them up, usually causing more destruction than individual suicide bombers on foot could. The insurgents also concealed explosives in or along roads and triggered them as American patrols or convoys passed by. Known as improvised explosive devices—IEDs—these took a heavy toll on Americans riding in vehicles that lacked sufficiently robust protective armor, as most of them did, especially during the first year of the American presence.[140] The insurgency set up factory-like facilities on the outskirts of Baghdad and in western Iraq to make the IEDs and assemble the car and truck bombs.

The Sunni insurgency began with attacks on the American divisions moving from Kuwait to Baghdad in March and April of 2003 and continued after the fall of the capital. It escalated dramatically during the summer of that year: truck bombs blew up the Jordanian embassy on August 7 and then, on August 19, the temporary headquarters of the United Nations in Baghdad, on the second occasion killing 22 people including the head of the mission, the Brazilian diplomat Sergio Vieira de Mello, injuring 150 others, and prompting the withdrawal of most UN personnel.[141]

On several occasions the insurgents fought sustained battles with American troops. The two most notable occurred in the city of Fallujah, 43 miles west of Baghdad.[142] The insurgency had a strong position in the city and on March 31, 2004, four American contractors were killed there. Their bodies were dragged through the streets and then hung on a bridge over the Euphrates River.[143] The CPA decided that this atrocity should not go unpunished and dispatched Marines to capture Fallujah. The operation required the kind of grinding, perilous urban combat that the United States had managed to avoid during the initial march to Baghdad. The American forces made steady progress, but before they could take full control of the city, the civilian authorities in Baghdad and Washington decided that the operation was doing unacceptable harm to the political standing of the United States in the country, the region, and elsewhere, putting the larger American mission in Iraq in jeopardy.[144] The civilians ordered the operation suspended, to the displeasure of the Americans in uniform who were doing the fighting. Seven months later, in November, with the city still functioning as a base for anti-American attacks, the Marines returned to Fallujah and this time succeeded in conquering it and driving out the insurgents. It was the bloodiest battle the United States fought in Iraq. A total of 95 Americans were killed and 560 wounded. A reported 2,175 insurgents died and an estimated 7,000 to 10,000 of Fallujah's 50,000 residential buildings were destroyed.[145]

In a battle against American troops the insurgents, even with the advantages of advance notice, concealment, and knowledge of the urban terrain where the fighting took place, could not hope to win. The Americans' advantages in firepower, surveillance, and communication, their total control of the air, and the discipline and bravery of their troops made it inevitable that, with sufficient determination, they would prevail. While the Army and the Marine Corps could capture territory anywhere in Iraq, however, they lacked the manpower to maintain control of the entire country. They could and did push the insurgents out of Fallujah, but the Sunni fighters they evicted regrouped elsewhere. The insurgency could sustain itself as long as it received adequate support, or at least tolerance, from the population among which it lived; and because of the reversal of fortune the Americans had imposed on them, the Sunnis of Iraq, by and large, sympathized with the insurgents and disliked the Americans.

The Shia population, the beneficiaries of the American occupation, had no comparable reason to oppose it. Freed from the domination of the Sunni Baathist regime, the Shia organized themselves along religious and sectarian lines.[146] Several of these organizations formed their own militias and used them to carve out domains of influence and power in the new Iraq. One of them came into conflict with the American authorities.

Moqtada al-Sadr was the son of a well-known Shia cleric whom Saddam had ordered murdered in 1999. Moqtada lacked his father's scholarly and religious credentials but inherited part of his following and used it as the base for a movement that functioned as a political party; he also created an armed force, which he called, the Mahdi Army.[147]

His fiery, populist rhetoric, which included a healthy dose of anti-Americanism, won him support among impoverished Shia throughout the country, especially in a part of Baghdad that was known as Saddam City in the Baathist era but that came to be called Sadr City after the fall of the regime. By early 2004, the Mahdi Army had established a visible and extensive presence there and in the south of the country.[148]

On March 28, 2004, Bremer ordered a Sadr-run newspaper shut down for inciting violence against American troops. In response, Moqtada's supporters staged protests that sometimes turned violent in Baghdad and in Shia-dominated southern cities.[149] They besieged the CPA headquarters in Najaf. The Sadrists eventually backed down, or calmed down, but in August they resumed their disruptive tactics and American units waged a full-scale battle with Mahdi Army forces in the heart of Najaf. As in Fallujah, the American side used its superiority in firepower and overall military competence to gain the upper hand; but to crush their adversary the Americans faced the prospect of attacking one of its redoubts, a shrine sacred to Shias located in a densely populated area. Such an attack could have triggered a fierce backlash against the United States among the Shia population. Before it happened, Moqtada agreed to end the fighting, but retained his militia.[150]

While he came into conflict with the United States when it attempted to check his power, his and the other Shia organizations considered Iraq's Sunnis to be their principal enemies. The Sunnis reciprocated. While continuing to attack Americans, in the months after the fall of the Baathist regime the Sunni insurgency and the Shia militias increasingly devoted themselves to killing and displacing members of the other sect.

Al Qaeda and the former Baathist insurgents turned the tactics used against the Americans on the Shia as well. They set off, for example, car bombs in crowded parts of Shia neighborhoods. They aimed to intimidate the Shias. Some Sunnis hoped to trigger a full scale sectarian war, which they were convinced they would win because of their superior martial qualities and because the conflict would draw in Muslims from the rest of the Middle East and around the world, where, in both cases—and unlike in Iraq—Sunnis outnumbered Shias.[151] The most spectacular and symbolically powerful Sunni terrorist attack on the Shias occurred on February 22, 2006, when bombs blew up the Al-Askari mosque, an important Shia holy site in the city of Samarra, 78 miles north of Baghdad.[152] The Shias responded with attacks of their own on the Sunnis. In the Shia-dominated Iraqi government, beginning in 2005, they used government agencies as bases for sectarian assaults. They formed death squads that sought out and executed Sunnis.[153]

In Baghdad, the violence led to large-scale ethnic cleansing of the kind that had taken place a decade earlier in Bosnia. Sunnis fled predominantly Shia neighborhoods and vice versa. The capital became what it had not been under Saddam: a city segregated by sect, with Sunnis in the west and Shia in the east.[154] The United States found itself not only under attack from both sects but also caught in the middle of their civil war.

Having come to Iraq with the intention of ending the kind of violence Saddam had routinely practiced, as well as with the goal of building a tolerant, non-sectarian government just as the Clinton administration had aspired to do in Bosnia, the Bush administration was dismayed by the killings and strongly opposed the ethnic cleansing. While the American military presence probably reduced the scale of the killing and expulsions, the United States could not stop them: it had too few troops to police the entire country, and the troops it did have were under attack from the Sunni insurgency even as the Sunnis and Shias battled each other.

Iraq's neighbors made the problems the United States encountered in Iraq even worse. The Arab media bombarded the country with commentary and reporting resolutely hostile to the American enterprise.[155] All neighboring countries, with the partial exception of Turkey, wished to see the American mission fail: none, except Turkey, found the prospect of a nascent democracy in their midst a pleasing one. They feared it would become precisely what the Bush administration hoped it would be: an example and an inspiration to the people the rulers of Iraq's neighbors were governing undemocratically.[156] For that and other reasons Iraq's neighbors worked actively, in various ways, to affect what happened in the country after Saddam's downfall, and much of what they did added to the difficulties with which the Americans had to contend.

The Islamic Republic of Iran sought to expand its influence, making use of the adherence to Shia Islam that the ethnic Persians who dominated Iran shared with the majority of Iraqis. At the same time it sought to reduce the influence of the United States, which the rulers in Tehran regarded as a particularly dangerous adversary. Their attitude was captured by the term they routinely applied to America: the Great Satan.[157] In addition, as a regime based on religion and led by clerics, the Islamic Republic supported Shia religious parties in Iraq with the hope of replicating, and thus reinforcing, its own system of government. During the Saddam era, Iran had sheltered a number of exiled Shia politicians. Some of them, such as Nouri al-Maliki, the prime minister from 2006 to 2014, became part of the Shia-dominated Iraqi governments. The Islamic Republic supplied Shia parties with money and political guidance. It also provided money, weapons, and training to Shia militias.[158] Here Iran was repeating, or at least trying to repeat, a pattern it had established in Lebanon, where the Shia militia it sponsored, Hezbollah, had come to dominate the country.[159]

Whatever its consequences for the United States, the American invasion of 2003 brought major benefits for the government of Iran. By overthrowing Saddam Hussein the invasion removed one of its most determined adversaries, who had initiated a bloody decade-long war against it in 1980. By bringing Shia to power it made possible a major expansion of Iran's influence in the Middle East. In this way the country that the Iranian mullahs had proclaimed their greatest enemy became, unintentionally, their greatest benefactor.

The government of Syria also gained from Saddam's downfall. While in theory the Baath Party governed Syria as it did Iraq, in fact, as in Iraq, a ruling family controlled in the country. Hafez al-Assad, a member of the Alawi sect, an offshoot of Shiism, seized power in 1970 and his son, Bashar, succeeded him on his death in 2000. Despite their common roots in Baathism, the two regimes became bitter adversaries. The American overthrow of Saddam therefore did a service to Assad as well as to Iran. This did not, however, engender Syrian goodwill toward the United States. To the contrary, the government in Damascus, an ally and client of Iran, made a major contribution to America's post-invasion troubles in Iraq. Like Pakistan in the Afghan war, Syria served as a refuge, a staging area, and a transit point for Islamic militants from all over the world eager to fight the Americans.[160] The Assad regime supported the insurgency in Iraq despite the fact that the insurgents it assisted were virtually all Sunnis, many of whom were violently opposed to Assad's sect.[161]

Unlike Iran and Syria, Saudi Arabia had good relations with the United States and had had very poor relations with Saddam. His occupation of Kuwait in 1990 made him a direct threat to their rule. The United States had gone to war in 1991 in no small part to relieve that threat so as to ensure that the Arabian peninsula's vast oil reserves remained in friendly hands. Yet the Saudis did not welcome Saddam's downfall, and not just because they feared that a democracy on Iraqi soil would inspire the people of the Arabian peninsula to seek a similar political system.

They regarded Shia rule in Iraq as an even more urgent danger. The extreme Wahhabi form of Sunni Islam that they professed, that they imposed on those they ruled, and that they spent billions of dollars to spread among Muslims around the world, made the ruling family in Saudi Arabia Sunni supremacists.[162] They saw themselves as engaged in a struggle with Iran for primacy in the Middle East and in the Muslim world more generally. In this struggle, the shift of Iraq from the Sunni to the Shia camp gave their adversary an advantage. They and many other Sunnis saw the Shia-dominated elected government in Baghdad as little more than a Persian puppet. Moreover, the Saudi kingdom itself harbored a Shia minority that happened to be concentrated where the oil on which the government depended was located, making the rulers all the more wary of Shia power in the region. The Saudi government therefore disapproved of the American invasion of Iraq; and although after the invasion it did not provide the kind of support to the enemies of the United States in Iraq that Iran and Syria did, like the hijackers of September 11 many of the Sunni insurgents fighting the Americans came from Saudi Arabia and private citizens of the kingdom sent money to the insurgency.[163]

As the violence against Americans increased in the months after the fall of Baghdad, the Bush administration initially denied that it faced a serious problem.[164] Paul Wolfowitz told a Congressional hearing on June 19, 2003, that those responsible for the violence were "the last remnants of a dying cause."[165] On July 2 the president said to reporters, with what came to seem, in retrospect, injudicious bravado, "There are some who feel like that the conditions are such that they can attack us there. My answer is: Bring 'em on. We've got the force necessary to deal with the security situation."[166] As late as November 11, when the CIA warned the administration's top officials about the growing insurgency in Iraq, Rumsfeld challenged the use of the term to describe what was happening there.[167] The administration hoped that the December 13, 2003, capture by American troops of Saddam Hussein, who was hiding in a village about 80 miles northwest of Baghdad, would dampen the insurgency. It did not. The causes of the insurrection ran far deeper than personal loyalty to the former dictator.[168]

When the administration did finally acknowledge—above all to itself—the seriousness of the challenge it faced, its strategy for reducing the insurgency emphasized turning power over to Iraqis more quickly than Bremer had initially planned. The accelerated June 30, 2004, deadline for the return of sovereignty would, the Americans hoped, reduce the hostility that was fueling the anti-American campaign.

The Bush administration devised a military plan to complement the political course on which it had embarked, a plan by which the United States would train an Iraqi army that would, as quickly as possible, assume responsibility for maintaining security in the country. "As the Iraqis stand up," went the American description of the policy, "we will stand down."[169] Rumsfeld was particularly anxious, in his words, to "take the hand off the bicycle seat" so that the Iraqis would learn, metaphorically, to ride the bicycle unassisted—to take responsibility, that is, for their own affairs[170]—and the American troops could come home.

The strategy relied on the presumption that American troops had the effect of an antibody in Iraq, a foreign object that triggered an internal reaction against it just as viruses and bacteria do in the human body, as General John Abizaid, head of CENTCOM, the American regional command that covered the Middle East, put it.[171] Removing the alien presence, the administration hoped, would make the countervailing response disappear. The United States could restore order to Iraq, according to the theory underlying the strategy American military commanders embraced, by leaving.

Neither part of the strategy worked as the administration desired. The installation of an elected Iraqi government did not end the insurgency.

If anything, the elections increased the violence because, by bringing the Shia to power, they further angered and alienated the Sunnis,
who were conducting most of the attacks. The new Iraqi army that
the United States was building grew more slowly than expected and
the soldiers the Americans did train did not perform as effectively as
hoped.[172] Here, too, the American nation-building mission faltered.

In Iraq, the wars that broke out in the wake of the 2003 American
war to overturn the Baathist regime brought death and destruction
on a large scale, ruined the hopes that Americans and Iraqis held for
democracy and prosperity in the country, and sharpened the bitterness,
suspicion, and outright hatred among Sunnis, Shias, and Kurds. The
violence also had important consequences far from the Middle East.
The anti-American insurgency had what would turn out to be a decisive impact 8,000 miles away. It provoked a strongly negative political
reaction in the place where the fate of the American enterprise in Iraq
would be decided: the United States.

The Home Front

In military terminology "the center of gravity" refers to whatever it is
that enables a party to a war to keep fighting it.[173] The military leaders of the United States identified the American public as the center
of gravity of their effort in Iraq.[174] They were correct. American public
opinion set limits on the scope and the duration of American military
operations. The insurgency could not and did not defeat the American
forces. It could and did, however, impose costs on the United States
that made the war increasingly unacceptable to the people who had the
ultimate power to decide how, and for how long, to wage it. As with the
American wars in Korea in the 1950s and in Vietnam during the 1960s
and 1970s, the downward trajectory of public support for the country's
involvement in Iraq determined the course of the American war there
in the first decade of the twenty-first century.

At its outset the war commanded very strong support in the United
States. In March 2003 more than 70 percent of the country favored military action in Iraq.[175] The shock and anger occasioned by the attacks
of September 11 and their association in the public mind, however
mistakenly, with Saddam, the animus toward the Iraqi dictator dating

from the 1991 war, and the example of what seemed to be the quick and easy success of the late-2001 campaign to depose the Taliban in Afghanistan all combined to make military intervention very popular.

President Clinton had not gone to the Congress for approval of any of his military interventions but his successor did so for Iraq. The administration scheduled the Congressional vote on the war in advance of the 2002 midterm elections, confident that, with the public so strongly in favor of it, few legislators would defy their constituents and publicly oppose the mandate the president was seeking. That confidence was vindicated.[176] In the November election, George W. Bush's Republican Party campaigned on both his vigorous response to the September 11 attacks the year before and the prospect of removing the threat that Saddam posed in the near future. The Republicans did unusually well at the polls. In off-year elections the incumbent president's party ordinarily loses seats, but in 2002 Bush's party gained two in the Senate and eight in the House of Representatives.

By the time Bush ran for re-election two years later, in November 2004, enthusiasm for his war had diminished. The insurgency had undercut the expectation of a smooth and rapid transition to democracy and to a government friendly to the United States. It had become apparent that the costs of removing Saddam and remaking Iraq would exceed what the public had expected to pay. Bush's Democratic opponent, Senator John Kerry of Massachusetts, ran for the presidency as a critic of the administration's conduct of the conflict,[177] although without calling for an immediate end to the American military presence in the country. Bush stressed his prosecution of the war on terror, which remained popular, rather than his supervision of the conflict in Iraq, which increasingly was not.[178] Iraq proved not to be a fatal drawback for him: he was reelected.

As with the Korean and Vietnam wars, in the case of Iraq the public became disenchanted not with America's goals—few doubted the value, in principle, of ending Baathist rule, defeating the insurgents, and building Western-style institutions—but rather with what turned out to be the costs of achieving those goals. Understanding the political dangers of rising costs, from the beginning the Bush administration worked to minimize what the American public had to pay.

Before the war the administration said—and, as with the confident but erroneous assertion that Saddam possessed weapons of mass
destruction, surely believed—that those costs would be modest. The
troops would conduct a short campaign to remove Saddam from power
and then return home. As for reconstruction, Paul Wolfowitz, ever the
optimist, suggested that the country's oil revenues would pay for it.[179]
In September 2002, the president's chief economic advisor Lawrence
Lindsey estimated the price of the impending (but then still hypotheti-
cal) conflict at between $100 billion and $200 billion. The administration's budget director, Mitch Daniels, hastened to disagree, saying that
that Lindsey's figure was "likely very, very high."[180] It turned out, in the
end, to be very, very low.

As the costs mounted, the administration found ways to soften their
immediate impact on the American public and thereby, it hoped, reduce
their political impact. Funding came through "emergency" appropriations outside the regular budget process.[181] The administration broke
with a long precedent in American history in the way it chose to pay
for Iraq. In the past, American governments that had taken the country to war had borrowed to defray the increased expenditures involved
but had also raised taxes and reduced or postponed social spending.[182]
The Bush administration paid for all the additional spending the war
necessitated by borrowing, pushing the burden of repayment on to the
taxpayers of the future. As for raising taxes and reducing non-military
spending, it did neither: to the contrary, it actually cut taxes and
enacted a significant expansion of the Medicare program.[183] One clear
purpose of all this was to ensure that the vast majority of Americans
did not have to make any sacrifice at all for the sake of the goals the
country was pursuing in Iraq.

In World War II and during the Korean and Vietnam wars, sacrifice had been more widely shared not only because taxes rose but also
because part of the fighting force was recruited through conscription,
for which all males between 18 and 26 years of age were eligible. By
2003 the draft had been gone for three decades and no serious attempt
was made to resurrect it. The burden of deployment to the Middle East
fell entirely on the all-volunteer regular forces of the United States and
the country's reserves, who also served voluntarily.[184]

A saying has it that when the United States fights it is not just its armed forces but the whole country that goes to war. That was not true of Iraq. It was sometimes called the "one percent war" because its direct costs fell only on those who served and their families, who together comprised a tiny fraction of the American population.

Beyond the burden borne by the troops and their families, the war took a toll in what economists call "opportunity costs." Every dollar spent in Iraq represented a dollar not spent on other government programs or for private purposes by citizens who paid the dollars originally through their taxes.[185] The war involved an opportunity cost of another kind as well. The attacks of September 11 made the invasion of Iraq possible for George W. Bush by investing him with more authority than he would otherwise have had, as the country rallied around the president, as it does on such occasions. They provided him, that is, with a windfall of political capital that enabled him to mobilize a degree of public support for policies that under normal circumstances would not have commanded it.

Bush chose to spend his September 11 windfall on Iraq. In retrospect, investing it in changing American energy policy to reduce reliance on imported oil through a gasoline tax, or in reforming Social Security and Medicare, the country's "entitlement" programs, to make them easier to sustain over the long term, would have contributed more to the nation's security and general well-being than the war did.[186]

The economic cost of the Iraq war soared far beyond the Bush administration's initial projections. By one detailed estimate, the United States will ultimately pay upwards of $3 trillion for the conflict, a total that includes direct expenditures for troops, consultants, military equipment and reconstruction projects, as well as on pensions and benefits that will be paid out over decades, and other effects on the American economy.[187]

Large as that sum is, the amount that the country had to pay annually during wartime turned out to be smaller as a percentage of the national output than had been the case for Korea and Vietnam.[188] Nor did its economic impact cause the increasing unpopularity of the Iraq war after 2003. Americans turned against it for the same reason that they had turned against the wars in Korea and Vietnam: the rising toll it took in American lives.[189]

Following the pattern of the Korean and Vietnam Wars, as American casualties rose, the percentage of Americans who considered the war to have been a mistake increased and support for the conflict among the American public declined. For Iraq, as for Korea and Vietnam, Americans decided that the price of fighting to achieve the nation's goals, in the currency that mattered most—American lives—had become too high.§

Unlike in Korea and Vietnam, none of the Americans who died in Iraq had been compelled to be there. None had been drafted: all had volunteered for military service. That did not make the American public more tolerant of their deaths, however.[190] In fact, public sensitivity to casualties was higher for Iraq: it took fewer deaths than in Korea and Vietnam to make that war unpopular. Americans were presumably willing to tolerate fewer of them because the threat in Iraq seemed less urgent even after September 11 than it had during the Cold-War-era conflicts in Asia, when the Soviet Union stood behind North Korea and North Vietnam.[191]

The domestic politics of Iraq differed from the politics of Korea and Vietnam in another significant way. Public opinion divided sharply, from the beginning, along partisan lines. Republicans and Democrats tended to take opposing positions—Republicans for the war and Democrats against it—to a greater extent than in either of the two previous conflicts.[192] As in those wars, however, as more Americans were killed, more and more Democrats, Republicans, and Independents came to oppose American participation in the conflict and to disapprove of the performance of the president responsible for it.

Although it became a subject of controversy and figured in much of the criticism aimed at the Bush Iraq policy, the absence of weapons of

---

§ Americans supported all three wars, when and to the extent they did support them, as a way of protecting the United States. In none of the conflicts did the goal of protecting or establishing democracy carry as much weight with the public as self-defense. "Americans have never been very supportive of putting American troops in harm's way for purposes that are primarily humanitarian. As with the wars in Korea and Vietnam, they did buy the war in Iraq for a while because they saw it, like Afghanistan, as a response to 9/11—a direct attack on the United States." John Mueller, "Iraq Syndrome Redux," *Foreign Affairs*, June 18, 2014, www.foreignaffairs.com/articles/14/141578/john-mueller-iraq-syndrome-redux.

mass destruction did not drive the course of public approval of the war downward. Had chemical weapons been found but events otherwise proceeded as in fact they did, with the American death toll mounting, the administration would have lost support for the war. On the other hand, had the Iraq operation gone as the administration had initially believed it would—with a quick victory over Saddam, a grateful Iraqi people forming a stable, representative government, and most American troops leaving the country in the fall of 2003—but without any weapons of mass destruction being found, the president's approval rating would not have suffered appreciably, if at all.

The absence of the weapons the administration had touted as a reason for war did precipitate a political scandal in Washington that led to the trial and conviction of a Bush administration official. It began when Vice President Cheney asked the CIA to check a report that Iraqi representatives had tried to purchase uranium, the material from which nuclear explosives are made, from the African country of Niger. The CIA sent former Ambassador Joseph Wilson to Niger to investigate and he concluded that the report was unfounded. Later, with the war under way and no sign of weapons of mass destruction, Wilson published an op-ed column about his experience in *The New York Times* that implied what many already believed: that the administration had not been straightforward with the public about what it did and did not know about Saddam Hussein's armaments.[193]

The administration mounted a political campaign to discredit him, in the course of which it was disclosed that Wilson's wife, Valerie Plame, worked at the CIA. (It was suggested, wrongly, that he had been sent to Africa only because she had arranged the assignment for him.) Divulging the identity of an undercover CIA operative is illegal and a special prosecutor was appointed to look into the revelation. Ultimately the Vice President's Chief of Staff, I. Lewis Libby, was indicted, convicted, and sentenced to 30 months in prison. President Bush commuted the sentence but refused Cheney's entreaties to grant Libby a full pardon.

Libby's defenders charged that he was the victim of a political witch-hunt and that prosecuting him was an attempt to put the war on trial. They had a point. The proceeding against him made no sense. Cheney, it turned out, had never seen what Wilson told the CIA or indeed even heard of Wilson, whose report in any case did not prove conclusively that Iraq had never sought uranium in Niger. Moreover, when her name became public Valerie Plame was no longer working under cover at the CIA. Furthermore, Libby was not the first person to disclose her name to the press. That turned out to be Deputy Secretary of State Richard Armitage, who, far from being a cheerleader for the administration's Iraq policy, was well known to harbor doubts about it. Finally, Libby was tried and convicted not of having made the disclosure, which was the reason for focusing on him in the first place, but of having lied to the grand jury investigating it. He was convicted, that is, of an illegal act that was triggered by a controversy about an issue that was not a major cause of the war or the opposition to it, an act that occurred during the investigation of an entirely different act that turned out not itself to be illegal and that somebody other than Libby had in any case committed.[194]

The war did not put the president in legal jeopardy but, just as had happened with Harry Truman and Korea and Lyndon Johnson over Vietnam, it did cripple his presidency. Having triumphed at the polls in 2002 on the strength of the impending Iraq war and having himself escaped the worst electoral punishment—defeat—in 2004 for the course it had unexpectedly taken, his Republican party received its comeuppance in the midterm elections of 2006. While Bush himself was not on the ballot, his war was the major issue.[195] The Democrats, by now almost unanimously critical of the war, won a sweeping victory; they gained 31 seats in the House of Representatives and 6 in the Senate, giving them control of both. The election served as a referendum on the Iraq war, and the American public voted against it.

The next month, the Iraq Study Group, a Congressionally authorized, 10-member, bipartisan panel of prominent retired officials co-chaired by former Secretary of State James Baker and former Indiana Congressman Lee Hamilton,[196] which was charged with assessing overall American policy in Iraq, issued its report. "The situation in Iraq," it said, "is grave and deteriorating." It recommended that the American military switch from fighting the insurgency to training Iraqi troops to do this and that all American combat forces be withdrawn by the first quarter of 2008,[197] which was more or less the policy, although on an accelerated schedule, that the top military officials were trying to carry out. The report put the imprimatur of the American foreign policy establishment on the public's wish to liquidate, although not precipitously, the commitment that Bush had initiated in 2003.

Ultimately the United States did withdraw, leaving the government it had helped establish to administer and defend the country without American military support. This was the pattern it had followed in Vietnam, although not Korea. Before that happened, however, the Bush administration executed a sharp and, for a time, successful change of strategy in Iraq.

Exit and Reentry

At the beginning of 2007 the Bush administration's Iraq policy was failing.[198] The level of violence in the country, both against Americans and between Sunnis and Shias, was high and in some places rising.[199] The American public had made clear its lack of faith in and support for what the administration was doing in the country. In response, President Bush ordered a change of strategy, one that, for a time, markedly improved American fortunes there.

Instead of simply training as large an Iraqi army as possible as quickly as possible, with an eye toward leaving the country as soon as possible, the United States adopted a strategy of counterinsurgency. It defined the American task as winning a political struggle with the insurgents for the allegiance of the civilian population. It aimed to win that allegiance by offering the civilians protection from the insurgents, which required a larger, more visible, ongoing American military presence among them, and by helping to furnish governance superior to what the insurgents could provide. It was more ambitious than the counterterrorism operations of the Joint Special Operations Command, whose mission was to eliminate terrorist leaders.[200] It differed as well from what had been, at least since late 2003, the dominant train-and-leave approach. This had involved removing American troops from populated areas and staying out of the day-to-day lives of the Iraqi people as much as possible. Counterinsurgency reversed this pattern.

The impetus for changing American strategy came partly from outside the government, from civilian specialists on military affairs working mainly in think tanks, and from retired officers. The outsiders drew on a body of hard-earned but largely forgotten Western experience.[201] The United States had waged a counterinsurgency campaign in Vietnam in the 1960s, the British had fought a similar kind of war, with greater success, in Malaya in the 1950s, and the French had had to cope with insurgencies in both Asia and Africa in their ultimately unsuccessful twentieth-century efforts to preserve their colonial empire.[202]

The impetus for change came as well from within the army, where its leader was General David Petraeus. He had served two tours of duty in Iraq. He had commanded the 101st Airborne Division stationed in Mosul, in the Sunni heartland, where he had employed some of the techniques of counterinsurgency.[203] He had returned to supervise the American training program for the new Iraqi army. Back in the United States, he had overseen the writing of the new army field manual, waging a bureaucratic campaign to give counterinsurgency a prominent place in it.[204]

The president himself, who had deferred to his secretary of defense and the military commanders throughout the Iraq operation, was ready to make a change. The course that his advisors had recommended, that he had authorized, and that the United States had followed for more than three years was not working. The entire enterprise, it had become clear, which he had begun with such confidence and high expectations in 2003, was doomed to failure without a major shift of direction. George W. Bush's personality also contributed to his decision to change course. The same traits of character—called boldness when they produce desirable results, recklessness when they do not—that had caused him to invade Iraq without taking the likely consequences into serious account and despite well-founded warnings about those consequences, made him willing to confound prevailing opinion on American policy there—expressed in the 2006 elections and embodied in the report of the Iraq Study Group—which wanted as quick a divorce from Iraq as was feasible.[205] Instead, Bush ordered an increase in the American troop presence in the country.

As part of the change of strategy the officials responsible for managing the war changed as well. Donald Rumsfeld resigned in the wake of the Republican defeat in the 2006 elections, and Bush replaced him with Robert Gates, who had served in his father's administration as deputy national security advisor and CIA director.[206] He also made

David Petraeus the commander of American forces in Iraq, with a mandate to implement a policy of counterinsurgency.

In 2007 the United States dispatched an additional five brigades— 20,000 troops—to Iraq. Some went to Baghdad; others were assigned to the area north of the city.[207] Following counterinsurgency principles, they established their bases in populated areas and began regular patrolling to demonstrate their commitment to protect people against the insurgents. They also worked with Special Operations forces to find, target, and eliminate the leadership of the insurgency.[208]

At the same time, Sunni tribesmen in western Iraq began to cooperate with the American forces stationed there. Revulsed by the predatory behavior of al Qaeda, many of whose cadres came from outside the country, dismayed and made increasingly insecure by the growth of Shia power in Iraq, and no doubt favorably impressed by the enhanced commitment of the United States to fight the insurgency, they turned to the Americans to help them protect their own villages and towns. The American effort to build modern, impersonal, rule-governed institutions in Iraq ran afoul of the country's tribal social structure. In this instance, by contrast, the tribal form of social organization proved to be an asset for the United States.[209]

In the past, proposals to American military leaders of ways to work with the Sunnis had encountered indifference, at best.[210] Local American commanders, however, came to ad hoc arrangements with them and Petraeus, when he assumed his position, accepted and encouraged this practice.[211] The Americans began paying the tribesmen, supplying them with light arms, and engaging in joint operations with them against their common al Qaeda enemy. The American armed forces had fought their fiercest battles in Iraq against Sunnis in the western part of the country; but in 2007 some of the former adversaries switched sides and became de facto American allies. The cooperation became widespread enough for the Americans to give it a name, taken from the Iraqi province where it began: the Anbar Awakening.[212]

The increase in troop strength and the new strategy the troops carried out also received a distinctive title—"the surge"—and the surge achieved its principal goal: the violence in the capital and the western part of the country dropped sharply.[213] The American undertaking in Iraq seemed to have turned a corner. With an elected government in place and what had been the most turbulent parts of the country more peaceful, the mission seemed closer to being accomplished than at any time since the 2003 capture of Baghdad.

In March 2008 another military operation in which American troops took part reinforced the favorable trend in the governance of Iraq that the surge had initiated. Shia militias loyal to Moqtada al-Sadr had come to dominate Basra, the largest city in the southern part of the country.[214] Prime Minister Maliki, also a Shia, decided to assert the government's authority there. He ordered the Iraqi army, which the Americans had built but that answered to him, to seize the city and flew to Basra to oversee the battle. The ensuing fighting went badly for the government forces and American troops had to come to their rescue. In the end, however, the Sadrists retreated,[215] and not only in Basra but in Baghdad as well, where they had also established a strong position in the eastern district known as Sadr City. Here, too, American troops played a key role.[216] For the first time since the fall of Saddam an Iraqi government—this one duly elected—appeared to exercise more or less effective control over the entire country.

Against this background of long-hoped-for political and military progress in Iraq, the 2008 American presidential election took place. Barack Obama, who had captured the Democratic nomination in no small part because he had opposed the Iraq war earlier and more ardently than his rivals, became the nation's 44th president. Yet, unlike the 2006 election, the war did not dominate this campaign, for three reasons.

First, a major crisis intervened. The failure of the large investment bank Lehman Brothers on September 15, 2008, brought the American financial system to the brink of collapse and plunged the country into a deep recession, events that preoccupied voters and pushed Iraq to the margins of their concerns. Second, Americans had arrived at a consensus of sorts about the war. They generally agreed that it was going better for the United States as a result of the surge but also still largely believed that the country had been mistaken to undertake it.[217]

Third, President Bush had neutralized what could have been a point of contention between Obama and his Republican opponent (and longtime supporter of the Iraq war) Senator John McCain of Arizona. While in the Senate Obama had called for a definite date for the withdrawal of

American military forces from Iraq.[218] The administration had opposed this. In 2008, however, the United Nations resolution (passed after the American invasion) that gave legal cover to the American military presence in the country was due to expire. The United States had to negotiate a new agreement with Prime Minister Maliki, who insisted on setting a date for withdrawal: despite having delivered power to them, the American presence had become unpopular with his Shia constituents. With little leverage at his disposal, Bush agreed, thereby reversing his own previous position and adopting Obama's. The two sides haggled over the precise date, with the Americans wanting to stay longer than the Iraqi government preferred. Eventually they agreed that American troops would vacate Iraq's cities by the end of June 2009 and leave Iraq altogether by the end of 2011.[219]

When the Obama administration took office, the American course in Iraq had been set; the timetable for leaving was in place. The new administration made an effort to negotiate an extension but was unable to conclude a Status of Forces Agreement with the Iraqi government giving American troops immunity from Iraqi law.** So it followed the Bush schedule, and by the beginning of 2012, more than eight years after American troops had first crossed the border with Kuwait, none remained in Iraq.

** "The collapsed talks had been a casualty of rising Iraqi nationalism, backroom machinations by Iraqi politicians, and a deep ambivalence about continued American military involvement in Iraq on the part of President Obama and his inner circle as they approached the election season at home." Michael Gordon and Bernard E. Trainor, *The Endgame: The Inside Story of the Struggle for Iraq from George W. Bush to Barack Obama*, New York: Pantheon, 2012, p. 3. See also pp. 665 and 670. "'We really didn't want to be there and he really didn't want us here,' said a former senior White House official. 'It's not like Maliki went out of his way to get a deal. It was almost a mutual decision, not said directly to each other, but in reality that's what it became. And you had a president who was going to be running for re-election, and getting out of Iraq was going to be a big statement.'" Peter Baker, "Relief Over U.S. Exit From Iraq Fades as Reality Overtakes Hope," *The New York Times*, June 23, 2014, p. A8. "Mr. Maliki was under pressure from the most powerful Shia leaders underpinning his government, as well as from his allies in Iran, to hurry the Americans out. According to an opinion poll at the time, only 16% of Iraqis wanted the Americans to stay on." "Why Iraq's army crumbled," *The Economist*, June 21, 2014, p. 47.

In the end, the United States did carry out the policy to which the American political authorities and military leadership had committed the country late in 2003, after the rosy vision of post-Saddam Iraq with which the Bush administration had gone to war had been decisively discredited, that the Baker-Hamilton Commission had recommended, and—most important of all—for which the American public had in effect voted in 2006. The Obama administration was able to carry it out, however, more smoothly and with a stronger sense of national accomplishment because of the success of the surge than would have been the case without it.[220]

In 2010 Iraq held, on schedule, its third general election. A party headed by Ayad Allawi, the first, appointed, prime minister, which had a secular rather than a religious orientation and, although led by a Shia, had strong Sunni support, won the highest number of votes. Had Allawi been able to form a government, it would have represented a major step toward the establishment of the kind of multisectarian, pro-Western regime that the Bush administration had—naively—believed would follow Baathist rule. Incumbent Prime Minister Nouri al-Maliki's Shia party finished a close second, however, and it and the other Shia religious parties refused to allow Allawi to take office. A prolonged stalemate followed, lasting 249 days. The United States tried to broker a compromise but finally weighed in on Maliki's side and he became prime minister again.[221] Like its predecessor, the Obama administration decided to bet on Maliki as the best feasible hope for the kind of Iraq that Americans had sacrificed blood and treasure to achieve. It proved to be a bad bet.

The architects of the surge were always clear that more American troops and different American tactics could not, by themselves, bring stability to Iraq. The insurgency these measures were designed to quell had its roots in politics, and to put an end to it required effective, responsible, widely accepted governance in order to assuage the grievances that had sent Sunnis and Shias into rebellion. The surge bought time and created political space for the Maliki regime to supply the kind of governance that was needed, the kind that would reconcile Iraq's three constituent communities to living together in a single state.[222]

It failed to do so. Instead of governing in an inclusive manner the prime minister created a narrowly based, intolerant, corrupt regime that favored his family, his political party, and the Shia population. His relatives and cronies used the control of the state institutions he gave them to enrich themselves[223] and to exclude and persecute the Sunnis of Iraq. For Maliki, the Sunnis remained a threat, to be contained and reduced in power in every way possible.[224] He had promised that the Sunni tribesmen whom the Americans had recruited in the Anbar Awakening would receive support from the Iraqi government, but he broke that promise.[225] He arrested, or tried to arrest, leading Sunni politicians.[226]

He himself amassed wide powers. Fortified with revenues from the sale of Iraq's oil, which accounted for almost all the country's income,[227] he established the kind of regime that governed almost everywhere in the Middle East, with power concentrated in the hands of one person, one family, and one sect. Especially after the Americans left, he turned into a somewhat less brutal Shia version of Saddam Hussein.[228] He might have succeeded in sustaining this kind of rule as long as Saddam had but for a development outside Iraq's borders that unseated him and drew the United States, reluctantly, back into a military role in the country.

What intervened to dislodge Maliki was a civil war in neighboring Syria, itself part of a larger revolt against autocratic regimes across the Middle East that began in Tunisia in late 2010 and came to be known as the Arab Spring.[229] The majority Sunnis in Syria rose up—at first peacefully—against the regime of Bashar al-Assad, a member of the Alawi sect that is an offshoot of Shia Islam and whose members make up a mere 12 percent of the country's population. Assad repressed the uprising brutally and a countrywide conflict ensued in which fundamentalist Islamic groups became prominent. One in particular, with its roots in al Qaeda in Iraq, captured Sunni-majority territory in Syria and extended its reach across the border into Iraq. There it received support from Sunnis alienated from Maliki's Shia-dominated government[230] and seized much of western part of the country, including, in January 2014, the city of Fallujah where American forces had fought their bloodiest battles of the war, and in June of that year, to the world's astonishment, Iraq's second biggest city, Mosul.

The Shia-dominated and American-trained Iraqi army charged with defending the city, although larger and equipped with far more powerful weapons, barely put up a fight. Its officers abandoned their troops, and the troops themselves either surrendered or fled south. Having swept across western Iraq, the Islamists threatened Baghdad and the Shia heartland.[231] The Iraqi government, which had earlier insisted that the American military vacate its territory entirely, asked the United States for assistance. The Obama administration made it clear that it would not assist a government headed by Nouri al-Maliki, whom it blamed for the sectarian policies that had allowed the Islamic fundamentalists to flourish. Maliki's Dawa party had won the 2014 parliamentary elections, but he was eased out of office and another figure from that party chosen to serve as prime minister.

The fundamentalist jihadis proclaimed the territory they held to be the Islamic State in Iraq and Syria (ISIS) and began to enforce, where they held sway, a very harsh form of what they defined as religious orthodoxy, in the manner of the Taliban in Afghanistan. ISIS captured the attention of the world by beheading captured westerners, filming the grisly acts, and posting the videos on the Internet.

In the summer of 2014, ISIS forces threatened both to eradicate the Yazidis, a small group in northwestern Iraq practicing an ancient religion related to Zoroastrianism, whom they had besieged, and to overrrun the main Kurdish city of Erbil. In response, the United States conducted a bombing campaign that checked the ISIS advance and rescued the Yazidis. In September of that year President Obama announced a larger military campaign, also to be confined initially to air power, to degrade and ultimately destroy ISIS. History is filled with ironies—the contrast between what is expected and intended and what happens—and these events, in the context of the eight long and frustrating years of American military engagement in Iraq, between 2003 and 2011, presented three of them.

The first was that Barack Obama, who had managed to become president in 2008 because of his opposition to the American war in Iraq and who had won reelection in 2012 on the strength of the fact that he had ended that war, found himself, contrary to his expectations and seemingly with mixed feelings, ordering American servicemen into combat in Iraq once again.

The second irony was that the American policies that the attacks on New York and Washington, DC, of September 11, 2001, had set in motion, which were all designed to reduce the power and reach of the group responsible for the attacks and those with similar aims, had, entirely unintentionally, made such forces even more powerful. ISIS had many more fighters than its ancestor, al Qaeda, had ever deployed and unlike al Qaeda it exercised effective control over a large swath of territory that had greater economic value and strategic importance than Osama bin Laden's Afghan refuge. ISIS could never have come into possession of the parts of Iraq and Syria it controlled, indeed it might well not have come into existence at all, if the United States had not deposed the Baathist government of Iraq and installed a Shia-dominated government in Baghdad.

The final irony that emerged from the events of 2014 is that while the American intervention of that year helped to preserve the one great success that the United States could claim for its long and costly involvement in Iraq, this was a success about which the American government displayed ambivalent feelings and to which its most intensive efforts in Iraq, between 2003 and 2011, contributed relatively little.

Unlike the rest of the country, the Kurdish region in the northeast, which enjoyed autonomy after 2003 both by virtue of provisions in the post-Saddam constitution (on which the Kurds had insisted)[232] and their own effective fighting force, known as the Pesh Merga, became what the United States tried but failed to build in Iraq as a whole. It was peaceful, relatively prosperous,[233] and partly democratic although dominated politically by two families and not without corruption.[234] Unlike the Sunnis and Shias, moreover, the Kurds were well disposed toward the Americans. In Kurdistan, the kind of nation-building that the United States had attempted, without success, throughout the country and, over two decades, in other places around the world, actually took place. In this corner of the Middle East the American mission succeeded.

The United States, however, had a limited, although not negligible, role in this success. The no-fly zone the American Air Force established over their territory in the wake of the 1991 war made it possible for the Kurds to conduct their own efforts at nation-building without interference from Baghdad, and the removal of Saddam 12 years later further strengthened their autonomy. But they did the rest themselves, with little in the way of American money, American weaponry, or official American advice.[235]

Had the United States maintained the no-fly zone but never invaded Iraq, the Kurdish region might well have developed more or less as it did after 2003. That development, however, which came closer to fulfilling the American vision of nation-building than what happened in any of the places where the United States made far more intrusive and expensive efforts, evoked ambivalence among America's political leaders. On the one hand, they appreciated what the Kurds had accomplished and appreciated even more the fact that the Kurdish homeland remained peaceful while much of the rest of the country was wracked with violence and thus required the presence of foreign troops. On the other hand, the American government actively opposed the goal to which the Kurds aspired and for the purpose of which they were building their state: sovereign independence. Confronted with the opportunity to assist in the emergence of what the Bush administration had made it the highest priority of its foreign policy to create—a democracy in the middle of the Arab world—the United States declined.[236]

Kurdistan aside, the United States did not achieve any of its goals in Iraq. It did not create a free-market democracy. It did not foster a government friendly to the United States or committed to Western-style governance or even able, in the end, to defend all of its territory. It did not leave in place a regime willing or able to take the steps necessary to reconcile Sunnis, Shias, and Kurds to living peacefully and voluntarily in the same state. Having stayed in the country after deposing Saddam Hussein to build a new, better Iraq, the United States could not be sure, three years after it had finally left, that there would, in the future, be any Iraq at all.

Could the American project have achieved greater success? The answer depends on whether the failure is thought to have come from American mistakes or the intractability of the country itself. Especially at the beginning of the occupation, the American government adopted policies that seemed to many to have been mistaken and ultimately counterproductive. Yet even with a more adept performance by the United States, the social and political material Iraq offered was considerably less than ideal for the kind of state- and nation-building on which the Americans embarked.

Iraq lacked the traditions, the historical experience, the political values and the social structures that elsewhere in the world form the basis for the Western institutions that the United States hoped to implant in the country the British had assembled after World War I. In 2006, Steven Hadley, the national security advisor in Bush's second term, returned from a trip to Baghdad and wrote a memo for the president that asked, "Do we and Prime Minister Maliki share the same vision for Iraq?"[237] It turned out that they did not, and even if they had, given the country's history, political culture, and social composition, implementing the American vision would have proven formidably difficult.

America's failure stemmed ultimately not from what the Americans did or did not do in Iraq but from who and what the Iraqis were.[238] The eminent scholar of the contemporary Middle East Fouad Ajami called the American enterprise there "a struggle between American will and the laws of gravity in the region."[239] The laws of gravity prevailed in Iraq, and they prevailed as well in other parts of the Middle East where the United States also undertook post-Cold War missions that failed.

5

The Middle East

The basic problem is that the Arabs have not recognized the basic right of
the Jewish people to a homeland.

— ARIEL SHARON[1]

. . . the United States has adopted a new policy, a forward strategy of freedom in the Middle East.

— GEORGE W. BUSH[2]

The Center of the World

In a 2008 survey that asked professors of international relations which
area of the world they considered to be of greatest importance to the
United States, 46 percent chose the Middle East, a higher total than
for any other region.[3] During the Cold War, the responses would have
been different. In that era Europe, where the largest American army
was deployed to deter a Soviet attack westward, and East Asia, where
the United States fought two protracted and costly wars in Korea and
Indochina, would have earned pride of place. With the conclusion of
the conflict with global communism, however, the threats to American
security in Europe and Asia disappeared—or at least seemed to do so.
Those two regions still had major economic significance but had ceased
to be the sites of major political or military challenges. The Middle
East, by contrast, continued to present both. Europe and Asia were,
or at least appeared to have become, peaceful. The Middle East had
not, and so claimed a great deal of American diplomatic and military
attention.

American policy in the region centered on Iraq but extended much farther. Senior officials of the Clinton, George W. Bush, and Obama administrations devoted innumerable hours to trying to resolve the conflict, between Israel and the Arabs, which long predated the post-Cold War period. Faced with the political dysfunctions of the region, which were rampant in, but hardly confined to, Iraq, President Bush launched an ambitious project to cure them by bringing democracy to the Middle East. And in the second decade of the new millennium popular uprisings erupted against long-ruling authoritarian governments there, some of them long-time friends of the United States. The Obama administration had to devise a policy—or set of policies—toward what became known as the Arab Spring.

As with its initial approaches to China and Russia in the 1990s, its interventions during that decade in Somalia, Haiti, Bosnia, and Kosovo, and its wars of the next decade in Afghanistan and Iraq, so in the Arab-Israeli conflict, with its democracy agenda, and through its responses to the Arab Spring, the United States sought to vindicate and to spread its own political values. In the broader Middle East, as elsewhere, America undertook the mission of fostering reconciliation, prosperity, and democracy. In the Middle East, as elsewhere, the mission failed.

It failed in a region that, before the twentieth century, had been dominated by three great empires one after the other: the Arab, the Persian, and that of the Ottoman Turks. The Ottoman Empire collapsed in defeat in World War I, and two of the victorious powers, Great Britain and France, became the arbiters of the Middle East. Together they drew the borders of the successor states to the Ottoman Empire, which were still in place (in some cases only nominally) in the second decade of the twenty-first century. The British gave the region its most widely used name: they called it the Middle East (or the Near East) to distinguish it from the countries of the western Pacific, such as China and Japan, which were more distant from the British Isles and so came to be known collectively as the Far East.

The British and the French governed parts of the Middle East, directly and indirectly, for several decades,[4] and the inhabitants of the region fell into the habit of blaming the legacy of Western rule for their many political and economic troubles. In truth, the period of

European governance was too brief to have a profound effect on Middle Eastern societies. Indeed, for the purposes of adapting to the pressures and opportunities of the modern era—the region's persistent unmet challenges—the Arabs of the Levant, Mesopotamia, the Persian Gulf, and the Arabian peninsula might have been better served by a longer and more intrusive European presence.

After World War II, British and French influence faded and the United States took their place as the leading outside power. Americans had long had cultural connections and sentimental attachments to the Middle East[5]—above all as the birthplace of Christianity—but until then had played a negligible role in the region's political affairs. That changed with the onset of the Cold War.

The conflict with the Soviet Union and the other communist countries became global in scope, drawing the United States into every part of the world including the Middle East. There American policy sought to check the advance of Soviet political influence and to protect the flow of oil from the region to America's allies in Western Europe and East Asia.

Oil played a crucial role in Middle Eastern affairs after 1945. The region had the largest readily accessible reserves on the planet—by some estimates as much as two-thirds of them—which the industrial democracies could not do without. The West, and its leading power, the United States, therefore developed a major interest in the Middle East. At the same time, the distribution of oil within the region did a great deal to determine the balance of power, influence, and ambition among its various countries. At one time or another oil gave Saudi Arabia, Iraq, and Iran a large measure of all three.

The initial oil-determined American policy in the Middle East dates from before the end of World War II. In 1943 President Franklin D. Roosevelt declared the defense of Saudi Arabia, the country with the largest proven reserves of petroleum, to be a vital American interest.[6] On February 14, 1945, while returning from a summit meeting with the leaders of America's two main wartime allies, Joseph Stalin of the Soviet Union and Winston Churchill of Great Britain, which had taken place at Yalta, a Soviet city on the Black Sea, Roosevelt met the king of Saudi Arabia on an American ship in the Great Bitter Lake near the Suez Canal. Thus began the alliance between the two countries—really the American protectorate of the Saudi regime—whose consequences included, among other things, the American war to evict Saddam Hussein's troops from Kuwait in 1991.

In defense of its interests in the Middle East during the Cold War, the United States sought to check radical regimes and movements that seemed susceptible to Soviet influence and that threatened America's friends. In the 1950s and 1960s that meant opposing Egypt's leader Gamal Abdel Nasser and his ambition to dominate the region under the banner of the ideology of pan-Arabism.[7] After 1979 the United States opposed the aggressive, fundamentalist, Islamic Republic of Iran, whose clerical leaders had seized power in that year. In the last decade of the twentieth century and the first decade of the twenty-first, the pursuit of American interests in the region, as the administrations of the time defined it, led to the two wars against Iraq.

In the Middle East the United States engaged in a version of the policy of containment that it carried out in Europe and Asia, bringing to bear military power and political influence for the purpose of protecting its allies and preventing military or political gains by hostile forces. After 1991, when the ranks of the unfriendly included both Iraq and Iran (which had recently concluded a decade-long war against each other), the United States practiced "dual containment," aimed at both of them.[8]

American Cold-War Middle East policy also resembled an older tradition, one associated with the British approach to the politics of the European continent. For centuries the British acted as the "offshore balancer," deploying their diplomatic and financial strength to keep any single power from dominating the continent and threatening the British Isles and the British Empire. Like this venerable British policy toward Europe and unlike the American policy of containment in Europe after 1945, the United States did not usually station its own troops in the Middle East during the Cold War.[9] The American government sold armaments and, like the British with Europe, provided economic support to its Middle Eastern allies.[10] Like Britain's offshore balancing over the centuries, which was guided by the precept that the nation had no permanent friends and no permanent enemies, only permanent interests, but unlike containment of the Soviet Union in Europe during the Cold War, America's portfolio of Middle Eastern allies and adversaries changed over time. Between the 1960s and the end of the Cold War, Egypt, Iraq, and Iran were alternately allies and adversaries of the United States.

On one point, American Cold-War policy in the region remained consistent. It did not seek to effect the internal transformation of the countries there. In fact, their domestic political systems had almost nothing to do with American policies toward these countries.[11] Whereas in Western Europe almost all of America's allies were democracies, so that in defending them the United States was also defending its own political values, in the Middle East, with the exception of Israel, none of the countries that received American protection was governed in anything like a democratic fashion. Instead, the autocracies that the United States befriended and sheltered qualified as "friendly tyrants,"[12] regimes with which the United States had interests but not political values in common. During the Cold War the United States aligned itself with anticommunist but undemocratic regimes in Asia, Latin America, and Europe[13] as well as in the Middle East, where all of its friends except Israel practiced tyranny at home.

The end of the Cold War did not do away with the Western world's need for Middle Eastern oil. Nor did the collapse of communism in Europe eliminate the radical threats to America's friends and America's interests in the region, which persisted because they did not draw their inspiration from the ideology of Marxism-Leninism or depend entirely for their military strength on the now-vanished Soviet Union. In the first decade of the post-Cold War era—until changed by the attacks of September 11—American policy in the Middle East continued much as it had before the fall of the Berlin Wall and the disappearance of the West's great communist antagonist.

One policy in particular proceeded more or less unaffected by the seismic, late-twentieth-century political events in Europe. The United States continued to devote diplomatic capital and an even more valuable resource—the time of its senior officials—to the effort to bring about a settlement to the ongoing conflict between Israel and the Arabs. That effort dated back to the 1970s. Like other American missions of the post-Cold War era, this one, too, failed. It failed in part because the American foreign policy establishment, which was responsible for it, did not recognize it as a mission. The Americans did not recognize that, as with China, Russia, the humanitarian interventions of the 1990s, and the wars in Afghanistan and Iraq, success in what was called the Middle East peace process depended on the internal transformation of one of the parties.

The Peace Process

In December 1991, in the Spanish capital city of Madrid, the United States convened a conference designed to foster peace between Israel and the Arabs. The conference brought together, in one hall, the governments of all the Arab states, most of which had refused to meet publicly with their Israeli counterparts. Also taking part were representatives, as part of the Jordanian delegation, of the Palestine Liberation Organization (PLO), with which Israel had declined to meet openly. The Madrid conference came on the heels of the first Gulf War and the American government considered it the logical sequel to that conflict.[14] The decision to invest the prestige and political capital the United States had earned through its most convincing military victory since World War II in the effort to resolve what was only one among several Middle East conflicts, one that was less destructive than others and presented no immediate threat to American interests there or elsewhere, testifies to the enormous importance the United States attached to it. From the first half of the 1970s to the first half of the second decade of the twenty-first century no international issue received greater sustained high-level American attention. The administrations of Richard Nixon, Gerald Ford, Jimmy Carter, Ronald Reagan, George H. W. Bush, Bill Clinton, George W. Bush, and Barack Obama all made the Arab-Israeli peace process a high priority.

It did achieve one major success: a peace treaty between Israel and its largest neighbor, Egypt, at the end of the 1970s. By eliminating the possibility of another major war between the two countries—in the quarter century between 1948 and 1973 they had waged four—that treaty made the region safer for each of them and for the interests of the United States. The more or less continuous negotiations thereafter, however, produced few tangible results. Indeed, the negotiations often coincided with, and in some cases actually caused, increases in Middle Eastern violence.

Like the failure to establish democracy in Iraq even with American troops occupying the country, the failure to resolve the Arab-Israeli conflict had its roots in the political culture—the values, traditions, and beliefs—of the Arab people. American sponsorship and direction of the effort to end the conflict generally proceeded, however, without regard to its fundamental cause. The conduct of the peace process resembled the medieval custom of treating a variety of diseases by placing leeches on the body of the affected person: it was based on an inadequate understanding of the pathology it was attempting to cure, it did not solve the problem it was intended to fix, and it sometimes made the problem worse.

The Arab parties to the conflict—the Baathist government of Syria and the PLO—whom successive presidents and secretaries of state tried to reconcile with Israel, repeatedly declared their interest in peace. They invariably refused, however, to take the steps that would have made peace possible, even—indeed, especially—when Israel offered concessions for this purpose. The American government invariably believed, or behaved as if it believed, that the Syrians and the Palestinians meant what they said, despite steadily accumulating evidence to the contrary. This evidence included not only what they did and refused to do but also the decidedly non-peaceful things they said, in Arabic, to the Arab publics. For this reason, the peace process qualifies as, to modify a line from the title and refrain of a song in the 1950 Broadway musical "Guys and Dolls," the oldest established permanent floating con game in the world.[15]

The conflict that the United States tried vainly to end began with the emergence, in the nineteenth century, of the modern Jewish national movement known as Zionism. The combination of four powerful, deeply rooted forces created Zionism: the Jewish sense of nationhood, which goes back to ancient times—the Jewish religion consists very largely of customs and rituals the citizens of the original Jewish state retained in exile; the powerful, age-old Jewish connection to the site of that state, centered on Jerusalem, where Jews had lived continuously, often as the majority of the population, since antiquity; the universal rise, in the wake of the French Revolution, of the desire of distinct national groups for their own state, making nationalism the most potent political force in the modern world; and the persecution of Jews in the nineteenth and twentieth centuries, most gruesomely in Europe but also in Arab countries, where substantial Jewish populations regularly suffered discrimination and worse.

From the beginning, Arab Muslims (and some Arab Christians) opposed Zionism. The fundamental cause of the Arab-Israeli conflict, through all its many phases spanning a hundred years and more, was the adamant Arab refusal to accept Jewish sovereignty in the Middle East. The refusal led to Arab violence, first against the Jewish community in Palestine, which Britain governed after World War I under a mandate from the League of Nations and then, after its establishment in May 1948 with the end of the mandate, against the Jewish state of Israel.

The refusal had religious roots. Muslims considered the territory of Israel to be an Islamic domain on which Jews, because they were not Muslims, had no sovereign rights.[16] The Arabs experienced the establishment of Israel as a particular humiliation, because it was the work not of the Western Christian world, which had surpassed them in power and wealth for the better part of two centuries, but rather of a people whom they had always known as a weak and despised minority. The tribal structure of Arab society, with its emphasis on group solidarity against outsiders, reinforced this refusal.[17] Since many Sunni Muslim Arabs did not believe that Shia Muslim Arabs were entitled to a political status equal to theirs, it is not surprising that they sought, as well, to deny this status to Jews, who were, after all, not even Muslims. Moreover, after Israel demonstrated that it could not be crushed militarily, Arab governments found it convenient to maintain their hostility to the Jewish state as a way of deflecting the attention, and anger, of those they governed from their own considerable shortcomings: their arbitrary and often brutal rule, their corruption, and the economic stagnation over which they presided. The Jews of the Middle East, after 1948 gathered into their own state, played, involuntarily, the same role that the Jews of Europe had for centuries: a scapegoat wrongly blamed for the failings of others. The conflict served the purposes of the Arab regimes in a way that peace could never do; and even when this was not so, none of the Arab leaders felt he could afford to appear less committed to anti-Zionism than his counterparts at the head of other Arab countries.

In November 1947, the United Nations voted to divide the British Mandate for Palestine into a Jewish and an Arab-Palestinian state and in May 1948, upon the expiration of the Mandate, the Jewish Agency for Palestine proclaimed the establishment of a Jewish state on part of its territory. This triggered an attack on the new state, Israel, by four Arab armies [18] that were confident of easily conquering it and parceling out its territory among themselves. As would happen regularly for the next seven decades, however, they miscalculated. Israel defeated the invaders and the war ended in 1949 with the Jewish state in possession of more territory than the UN partition resolution had assigned to it.

In 1956 came the second Arab-Israeli war. In response to regular, low-level attacks by its neighbors, Israel joined with France and Great Britain in a campaign against its chief tormenter, Egypt. The Israeli army took over the Egyptian-controlled Sinai peninsula to its south, while the British and French used the Israeli initiative as a pretext to seize the Suez Canal.[19]

War broke out again in 1967.[20] Nasser evicted the peacekeepers the UN had deployed in the Sinai in the wake of the 1956 conflict, massed troops on the border with Israel, and closed the Straits of Tiran, Israel's outlet to the Red Sea. The closure imposed a blockade that qualified, under international law, as an act of war. Israel responded with military operations in three directions that produced a sweeping victory in only six days. That victory left Israel in possession, once again, of the Sinai peninsula and of the Egyptian-occupied Gaza Strip to its south; of the territory between the 1967 ceasefire lines and the Jordan River to the west that the Kingdom of Jordan had controlled, territory the Israelis called by the Biblical names of Judea and Samaria and that much of the rest of the world knew as the West Bank; and of a plateau to its north overlooking northern Israel that Syria had governed, which was known as the Golan Heights.

The United States played a role, but not a central one, in each of the first three Arab-Israeli wars. In 1948 the American government became the first to accord official diplomatic recognition to the new Jewish state,[21] but it steered clear of the war the Arabs started. In 1956 the Eisenhower administration, fearing that the British, French, and Israeli attacks on Egypt would pave the way for Soviet political gains in the Middle East, forced the return of the Suez Canal and the Sinai peninsula to the Egyptian government. Having promised Israel at that time to help keep the Straits of Tiran open, the United States launched a diplomatic initiative for this purpose when Nasser closed them in 1967. When the initiative failed, Israel acted alone.[22]

In 1973 another war opened a new chapter in the American involvement in the Middle East. On October 6 of that year, on Yom Kippur, the holiest day on the Jewish calendar, Egypt and Syria launched surprise attacks on Israel. Initially both made headway. After a week of fighting Israel was running low on ammunition and weaponry and the United States rushed military supplies to it through a large-scale airlift. By the end of another week, the Israeli army and air force had gained the upper hand, driving the attacking armies back beyond the positions they had held at the start of the war and surrounding Egypt's Third Army.

At the war's end, evidently alarmed by Egypt's precarious military position, the Soviet leader, Leonid Brezhnev, sent a note to President Richard Nixon, which the American government interpreted as a threat that the Soviet Union would send troops to rescue the Egyptians. The United States, itself now alarmed by the prospect of Soviet forces on the ground in the Middle East, put its own military forces on worldwide alert to deter Moscow. In the wake of the war, moreover, the Arab oil-exporting countries, in an attempt to punish the United States (and the Netherlands) for supporting Israel, reduced their production of oil. As a result, in what became known as the first oil shock of the decade (the Iranian revolution of 1979 and the drop in that country's oil production caused the second), the global price of oil rose substantially. The United States experienced a temporary shortage of gasoline, leading to long lines at the country's service stations.

The guns fell silent on October 25 with the Israeli and Egyptian armies positioned in ways that had the potential to trigger more fighting. The American Secretary of State Henry Kissinger traveled to the region to try to disentangle them, as well as to give the Arab oil producers reason to increase their output. He succeeded in negotiating a disengagement agreement between the two sides. Based on his success, and with the encouragement of the warring parties themselves, he spent extended periods in the region traveling back and forth—"shuttling"—among the capitals of the belligerent countries. He managed to broker five additional agreements between Israel and Egypt and one between Israel and Syria.[23] A new American role in the Middle East was born: mediator between Israel and the Arabs.

That role continued in the administration of President Jimmy Carter, which brought the Egyptian president Anwar Sadat and the Israeli Prime Minister Menachem Begin together for direct negotiations in September 1978 at Camp David, a meeting triggered by a dramatic and unprecedented visit by Sadat to Jerusalem to address the Israeli parliament.[24] The Camp David meeting gave an impetus to negotiations between the two countries that led eventually to a peace treaty in 1979.[25] Having been a Soviet client, Egypt realigned itself with the United States. In return it began to receive a generous annual American subvention, most of which went to the army. In this way American taxpayers underwrote the peace between Israel and Egypt.[26]

Kissinger's "shuttle diplomacy" and the efforts of the Carter administration to secure a settlement between Israel and Egypt established a pattern that would continue for decades. It became known as the peace process. Underlying it was the assumption that the second part of the term would lead to the first: the process of American-sponsored negotiations between Arabs and Israelis would increase trust between them, identify or create areas of agreement and common interest, and yield, at the end, peaceful relations. The American foreign policy establishment, in both major political parties in every administration from Nixon's to Obama's, became deeply—sometimes obsessively—committed to the peace process.

The Americans found it irresistible because it put them in the position of mediator, using America's power and good offices to bring about the most precious of all international conditions: peace. The United States had a pre-Cold War history of mediation, dating back to 1905 when President Theodore Roosevelt presided over a negotiated end to the Russo-Japanese War of 1905 at a conference in Portsmouth, New Hampshire. For that he received the Nobel Peace Prize, the hope for which was not entirely absent from the minds of the American officials involved in the perpetual pursuit of Middle East peace.

The wider American public had a lesser stake in the peace process than did the foreign policy community but certainly did not oppose it. It cost the United States very little and entailed no obvious risk to vital American interests. In addition to the psychological satisfaction that those directly engaged in it derived from doing, as they saw it, important and entirely beneficial work, the peace process sometimes brought a strategic benefit to the United States. It made easier the diplomatic task of maintaining good relations with Arab governments while at the same time sustaining close ties with Israel. It gave the Arabs, who declared Israel to be an abomination, political cover for proper and often cordial dealings with Israel's greatest friend. The American government could tell the Arab rulers, and those rulers could tell their often fervently anti-Zionist publics, that the United States was, after all, working hard at addressing at least some of the Arabs' grievances.[27]

The American peace processors did not regard their project as only, or even mainly, a protective shield for their country's diplomacy in the Middle East, however. They undertook it for its own sake. Their commitment rested on three premises. While each of them had been true of the Israeli-Egyptian negotiations of the 1970s, none turned out to be valid for the peace process thereafter. They nonetheless congealed into an orthodoxy that the American foreign policy elite embraced.

These Americans believed, first, that protecting the interests of the United States urgently required a comprehensive Arab-Israeli settlement. The 1973 war and its aftermath had placed major American interests in jeopardy. A direct military clash with the Soviet Union had seemed distinctly possible, as did a permanent global shortage of oil. Then the Cold War ended and the Soviet Union disappeared, eliminating the risk of a Soviet-American conflict. In addition, the evolution of global energy production and consumption, combined with the escalating requirements for revenue of the Arab oil producers, dramatically diminished the prospects for an oil shock comparable to the two that occurred in the 1970s.

Despite these radically changed, and improved, circumstances, the American government continued to give high priority to the peace process. It did so on the basis of the theory of "linkage," according to which the Arab-Israeli conflict affected—was linked to—everything else that happened in the Middle East.[28] Because of its ties to Israel, the theory went, the United States was fated to operate under a substantial handicap there unless and until the conflict ended. A successful peace process, therefore, held the key to protecting American and Western interests in the Arab world according to this view.[29]

The Arab governments certainly complained about Israel to their American counterparts, for the same reason that they advertised their hostility to the Jewish state to the people they ruled: to deflect attention from other issues.[30] Alleged Israeli misdeeds served as a convenient excuse for not doing whatever, at any given moment, the United States wanted Arab leaders to do but that they did not wish to do. These leaders determined their actual policies, however, based on their interests—above all their common interest in remaining in power—which seldom had anything to do with the Arab-Israeli conflict.[31] During the Iraq War, when the many costly problems the United States encountered in attempting to pacify that country manifestly had no connection with Israel, the idea of linkage lost some of its popularity in American policy circles; but it did not disappear entirely.[32]

The second premise on which the peace process rested was the confident assumption that a settlement was feasible because all the parties to the conflict desired one. This was true of Israel, which had not sought the conflict in the first place, had not begun it, and was usually willing to end it on almost any terms consistent with its own security. Because Egypt posed a greater military threat to the Israelis than any other country, moreover, and since without Egypt the Arabs could not hope to form a coalition capable of a militarily effective assault on the Jewish state, Israel was especially eager to conclude a peace agreement with the government in Cairo. For his part, President Sadat also had strong motives for reaching an agreement. He wanted to extract Egypt from the conflict with Israel, which would assist him in sealing a close relationship with the United States.[33]

The other Arab parties to the peace process, however—the government of Syria and the leadership of the PLO—although willing to regain territory lost in the 1967 war, had higher priorities than peace with Israel. Indeed, a settlement of the kind the American peace processers envisioned would, at least as they seemed to see it, have weakened rather than strengthened their personal political standing, which was why they never agreed to one.

The peace process rested, third, on the premise, also an article of faith with Americans officials, that a formula for peacemaking acceptable to all parties to the conflict was available: the exchange of the land Israel had captured in June 1967 for a credible, irreversible commitment to peace by the Arabs. United Nations Security Council Resolution 242, passed soon after the end of the Six Day War, incorporated the land-for-peace formula and became the touchstone of the peace process.

To get the treaty with Egypt, Israel returned to Egyptian control the Sinai peninsula, a largely uninhabited stretch of desert on which the Egyptian government agreed not to station military forces. Israel did not need or want the Sinai and for Egypt what mattered was the symbolism of regaining title to it, not any practical use to which it might be put. The exchange was therefore, in the end, a relatively easy one for each side to make.

By contrast, the Golan Heights had considerable strategic value for Israel: the plateau could be used (and had been used before 1967 by the Syrians) to shell the towns of northern Israel and as the starting point for an all-out assault on the Jewish state. The West Bank had even greater strategic significance, situated as it was close to Israel's major population centers. It had considerable emotional and therefore political importance as well, as the heartland of Biblical Israel. The Israelis were not willing to relinquish either piece of territory without strict and elaborate measures to safeguard their security. The Syrians and Palestinians would have found it politically difficult to accept what Israel demanded even if they had been willing to make peace, which they were not. The normal meaning of the peace for which Israel was being asked to give up land, and certainly Israel's understanding of its meaning, is the end of conflict. This, the Arabs refused to offer.

The differences between the conditions in which the negotiations between Israel and Egypt took place and those surrounding the peace process thereafter account for its history: first success, then sustained failure. Despite these differences, American administrations, one after another, pressed doggedly ahead with it. While the American fixation on it received remarkably little criticism—for most of its existence the peace process had the same politically sacrosanct status in the United States as motherhood, apple pie, and the flag—America's relations with

Israel did arouse a certain amount of controversy, generated mainly by those who blamed the Israelis for the failure of peace negotiations or disliked the Jewish state for other reasons, or both.* It arose from, or at least was justified by, three myths about relations between Israel and the United States.

The first of them held that Israel was not only an American ally and not merely an American client, but in fact was an American puppet. From this it followed that Washington could, if it wished, impose a peace settlement on the government in Jerusalem if it chose to do so.[34] The failure to do so, this myth implied, was responsible for the continuation of the conflict.

While the United States certainly had influence on the Israeli government, it did not have, and could not have, enough of it to get Israel to adopt policies that Israelis believed would compromise their own security. All countries resist suggestions to take measures that they consider dangerous, no matter how powerful or well-intentioned the party making the suggestion. The United States would no more use the ultimate means of moving another country—force—against Israel than it would against any other democratic ally. Washington could of course threaten to withdraw political support for Israel, or abandon it altogether, as some critics proposed; but these forms of pressure were less likely to work on Israel than on other democracies because one of Zionism's founding precepts was the need for the Jewish state to rely, ultimately, only on itself for its defense. As a matter of principle Israel

---

* The attention Israel received both in the United States and other countries, was excessive by almost any reasonable standard: "When I was a correspondent at the AP, the agency had more than 40 staffers covering Israel and the Palestinian territories. That was significantly more news staff than the AP had in China, Russia, or India, or in all of the 50 countries of sub-Saharan Africa combined." Matti Friedman, "An Insider's Guide to the Most Important Story on Earth," *Tablet*, August 26, 2014, www.Tabletmag.com/jewish-news-and-politics/183033. This was due not only (perhaps not mainly) to its conflict with the Arabs but also to the world's ongoing fascination with its only Jewish state. On the broader fascination with Jews, from which the emphasis on Israel derives, see Adam Garfinkle's classic study *Jewcentricity: Why the Jews are Praised, Blamed, and Used to Explain Just About Everything*, New York: John Wiley & Sons, 2009. On the American approach to Zionism prior to the establishment of Israel see Peter Grose, *Israel in the Mind of America*, New York: Alfred A. Knopf, 1983.

was prepared to stand alone in the world if it had to. In any event, the Israelis almost always did offer the concessions that the United States believed were necessary to achieve peace; the Arab side invariably deemed them insufficient.

A second myth, the opposite of the first, held that Israel manipulated the United States: when the two countries disagreed, as they sometimes did, the weaker party invariably got its way. The Israelis had in this way avoided doing what was necessary for peace in the Middle East, according to Israel's critics and enemies. This belief does not stand up to the evidence: on one issue after another, from the Reagan administration's plan to sell advanced aeronautical technology to Saudi Arabia to the Obama administration's insistence on a total freeze on Israeli housing construction outside the 1949 ceasefire lines, when the two sides clashed, the Americans prevailed.

The third myth, closely related to the second, held that Israel was able to exercise great and undue influence over American foreign policy because of the machinations of a powerful lobby, which distorted the policymaking process in Washington DC.[35] This theory had particular purchase in the Arab world, where conspiracy theories are common, because it provided a comforting explanation of tiny Israel's ability to defeat the far larger and more populous Arab states.

Israel did have some influence in the American capital, and more than one group there was dedicated to enhancing and wielding that influence, as was the case for many other countries as well as various domestic and foreign economic interests. This is normal in the American political system. That influence, however, such as it was, had a far broader base than lobbyists. Polls showed the Jewish state invariably stood high in the affections and esteem of the American public as a whole, and not because of the exertions of any pro-Israel lobby.[36] Israel's popularity stemmed from its status as a staunchly pro-American democracy in a region in which most countries were neither. Unlike the other countries of the Middle East, and to a greater extent than most countries around the world, Israelis shared American values.

Moreover, as a militarily capable ally, Israel served American strategic purposes in its region. It contributed to the American strategy of offshore balancing.[37] Its sweeping 1967 victory dealt a severe blow to the power and prestige of the Soviet Union, which had armed the

Arabs. In 1970 Israeli military mobilization helped to halt an attack by anti-American Syria on pro-American Jordan.[38] In the wake of the Cold War, Israel opposed, and helped to keep in check, America's radical adversaries in the Middle East. Common interest as well as common values bound the two countries together.

The post-Cold War era in the history of the peace process began with the Madrid conference. It continued with the advent of the Clinton administration, which came to office with a commitment to it that was, if anything, even stronger than that of the outgoing administration of George H. W. Bush, which had organized the Madrid meeting. The new administration also inherited a new Israeli government, formed by the Labor Party and led by Prime Minister Yitzhak Rabin. He had served as the army chief of staff during the 1967 war and was assuming the leadership of the country for the second time. Rabin and Labor were better disposed to the energetic pursuit of a settlement with the Arabs than the preceding government, which had been dominated by the more hawkish Likud Party.

Rabin set his sights on a deal with Syria and the United States threw itself into the effort to secure one. As talks between Syrian and Israeli representatives proceeded in Washington and other cities, Secretary of State Warren Christopher, during his four years in office, traveled to the Syrian capital, Damascus, 28 times to meet with that country's leader, Hafez al-Assad. In 2000, Clinton himself made a special trip to Geneva to meet with Assad in the hope of coaxing him toward a settlement with Israel. The Syrian leader was willing to engage in the peace process—largely, no doubt to improve his relations with the United States, which, with the collapse of the Soviet Union and the decisive American victory in the 1991 war with Iraq, had become the predominant power in the Middle East, as elsewhere. Assad was unwilling, however, to make peace.

Through his slow, deliberate, obstinate conduct of the negotiations he made it clear that, at the very least, he was in no hurry to change the territorial status quo, even in order to regain the Golan Heights.[39] Moreover, the opening of Israeli talks with the PLO in the second half of 1993 complicated the Syrian-Israeli negotiations, which foundered on a dispute about where the final border between the two countries should be. The Israelis stipulated an internationally recognized line of

1923; Assad insisted on a return to the ceasefire line of 1949, which had been in force before the 1967 war (although there had been no internationally-agreed definition of it) and that would have given Syria slightly more territory and made northern Israel far more vulnerable to attack.[40]

The Americans and the Israelis told the Syrians that in order to persuade the Israeli public to assume the risk of retreating from the elevated defensive position that possession of the Golan conferred it would be helpful, perhaps even necessary, for Assad to make a dramatic conciliatory gesture, like Sadat's trip to Jerusalem and address to the Israeli parliament. The Syrian dictator displayed no inclination to do any such thing.[41] The nature of his own government—an often brutal tyranny—gave him no basis for understanding the crucial role of public opinion in democracies such as Israel, and the need to cater to it; but the character of the Syrian regime obstructed peace with Israel in another, deeper way.

Nominally a government, like Saddam Hussein's Iraq, of the Baath party, Assad's regime was in fact a narrowly based sectarian one. He himself belonged to the Alawite sect, an offshoot of Shia Islam. The Alawites made up a mere 12 percent of the Syrian population. They ruled the three-quarters of all Syrians who were Sunnis—many of whom did not consider the Alawites to be Muslims at all—through coercion, not consent. In February 1982 the Sunni Muslim Brotherhood rose up against the Alawite regime in the city of Hama and Assad's forces massacred as many as 20,000 of them.

For all their often-poisonous differences, all Syrians were Arabs, and Assad attempted to win a measure of legitimacy among non-Alawites by presenting himself as the foremost champion of Arab causes, above all the cause of anti-Zionism.[42] His grip on power depended, that is, beyond his demonstrated willingness to kill any and all Syrians who opposed him, on the ongoing confrontation with Israel. The price he would have to pay to regain control of the Golan, he had reason to believe, might well threaten his control of Damascus.[43] Thus, to regain territory that Israel held in exchange for reconciliation with the Jewish state carried more risks than benefits for him. Assad did not want what the Americans assumed he should want and therefore believed he did want. He did not want the return of the Golan enough to pay the obvious and internationally agreed price for it. The peace process in which Syria, Israel, and the United States engaged did not, therefore, bring peace.

As the effort to reconcile Israel and Syria faltered, the Clinton administration, and its successors, shifted the emphasis of the peace process to negotiations between Israel and the Palestinians. A breakthrough in Israeli-Palestinian relations seemed to occur in 1993. Several Israelis, acting without the official sanction of their government, met secretly in the Norwegian capital, Oslo, with representatives of the PLO. The Arab states had recognized the PLO, at a summit meeting in Rabat, Morocco, in 1974 as "the sole legitimate representatives of the Palestinian people," dismissing the claim to this role of the Kingdom of Jordan, which had controlled the West Bank between the 1948 and 1967 wars. Since the PLO refused to recognize the right of the Jewish state to exist at all, the Israelis had refused to deal with it. The two sides abandoned these positions at Oslo and their meetings there yielded a framework for further negotiations that were intended to lead to an ultimate settlement of their conflict. Prime Minister Rabin chose to accept the framework and committed the Israeli government to those negotiations.

As with the Sadat visit to Jerusalem in 1977, the decisive event in Israeli-Egyptian relations, the American government had no role in the deliberations in Norway and did not even become aware of them until they were almost completed. The Clinton administration embraced the Oslo accords, however, and staged the ceremony at which they were signed on the south lawn of the White House on September 13, 1993. The ceremony featured an awkward handshake between Rabin and Yasir Arafat, the PLO leader. The framework agreement called for a division of the West Bank into three different zones and, over time, the withdrawal of Israel from each of them, with the implicit final goal of an independent Palestinian state.[44]

The negotiations within that framework proved difficult— protracted, subject to delays in implementing the measures on which the two sides managed to reach agreement, and punctuated with periodic crises. Over the course of the next six years, however, the two parties did conclude five agreements of various kinds. A Palestinian governing body, the Palestinian Authority, which the PLO dominated, was established in the West Bank and Gaza. Israel withdrew from part of the territory between the 1967 border (in reality the 1949 ceasefire line) and the Jordan River. Particular difficulties arose over the status of the city of Hebron, located in a solidly Arab part of the West Bank but of historical and religious importance to Israel; but an accord concerning the city was concluded in early 1997.

The most beneficial consequence of the Oslo negotiations turned out to be a byproduct of them: a peace treaty, signed in 1994, between Israel and Jordan, which continued to share a border even after the Jordanian government had formally abdicated responsibility for the West Bank. The peace process gave Jordan's King Hussein political cover to turn what was a de facto peace into an official one. Since the establishment of Israel, the governments of the two countries had maintained secret contacts and had an important if unstated common interest beyond avoiding another war: a deep suspicion of the PLO.[45] The conditions that had made possible an Israeli peace treaty with Egypt—an Arab leader close to the United States who saw the end of the conflict as serving his and his country's interest and whose political authority did not depend on adamant opposition to Zionism—were present in the Jordanian case as they were not for the Syrian one or, as events were to show, that of the Palestinians.

A severe shock to the peace process occurred in November 1995, when a Jewish fanatic assassinated Yitzhak Rabin. The foreign minister, Shimon Peres, succeeded him. A veteran of Israeli politics who had once been prime minister himself, Peres lacked the political strength and credibility as a negotiator that Rabin's military background had earned him among Israelis. Nonetheless, Peres led the Labor Party in the 1996 Israeli elections and the Clinton administration, believing his continuation in office to be vital for the peace process, did everything it could to help him win. Despite American efforts, he lost. The new Likud government was headed by Benjamin Netanyahu, whose skepticism about Palestinian intentions made him unpopular in Clinton's Washington.[46] Still, during his term in office between 1996 and 2000, the peace process continued.

Netanyahu's election reflected the growing doubts and divisions within Israel about the good faith of the Palestinians, doubts made all the more acute by the terms of the exchange that circumstances required Israelis to contemplate: they had to give up something tangible and strategically valuable—land—to get something intangible—an Arab promise to launch no further wars. Their experience with their neighbors over the five decades since the creation of the Jewish state had not been such as to give them much faith in Arab promises. Because they had no goal higher than peace, however, and because of the strength of their connection to the United States, whose government made the peace process such a high priority, the Israelis persisted in the negotiations despite their reservations; and in the end they offered major concessions in order to achieve a final agreement. No such agreement was reached, either during the Clinton administration or thereafter, because of the priorities, rooted in their political culture, of the Palestinians and especially of their leader, Yasir Arafat.

Arafat spent most of his early life not in Mandatory Palestine but in Egypt. He trained as an engineer but gravitated toward politics and became the head of al Fatah, the largest group within the PLO. Ultimately he rose to be the supreme Palestinian leader. He began his political career as a would-be Third World revolutionary, patterning himself after Mao Zedong, Ho Chi Minh, and Fidel Castro.[47] Over time he shifted his emphasis from revolutionary socialism to Palestinian nationalism. To these he added, in his public persona, conspicuous elements of Islamic piety.

Arafat led the Palestinian cause, which he came to embody in the eyes of the world, from one disaster to another. He established a beachhead in Jordan, then started a war with the Jordanian government in 1970 that resulted in the defeat and expulsion of the PLO. He transferred his operations to Lebanon and used that country as a base from which to attack Israel as well as to help to trigger a Lebanese civil war. The Israelis struck back in 1982 and, despite Arafat's boasts about his organization's military prowess and the weapons it had received from the Soviet Union, routed the Palestinians. Arafat and his associates fled into exile in Tunis, the capital of Tunisia in North Africa, far from the territory they proclaimed it their mission to conquer. In Tunis, the PLO leader committed yet another strategic blunder. His enthusiastic support for Saddam Hussein's invasion of Kuwait in 1990 alienated the oil-producing states of the Persian Gulf that were his financial sponsors, whom Saddam threatened. They withdrew their subventions (as well as evicting the Palestinians residing within their borders), pushing the PLO to the brink of destitution. The Oslo process rescued Arafat;[48] as part of its terms he moved from Tunisia to the West Bank.

Once installed as the head of the Palestinian Authority he presented two contradictory faces to the world. To the West he played the role of a stubborn and often erratic negotiator who nonetheless accepted the basic assumption of the peace process: that he was intent on an agreement with Israel that would leave two states—predominantly Jewish Israel and Arab Palestine—living side by side in harmony. To the Arab world, by contrast, and especially to the Palestinians he purported to lead, he broadcast a different message: It was a message of rejection of Israel, an adamant version of the attitude the Arab world had adopted toward Zionism from its beginnings.

Arafat consistently refused to condemn, and sometimes praised, acts of violence against Israelis,[49] 300 of whom died in terrorist attacks between 1993 and 1996.[50] The Palestinian Authority over which he presided practiced what came to be known as "incitement," which consisted of derogatory propaganda about Jews and Israel,[51] the denial of any historical Jewish connection to Jerusalem and its environs,[52] and the insistence that all the territory between the Jordan River and the Mediterranean Sea belonged to the Arabs, making the Jews living there contemptible interlopers to be evicted. To the Europeans and Americans, that is, Arafat conveyed the impression that he had abandoned the unremitting hostility to Israel's very existence that he and other Arab leaders had maintained prior to Oslo. To the Arabs he sent, clearly, powerfully, and persistently, the message that he had not abandoned it at all.

Committed as they were, personally, professionally, and politically, to the peace process, whose success required that the message Arafat sent to the West be the authentic one, the leaders of Western governments, including the officials of the Clinton administration, had a strong interest in believing what he told them; and so they did believe it. If they persevered with the negotiations, they convinced themselves, those negotiations would eventually succeed: peace was just around the corner.

The Arab version of Arafat turned out to be the genuine one. The Palestinian leader saw himself as a transcendent historical figure,[53] and he did achieve at least one singular distinction in the annals of the twentieth century. For taking part in the Oslo process he received, along with Rabin and Peres, the Nobel Peace prize, making him, at the time he accepted it, the least-deserving recipient in the long and checkered history of that award.

As the president of the Palestinian Authority, Arafat built none of the institutions that states require to flourish.[54] His domain did not have impartial courts, or effective administrators, or a working financial system, or the rule of law. Like many other leaders, and more than most, Arafat turned out to be personally corrupt, amassing a net worth estimated at $300 million, much of it by diverting to himself international aid intended for the Palestinian people.[55] Like the leaders of the Arab states, he established large security forces that were responsible only to him.[56] As in the Arab states, Arafat permitted no opposition to his policies or his personal rule.

Still, the American side pressed ahead with the negotiations, expecting, or at least hoping for, a breakthrough. During the Clinton administration, Arafat visited the White House 13 times, more than any other foreign leader.[57] The Americans' hopes rose in 1999 when, in elections held in May of that year, the Israeli electorate turned the Netanyahu government out of power and replaced it with one dominated by Rabin and Peres's Labor Party and headed, as prime minister, by another former army chief of staff, Ehud Barak.

Barak was as committed to a settlement with the Palestinians as his Labor predecessors in the office and more impatient for one than Rabin had been. He pressed for an Israeli-Palestinian summit meeting to address the most difficult issues dividing the two sides. Seeking to repeat the success of the 1978 Israeli-Egyptian summit that the Carter administration had organized, the Clinton administration convened such a meeting in the same place, the presidential retreat at Camp David.

The summit meeting lasted two weeks, from July 11 to 25. It preoccupied the president himself and his senior foreign policy officials.[58] They spent long hours with the two leaders, Barak and Arafat and their advisors, both separately and together. The deliberations addressed the "final status" issues, the ones hardest to resolve that had to be resolved to establish peace between Israelis and Palestinians.

The two intensive weeks at Camp David failed to produce an accord on these issues. Undaunted, the American peace processers continued to seek agreement on them, in a series of different venues, until the end of the year and even into the first month of the next one, Bill Clinton's last as president. He himself offered an American proposal for the resolution of the conflict, which became known as the "Clinton parameters."[59] The Israeli cabinet accepted the parameters. Arafat did not.[60]

Other than prosecuting wars and managing the great nuclear crisis over Soviet missiles in Cuba in 1962, to no other international issue in the twentieth century did the American government devote as much sustained, high-level attention as it did to the peace process in the year 2000. It was all to no avail. At the end of the Clinton administration in 2000, Israel and the Palestinians were no closer to a settlement of their conflict than they had been at the beginning of the Oslo process in 1993. Indeed, in one important way they were considerably further from a peace agreement: they were at war. Arafat responded to the failure of the talks with an assault on Israeli civilians.

Four issues dominated the failed deliberations: the question of where to draw the border between Israel and a Palestinian state; the nature of the security arrangements in the West Bank to ensure that it would not be used as a platform for attacks on Israel; the status of and division of control over Jerusalem, Israel's capital and the holiest of all places for Jews, which the Palestinians also wanted as the seat of their government and that had religious significance for Muslims as well; and last but not least, the disposition of the Palestinian "refugees."

This last item demonstrated the peculiarity, and peculiar difficulty, of ending the conflict. During the 1948 War an estimated 400,000 Arabs fled what became Israel, going not only to Gaza and the then Jordanian-controlled West Bank but also to Jordan itself, Lebanon, and Syria. Arafat asserted that, as part of the settlement, all of them who remained alive, and their descendants—who numbered, by his count, several million people—would have to be allowed to settle in Israel.

It was an extraordinary demand: the original refugees had left because of a war started by the Arabs, not the Israelis. The new Israeli government had even urged them to stay; Arab leaders had told them to leave, promising that they would return after the anticipated destruction of the new state.[†] The twentieth century had seen other such large-scale flights—of Hindus from Pakistan and Muslims from India at the time of the partition of South Asia in 1947, for example—and in no case had the countries the refugees had abandoned been expected to take them back.[61] Those who left had instead been resettled in the places to which they fled. This happened with one such exodus in particular, that of the Jews from the Arab countries, who were expelled, in many cases from places where their ancestors had lived for centuries, in numbers comparable to if not greater than the total number of Arabs who left the new Israel in 1948. Israel welcomed and absorbed the Jewish refugees from Arab countries. By contrast, with the exception of Jordan, the Arab countries did not permit those who left Israel to become citizens and the Arab governments forced them to live, from one generation to the next, in refugee camps. Arafat insisted that they had the "right of return," although no such right existed in international law or custom[‡] and although by the 1990s the majority had never set foot in the place to which Arafat demanded that they be permitted to "return." He repeatedly promised that they would eventually be able to relocate from wherever they were to Israel.[62]

The demand that the Palestinians scattered around the Arab world be allowed to live in Israel (rather than in a Palestinian state

[†] The circumstances surrounding the departure of many of the Arabs living in what became Israel in May 1948, has been extensively and often acrimoniously debated by Israeli historians. For an overview of this episode see Efraim Karsh, *Palestine Betrayed*, New Haven, Connecticut: Yale University Press, 2012. Neither this issue nor any other connected to the Arab-Israeli conflict has been seriously studied or honestly debated in any Arab country.

[‡] The Palestinians claimed that the right to return stemmed from United Nations General Assembly Resolution 194 of 1948, which, while devoted chiefly to other matters, included a paragraph suggesting the return of all refugees—implicitly including Jews who had resided in Arab countries—to their homes. The resolution was not written to be mandatory and was never intended to have the force of law. The Arab governments never made any effort to extend the "right" to Jews who had had to flee their countries and in any event did not vote for the resolution when it came before the General Assembly. See Efraim Karsh, "The Palestinians and the 'Right of Return,'" *Commentary*, May 2001; and Richard Schifter, "Origins of the Palestinian Claim of a 'Right of Return,'" *Washington Jewish Week*, February 28, 2014.

on the West Bank and Gaza) not only violated historical precedent and basic notions of justice. By forcing the Israelis to bear the costs of a problem for which they were not responsible it also constituted an assault on the sovereignty of the Jewish state. It asserted that Israel should not be allowed to exercise the fundamental, indeed defining property of sovereignty—the control of its own borders. It also denied Israel another sovereign prerogative, deciding who has the right to citizenship. Further, by flooding the country with people hostile to it, the consequence of acceding to Arafat's demand would be the destruction of Israel, which was surely one of the reasons he made it.

In an effort to achieve a settlement, the Israeli government ultimately offered to resettle some Palestinians from other countries, but Arafat would not budge from his insistence that everyone he defined as a refugee be admitted to Israel, a demand that no government had ever accepted or could accept. Indeed, Barak made major concessions on all four issues. Arafat rejected them, and made no counterproposals of his own.[63] Moreover, he gave no indication that he was prepared to end the conflict on any terms.[64]

The Clinton-era peace process between Israelis and Palestinians failed because of the shortcomings of the Palestinian leader, but not for that reason alone. Arafat showed himself to be a grandiose,[65] unrealistic, erratic, and duplicitous negotiator; but his refusal to modify his positions in order to reach agreement with Israel reflected the Palestinian political culture over which he presided, which he himself had of course done a great deal to foster. The Palestinians saw themselves as victims, justice for whom required the abolition of Israel.[66] They did not recognize any Jewish rights at all in the Middle East and regarded any compromise of their maximal demands as a betrayal. In 1998, following a custom that had developed after 1948, Arafat designated May 15 as a Palestinian holiday, which came to be called "Nakba Day." On the day before, May 14, in 1948, Israel had declared its independence, and "nakba" means, in Arabic, catastrophe. This made the Palestinians the only people whose national day is devoted not to celebrating themselves but to vilifying another group. It suggests that organized Palestinian politics in the Arafat era did not really constitute a nationalist movement at all, since it was dedicated not to establishing a Palestinian state, opportunities for which the Palestinian leadership had several times rejected, but rather to destroying the state of another people.

Given the fundamental features of Palestinian political culture, it is not surprising that Arafat refused any and all offers of compromise on the most difficult and divisive issues. What is surprising, what requires explanation, is the enduring American conviction, in the face of relentlessly mounting evidence to the contrary, that he would ultimately agree to a settlement. To be sure, in sponsoring the peace process the Americans were, up to a point, carrying out the wishes of the Israelis, or at least, at the end of the Clinton administration, of the Israeli prime minister, Ehud Barak. The Americans involved in the peace process also had developed personal stakes in the process. They had devoted large parts of their careers to it; their professional reputations rested on it. Moreover, the Americans paid no personal price for the failure to achieve peace. To the contrary, the investment of American political capital in this particular unsuccessful venture came to be considered noble rather than feckless. This was so in no small part because, unlike in Iraq—an equally ineffectual American effort that had at least an equal claim, based on its motives, to nobility—the United States as a whole suffered no obvious damage for the negative results of the peace process.

Perhaps the most important reason for the American persistence, as well as for the American failure, was a misidentification of the problem. In the eyes of American officials the peace process involved a series of transactions, like a labor negotiation. The trick was to find a happy medium, a set of arrangements that both sides, each of which wanted the conflict to end, could accept. That analysis was accurate for Israel but not for the Palestinians. Their supreme interest, as they defined it, was not the end of the conflict but the end of Israel. They would not accept a final settlement that ratified the legitimacy and the continued existence of a Jewish state in the Middle East.

In this sense the American failure in the peace process had the same underlying cause as the American failure to bring democracy, or even stability, to Iraq, Afghanistan, Somalia, Haiti, and the Balkans: namely, the inability of the local political culture to sustain what the United States was trying to bring into being. In all of these cases, the local people did not want what the Americans believed they should want and so assumed, wrongly, they did want. Properly understood, the peace process was not simply a complicated transaction: it was a mission of transformation. The success of the American enterprise there required, as it did in other parts of the world where post-Cold War American foreign policy faltered, the transformation of the local society. As in Iraq, Afghanistan, Somalia, Haiti, and the Balkans, that mission failed. Unlike in the other places, the American government did not understand—or would not admit to itself—that transformation was what was required and thus never seriously attempted it.

Having rejected American entreaties and Israeli concessions at Camp David and thereafter, Arafat fell back on the tactic he had historically favored: violence. He orchestrated what came to be called the Second Intifada—the Arab term for uprising. The first one, in the late 1980s, had broken out spontaneously, as a protest against the Israeli presence in the West Bank, with Palestinian teenagers throwing stones at Israeli police and soldiers. Beginning in 2000, armed Palestinians, with Arafat's encouragement and support, sought to kill Israeli civilians.

The Second Intifada opened a new chapter in Arab-Israeli relations. Whereas between 1948 and 1973 Arab states had sent armies to defeat the Israeli military, in 2000 and thereafter groups that were not states employed irregular forces to murder Israeli men, women, and children as well as visiting tourists, most of whom were not in uniform. In the decade and a half after the collapse of the Oslo process the Israeli public discarded its illusions about the prospect of peace with the Palestinians. The American government, however, with one notable exception, retained an unwavering faith in the peace process. The Arabs, for their part, waged five small-scale wars against Israel, designed not to conquer the Jewish state but to terrorize and demoralize its citizens. Like the conventional assaults of 1948, 1967, and 1973, Israel won all these wars. As with the bigger conflicts, however, Israeli success in the later, smaller ones did not bring peace.

Land for War

According to the diagnosis made by the government of the United States and shared by much of the rest of the world, Israel's continuing possession of the territories it had captured in the 1967 war caused the Arab-Israeli conflict. Returning those territories to Arab control, it followed, would eliminate the Arab grievance against the Jewish state. Israel therefore could and should trade land for peace.[67]

Despite the absence of formal peace agreements with the Palestinians or the government of Syria, Israel did, beginning in the 1990s, vacate territory that it had occupied during the course of waging its defensive wars. It left parts of the West Bank, the sliver of southern Lebanon it had held since the 1982 war against the PLO there, and the Gaza Strip that it had taken from Egypt in 1967 but that the Egyptian government declined to reclaim. These withdrawals did not lead to reconciliation. To the contrary, the Arab groups that took control of the places that Israel left used them to mount attacks on the Jewish state in pursuit of their professed goal of eliminating it altogether.

The American-sponsored peace process proceeded on the assumption that the Arab grievances against Israel stemmed from 1967. The events of the post-Cold War era revealed that they had their roots, instead, in 1948. What was at issue from the Arab point of view was not the country's post-1967 borders but rather its post-1948 existence. The trade that Israel made, therefore, turned out to involve not land for peace but land for war.

Those wars did not directly threaten Israel's existence. Without any hope of defeating the powerful Israeli army, Israel's Arab enemies sought to bypass that army and kill Israeli civilians. The Arab groups employed two instruments in particular for this purpose: suicide bombers, who infiltrated Israel and detonated their explosives with the aim of killing as many Jews as possible as well as themselves; and rockets hurled at Israeli cities, some of them crude, home-made, and inaccurate but others more sophisticated and dangerous. Increasingly, the rockets were given to the Palestinians by the Islamic Republic of Iran, which made itself Israel's most formidable enemy both because of the deep anti-Semitism of its clerical rulers and in order to render its ambition for Middle Eastern dominance more acceptable to the historically anti-Persian Arabs by assisting the Arab campaign against Israel.

The attacks were intended to demoralize the Israeli population: those launching them repeated the error of the Arab states after 1948 of believing their own propaganda about the cowardly character of the Jews and the weakness of Israeli society, which, they imagined, would collapse when challenged.[68] They had another goal besides demoralization: delegitimization. When the Israelis fought back, the attackers claimed that Israel was acting in brutal, illegal fashion that deserved international censure.[69] By this tactic they hoped ultimately to isolate the Jewish state politically and, through boycotts, economically. The tactic relied on vastly exaggerating the number of civilian casualties Israeli self-defense caused. It also involved taking steps to maximize the actual number of people killed by Israeli retaliation by locating weapons and commanders in heavily populated areas and preventing the civilians from leaving. The Arabs presiding over the attacks calculated that they gained not only when Jews died but also when Arabs died.[70] In fact, Israel's armed forces surpassed any other, including those of the United States, in the care they took to avoid civilian casualties, but the charges of brutality and illegality leveled against them did resonate among those ill-disposed to the Jewish state in the first place,, in Arab and Muslim countries, and in some sectors of European opinion.

While the wars of the twenty-first century did make some headway in tarnishing Israel's international reputation—although not in the United States, where its standing with the public remained high—they did not shake the country's morale, and here the United States made an important contribution. Contrary to what its Arab enemies believed, or at any rate said, Israel had one of the most cohesive and resilient societies in the world. The Israelis not only weathered the five wars launched against them, they came out ahead in each one. They did so by sending troops into the West Bank, southern Lebanon, and Gaza, but also through two other militarily effective responses.

Precision bombing of enemy targets knocked out many of the rockets aimed at their cities and crippled the crews trained to launch them. Israel also developed two defensive techniques, one a familiar feature of the long history of warfare, the other a contemporary innovation. Just as governments from time immemorial had built berms, moats, and stout walls to protect their populations from invaders, so the government of Israel built a barrier, a security fence, to keep suicide bombers from the West Bank from entering Israel. At the same time, it developed an anti-missile system, given the name "Iron Dome," that compiled an impressive record in repelling rockets targeted at its citizens.

Israel owed its success in these conflicts to its own ingenuity and determination but also to the assistance of the United States. While the American government at first criticized the security fence, it came to regard the barrier as both effective and legitimate. America also provided financial and technical assistance in the development of Israel's air power and its anti-missile technology. Israel could and would have survived the Arab wars of demoralization and delegitimization without American help, but that help made the price of survival considerably lower than it would otherwise have been. In military and strategic terms, the United States proved to be a steadfast ally.

The first test of that alliance in the new century came with the violence that erupted in the wake of the failure of the negotiations at Camp David and thereafter. Palestinians attacked Israelis with rocks, rifles, and suicide bombings. Arafat claimed to be powerless to stop this violence but evidence came to light that he himself had planned and instigated it. He certainly did nothing to discourage it, and the Palestinian Authority that he controlled paid the salaries of some of those committing it.[71] In the eyes of Israelis the assault against them discredited the peace process, and Ehud Barak, its champion, lost a special election he had called and resigned as prime minister. Ariel Sharon of the Likud Party, a forceful and controversial former general, succeeded him.

After another year of violence marked by a wave of suicide bombings, and in the wake of the deadliest month of killing yet, in March 2002 Israel struck back with Operation Defensive Shield, the largest military undertaking in the West Bank since 1967. Israeli forces entered cities throughout the territory, imposed a strict curfew, and laid siege to Arafat's headquarters in the city of Ramallah. The new American administration of George W. Bush registered some objections to the Israeli operations,[72] but they succeeded in quelling the violence. The number of Israelis killed by Palestinian terror declined sharply.[73] While it was eventually quashed, however, the Second Intifada established a pattern that would recur in Arab-Israeli relations for the next decade and a half. The West Bank remained relatively calm, in part because the Israeli military kept a close watch over it, but Israel had to fight similar wars to its north and its south.

To the north, in 2000 Barak removed the small Israeli military contingent that had been stationed in southern Lebanon since the 1982 war. The area came under the control of the Shia Muslim militia Hezbollah—Arabic for the Party of God—which Iran had organized, trained, and equipped. Hezbollah asserted that Lebanon's confrontation with Israel would continue because the Israelis still held a tiny piece of Lebanese territory known as Shebaa Farms, even though the United Nations had certified that the Israelis had withdrawn completely from that country: the militia used this claim as a pretext for keeping its armaments, which made it a disruptive and ultimately dominant force in the affairs of a country where none of the different groups—Sunni, Shia, Christian, and Druze—constituted a majority of the population.[74] The arms it retained also enabled Hezbollah to serve Iran's political aims, which was one of its founding purposes.

On July 12, 2006, Hezbollah launched a cross-border attack, kidnapping two Israeli soldiers and killing three others. Israel retaliated and the conflict lasted for 34 days. Hezbollah fired Iranian-supplied missiles into northern Israel. The Israeli response began as an air campaign, but after several weeks the Israeli prime minister, Ehud Olmert, who had succeeded to the office after Sharon had suffered an incapacitating stroke in January 2006, ordered a ground invasion.

The Bush administration supported Israel and worked diplomatically to give its armed forces as much time as possible to degrade Hezbollah's fighting strength: the Shia militia was one of the world's most active terrorist organizations, responsible for killing Americans as well as Israelis. The predominantly Sunni Arab countries with which Washington had close ties, in particular Saudi Arabia, regarded Hezbollah as a pawn of their chief adversary, Iran, and wanted Israel to weaken it.

Ultimately the Bush administration concluded that the war had gone on long enough and pressed Israel for a ceasefire.[75] Hezbollah lost part of its force but emerged with much of it intact and claimed victory in the conflict. Israelis generally regarded what they called the Second Lebanon War as a defeat, at least initially. The damage Israel inflicted on Hezbollah, however, discouraged the Shias from launching further assaults. The war reinforced Israeli deterrence to its north. In a moment of unaccustomed candor the Hezbollah leader, Hassan

Nasrallah, admitted that starting the war had been a mistake.[76] While Israel's border with Lebanon remained generally quiet, however, the one with Gaza, to the south, did not.

In 2005, Prime Minister Sharon decided to withdraw both Israeli troops and Israeli settlements, unilaterally, from the Gaza Strip, an undertaking he carried out in coordination with the United States.[77] With the Israelis gone, Gaza came under the control of a virulently anti-Israeli and anti-Semitic Islamist organization called Hamas, its name an acronym for the Islamic Resistance Movement, an offshoot of Egypt's Muslim Brotherhood. Its principal tactic for advancing its aims was terror. Those aims, stated in the Hamas charter, centered on the destruction of Israel and the establishment not of a Palestinian state but of an Islamic caliphate.[78]

Elections for the parliament of the Palestinian Authority in 2006 began the Hamas takeover of Gaza. As a terrorist organization it had dubious credentials for taking part in them; both the Israeli government and (privately) the leaders of the Palestinian Authority, who belonged to Hamas's Palestinian rival, Fatah, wanted it barred. The American government, however, insisted that Hamas be permitted to participate and it won the largest number of seats.[79] A small war in Gaza between Hamas and Fatah followed the next year, in which Hamas prevailed, took control of the territory, and established a dictatorship.

Hamas in power concentrated not on building the institutions of government but on waging war against Israel, mainly by launching rockets into Israeli territory, which it did on three separate occasions: in 2008–2009, in 2012, and in 2014. On each occasion Israel got the better of the exchange, on the third destroying an elaborate system of tunnels Hamas had dug beneath the border between Gaza and Israel for the purpose of mounting terrorist attacks against Israeli civilians. On each occasion the United States provided diplomatic support for Israel against Hamas, which the American government designated, as it did Hezbollah, a terrorist organization.

Through all these conflicts, however, the American foreign policy establishment held fast to the orthodoxy of the peace process, continuing to believe it both urgent and feasible for Israel to trade land for peace with the Palestinian Authority in the West Bank. One senior American official did dissent from this orthodoxy and proposed modifications to American policy toward the Arab-Israeli conflict. He had considerable—although not, as it turned out, decisive—influence because he held the office of president of the United States.

George W. Bush entered office without the initial commitment to the peace process that his predecessor and his successor both displayed. Indeed, his lack of enthusiasm owed something to his predecessor's experience: in a pre-inauguration conversation at the White House, Clinton made clear to Bush his sense of betrayal by Arafat.[80]

Two other episodes shaped his approach to the Arab-Israeli conflict. The terrorist attacks on the United States of September 11, 2001, made him wary of leaders and organizations, such as Arafat and the Palestinian Authority, that were themselves involved in perpetrating terrorism; and he ultimately had his own personal experience with Arafat's duplicity. In January 2002 the Israeli navy, operating in the Red Sea, seized a Palestinian freighter, the *Karine A*, carrying Iranian weapons to the Palestinian Authority that were clearly intended for use in attacking Israelis. Arafat denied that he had had anything to do with the shipment. The Israelis produced irrefutable evidence to the contrary, enhancing Bush's skepticism about the Palestinian leader and the peace process orthodoxy.[81] He proceeded to make four changes in American policy toward the conflict between Israelis and Palestinians.

One of them favored the Palestinians. He became the first American president to go firmly on record in favor of what the Oslo process had implied: the creation of an independent Palestinian state.[82] The other three innovations that Bush introduced aligned the United States with Israeli positions; but they also brought American policy into closer conformity with the realities of the region because they involved endorsing conditions without which Israel would not agree to withdraw from the West Bank.[83]

Bush acknowledged that all of the people the Palestinians counted as refugees would not be relocated to Israel under the terms of any settlement: the professed right of return, the United States said, did not exist.[84] In addition, the United States and Israel came to an agreement about the status of Israelis living outside the 1967 borders (the 1949 ceasefire lines) known as the "Green Line."

After 1967, Israel had built settlements of three kinds: in Jerusalem; in close proximity to both Jerusalem and Tel Aviv, Israel's other major city; and in places further from the Green Line, some of them in areas populated by Palestinians. The settlements became controversial. Much of the world deemed them illegal, although the territory between the Green Line and the Jordan River had had no settled, recognized legal status after 1948.[85] The American government considered them an obstacle to a land-for-peace trade with the Palestinians on the grounds that Israel would not vacate land where it had implanted settlements. In fact, however, the Israeli government had uprooted settlers in 1982 when it withdrew from the Sinai peninsula as part of the peace treaty with Egypt, and again as part of the withdrawal from Gaza in 2005; and anyway, as Camp David and its aftermath had demonstrated, the Palestinians were not prepared to make a lasting peace with Israel on any terms.

Still, the settlements generated friction between the United States and Israel[86] and Bush, working with Prime Minister Sharon, found a formula that both countries could accept that preserved the possibility of a Palestinian state on the West Bank should the Palestinians ever come around to the idea of peaceful coexistence with Israel. The agreement stipulated that Israel would build no new settlements and that incentives to Israelis to move beyond the Green Line would end, but that natural growth in existing settlements and in Jerusalem would continue.[87] Under these terms the vast majority of Israelis outside the 1967 lines, who lived in what were in effect suburbs of Jerusalem and Tel Aviv that took up a tiny fraction of the territory, would remain in place. This left open the possibility of creating a Palestinian state on almost all of the West Bank should that ever become politically feasible.[88]

Finally, while advocating the creation of a Palestinian state Bush insisted that it be a state of a certain kind. It should, he said, be a democracy, and toward that end he called for political reform in the corrupt, autocratic Palestinian Authority.[89] Stipulating this condition had the advantage of directing attention to what was, after all, the root cause of the Israeli-Palestinian conflict: Palestinian political culture.

The Bush administration negotiated, along with Russia, the European Union, and a representative of the United Nations—a group known in the parlance of Middle East diplomacy as the Quartet—a multi-stage Roadmap to a Palestinian state in which political reform would come before the creation of such a state.[90] Despite the failure of Camp David and its aftermath, and despite the violence of the Second Intifada, a major development in the Palestinian camp gave the Bush administration grounds for optimism that the steps of the Roadmap could and would be carried out. In November 2004 Yasir Arafat died and in January 2005 Mahmoud Abbas was elected to succeed him as president of the Palestinian Authority.

Abbas had long traveled in Arafat's orbit as a member of the upper echelon of the PLO. Under pressure from the United States to make political reforms in the Palestinian Authority, Arafat had in fact appointed him the Palestinian prime minister in 2003 but kept him (like all other Palestinian officials) powerless, and he resigned after six months. Abbas seemed to be Arafat's opposite in temperament and political outlook and thus a far more promising interlocutor for Israeli-Palestinian peace negotiations: he was modest not histrionic, steady rather than mercurial, and straightforward instead of reflexively mendacious. He spoke out more strongly than Arafat had done against Palestinian violence against Israelis.

Yet Abbas proved no more willing or able than Arafat to make the compromises necessary to settle the conflict, including what was, from the Palestinian perspective, the greatest compromise of all: the acceptance of the legitimacy and permanence of Jewish sovereignty in the Middle East. He turned out to be a weak leader who did not command the allegiance of the Palestinians that Arafat had achieved. Arafat had made himself, in their eyes, the heroic symbol of their cause; Abbas had the aura, and the charisma, of a bureaucrat.[91] He turned out to be personally corrupt,[92] and, despite his promises to do so, he did not reform the Palestinian authority. He appointed a reformist prime minister, Salam Fayyad, an American-trained economist, but then did to Fayyad more or less what Arafat had done to him, opposing or ignoring his initiatives. Fayyad finally resigned.

All apart from his personal shortcomings, Abbas had to operate within the confines of Palestinian opinion, with its deep hostility to the very idea of Israel, which he did nothing to try to change. Instead, he pandered to it. He insisted, for example, on the "right of return." Moreover, he continued Arafat's policy of fostering incitement.[93] In the Arafat tradition of conveying different messages to different audiences, while Abbas proclaimed, for the benefit of the West, his opposition to violence, he paid tribute (and sometimes money) to terrorists who committed it—calling those who died in carrying out terrorist acts "martyrs."

The loss of Gaza to Hamas further weakened him. He could no longer negotiate on behalf of part of the territory that was to be included in a Palestinian state, and he had to compete for the loyalty of the Palestinians, with their radically anti-Israel mind-set, with a group far more active in perpetrating acts of violence—which they called "resistance"—than his own Palestinian Authority.

Despite his disappointing performance as the Palestinian leader, and despite Bush's modifications of the American position on the Israeli-Palestinian conflict, peace process orthodoxy staged a resurgence in the second Bush presidential term: it enjoyed the patronage of Condoleezza Rice, who became secretary of state in 2005. She came to government service from an academic background and had specialized in the study of the Soviet military, which meant that the end of the Cold War eliminated her subject. Unlike Madeleine Albright, who also held a PhD degree (and with whose father she studied at the University of Denver), Rice had had a career as a serious scholar, with well-regarded publications to her credit. Unlike her immediate predecessor, Colin Powell, she had a close personal relationship with the president, an important asset for any secretary of state or indeed any cabinet official.

Rice had grown close to Bush while serving as national security advisor in his first term. In that position she had had to contend with a set of unusually powerful and experienced senior foreign policy officials: a vice president who had served as secretary of defense, a secretary of defense who had held the job previously, and a secretary of state who had been both national security advisor and chairman of the Joint Chiefs of Staff.[94] She did not always find it easy, or indeed possible, to carry out the work of the national security advisor, which is to coordinate among the relevant departments and senior officials.[95] Partly for that reason, however, she largely escaped public blame for the problems in Iraq and arrived at the State Department in an unusually strong position. She decided to use her authority to press for an Israeli-Palestinian settlement.

Indeed, Rice's stewardship at the State Department testifies to the powerful grip the orthodoxy of the peace process had on the American foreign policy establishment, even in the face of the repeated failures of the negotiations that that orthodoxy deemed both enduringly essential and perennially promising. When she accepted the offer of the State Department post from Bush, of all the issues in all the world she chose to mention the Arab-Israeli conflict. Recalling that Oval Office meeting in her memoirs, she wrote that "I then turned to one substantive issue that was on my mind. 'Mr. President,' I said, 'we need to get an agreement and establish a Palestinian state.' "[96]

The Middle East became her most frequent destination: she made 20 trips there in four years.[97] She jettisoned Bush's commitment to making democratic Palestinian reform a precondition for creating such a state[98] and tried, like the Clinton administration—and in cooperation with the Israeli government of Ehud Olmert—to resolve the final status issues. At her behest, an international conference convened in Annapolis, Maryland, in November 2007, in an effort to generate momentum in the negotiations. She spearheaded negotiations that continued, as had happened during the Clinton administration, to the very end of the Bush presidency. Like Ehud Barak, the Israeli prime minister at Camp David, Ehud Olmert made major concessions to the Palestinians. They were in fact so sweeping that, as with those Barak had made in 2000, it was not at all clear that the Israeli public would agree to support them.[99] Like the previous last-ditch effort, the one that the Bush administration made failed. Like Arafat before him, Abbas deemed the Israeli concessions inadequate but made no counterproposals of his own. In the end he simply refused to respond at all to what Olmert put on the table.[100] In one respect, however, he departed from the precedent Arafat had established eight years previously: he did not start a war.

Barack Obama entered office committed to reversing or abandoning the foreign policies of the Bush administration, with the exception of the peace process, to which the new president displayed an even greater devotion than that of his predecessor. He demonstrated the importance he assigned to it by placing telephone calls to Israeli and Arab leaders on his first day in office.[101] He appointed as a special envoy to pursue it former Democratic Senator George Mitchell, who had served as a mediator in Northern Ireland during the Clinton administration. In addition to meeting with the Israeli government and the Palestinian Authority, Mitchell made frequent visits to Damascus to confer with the Syrian dictator, Bashar Assad, who had succeeded to power upon the death of his father, Hafez, in 2000. None of his ventures bore fruit, and Mitchell resigned in 2011.

Obama subscribed to what might be called the orthodox version of the peace process orthodoxy, according to which the chief obstacle to resolving the Israeli-Palestinian conflict was the Israeli settlements outside the 1967 lines. He therefore demanded a total freeze on all construction there, including in Jerusalem. The demand contradicted the Bush-Sharon agreement, which the American government had put in writing, on where construction would and would not take place;[102] and Obama made the demand despite the fact that the Palestinian side had never made such a freeze a condition of dealing with Israel.

The Israeli government, once again headed by Benjamin Netanyahu, who became prime minister in March 2009, balked at this demand but eventually agreed to a freeze of 10 months. True to form, Abbas refused to engage in serious negotiations and the initial Obama management of the peace process, like the efforts of Clinton and Bush before him, ended in failure.

Obama won a second term in 2012 and appointed as secretary of state John Kerry, the chairman of the Senate Foreign Relations Committee who had himself run, unsuccessfully, for president in 2004. As Kerry assumed the office in 2013, the world had become less stable and predictable. New challenges to the United States were appearing in Europe and Asia, as well as in the Middle East. A civil war was raging in Syria, the Islamist terrorist organization Hamas controlled Gaza, and Mahmoud Abbas was serving the ninth year of the four-year term as Palestinian president to which he had been elected. In these circumstances the new secretary decided that the issue most in need of American attention, the one where the investment of the time of senior officials and of American political capital was likeliest to bring success, and in which his direct, intensive, personal involvement would pay dividends, was none other than the Israeli-Palestinian conflict.

Kerry threw himself into yet another round of the peace process, with precisely the same result that his predecessors had achieved. He announced a deadline to complete a peace agreement. The deadline passed without any agreement.[103] History repeated itself, with one difference. Clinton and Bush had held the Palestinian side, which had never budged from its maximalist positions or even, in the end, seriously negotiated on the final status issues, chiefly responsible for the continuation of the conflict. The Obama administration blamed Israel. When it came to the peace process, the American foreign policy establishment had, over a quarter century, like the French royal house of Bourbon learned nothing and forgotten nothing. Albert Einstein defined insanity as doing the same thing over and over again while expecting a different result. According to his standard, by 2014 American policy toward the Israeli-Palestinian peace process did not enjoy robust mental health.

By 2014 a consensus had formed among Israelis about their relations with the Palestinians. In the past that issue had sharply divided the country, with some favoring retaining the territories won in 1967 that had been the heart of the Biblical land of Israel while others wished to divest Israel of them in order to avoid governing a large number of Arabs. Now, a majority believed that holding onto the West Bank brought high costs but that turning it over to Palestinian control, given the attacks that had come from the lands to the north, west, and south that the Israelis had vacated over the previous two decades in an effort to make peace, would increase the dangers to their country. Israel's critics cited the Israeli presence in the West Bank as the cause of the Israeli-Palestinian conflict. In fact, by 2014 it was the other way around: the Israelis remained there to protect themselves from armed Palestinian efforts to destroy their state. The status quo, most Israelis had concluded, was undesirable, but the alternative to it would be worse.

The Palestinians had a consensus, as well, although it was more difficult to verify because they had no democratic opportunity to express it. It was the same consensus that Yasir Arafat had helped to create, over which he had presided, and to which he and Mahmoud Abbas had geared their policies: under no circumstances would the Palestinians agree to live peacefully, side by side, with a Jewish state. The conflict would continue, as far as they were concerned, until the state of Israel disappeared from the Middle East.[§]

The Palestinian consensus had multiple and powerful sources: the tribal nature of Palestinian society, which promoted hostility to other groups and an aversion to compromise;[104] the conviction, stemming from the Arab version of Islam, that the land on which Israel stood was rightfully Muslim territory; and the structure of Palestinian politics, in which different factions competed for the distinction of having the most extreme anti-Israeli position.[105] The leadership of the Palestinian Authority found the peace process useful but peace itself unattractive.[106]

Yet among Americans the peace process orthodoxy endured, in part for the same reason that the United States did not anticipate the attacks of September 11, 2001: a failure of imagination. Americans could not conceive that the Palestinians would give priority to the refusal to countenance Jewish sovereignty in the Middle East over peace, the opportunity for prosperity, and the creation of their own state. From the American point of view that was irrational and therefore could not be the real Palestinian position; but it was. The reality of the Palestinian position was all the harder for Americans to accept because to accept it meant accepting as well that the Israeli-Palestinian conflict was a

[§] See David Pollock, "Hardline Views, But Also Pragmatism," PolicyWatch 2276, Washington, DC: The Washington Institute for Near East Policy, June 25, 2014. "In a recent poll by the respected American firm of Greenberg, Quinlan, Rosner, two-thirds of Palestinians affirmed that 'over time Palestinians must work to get back all the land for a Palestinian state' and 60 percent agreed that 'the real goal should be to start with two states but then move it to all being one Palestinian state.'" Peter Berkowitz, "One State?" *Jewish Review of Books*, Winter, 2011, p. 38. Shlomo Avineri, a distinguished Israeli academic, former director general of his country's Foreign Ministry, and staunch supporter of the Oslo process, summarized the lessons of two decades of the peace process as follows: "We thought [the Palestinians] wanted a two-state solution, but it turns out that they want to destroy Israel, because they cannot/will not accept any form of Jewish national self-determination . . . All of those who supported the Oslo process believed that we were talking about a dispute between two national movements, and that the other side felt the same way. We were mistaken. The Palestinian side . . . believes that we are talking about a dispute between one national movement— the Palestinian—and a colonial imperialistic entity that will eventually die off." *FrontPage Magazine*, July 14, 2014, www.frontpagemag.com.

problem that could not be solved. In the American world view, by contrast, one rooted in American experience, every public problem has a solution, which the application of sufficient ingenuity, goodwill, and political leverage will eventually produce. Even with its consistent lack of success, partisans of the peace process insisted that it was better to try to resolve the conflict and fail than not to try at all.[107] The failed American initiatives did, however, have costs.

The way the United States conducted the peace process deflected attention from the real cause of the conflict. Especially during the Obama administration, the American government frequently criticized Israeli housing construction outside the Green Line, which might conceivably have obstructed a peace agreement had the Palestinians been willing to make one, but almost never mentioned Palestinian anti-Zionist and anti-Semitic incitement, the symptom and cause of their unwillingness to make peace and therefore the root cause of the conflict. This misplaced emphasis, in turn, reinforced the Palestinian strategy of attacking Israel by branding the Jewish state as illegitimate, hoping thereby to weaken it politically.[108]

This Palestinian strategy was aimed, in particular, at Europe. A constituency for this charge existed in the European countries because of historical attitudes toward Jews, the need to placate their own growing and restive Muslim population, and reservations about Israel's powerful national ethos and military capacity. Nationalism and military power had brought disaster to Europe twice in the twentieth century and so had become discredited there but the Israelis considered them necessary for their own survival. The more support the strategy of delegitimization gained, the weaker became the already dim prospects that the Palestinians would consider making the compromises necessary to end the conflict: they could tell themselves that their intransigence was succeeding. In this way the peace process became an obstacle to peace.

In the initial post-Cold War policies toward China and Russia, in the humanitarian interventions of the 1990s in Somalia, Haiti, and the Balkans, and in the American occupations during the next decade of Afghanistan and Iraq, the mission of transformation failed. The same mission was the necessary condition for the peace process to succeed: peace between Israel and the Palestinians required the transformation of Palestinian political culture. This would have been no easier than transforming the countries that became the objects of American political missionary efforts if the United States had attempted it among the Palestinians; but the attempt was not made because the senior officials of the American government did not recognize the need for it—with one notable exception. President George W. Bush did recognize what was needed. The unsuccessful effort to change Palestinian politics that he initiated formed part of a larger project to transform the Middle East as a whole. That, too, failed.

The Democracy Agenda

George W. Bush made the promotion of democracy, worldwide but especially in the Arab Middle East, the signature initiative of his second presidential term. The impulse to foster democratic institutions and policies beyond the borders of the United States has, of course, a very long pedigree in American history, going all the way back to the founding of the republic and even to the Pilgrims' arrival in the New World.[109] Bush's democracy agenda was also very much in keeping with the dominant theme of post-Cold War American foreign policy. It sought to do across the Arab world what the United States was already trying to do in one of the region's countries, Iraq, as well as in Afghanistan. Its aims were similar, if not always identical, to those the American government had pursued in China, Russia, Somalia, Haiti, and the Balkans. The direct inspiration for the Bush initiative, however, came not from the Clinton administration's failed efforts but rather from the attacks of September 11. Democracy, the president came to believe, provided the surest antidote to terrorism. Promoting it therefore became a way of defending the United States. The credit for the Bush democratic agenda, like the war on terror and the occupations of Afghanistan and Iraq, belonged to Osama bin Laden.

Bush made several major speeches committing the United States to the spread of democracy abroad, most notably his second inaugural address.[110] At the beginning of that speech, referring to the terrorist attacks, he set out the rationale for what he hoped would be a major legacy of his presidency:[111]

> We have seen our vulnerability—and we have seen its deepest source. For as long as whole regions of the world simmer in resentment and tyranny—prone to ideologies that feed hatred and excuse murder—violence will gather, and multiply in destructive power, and cross the most defended borders, and raise a mortal threat. There is only one force of history that can break the reign of hatred and resentment, and expose the pretensions of tyrants, and reward the hopes of the decent and tolerant, that is the force of human freedom.
>
> We are led, by events and common sense, to one conclusion: The survival of liberty in our land increasingly depends on the success of liberty in other lands. The best hope for peace in our world is the expansion of freedom in all the world.

He launched a series of programs for this purpose: a proposal for a Middle East Free Trade Area; the Middle East Partnership Initiative, which made grants for the purpose of fostering democracy in the region; and the Broader Middle East North Africa Initiative, which operated under the auspices of the Group of Eight, the association of democratic countries (with Russia added in 1998) that met annually mainly to discuss global economic issues.[112]

The prospects for Middle Eastern democracy appeared promising at first. On February 14, 2005, Rafik Hariri, the prime minister of Lebanon, was assassinated in Beirut by a car bomb. In the following days, hundreds of thousands of Lebanese took part in public demonstrations demanding the end of the 30-year occupation of the country by Syria, which was widely blamed for the killing. The Syrian troops did leave, the pro-Syrian government in Beirut fell, and a new one took office.

The Egyptian ruler, Hosni Mubarak, made gestures of accommodation, mainly rhetorical in nature, to his country's small democratic movement.[113] In February 2005 he called for direct, multi-candidate elections to parliament for the first time.[114] Saudi Arabia held an election to choose half of the members of its (relatively powerless) municipal councils.[115] The Crown Prince of that country, in which women were not permitted to drive, told Condoleezza Rice that Saudi women might someday be able to vote and even run for office.[116]

The democracy agenda had even wider ambitions than the three American wars that September 11 triggered: it aimed at the political transformation of an entire region. It produced, however, only very modest results. Despite the early signs of success, the democracy initiative foundered. It did not come close to transforming the region in the way that Bush had intended. Although Syrian troops left Lebanon, the pro-Iranian terrorist organization Hezbollah, a Syrian ally, retained a powerful position in the country. Free and fair elections among Palestinians in January 2006 yielded a victory for Hamas, another terrorist organization that had no intention of abiding by the rules of democratic politics, as it demonstrated thereafter by seizing all power in a violent coup and establishing an Islamist dictatorship.

Mubarak did not open up the Egyptian political system. In advance of the elections scheduled for 2005 he arrested some of the most outspoken proponents of democracy. Saudi Arabia held no meaningful elections, let alone meaningful elections in which women were permitted to vote. The trade initiative did not engage the largest economies of the region[117] and the programs to assist and encourage the growth of democracy in the Middle East failed to win wide bureaucratic support or generous funding within the American government. Secretary Rice had termed the effort to bring democracy to the Middle East a "generational commitment."[118] In fact, it barely lasted a single presidential term.

The democracy initiative labored under a particular handicap that did not affect the other American post-Cold War missions: ambivalence about its goals. The United States had close, productive, important relations with several of the governments that, according to its stated goals, it was trying to replace. Egypt and Saudi Arabia, in particular, were ruled by "friendly tyrants." Like the anti-communist friendly tyrants of the Cold War era, which the United States had embraced even though they shunned democracy, the Mubarak regime and the Saudi royal family shared geopolitical interests although not political values with the United States. The Bush democracy promotion policy in the Middle East presumed that the end of the global conflict with the Soviet Union and the advent of the threat of terrorism had done away with the dilemma that dealing with the friendly tyrants had posed for the United States. "America's vital interests and [its] deepest beliefs are now one," Bush said in his second inaugural address. In the wake of September 11, that is, defending the United States, the supreme national interest, against the chief threat to it, terrorism, required the promotion of America's highest political value—democracy.

It was one thing to say this in a speech, however, and quite another to make it the basis for American policy in the Middle East. "For sixty years my country, the United States, pursued stability at the expense of democracy in this region here in the Middle East," Rice proclaimed in a speech she gave in Cairo in June 2005, "and achieved neither."[119] In fact, the United States had helped to keep the Middle East stable enough to safeguard American interests,[120] it continued to have such interests, and the friendly tyrants helped to protect them. The Egyptian government served American interests (not as a favor to the United States but in pursuing what it regarded as its own interests) by maintaining its peace treaty with Israel, keeping the Suez Canal open to international shipping, and opposing radical, anti-American forces in the region. Saudi Arabia reliably supplied oil from its large reserves to the international market. Influential individuals and institutions, both within and outside the American government, therefore favored continued support for both countries.

Public and private pressure in the United States for such support was all the greater because it was far from clear that if the friendly tyrants were to fall from power their successors would be either less tyrannical or equally friendly to American interests. The Cold War offered two cautionary precedents: the anti-American, pro-Cuban and authoritarian Sandinistas had succeeded the pro-American dictator Anastasio Somoza in Nicaragua; and the unfriendly tyranny of the clerical leaders of the Islamic Republic had unseated the Shah, a prototypical friendly tyrant, in Iran.

The pro-American but undemocratic governments of Egypt and Saudi Arabia seemed all too likely, if they lost power, to give way not to Western-style democracy but to Islamism. In part, to be sure, because the Mubarak regime suppressed democratic political activity of all kinds, the strongest opposition to it in Egypt came not from democrats but from the Islamist Muslim Brotherhood.[121] In Saudi Arabia, Osama bin Laden's home country, radical Islamists commanded considerable sympathy, and the regime enshrined as its official doctrine, with which it bombarded the populace through the educational system and the mosques, the Islamist principles of Wahhabism. An Islamist group did in fact take advantage of the American commitment to democracy in the Middle East to seize power in 2006 when Hamas won the elections in the Palestinian territories on which the United States had insisted.

Because of the risks of doing so, the United States did not, in the end, make the promotion of democracy the only consideration, or even the major one, governing its relations with Egypt and Saudi Arabia.[122] Even if it had done so, this would scarcely have guaranteed the conversion of either to democratic governance, for reasons similar to those accounting for the failure of the other post-Cold War American missions.

For one thing, retaining their undemocratic political systems had far greater importance for the Egyptian and Saudi rulers than changing them had for the United States. The local elites were prepared to invest much more political capital, money, and even blood in blocking democracy than the government in Washington could muster to try to implant it. The autocrats would not give up power voluntarily and the American government was not about to remove them by force as it had Saddam Hussein.

For another, even if the governments of these two countries had wanted to install democracy, the effort to do so would have faced the same kinds of obstacles that had impeded the American efforts to foster the other political transformations it had attempted since 1993. One reason that the American government did not fully appreciate the difficulties of constructing democratic governments in the Middle East, where none existed or ever had existed, was that it operated with an erroneous—because incomplete—definition of the political system it sought to create across the region.

Bush was prone to conflating democracy with freedom: he called the initiatives he launched, collectively, the "forward strategy of freedom."[123] In practice that strategy concentrated on promoting free elections in the Middle East. Freedom—that is, liberty: the areas of social and political life fenced off from government control—and elections each form part of the political system known as democracy, but neither, by itself, defines that system. Democracy, properly understood, combines the two. A government that wins an election but does not respect political, religious, or economic liberty, such as the Hamas regime in Gaza, does not qualify as democratic.

The proper, hybrid definition of democracy[124] illustrates the principal barrier to constructing it in the Arab Middle East. Elections are easy to stage. Liberty, by contrast, is difficult to create. Freedom of religion, freedom of economic activity including the institution of private property, and political liberty—the rights enumerated in the first 10 amendments to the Constitution of the United States—depend for their existence on the appropriate values, above all on tolerance for differences and a regard for individual independence. Freedom also requires a particular set of habits, notably the habit of compromise. It needs, too, traditions, such as the responsiveness of leaders to those they lead. It requires, finally, institutions: legislatures, a criminal justice system with an impartial judiciary, and especially the institution that undergirds all the others—the rule of law. As the American experiences in Somalia, Haiti, the Balkans, Afghanistan, and Iraq demonstrated, these cannot be conjured out of thin air or readily transplanted from abroad.[125] They require time to take root and grow. They are the work of generations. Liberty cannot flourish in the absence of the necessary social conditions.

Of all the different parts of the world, the road to Denmark—that is, to effective Western-style institutions—was longest in the Arab Middle East.[126] The region qualified as the least democratic one in the world,[127] with no stable, functioning political system offering citizens regular opportunities to choose their leaders and scrupulously protecting religious, economic, and political liberty. According to the eminent specialist on the Middle East Bernard Lewis, historically the concept of liberty as Westerners understand it did not really exist in Middle Eastern societies.[128] The Bush administration was trying to bring democracy to a region that had been vaccinated against it. The vaccine included several components.

In common with other places where the American mission to create modern, decent, prosperity-supporting states had failed, the social structure of the region worked against democracy by giving rise to loyalties too narrow to support institutions based on impersonal norms, a requirement for democratic government. Arab societies had as their basic unit the tribe.[129]

Beyond kinship lineages, other parochial allegiances—sectarian, religious, and ethnic—dominated the Middle East. Sunnis and Shias, Muslims and non-Muslims, and Arabs and non-Arabs did not regard it as natural or desirable to live in a country in which each group had equal political rights, which is the necessary condition for democracy. The other Middle Eastern countries reproduced the kinds of divisions that the United States encountered in Iraq. The Bush administration could not change these basic social facts.

The region's large deposits of oil also obstructed the development of democratic politics. With oil wealth, governments have no need to do what is fundamental to democracy: take into account the preferences and opinions of those they govern. On the one hand, these governments get so much revenue from the sale of the country's oil that they can win popularity, or at least acceptance, by providing social services without taxing those who receive them. On the other hand, oil wealth gave these governments the resources to build institutions of repression to keep themselves in power. Arab regimes came to be known as "mukhabarat" states, the Arabic word for intelligence that in this context connoted the dominance of intelligence agencies or secret police. Moreover, much of the revenue from oil found its way into the bank accounts of the rulers, giving them a powerful incentive to retain power indefinitely rather than allow it to be conferred by democratic competition. A concerted effort to reduce American consumption of oil might have weakened the Arab autocracies; but such an effort proved politically impossible during the Bush administration, as it had before and afterward.

The economic systems of the region also inhibited the growth of democracy. Free-market economic institutions and practices foster political democracy by enshrining one basic form of liberty—private property—and by creating a middle class, the bulwark of democracy almost everywhere it is found.[130] Arab countries did not have genuinely free markets. The government dominated the economy in all of them, and economic success came not from providing popular products or services, as in Western economies, but rather through political connections to the rulers, an arrangement widely known as "crony capitalism."[131]

Not only the twenty-first-century features of Middle Eastern countries but also the region's past created a bias against democracy. Historically, Western Christendom had been the great rival of the Middle Eastern Islamic world,[132] and democracy bore the stigma, for the people of the Middle East, of its Western origins. While they welcomed some Western innovations such as weaponry, automobiles, telephones, and modern medicine, Arab Middle Easterners had at best mixed feelings about the ideas and institutions that their historic rivals for global power had invented and then spread around the world. The fact that it was the greatest Western Christian power, the United States, that was promoting democracy did nothing to enhance its popularity in the region.[133]

Islam itself, which exercised as much influence in the Middle East as any religion did anywhere else in the world, inhibited the growth of democracy. Because it lacks the separation of the sacred and the secular that is integral to Christianity,[134] strictly speaking religious law applies everywhere, leaving no room for the lawmaking by elected officials that democracy features. Since religious law handed down from the faith's founding years is deemed to be perfect, moreover, in principle Muslims have no need of further legislation of any kind.[135]

Like other major religions, Islam has had many incarnations and has many traditions, not all of them incompatible with democracy. Indeed, many twenty-first-century Muslims live in countries, some of them with Muslim majorities, governed by democratic rules and procedures.[136] The Arab version of Islam, however, tended to hew closely to the oldest and strictest interpretations of the faith because the Arab world—and specifically the Arabian peninsula in what became in the twentieth century Saudi Arabia—is where the religion originated.[137]

Moreover, the Middle East felt the full force of the Islamist wave of the 1970s,[138] which propounded a strict, backward-looking interpretation of the faith and a very large role for it in political affairs, both incompatible with liberty and popular sovereignty. Three events in the year 1979 made this movement particularly powerful: the Iranian Revolution, which brought to power in Tehran an Islamist government determined to expand its influence and spread its version of Islamic rule; an attack on the holy city of Mecca by fundamentalists opposed

to the Saudi royal family on the grounds that it had strayed dangerously far from the true faith, in response to which the regime enforced
and sought to disseminate more harshly Islamic interpretations and
practices; and the second oil shock, which, along with the first one
earlier in the decade gave both the Iranian and Saudi governments far
more money with which to spread their versions of Islam.

The rise of Saudi Arabia, a Sunni country (unlike Shia Iran) and thus
representative of the vast majority of Muslims, to a position of prominence, if not dominance, in the Islamic world[139] had a pronounced
and, by the standards of most of the 15 centuries of Islamic history,
distorting effect. As Bernard Lewis, describing Saudi influence, put it:

> Imagine then that the Ku Klux Klan gets total control of the state
> of Texas. And the Ku Klux Klan has at its disposal all the oil rigs in
> Texas. And they use this money to set up a well-endowed network of
> colleges and schools throughout Christendom, peddling their pecu-
> liar brand of Christianity. You would have an approximate equiva-
> lent of what has happened in the modern Muslim world.[140]

Like that of the Ku Klux Klan, the message of Saudi Islamism was
not a democratic one. Far more deeply rooted in Middle Eastern history and society, and with much more money to spread its message,
Islamism exerted wider and deeper influence across the region than did
the American mission of democracy promotion.

All of these countervailing forces—the American political investment in the friendly tyrants of the Middle East, the difficulty of
implanting the necessary institutions, the tribalism, oil, economic systems and anti-Western history of the region, and the features of Islam
inhospitable to democracy—pushed back against the Bush forward
strategy of freedom. That initiative, like the other, similar, post-Cold
War American missions in other parts of the world, had made little
headway when the Bush administration ended at the outset of 2009
and the Obama administration took office.

Like previous presidents succeeding a chief executive of the other
party, Barack Obama interpreted his election as a mandate to modify
or discard many of the foreign policies of his predecessor.

In the Middle East, this meant completing the withdrawal of American troops from Iraq that Bush had begun and abandoning, without the fanfare that accompanied that withdrawal, the Bush emphasis on promoting democracy in the region.[141] When, in 2009, peaceful protests on a large scale against the clerical dictatorship in Iran erupted, the Obama administration said and did almost nothing to encourage them.[142] The new president did aspire to transform, if not the Middle East as a whole, then at least the image of the United States there. His chosen instrument, however, was not American political institutions. It was a single American public official: himself.[143]

Six months into his presidency, on June 4, 2009, he delivered a speech in Cairo on the subject of American relations with Muslims that departed from previous presidential presentations in two striking ways.[144] First, it was addressed not to the people of Egypt, or to any particular country or set of countries, but to the "Muslim world" as a whole.[145] In so doing, Obama implied something that no other president had believed or at least said, and that was in fact of dubious accuracy when he himself said it: namely, that there is, for the purpose of statecraft, such an entity as a single, politically coherent Muslim world. (Ironically, the other international figure who spoke in those terms was Osama bin Laden.) Second, Obama presented himself as the solution to the problem of tension between Muslims and America. He had lived as a boy, he said in Cairo, in a Muslim country—Indonesia—and he considered it "part of my responsibility as President of the United States to fight against negative stereotypes of Islam wherever they appear,"[146] a responsibility not previously part of the job description for the position he held and one no leader of a Muslim-majority country had found it necessary to assume.

While in these two respects a break with presidential precedent, in other ways the Obama Cairo speech followed a familiar pattern. American presidents tend to impute great importance to their own words. It is, after all, largely their own rhetoric that takes them to the most powerful office in the world. They also come to believe that the force of their personalities, upon which their political careers also depend, can have the kind of impact abroad that it often has at home.

Franklin Roosevelt and Richard Nixon, for example, each believed himself to be uniquely equipped to manage policy toward the Soviet Union by virtue of his special personal relationship with his Soviet opposite number, Joseph Stalin in the first instance, Leonid Brezhnev in the second.

Along with Obama's personal initiative to repair what he saw as the broken relationship between the United States and the world's Muslims, and in keeping with his initial impulse to break new ground in American foreign policy, he committed himself to two other major changes. During his presidential campaign he had pledged to meet, without preconditions, with the leaders of hostile countries such as Cuba, Iran, and North Korea, in contrast with existing American policy.[147] The pledge arose from the apparent belief that such meetings, like his address to the Islamic world, would improve America's standing among people—in this case the autocratic leaders of these countries—hitherto hostile to the United States. In addition, he gave a speech in Prague on April 4, two months before his Cairo address, calling for the abolition of nuclear weapons everywhere. In recognition of and appreciation for the new course that Obama announced he wanted to follow, he received, from the Norwegian Nobel Committee, the Nobel Peace Prize for 2009.

Like the Bush forward strategy of freedom, the Obama initiatives were, in the end, largely set aside. The new president did not meet with the leaders his predecessors had shunned. The countries that had nuclear weapons, including the United States, showed no sign of giving them up.[148] The Muslims of the world displayed no enduring upsurge of enthusiasm for the international activities of the United States.[149]

That did not mean, however, that nothing changed in the Middle East during Obama's presidency. To the contrary, homegrown protest movements there seemed, for a brief, hopeful moment, on the verge of achieving what American policy had failed to accomplish. A series of upheavals across the Middle East unseated rulers long entrenched in power. Where the United States had failed to bring democracy to the people of the Arab world these people themselves seemed, for a brief historical moment, ready and able to install democratic governments for themselves by themselves. They, too, failed.

The Arab Spring

On December 17, 2010, Mohamed Bouazizi, a fruit peddler in the Tunisian city of Sidi Bouzid, set himself on fire to protest the harassment to which local officials had subjected him. The act sparked anti-government protests in Tunisia that spread rapidly across the Arab world to Yemen, Egypt, Bahrain, Libya, Syria, and other countries.[150] Severe and widespread public discontent with incumbent governments inspired the demonstrations, and many of the demonstrators demanded democratic political changes in places that were, without exception, undemocratically governed. It therefore seemed, at first, that democracy was finally coming to the Middle East; and in Mohammed Bouazizi's country a democratic political system did eventually take root. Elsewhere, however, that is not what happened.

The discontent that exploded across the Middle East at the end of 2010 and in 2011 had a number of interrelated causes: a large cohort of young men without jobs or economic prospects;[151] stagnant economies, especially in countries without oil, that offered no hope of future employment, let alone prosperity; oppressive, abusive regimes that remained in power through repression; and new technologies, especially social media, that made it possible to communicate more widely and organize demonstrations more rapidly than ever before.

The American response to the Arab Spring had, in turn, several not always consistent features: wariness, because governments friendly to the United States found themselves under siege; high hopes for the development of political systems committed to liberty and popular sovereignty; and uncertainty about how best to advance American values and interests in what became, across the region, increasingly chaotic conditions. American policy included both efforts to intervene to guide the course of events in the region and a determination to steer as clear of them as possible. Sometimes Washington adopted both approaches, at different times, to the same country. In the end, the United States had little influence on the Arab Spring and its aftermath, except in one country—Libya—where American military power did have a decisive effect but failed to bring democracy or even stability.

On January 25, 2011, evidently inspired by the Tunisian example, crowds began to gather in Tahrir Square in the heart of Cairo, demanding the resignation of President Hosni Mubarak, which was more or less what the Bush administration had suggested six years earlier. The protests spread to other Egyptian cities. Security forces cracked down on some of them, and several hundred people were killed.

The ambivalence on the part of the American government that had marked its democracy initiative carried over to its approach to the Egyptian chapter of the Arab Spring.[152] On the one hand, given America's political values, the Obama administration could hardly oppose removing a dictatorship, especially since the pressure to do so came from a grass-roots movement that appeared to favor replacing it with a democracy. On the other hand, the friendly tyrant who had wielded power in Egypt for three decades had consistently accommodated American interests. Eventually the administration decided that the Egyptian leader had to leave office. Obama called Mubarak to convey this message and shortly thereafter, on February 11, he did resign.[153] It was not pressure from the American government that forced him out, however, but rather the withdrawal of the support of Egypt's armed forces. Mubarak had come originally from the upper ranks of the military—he had been an air force general—but his former colleagues abandoned him because, among other reasons, of his apparent plan to have his son Gamal, who had no military background, succeed him as president.[154]

The next year, in May and June 2012, Egypt staged what the Bush administration had wanted: a free and fair election, as a result of which Mohammed Morsi, a member of the best-organized opposition group, the Muslim Brotherhood, became president of the country. The Brotherhood's Islamist ideology made it an unlikely partner of the United States but the Obama administration, committed to honoring the outcome of a democratic election and without more attractive options, sought to develop a good working relationship with the new regime.[155] It had some success: the United States and Egypt managed to cooperate, to a limited extent, during the second Gaza war in 2012.

If the United States was prepared to tolerate the new government of Egypt, however, a great many Egyptians were not. The Muslim Brotherhood in power proved to be both autocratic and incompetent,[156] a combination that ignited large anti-government demonstrations in late June and early July 2013. In response, the army removed Morsi from power, killed or imprisoned several thousand members of his organization, and took control of the country. In May 2014, the army's leader, Abdel Fattah al-Sisi, was elected president. These events again evoked ambivalence on the part of the United States, which found itself simultaneously relieved that an Islamist party had lost power and offended by what was, in effect, a military coup, in response to which the Obama administration imposed mild economic sanctions.

By 2014, over the course of three tumultuous years Egypt had come full circle, going from military rule, through a nation-wide uprising, the resignation of a long-serving autocrat, the election of an Islamist president, more demonstrations, and the forcible removal of that president leading back ultimately to military rule. Throughout all this the American government had been an interested bystander but not an active participant. It had had almost no impact on the dramatic events in Egypt,[157] where the United States was no better positioned to create democracy between 2011 and 2013 than it had been in 2005. The Egyptian round trip away from and then back to the kind of military rule that the country had had for six decades prior to 2011 left the United States with less influence there than it had had before. Both the triumphant military and the defeated Muslim Brotherhood regarded the Americans as having shown inadequate sympathy for their respective causes.[158] Moreover, the country's political trajectory had left Egypt in perilous economic straits, with a dwindling store of the hard currency needed to purchase the food and fuel its people required.[159] It was not the United States but rather the government of Saudi Arabia, bitterly hostile to the Muslim Brotherhood[160] and therefore fully supportive of the military, that stepped in after 2013 to provide crucial and generous financial assistance.

Elsewhere in the Middle East, when protests erupted against the autocratic ruler of another Arab country with which the United States had close ties, the Obama administration did not even display ambivalence: it supported the autocrat. Bahrain, a tiny oil-producing country on the Persian Gulf, had a majority-Shia population but a Sunni king. It also served as the home base of the United States Fifth Fleet, which made the ruler an important ally of the United States.

When, in the first part of 2011, the country's Shia launched peaceful demonstrations in favor of more democratic governance—that is, more power for themselves—military forces from Saudi Arabia marched across the causeway that connected that country to Bahrain to suppress them. The United States made no serious gesture of opposition.[161]

Also in February 2011,[162] a revolt against the government occurred in Libya. A big country geographically—the fourth largest in Africa—with its six million people concentrated in a narrow band running along the Mediterranean coast, and far less important to the United States than Egypt, Saudi Arabia, or even Bahrain, Libya had had, in the previous five decades, two claims on American attention: it possessed the tenth largest oil reserves in the world; and its dictator, an eccentric, megalomaniacal former army colonel named Muammar Qaddafi, had pursued rabidly anti-American policies that included sponsoring acts of terror against the United States. By 2011, however, Qaddafi had repaired his relations with Washington, renouncing terrorism and shutting down a program designed to make nuclear weapons.[163]

The uprising against him began in the western part of the country and centered on the city of Benghazi. Qaddafi's support came from eastern Libya, and especially the capital city of Tripoli. The anti-government movement quickly became an armed insurrection against which Qaddafi sent his army, producing a civil war. In early March the government forces gained the upper hand, pushing westward toward Benghazi. It seemed only a matter of time before the troops loyal to Qaddafi would crush the rebellion. They did not do so, however, because the West, including the United States, intervened to stop them.

The impetus for intervention came first from the leaders of Great Britain and France, Prime Minister David Cameron and President Nicolas Sarkozy. Alarmed at the possibility of a massacre of civilians like those that had taken place in the Balkans in the 1990s, they pressed for a United Nations resolution authorizing a no-fly zone over Libya, similar to the one that the United States had enforced over northern Iraq in 1991. While intended to protect civilians, such a measure was bound to help the rebels since Qaddafi controlled all of the country's military aircraft. The Arab League, whose members were not fond of the Libyan dictator, endorsed the measure. President Obama decided to adopt the British and French policy, and the Security Council passed a resolution calling for the use of "all necessary means" to protect Libyan noncombatants.

The United States then led an air campaign against the Libyan military that disabled its air force and gradually reduced its supply of tanks and other weapons. The war on the ground became a stalemate, but in August, as Western bombardment continued to take its toll, the rebels started to make progress and ultimately captured Tripoli. Qaddafi himself escaped from the capital and hid in the countryside for two months, but in September NATO warplanes struck a convoy of vehicles carrying him and the remnants of his inner circle, and forces loyal to the new Libyan regime located and killed him.

The Obama administration's involvement in the Libyan civil war repeated the policy of humanitarian intervention that had been the hallmark of the Clinton administration. Although American military intervention led to Qaddafi's overthrow, its initial and ostensible purpose—the one for which the UN authorized it—was different: it was to save the lives of civilians who, Western governments came to believe, the Qaddafi forces would kill once they had disarmed the rebels.

The administration was divided on the wisdom of intervening, with the three officials with primary responsibility for military policy—the secretary of defense, the chairman of the Joint Chiefs of Staff, and the national security advisor—as well as Vice President Joseph Biden all opposing it.[164] Against their advice, Obama decided to contribute American forces to the operations over Libya. Perhaps not coincidentally, the strongest proponents of this course of action within the executive branch all had connections to the humanitarian interventions of the 1990s. Susan Rice, the ambassador to the United Nations, had served in the Clinton administration and regretted that it had not intervened in Rwanda. Samantha Power, a member of the staff of the National Security Council, had worked as a journalist in the Balkans and subsequently written a book critical of the American failure on several occasions to use military force to prevent the killing of civilians.[165] The two of them alone would probably not have been able to prevail in the dispute over Libya policy, but they had a senior ally: the secretary of state.[166]

At the end of her husband's administration, Hillary Clinton had won a senate seat from New York. She had begun the contest for the 2008 Democratic presidential nomination as the favorite but had lost out to Obama. After his election he had asked her to serve in the senior position in his cabinet, and she had accepted.

By including a major political opponent in his cabinet Obama was following in the footsteps of one of the nation's greatest presidents, Abraham Lincoln, who assembled what came to be known as a "team of rivals" during the American Civil War.[167] Mrs. Clinton qualified as a political rival of Barack Obama but she, along with the other cabinet officers, turned out not to be an important part of his foreign policy team. More than most presidents he concentrated policymaking, especially the making of foreign policy, in the White House. The secretaries of state and defense had less power, and less say in major decisions, than their predecessors in other administrations

Mrs. Clinton spent much of her time at the State Department flying around the world giving speeches on subjects, such as women's rights, that, whatever their impact on the audience she happened to be addressing directly, enhanced her popularity in the United States. When she left the Obama administration at the end of its first term, she immediately became the leading contender for the 2016 Democratic presidential nomination. Years earlier, during the Vietnam War, her husband had written a letter explaining that his hope of a career in electoral politics had led him to make himself available for the military draft despite his opposition to the ongoing war to which draftees were being sent: he sought, he wrote, "to maintain my political viability." Four decades later his wife achieved the same goal by serving as secretary of state.

In justifying the decision to intervene in Libya, Obama invoked the same rationale that Clinton had used for the Balkan operations:

To brush aside America's responsibility as a leader and—more profoundly—our responsibilities to our fellow human beings under such circumstances would have been a betrayal of who we are . . . As president I refused to wait for the images of slaughter and mass graves before taking action.[168]

The commitment of the British and the French satisfied the administration's stated preference for taking military action on a multilateral
basis whenever possible. Obama also portrayed the intervention as a
way of supporting the then-promising trends of the Arab Spring:

> A massacre would have driven thousands of additional refugees
> across Libya's borders, putting enormous strains on the peaceful—
> yet fragile—transitions in Egypt and Tunisia. The democratic
> impulses that are dawning across the region would be eclipsed by
> the darkest form of dictatorship, as repressive leaders concluded that
> violence is the best strategy to cling to power.[169]

Leaders in other Arab countries, in fact, drew precisely that conclusion
despite the American intervention in Libya.

For a president who had come to office promising to end the wars
begun by his predecessor, inserting the United States into another conflict in the Arab world seemed out of political character; but Obama
promised to avoid the major, politically unpopular costs of the Bush
wars by refraining from putting American troops on the ground in
Libya. Clinton had made the same promise for the Balkans but had
dispatched American forces to police Bosnia and Kosovo after the wars
there had ended. Obama, by contrast, sent no American soldiers to
Libya, even after Qaddafi had fallen.

His fall did not bring peace to the country. To the contrary, fighting
continued among a variety of militias, some based on regional or
tribal affiliation, others embracing an Islamist creed. Qaddafi had
managed to impose a brutal form of stability on Libya. The end of
his rule left the country without any effective government at all.[170]
The violence spilled across Libya's borders. Tuareg soldiers, whom
Qaddafi had recruited from Mali, fled there with their weapons, fueling an insurgency against the Malian government.[171] With Qaddafi
gone, American attention shifted away from Libya only to be refo-
cused there on September 11, 2012, the eleventh anniversary of the
al Qaeda attacks on New York and Washington, when Islamist
militants attacked two American diplomatic facilities in the city of
Benghazi and killed four people, including the American ambassador
J. Christopher Stevens.

The Libyan operation not only did not replace the Qaddafi dictatorship with a democracy or even a stable government, it turned out not even to qualify as a successful humanitarian intervention. There had been, subsequent analysis suggested, no good reason to believe that Qaddafi's forces would have massacred civilians had those forces prevailed in the civil war;[172] and the Western intervention prolonged the conflict so that, by one estimate, seven to ten times more Libyans died than would have been the case if the United States and its allies had steered clear of the conflict and Qaddafi's forces had won it, as they were poised to do in March 2011.[173]

In Libya, once again, an American mission failed. The efforts of the government of the United States did not put Libya on the road to Denmark. Instead, they helped turn the country into a North African version of Somalia.[174] With unintentional assistance from the Obama administration, what was once one of the bright lights of the Arab Spring became a failed state. With Qaddafi gone, however, with the exception of the Benghazi attacks the American government, not to mention the American public as a whole, largely ignored the chaos there. That proved harder to do with another Arab country in which the people rose up against the government in 2011.

That country was Syria. In March 2011, peaceful protests against the government in Damascus began. The Assad regime responded with violent repression, initiating the bloodiest fighting of the Arab Spring. The conflict became a multi-sided civil war and a great humanitarian disaster. At the end of 2014, after three and a half years, it had the taken the lives of more than 200,000 people, most of them noncombatants murdered by forces loyal to Assad. Out of a population of about eighteen million, roughly two million Syrians had fled to Jordan, Lebanon, Turkey, Iraq, and Iraqi Kurdistan, and many others had been displaced within the country. The fighting effectively partitioned the country, with the regime controlling the western part and various opposition groups holding sway over much of the rest.

At first, the conflict pitted poor Syrians living in rural areas or forced off the land and into the cities—both groups harmed by a serious drought—against a government indifferent to their plight.[175] It soon became a sectarian war, with the majority Sunnis fighting to overthrow a government in which the minority Alawis monopolized power.[176]

Other countries became involved. Iran supported the Assad government, its long-term ally and fellow Shia regime, and dispatched Hezbollah forces from Lebanon to fight on Assad's behalf. Russia, whose alignment with the Syrian regime dated back to the Cold War era, also supported it. On the other side, Saudi Arabia and other Gulf states, out of solidarity with their fellow Sunnis and in opposition to their Shia and Persian archenemy Iran, sent arms and money to the rebels. Some of these funds found their way to Islamist groups, which figured prominently in the anti-Assad insurgency and attracted to their ranks Sunni Muslims from around the world eager to wage holy war against the Shia.

The Syrian civil war killed many more civilians than did the conflict in Libya. Unlike Muammar Qaddafi, moreover, Bashar Assad, who had spurned the entreaties of the Obama administration to make peace with Israel, remained both an adversary of the United States and an ally of America's greatest Middle Eastern nemesis, Iran. The administration therefore had more compelling humanitarian and strategic reasons to intervene in Syria than in Libya. Obama was, however, reluctant to involve the United States there. It was not until August 2011 that the administration expressed the view that Assad should leave power.[177] The president resisted calls either to arm opponents of the regime who were friendly—or at least not unfriendly—to the United States or to use American power directly to rescue the people the Assad regime was attacking. Syria looked all too much like its neighbor Iraq: that is, a country in which the serious pursuit of American values, including the humanitarian value of protecting civilians threatened by their government, would require an American occupation, as well as a country where the United States would have difficulty finding local allies willing and able to help achieve American goals.

Obama did make one rhetorical exception to his determination to remain aloof from the fighting in Syria. The Assad regime had a large stockpile of chemical weapons and in August 2012, Obama announced that their use would cross a "red line" for the United States and "change my calculus" about the American approach to the war. A year later the regime did launch chemical attacks on Sunni civilians in several cities. There followed one of the strangest and most embarrassing episodes in the history of American foreign policy.

Obama decided to respond to the attacks by bombing Syrian military targets. David Cameron promised that British forces would take part as well. The British House of Commons, however, voted against authorizing such an operation. Obama sought Congressional approval for an American bombing campaign but it soon became clear that he would not get it, in no small part because a large majority of the American public opposed such a venture.[178] So, abruptly and without consulting anyone except his closest aides, he reversed himself, saying that the United States would not attack Syria after all.

At a press conference in London, Secretary of State Kerry had been asked whether anything could be done to prevent the attack. He replied—more than a little facetiously, those who heard him thought—that the United States would hold its fire if Assad agreed to relinquish all of his chemical weapons, something that seemed entirely unlikely. Russian President Vladimir Putin, not only an ally of Assad but increasingly an adversary of the United States, declared that he was prepared to broker an agreement to achieve precisely that, and the administration accepted. The Russian proposal offered a way out of the corner into which Obama had painted himself by announcing and then renouncing his intention to strike. The maneuver did not enhance the credibility or the prestige of the United States or of its 44th president but it did keep America out of the Syrian civil war—for a time.[179]

What finally drew the United States into the Syrian conflict was not the depredations of the Assad regime but the successes of its adversaries. Having become increasingly prominent in the opposition to the regime, Islamist groups, including al Qaeda affiliates, crossed the border to conduct military operations in Iraq, scored dramatic victories, and proclaimed the establishment of the Islamic State of Iraq and Syria (ISIS)[180] with the goal of extending its reach across the Middle East.[181]

The bombing campaign the United States launched had the humanitarian goal of rescuing beleaguered minorities and the strategic aim of assisting pro-American Kurds. It had another motive as well: the fear that if ISIS, with its 20,000 to 30,000 fighters and an apparently devoted following among many Sunni Muslims around the world, consolidated its hold on the territory it had managed to overrun it would use that territory as a base from which to launch attacks on the United States, just as al Qaeda had used Afghanistan for this purpose 13 years before.

In a speech to the nation in September, Obama announced that the United States would "degrade and ultimately destroy" ISIS. This would be done, he said, by assembling a coalition of other countries to fight the Islamists. He would not, the president assured Americans, deploy American ground forces in Syria. This strategy had three major problems, the solutions to which the president did not immediately provide. First, it was not at all clear that ISIS made attacking American targets as high a priority as had Osama bin Laden's al Qaeda. Although hostile in principle to the United States, ISIS faced the challenge, on which it might have been expected to concentrate, of holding and governing the territory it had conquered, as al Qaeda in Afghanistan had not.

Second, destroying ISIS meant replacing it as the government of the parts of Syria and Iraq over which, at the end of 2014, it held sway; but no plausible replacement was available. The officially recognized governments of Iraq and Syria were the obvious candidates, but no matter how disenchanted the Sunnis of Syria and Iraq became with the harsh rule of ISIS they were unlikely to submit themselves again to the Assad family or to the Shia of Baghdad. Other countries in the region were not about to occupy the territory that ISIS had seized. If the United States was determined to oust the Islamists, the only immediately feasible way to do so was with its own troops.

The air campaign the United States began against ISIS had the unintended effect of assisting the governments in Damascus and Tehran, which was its third problem. The American military action stood to benefit, in the Syrian case, parties that were otherwise its adversaries: the Assad regime, its Hezbollah allies, and their common patron, the Islamic Republic of Iran. In 2014 the United States intervened in a sectarian conflict on the side of the Shia and therefore against the interests, or at least the preferences, of the Sunni countries of the Middle East, which happened to be the ones with which the United States had, or sought to have, good relations: Saudi Arabia, the smaller Gulf states, Turkey, Egypt, and Jordan. Thus, while the fear of another September 11 drew the United States into Iraq and Syria, the policy that Obama chose to prevent such an eventuality had the potential to become what the response to the September 11 attacks could be seen, in unhappy retrospect, to have been: excessive, expensive, and counterproductive.

By the end of 2014 the United States had failed, in Syria, to achieve the principal aim of any of the three post-Cold War presidencies. It had not rescued distressed people from their government, as the Clinton administration had sought to do. It had not planted the seeds of democracy, the ambition of the Bush administration. America's policy toward Syria in the Obama administration had not even done what Barack Obama had announced he would do upon assuming office: get out and stay out of Middle Eastern wars.

If the Bush democracy initiative had demonstrated that the United States could not implant democratic government in the Arab Middle East, the Arab Spring showed that the Arabs themselves could not do so, either. The local political culture proved resistant to liberty and popular sovereignty. What had begun at the end of 2010 had, four years later, plainly failed to fulfill American hopes for it in any country except Tunisia. The outcome of the Arab Spring did settle the debate with the region's friendly tyrants that the Bush democracy initiative had begun—by vindicating both sides. The Americans had said that the political status quo in the Middle East could not endure, and they were proven right. The Arab autocrats had said that the alternative to their rule would be worse, and they were proven right as well.

The early stages of the Arab Spring resembled the anti-communist revolutions in what was then called Eastern Europe. In 1989 largely peaceful uprisings removed the unpopular communist governments of Poland, Hungary, Czechoslovakia, East Germany, Bulgaria, and Rumania.[182] All became democracies that protected religious, economic, and political liberty and conducted regular, free, and fair elections. Czechoslovakia split into two separate countries, the Czech Republic and Slovakia; but otherwise post-communist Eastern Europe, which came to be known by the geographically more accurate name Central Europe,[183] made a relatively smooth transition to coherent, democratic nation-states commanding the loyalty of people of different ethnicities and religions living within their borders. Indeed, the citizens of these countries displayed an even broader (if often modest) allegiance: all of them joined the European Union.

The year 2011 began in the same way as 1989. Long-ruling dictators lacking popular legitimacy fell from power one after another. It ended differently, with renewed repression and war. While Europe continued to build a post-modern, transnational structure of governance and cooperation—the EU—the Arab Middle East, between 2011 and 2014, melted down to what had been its basic elements before the modern age: the sect, the tribe, the clan, the Islamic faith. In the terms in which Americans tended to see the world, the Middle East was moving in the opposite direction from the one in which the United States had believed history was traveling. It was going backward.

The destructive impact of the course of the Arab Spring on the optimism that the march of history had made the entire world receptive to American efforts to transform it is one of the reasons that the year 2014 marked the end of the period in which such efforts dominated the foreign policy of the United States. There is another. The American emphasis on the internal transformation of other countries became possible with the end of the Cold War because the traditional preoccupations of the foreign policies of all great powers before then, the external behavior of their peers, had declined sharply in importance. After 1993 the United States was free to conduct a missionary foreign policy because it faced no serious challenges to its security, to its basic international interests, or to the global rules and institutions that it had done so much to establish and in which it believed. In 2014 that happy circumstance came to an end.

6

The Restoration

Ninety percent of [the Chinese Navy's] time is spent on thinking about new and interesting ways to sink our ships and shoot down our planes.

— US ADMIRAL DENNIS BLAIR[1]

Who would have thought it possible 25 years after the fall of the Berlin wall . . . something like this [the Russian invasion of Ukraine] could happen in the middle of Europe?

— ANGELA MERKEL[2]

The End of the Post-Cold War Order

In 2014 the world observed the centenary of the outbreak of World War I, which brought to an end 100 years, dating back to 1815, without a war in Europe involving all the great powers and began a period of continual, all-encompassing conflict: the two world wars and the Cold War. The year 2014 turned out itself to have a similar historical significance. Then, too, an era came to an end, the period after the Cold War during which Europe and the world enjoyed an even deeper peace than in the nineteenth century. The year 2014 concluded, as well, a particular era in American foreign policy, one in which, as never before, the effort to transform the internal politics and economics of other countries took precedence over the defense of the United States and its interests.

By the close of that year the missions of transformation that the American government had undertaken toward China and Russia and in Somalia, Haiti, Bosnia, Kosovo, Afghanistan, Iraq, and in the wider Middle East had all failed. None of the countries involved had become what the United States had sought to make it. It was not these failures, however, that brought the post-Cold War era to an end. Just as a missionary's failure to make converts does not ordinarily shake his or her basic faith, so these countries' resistance to American efforts to make them more like the United States did not eliminate the American conviction, which dated back to the earliest European settlers in North America, that effecting such transformations was a worthy goal.

The failed missions, especially those in Afghanistan and Iraq, had proven costly, and their costs made Americans wary of attempting them elsewhere; but costs alone do not account for the end of the mission-dominated period of American foreign policy. During the Cold War, after all, the American wars in Korea and Vietnam had had even higher costs than the failed post-Cold War missions, yet the United States did not abandon the overall policy that gave rise to those conflicts, namely the containment of international communism and of the Soviet Union.

American foreign policy changed in 2014 because the world changed. The global condition that had made possible the two-decades-long emphasis on missions of transformation disappeared.[3] That condition was the deepest, most pervasive peace the world had experienced in centuries, if ever. It was a peace that arose from the absence not only of war but of the threat of war, of urgent preparations for war, of serious thoughts of war among the most powerful political leaders on the planet. It arose from the absence of what is sometimes called security competition, or power politics—that is, political and military rivalry among the most powerful countries. Because countries must assure their own survival before all else, historically, power politics, including its ultimate expression, war itself, has shaped relations between and among them. With the end of the Cold War this ceased to be the underlying fact of international life, freeing the world's richest and strongest country, the United States to devote its international efforts to improving other countries rather than protecting itself and its allies. Liberated from concerns about security, it could turn foreign policy into social work.[4]

So unusual and far-reaching in its effects was the disappearance of security competition after the Cold War that it bears comparison with revolutions within sovereign states, indeed to the first and greatest of them all, the French Revolution of 1789. Before then monarchs had come and gone in Europe but the institution of monarchy had remained. The Revolution transformed France's form of government: it overthrew not only the king, Louis XVI, but the centuries-old system of kingship. Similarly, throughout history great powers had risen and fallen, the hierarchy of countries in the international system had changed, but the system's basic feature, the dominance of security competition, had endured. International politics was a game in which the players came and went but the rules, and therefore the conduct of whichever sovereign states happened to be playing, remained.

With the end of the Cold War the rules did change, which gave the most powerful player of all the freedom to ignore the standard business of foreign policy—coping with the international behavior of other governments—in favor of trying to transform the way governments behaved toward those they governed.

Power politics came to what turned out to be a temporary conclusion after the Cold War in part because of a trend that had begun well before then: the growing unattractiveness of war due to the damage that ever more powerful weapons could inflict.[5] The freedom available to American foreign policy after the collapse of European communism stemmed as well from the distribution of power in the wake of that great historical event: the United States vastly exceeded all other countries in military and economic prowess.

American power defined what President George H. W. Bush called the "new world order," along with three other features of international relations after the Cold War. One of the three was the increased importance of the global economy, to which virtually every country belonged and that, by generating material benefits for its members, helped to suppress the impulse for security competition. The second was the fact that the possession of nuclear weapons, the most dangerous armaments in the history of mankind, was limited to countries that could be relied upon not to use them for the purpose of traditional power politics. The third signal feature of the new world order was the lack of interest on the part of China and Russia, each with the capacity to act as a traditional great power, in pursuing the assertive policies that in the past had put rivalry, security, and military competition at the center of international relations.

Even as it was engaged in its missions of transformation, the United States played a part in reinforcing each of these three features of the post-Cold War world. By the end of 2014, however, both despite American efforts and because of American mistakes, all had become unstable. The new world order of 1993 had come to look, two decades later, all too much like the old international system of the Cold War and indeed of all the preceding centuries. Like France several decades after the Revolution, when the monarchy had been restored, the old ways had returned: the world at the end of 2014 had become a place in which the United States could no longer afford to indulge its values; it had, instead, to seek, as in the past, to protect its interests.

Taking part in the global economy reduces the incentives for conflict because by trading with and investing in one another countries become partners rather than rivals. States trade and invest across borders in order to become richer; the ultimate form of rivalry, war, makes them poorer. In the first era of a truly integrated international economy, the nineteenth century, the idea that trade guarantees peace gained currency in the world's greatest trading country, Great Britain. The outbreak of World War I in 1914 showed that idea to be excessively optimistic but as global economic interdependence grew in the ensuing century, and especially in the wake of the Cold War, it provided an antidote, although not a perfect one, to international conflict.

Beginning after World War II, the United States assumed greater responsibility than any other country for organizing and managing the international economy.[6] For the first decade and a half after 1993 that economy functioned remarkably well, generating higher and more widely shared growth than ever before. Then came the near-meltdown of the American financial system of 2008 and the crisis of Europe's common currency, the euro, beginning in 2010, both the result in part of policy errors by the richest countries. The period of glorious prosperity ended.

This reversal of global economic fortune weakened the new world order. Because it did less well at generating prosperity, membership in that order became less attractive. Its champions and mainstays, the United States and the European Union, became economically less buoyant and politically less inclined to assert themselves on its behalf.

After 2008 the international system was less safe for American missions of transformation around the world than it had been before.

Not every country took the end of the Cold War as an opportunity to forswear the traditional quest for increased power through the use of force and settle happily into the peaceful, cooperative routines of economic interdependence. The new world order included a few pockets of rejection and resistance. The resistance that attracted the most attention, especially from Americans, came from the Islamist terrorists responsible for the attacks on New York City and Washington, DC of September 11, 2001. Terrorists were not, however, the most dangerous rejectionists. That distinction belonged to two countries, North Korea and Iran. The regimes of each embraced ideologies committed to the aggressive pursuit of power at the expense of other countries. Because they governed states and controlled territory, the two regimes had greater potential for causing disruption beyond their borders than terrorist groups such as al Qaeda. Most importantly, both had a far greater capacity than did terrorists for acquiring the most destructive and dangerous feature of contemporary international politics, nuclear weapons.

Because they can wreak so much destruction, these weapons make their possessors militarily formidable. North Korea and Iran both sought, throughout the post-Cold War period, to develop nuclear weapons for the purpose, at the very least, of threatening other countries. Full-fledged nuclear arsenals under their control had the potential to restart serious security competition in their regions and beyond. The United States led international efforts to deny nuclear armaments to these two countries. These efforts began during the Cold War, they continued after its end, and they had some success in slowing the progress made in each case.

By 2014, however, each country was approaching a nuclear tipping point, beyond which it would pose the kind of threat to global stability and American interests with which the United States had not had to contend since the Western triumph over European communism. The North Korean and Iranian nuclear programs produced cracks in the foundation of the post-Cold War order.

The heart of that order, the feature that most sharply distinguished it from what had gone before, was the absence of the military and political competition between and among the strongest states around which international politics had traditionally revolved. The governments of China and Russia eschewed the foreign policies practiced by their communist and imperial predecessors. They did so in part because of the intimidating power, in the wake of the Cold War, of the United States, but for other reasons as well.

In the 1990s the United States launched initiatives—linking trade with China with its human rights policy and working to implant a free-market economy in Russia—designed, among other things, to restructure the domestic political and economic arrangements of those countries in ways that would reinforce their pacific foreign policies. The initiatives failed, but the American government believed, or hoped, that the prevailing political and economic trends of the twenty-first century would have the same effect.

This did not happen. By 2014 both countries had abandoned their reticence and restraint in favor of the classic great-power quest to control more territory.[7] In so doing, each showed itself willing to approach the threshold of war and, in the Russian case, to cross it. China's aggressive naval maneuvers and Russia's invasion and occupation of parts of neighboring Ukraine put an end to the world in which the United States faced no serious threat to its own security or that of its allies, the world in which it could afford to devote attention and resources to trying to transform countries with little capacity to affect vital American interests. Chinese and Russian foreign policies reversed the revolution in international politics that had taken place at the end of the Cold War. They restored the old international regime of power politics, thereby presenting the United States with challenges that differed from the ones with which it had been preoccupied for two decades.

The Bubbles Burst

The international economy helped win the Cold War. That great global rivalry took place in three dimensions: it was a military, a political, and an economic contest. The West won the economic competition decisively, and its economic success discredited its communist adversary politically, which in turn diminished the impact of communism's military strength.

The American-centered Western coalition owed its economic triumph to the superiority in generating economic growth of its system of economic organization, the free market, in comparison with communist central planning. Free markets lend themselves to cross-border economic activity. Accordingly, during the Cold War the West's free-market economies traded with and invested in one another. Together the North Americans, the Western Europeans, and the Japanese formed an integrated international economic community, and their integration enhanced their economic performance, contributing to their decisive advantage over the communist bloc.

When the Cold War ended, the global economy became a central feature of the new world order that succeeded it.[8] With a few isolated exceptions, all countries took part in the pursuit of what became the supreme national goal almost everywhere: economic growth. Beyond fostering growth, international economic integration contributed to the suppression of power politics and so to sustaining the international conditions in which the United States could devote itself to missions of transformation. The global economy encouraged peaceful international conduct by separating power from wealth. Countries could and did become rich without deploying military power against others. This was not possible before the Industrial Revolution (which laid the basis for a genuinely integrated global economy), when wealth came from the control of land, which in turn required military might to secure. Whereas in the past sovereign states had gotten rich through war, with the growing importance of cross-border economic activity, armed conflict came to have the opposite effect: war made them poorer. International economic integration involves cooperation rather than rivalry. Among countries participating in the global economy in the wake of the Cold War such cooperation was more widely practiced and was more important to its practitioners than ever before.

Free markets do not operate in a vacuum. Whatever their scope—local, national, or international—they require a sturdy political framework that fosters the confidence that people need to engage in economic transactions. Ordinarily, governments provide the framework. Because there has never been an effective global government, however, the global economy has depended on a single country to supply the needed political underpinning.

During the first great age of global economic integration, in the nineteenth century, Great Britain was that country. Trade and investment flowed within the far-flung British Empire, the British Navy protected the seaborne trade of other countries as well as Britain's, the London financial community—using the world's most powerful currency, the pound sterling—supported trade and channeled investment around the world, and the great idea underlying global economic integration, the universal economic advantages of free trade, was born and first gained political currency in the British Isles.

After World War II, the United States assumed Britain's international economic responsibilities. It took the lead in recreating the institutions and practices that the two world wars and the Great Depression had destroyed. American military power, deployed around the world to check communist aggression, had the added effect of protecting international commerce. The United States underwrote international economic activity as well by supplying a widely used currency, the dollar, and by opening its home market to imports from Europe and Asia.[9]

With the end of the Cold War and the collapse of communism, the American-supported economic order expanded, becoming truly global in scope. China, India, and formerly communist Europe joined it. The United States continued its policies of support, which became, in one way, more difficult to provide because the system had grown larger, with far more cross-border trade and investment, but in another way easier to supply because America no longer had to confront powerful communist adversaries.

Properly understood, therefore, post-Cold War American foreign policy had a dual focus. The United States protected and helped to manage the global economic order to which almost all countries—and all the important ones—belonged. The policies that it undertook for those purposes were the most important ones the country implemented beyond its borders. Because it had become routine, however, carrying over as it did from the Cold War era, and because it encountered no serious challenges, what America did in support of cross-border economic activity attracted little notice in the United States or elsewhere.

At the same time, a few far less consequential but politically unstable places—Somalia, Haiti, the Balkans, Afghanistan, and Iraq—became the objects of American attention. While sustaining the global economy was important for the United States and the world, pacifying and trying to transform these trouble spots seemed to officials of the American government to be urgent; and, as so often in human affairs, the urgent took precedence over the important.

Countries took part in the international economy in order to achieve economic growth, and at first rapid economic growth is what they got. Between the end of the Cold War and 2008, growth boomed almost everywhere, which reinforced global allegiance to the post-Cold War order and respect, if not always affection, for its principal guardian, the United States. Then, in 2008, because of the United States, the period of high growth came to an abrupt end.

On September 15, 2008, the collapse of the American investment bank Lehman Brothers caused a near-meltdown of the country's financial system. Lehman was so closely connected to so many other major financial institutions that its demise sowed panic, which spread like a computer virus on the Internet. Its trading partners could not be certain of their own solvency. Credit froze and, because credit is the lifeblood of a modern economy, this jeopardized American economic activity of all kinds. It was the equivalent for the economy of a heart attack for a human being.[10]

The Lehman failure triggered the heart attack because it burst an enormous version of the kind of financial bubble to which free-market economies are susceptible. A bubble forms when overconfident investors bid the price of an asset ever higher:[11] one of the earliest and perhaps the best known of all such bubbles was the one based on tulip bulbs in the Netherlands in the seventeenth century. In the twenty-first-century-United States the asset in question was real estate. The housing bubble expanded to epic dimensions and endangered the entire financial system when it burst because so much borrowed money helped to inflate it, as did recently devised and poorly understood financial instruments.[12]

While severely damaged, the American financial system did not break down completely in the wake of the Lehman failure; but its difficulties brought on the deepest economic downturn in the United States since another financial disruption had led to the Great Depression of the 1930s. Moreover, the American economic distress spread around the world: to Europe through that continent's close connections with financial institutions in the United States and to Asia because the American recession sharply reduced American purchases of Asian exports.

The financial crisis that erupted on September 15, 2008, administered almost as great a psychological and political shock to the United States as—and a greater one to the rest of the world than—the terrorist attacks on New York and Washington, DC of almost exactly seven years before. The two events had a cause in common: a failure of imagination. The American political authorities, despite previous terrorist assaults, could not, or at any rate did not, conceive of an attack as devastating as the one al Qaeda launched on September 11, 2001.[13] Similarly, seven years later the country's economic officials, and experienced economic observers as well, despite warnings that real estate values had risen to unsustainable heights, did not believe that this would lead to the thunderous crash that in fact occurred.[14] Asset prices had plunged in the past, but investors and officials responsible for overseeing the economy embraced a familiar, and dangerous, mantra of the financial community when the signs of a bubble appear: "this time it's different."

Both events shook the American government and the American public. Both gave rise to extraordinary measures—to guard against further attacks in the earlier case and to prevent catastrophic financial disintegration in the later one—that involved expanding the power of the American government in ways that approached, if they did not exceed, the boundaries set by American law and the American Constitution.[15] The response in both cases, whatever its constitutional standing, proved effective. The worst did not happen. The United States suffered no further serious terrorist attacks and credit, with the assistance and encouragement of the federal government, became available again.

Indeed, in retrospect the American government did well in coping with the consequences of September 15. Drawing in part on American experiences with the Mexican and East Asian financial crises of the 1990s,[16] the actions it took succeeded in preserving its largest financial institutions, restarting the flow of credit, and restoring a measure of confidence in the financial system as a whole. Without the frequently ad-hoc policies adopted by the Treasury Department and the Federal Reserve, the American economy would almost surely have suffered more damage than it did. The American authorities also helped the governments of other afflicted countries to cope with the challenges its own financial crisis had imposed on them.[17]

While the damage from the bursting of the real estate bubble could have been worse, the damage it did do, for all the American government's rescue efforts, was considerable. Virtually every country around the world felt its effects, some more than others, and the losses it caused dimmed the luster of the global economic order. Membership in that order, it turned out, brought costs as well as benefits.

The crash of 2008 lowered the global standing of the United States.[18] To be sure, the financial crisis had diverse and complicated causes, not all of which stemmed from American mistakes. A number of countries, chief among them China, for their own economic and political reasons and contrary to the interests of the global economy as a whole, ran large, persistent current account surpluses with the United States. Many of the dollars they earned found their way back into the American economy and helped to inflate the housing bubble.[19] Still, the United States received the lion's share of the blame for the global economic disaster of 2008 and afterward, and rightly so. The crisis exploded in the American financial system, after all. It was the American government that had ignored what appeared in retrospect to have been clear warning signs of peril.[20] The American economic authorities and economic experts also contributed to the financial crash through a mistake similar to the one that doomed the country's missions of transformation between 1993 and 2014.

In both cases mistaken ideas about how the world worked, ideas rooted in both American preferences and recent experience, led to failure. Behind the failed missions in Somalia, Haiti, the Balkans, Afghanistan, and Iraq lay the belief, fortified by the late-twentieth-century spread of democracy and the near-universal appeal of membership in the global economy, that peoples everywhere could and would adopt Western political and economic institutions and practices. The societies in which the missions of transformation took place, however, most of them dominated by kinship ties and riven by ethnic, religious, and sectarian divisions, proved inhospitable to the Western implants the United States attempted.

Similarly, many of the Americans involved in finance in both the private sector and the government believed that financial markets were self-regulating and so did not require active supervision.[21] For this they could cite some evidence: at the end of the twentieth century and the beginning of the twenty-first the United States and other countries had engaged in extensive deregulation of finance, and until 2008 their economies had thrived. In that year, however, it turned out that, just as the idea of the universal receptivity to democracy and free markets was mistaken, so, too, was the conviction that financial markets would function smoothly indefinitely without serious regulation.

Ignorance played a part in both failures. American political leaders knew little about the societies they proposed to transform; American economic officials and professional economists did not fully understand the country's twenty-first-century financial system, with its array of institutions other than banks that came to be known as the "shadow banking system" and its new and complicated financial instruments.

The financial crisis and its aftermath undermined faith in the global economy around the world. That faith had rested on the assumption that participation in cross-border international economic activity would deliver steady growth. After 2008, to the contrary, many countries suffered major economic losses.

The crisis also damaged the American reputation for competent economic management.[22] In addition, it aggravated preexisting sentiments in two large, important, countries. Drawing on other sources as well, these sentiments pushed those two countries, by 2014, toward challenging rather than upholding the post-Cold War order. In the short term China escaped serious economic damage from the financial crash and the ensuing recession, which strengthened its leaders' confidence that they could expand Chinese power and influence in Asia and beyond, whatever the wishes of other countries including the United States. Russia, by contrast, did suffer a major economic setback as a result of the financial crisis and the recession, which only increased Russian resentment of the United States, the West, and the global political and economic orders for which they were responsible.

The economic costs to the United States of what happened in 2008 and thereafter were very high, which made the world's leading power both less willing and less able to serve as the custodian of the global economy and the wider post-Cold War order.[23] With the near-death experience of its financial system and the prolonged slump in output that followed coming on top of the disappointments of Iraq and Afghanistan, America turned inward. The public strongly favored concentrating on problems at home rather than addressing instability abroad.[24] Weakened by the events of 2008, the global economy, and therefore the international order in which the United States had concentrated on missions of transformation, suffered another major blow in the following years: a financial crisis in Europe.

The virtues of international economic integration, and therefore the benefits of participation in the global economy, have—or had—no better, more persuasive advertisement than the European Union. The process of integration in Europe began shortly after the end of World War II and progressed so far that European countries pooled their sovereignty to create, in 1999, a single currency. By 2014, 19 of the EU's 28 members used that currency, the euro. As economic integration in Europe proceeded, the security competition that had dominated the international relations of the continent for centuries came to an end. Between 1870 and 1945, France and Germany fought three increasingly destructive wars. By the end of the Cold War, because, among other reasons, their economies had become so closely intertwined, another such conflict between them had become unthinkable.

European economic integration following World War II also coincided with, and received credit for, rapid economic growth. Shortly after the American real estate bubble burst, however, Europe had its own financial crisis, which ushered in hard economic times on the continent. Like the American crisis and its aftermath, the European economic troubles made participation in the global economy, and the peaceful conduct that participation encouraged, less broadly compelling.[25]

As in the United States, a bubble caused Europe's economic difficulties, in the European case a bubble in the government bonds sold by the southern European members of the common currency to finance their deficits. With the euro's formation these bonds seemed entirely safe, and investors, including many northern European banks, rushed to buy them. Then investor psychology changed and the interest rates the southern Europeans had to offer to attract purchasers rose sharply, which placed enormous stress on their economies. Greece effectively went bankrupt and other, larger, more important countries—Italy, for example—drifted in that direction. National bankruptcies on a large scale had the potential to ruin bond-holding banks in Europe and their counterparts in North America and elsewhere.

The EU moved to forestall this possibility by making loans to the distressed countries; ultimately the European Central Bank declared that it would buy the bonds in question without limit. The EU addressed its crisis more slowly and less decisively than the American government had responded to its own in 2008 because it was not itself a unified state but rather an association of governments, each of which had to approve whatever action was taken.

By the end of 2014 the measures the EU had adopted had succeeded in preventing the worst case: national bankruptcies beyond Greece, a financial panic, and the collapse of the euro; but the crisis had not ended. The terms that the southern Europeans had had to accept to receive their loans had pushed their economies into deep recession, generating a populist political backlash within their borders.

Like the American financial crisis of 2008 and the failure of America's missions of transformation around the world, the crisis of the euro stemmed from an initial, fundamental mistake. Both historical experience and the studies of professional economists had led to the conclusion that a currency, in order to function successfully, requires certain political conditions that were not present in the case of the euro. Its members did not comprise an "optimal currency zone" because, among other things, they did not have a single overarching government.

Just as American economic officials did not respond to the signs that a dangerous real estate bubble was forming, so the leaders of Western Europe, in creating the euro, ignored what history had taught and economists had learned about currencies. Indeed, they created it as much to intensify political integration on the continent, and thus enhance Europe's political role in the world, as to accelerate economic growth;[26] but the euro's troubles set Europe back on both fronts, fostering political dissension and economic stagnation. As a result, Europe, like the United States in the wake of its own financial shock, became less powerful and influential in international affairs. This in turn diminished the appeal of the post-Cold War order of which it was, along with the United States, one of the two main pillars.

In general, the financial troubles of the West had the same effect on the post-Cold War international order, the framework for the American missions of transformation, that the weakening of the immune system has on a person. They enhanced the international system's vulnerability to challenges to its defining norm—the absence of security competition. Just as a weakened immune system does not by itself constitute a disease, the two financial crises did not by themselves bring back such competition; but they made it more feasible for countries that were so inclined to restore it, just as a weakened immune system increases the vulnerability to pathogens. Four countries proved to be so inclined. Two were once and future great powers, with large territories, substantial military resources, and long histories of conducting the kind of aggressive foreign policies that had not been in evidence in the wake of the Cold War. By 2014 China and Russia had resumed such policies. The two other countries, North Korea and Iran, did not qualify as major powers and serious potential disturbers of the international peace in any way except one: their common aspiration to acquire the most destructive weapon in human history.

By 2014 the challenges that China, Russia, North Korea, and Iran had mounted had become serious enough to restore to the international order, and to the foreign policy of the United States, the historically familiar imperatives of power politics. The future had become the past. China and Russia's territorial aspirations, along with North Korea and Iran's pursuit of nuclear armaments, shifted the agenda of American foreign policy away from the promotion of its values in countries that could not affect the United States in any serious way and back to the defense of its interests against states that most certainly could.

The Rogues

New circumstances beget new terminology. The unusually peaceful condition of the post-Cold War world inspired a term for the few countries that did not place a high value on peace, or on peaceful economic relations with others. The "rogues" got their name, presumably, from rogue elephants, which separate from the herd and behave dangerously. The rogue states, similarly, distinguished themselves from the vast majority of the other members of the international community in the goals they sought and the strategies they employed in seeking them.[27] They wanted more power, territory, and influence and were willing to use force to get them. Since this was historically true of most countries most of the time, their designation as outliers and rebels against the prevailing international norms testified to how historically unusual those norms in fact were.

Two rogues in particular, North Korea and Iran, commanded the attention of the United States. Both professed ideologies whose aggressive implications harked back to the great, poisonous, destructive political creeds of the twentieth century, fascism and communism. North Korea remained an orthodox communist country and overlaid its commitment to its own version of Marxism-Leninism—which in practice meant total control of all aspects of political, social, and economic life under the reign of a single family—with a virulent form of nationalism and self-reliance known as "juche." Iran was ruled by Islamic fundamentalists dedicated, at least nominally, to enforcing Islamic law throughout their country and beyond, spreading Iranian influence, and destroying the state of Israel. It differed from al Qaeda and Saudi Arabia, both of which also embraced fundamentalism and sought to impose religious law, in that its rulers (and citizens) were Shia, not Sunni. Unlike the terrorist group, moreover, the Iranian clerics, while dedicated sponsors of terrorism, also controlled a state; and unlike the al-Saud family that ruled Saudi Arabia, the mullahs in Tehran made it their goal to expand their power and influence by force.

Both North Korea and Iran defined their foreign policies by opposition to the United States, with which both had a history of conflict. The Truman administration had dispatched troops to the Korean peninsula in June 1950 to repel the invasion of the south by communist North Korea. American forces had remained there in strength after the 1953 armistice for the purpose of deterring another attack. The 1979 Iranian revolution that overthrew America's ally, the shah, and brought the radical clerics to power in Tehran had a decidedly anti-American cast. Students supporting the new regime took American diplomatic personnel hostage and held them for more than a year, establishing a relationship of mutual hostility with the United States that outlasted the Cold War.

The American government concerned itself throughout the post-Cold War period with these two countries because of their eager embrace of aggressive policies and tactics that, with the end of the Cold War, had gone out of fashion almost everywhere else. American attention also stemmed from the fact that each was located in an economically important region, disruption in which had the potential to harm the United States and its allies and friends. Above all, the two became increasingly important in American eyes during the course of the post-Cold War era because of their dogged pursuit of the weapon that, if they managed to acquire it, would turn them from annoying international nuisances into major threats to American interests and to the United States itself.

Although not fired in anger after 1945, nuclear weapons had a pervasive effect on the Cold War. They prolonged it: with their large nuclear arsenals neither the United States nor the Soviet Union could overthrow the other militarily. At the same time, nuclear weapons kept the rivalry from erupting into a military conflict because a war against the other would have been an act of suicide for each. The two main Cold War antagonists had by far the largest stockpiles of these weapons, which ratified their joint status as the world's "superpowers" and made the structure of the international system "bipolar."

Yet the nature of nuclear armaments makes them a weapon of choice not—or not only—for the strongest countries but for weak ones as well. Such weapons offer a shortcut to wielding power in the international system. By themselves, and even in the absence of the basic sources of military power in the modern age—a large population, a broad industrial base, the mastery of advanced technology—they can make their possessors militarily formidable. They can turn Lilliputians into Gullivers.[28]

Because an increase in the number of nuclear-weapon states seemed likely to increase the chances of nuclear war, and a wider distribution of such armaments reduced their own margins of military superiority over all others, both the United States and the Soviet Union opposed the spread of these weapons. The term that came to denote their spread, nuclear proliferation, made the process sound like the international political version of a communicable disease; and that is more or less how the two superpowers and much of the rest of the world saw it.

From the widespread opposition to the dispersion of these armaments emerged the 1968 Nuclear Nonproliferation Treaty (NPT), according to whose terms countries with nuclear armaments could keep them but had to promise not to give them to others, while the many more countries without these weapons pledged not to acquire them. By 2011, the NPT had 189 signatories. A number of countries, including some eminently capable of making them such as Germany and Japan, felt free to renounce these weapons because they enjoyed the nuclear protection of the United States. Just as important to the Cold-War nonproliferation system as the NPT, therefore—indeed even more important—was the American system of alliances.[29]

Still, the appetite for these armaments persisted in a few corners of the world and, with the end of the conflict with the Soviet Union, preventing proliferation replaced deterring a Soviet attack as the chief American goal for nuclear weapons. Acquiring them involves three tasks: fabricating the material that can generate nuclear explosions; turning that material into a bomb; and building a system for delivering the bomb—the most effective vehicle being a ballistic missile. Of these the first is the most difficult. It requires either enriching uranium to a level necessary for a nuclear explosion or purifying another element named after a distant former planet, plutonium.[30]

To complicate the politics of nonproliferation, both uranium and plutonium are used in what the NPT designated a peaceful and therefore legal use of nuclear material: the generation of electricity. Uranium enriched below the level of bomb material fuels electric-power reactors, and one of the waste products of nuclear power plants is plutonium. To ensure that countries employing these materials for power generation do not take the steps necessary to convert them to bomb material, the International Atomic Energy Agency (IAEA) was established. Signatories to the NPT agree to allow IAEA personnel to inspect their nuclear power-generation facilities.

The end of the Cold War made preventing proliferation more difficult for two reasons: the disappearance of the Soviet Union removed a check on its former clients, notably North Korea, that harbored nuclear ambitions; and the tens of thousands of Soviet nuclear weapons were suddenly dispersed among what became several different countries. During the Clinton administration, the United States developed a program to safeguard the nuclear armaments on the territory of what had been the Soviet Union.[31] In part no doubt due to this program, the fear that some of the Soviet-era weapons would find their way into the hands of governments or groups that would use them for nefarious or even catastrophic purposes were not realized.

The administration of George W. Bush added two new anti-proliferation programs. Its Proliferation Security Initiative (PSI) launched robust efforts to interdict the clandestine transfer of nuclear materials. The Bush administration also withdrew from the 1972 Anti-Ballistic Missile Treaty that effectively prohibited systems of ballistic missile defense, which the United States had signed with the Soviet Union, and began to deploy such systems. With available technology, defensive systems had no chance of stopping the kind of large-scale attack that Russia, which inherited the Soviet nuclear stockpile, could mount; but they would be effective, or so it was hoped, against one or two nuclear-armed missiles fired at an American ally by a rogue state.

American anti-proliferation efforts did not prevent the number of nuclear weapon powers from increasing during the post-Cold War period. In May 1998, first India and then, in response, Pakistan detonated nuclear explosions. The United States protested but then accepted their new status, in part because Washington had no better choices in the matter—it could not undo what they had done—but also because neither country, even equipped with nuclear armaments, seemed to pose a serious threat to American interests.[32] India was a friendly democracy, Pakistan only intermittently democratic but an ally and client of the United States for much of the Cold War and the post-Cold War era.

North Korea and Iran, by contrast, were neither democratic nor friendly. Both sought to obtain nuclear armaments and that aspiration came to seem even more dangerous in the wake of September 11, 2001. The terrorist attacks of that day raised the awful prospect of a group such as al Qaeda in possession of an atomic bomb. In his 2002 State of the Union speech, President George W. Bush referred to this possibility in grouping North Korea and Iran together with Iraq as the "axis of evil."[33] The American invasion of Iraq crossed that country off the list of would-be proliferators and the United States led multinational campaigns to keep the other two from getting the bomb, which slowed but did not stop their nuclear progress. By 2014, the North Korean and Iranian programs had reached the brink of posing the kinds of threats to the security of the United States that had seemed to have vanished with the Cold War.

After the Korean War left the Korean peninsula divided in 1953, South Korea adopted free markets, joined the American-led global economy, and prospered. North Korea clung to communist economic practices and became increasingly oppressive, poor, and isolated. It also continued to be aggressive, launching occasional terrorist attacks against the South. In 1965, the North Korean regime received a small nuclear reactor from the Soviet Union. In 1985, at the Soviets' request, it signed the NPT. In 1986 it built another, indigenously engineered, reactor in the place where the first one was located, Yongbyon. In 1988, American intelligence detected a plant there designed to extract plutonium from spent fuel, which could have no purpose other than making bombs.[34]

Then, in 1993 and 1994, a series of North Korean initiatives so alarmed the American government that it seriously considered attacking the Yongbyon facilities. First the North Korean government announced its intention to withdraw from the NPT. Then it said that it would shut down the reactor there and remove the irradiated fuel rods from it. Having done this, it would then be able to reprocess the plutonium they contained, which would provide the basis of a nuclear weapon.[35]

In response, the American government pressed for UN-imposed sanctions, which the communist regime in Pyongyang asserted would amount to a declaration of war. The American secretary of defense at the time, William Perry, concluded, in retrospect, that there was "a real risk of war."[36] As he was to do several months later when the United States was preparing to send troops to Haiti,[37] former president Jimmy Carter inserted himself into the middle of the crisis. In June, he traveled to Pyongyang, met with the country's leader, Kim Il-sung, and announced that he had found a formula for resolving the dispute and avoiding the use of force. Although dissatisfied with the terms Carter had obtained, the Clinton administration decided to use them as the basis for further negotiations and eventually concluded what came to be known as the Agreed Framework. Under its terms the United States agreed to furnish the North Koreans with two proliferation-resistant reactors and shipments of fuel oil in exchange for an end to Pyongyang's nuclear weapons program.[38] The North Koreans cheated on the agreement, obtaining bomb-making technology from Pakistan in the late 1990s, but the Clinton administration pressed ahead, during its second term, with negotiations to end the North Korean ballistic missile program.[39] Its time in office ended, however, without reaching an accord.[40]

The administration of George W. Bush entered office skeptical of the value of negotiations with North Korea[41] but decided to continue them nonetheless. In October 2002, however, the administration made public its discovery of a secret North Korean uranium enrichment facility, which violated the Agreed Framework.[42] In 2003 the North Koreans withdrew from the NPT, discarding the obligation to permit IAEA inspections of their nuclear facilities, and began to remove fuel rods from the reactor at Yongbyon. This was a watershed, and not a good one, in American nonproliferation efforts. In response to the threat to take precisely the same step a decade earlier, the Clinton administration had seriously contemplated war. The Bush administration did no such thing. Instead, it entered into six-party talks, involving North and South Korea, China, Japan, and Russia, to try to limit the North Korean nuclear program.

These talks failed to accomplish their aim. On October 8, 2006, North Korea detonated an underground nuclear explosion, albeit apparently an only partly successful one. The negotiations nonetheless continued. In 2007 the North Korean government agreed to dismantle Yongbyon and give what it promised would be, but turned out not to be, a full accounting of its nuclear program. In return for the partial disclosure the regime did provide, the next year the United States removed North Korea from its list of state sponsors of terrorism.[43]

Upon coming to office in 2009, the Obama administration adopted a conciliatory approach to North Korea, as it did to other countries with which the United States was at odds. This, too, failed. The communist regime tested a long-range missile and conducted another nuclear explosion in 2009 and built a uranium enrichment facility in 2011.[44] In 20012, with Kim Il-sung's son and successor Kim Jong-il dead and the country's leadership in the hands of a third-generation Kim, his young, inexperienced, untested son Kim Jong-un, the regime launched yet another missile, with an intended range sufficient to strike

North America, and restarted the reactor at Yongbyon that it had shut down five years earlier. In 2013 it conducted a further nuclear test. Despite the explicitly declared American determination to prevent such a development, during the post-Cold War era North Korea made the transition from rogue state to rogue state capable of building nuclear weapons.[45]

The American engagement with North Korea followed a pattern: the communist regime would take or threaten to take a step that would bring it closer to the possession of usable nuclear weapons. The United States, usually in concert with other countries, would respond by negotiating with Pyongyang. The negotiations would reach an agreement in which North Korea promised to halt whatever the Americans found threatening in return for a material reward: the North Koreans in fact received over $1 billion worth of aid from the United States.[46] Invariably, however, they would renege on the bargain that had been struck and the "cycle of extortion" would start again.[47] Through all the iterations of this cycle the North Korean nuclear weapons program moved ahead. Over two decades, from 1994 to 2014, the United States paid North Korea repeatedly to give up its nuclear weapons program. The North Koreans pocketed the payments and kept the program. The Americans paid ransom, again and again, for a hostage that was never freed.

The experience demonstrated that even a very poor, largely isolated, technologically backward country can find a way to become a nuclear power if it is sufficiently determined to do so. The only certain way to prevent nuclear proliferation is through the use of force—by destroying the would-be proliferator's nuclear facilities, as Israel did to Iraq in 1982 and to Syria in 2007, or by removing from power the regime whose possession of nuclear weapons would pose a serious threat, as the United States did to Iraq in 2003, or both.

The United States chose not to go to war to stop North Korea from getting the bomb. In 1994 the Clinton administration came close but then secured an agreement that was supposed to achieve that aim. In 2003, in the same circumstances, the Bush administration did nothing. It was by that time preoccupied with Iraq, but another consideration restrained the United States then and thereafter.

A war against North Korea would have proven costly, above all for South Korea. The North Korean regime had an army that numbered more than a million men. It also had hundreds of artillery pieces deployed along the Demilitarized Zone, the de facto border between North and South. These were aimed at the South Korean capital Seoul, with its population of 9.8 million (in 2014), only 35 miles away. In a war the North Koreans, while they would eventually have lost it, could have inflicted terrible damage on the South.[48] North Korea, in short, had the military forces to deter a direct attack even without nuclear armaments. It sought these weapons to reinforce its deterrent power, to solidify the Kim family's rule, and to provide a shield behind which it could launch terrorist assaults or even cross-border invasions, in addition to using the threat of getting nuclear armaments to blackmail the rest of the world.

With negotiations ineffective and war prohibitively expensive, successive American administrations placed their hopes for shutting down the North Korean nuclear program on a change of regime in Pyongyang. Nuclear nonproliferation in North Korea turned out to require what the United States had attempted, unsuccessfully, in Somalia, Haiti, the Balkans, Iraq, and Afghanistan: the transformation of another country's domestic arrangements.

The Bush administration hoped the pressure of economic sanctions would loosen the communists' grip on power. The South Koreans, sometimes with the support of the United States, adopted the opposite approach. Through its "sunshine policy" Seoul offered the North economic cooperation. South Korea expected, or hoped, that this would encourage Chinese-style economic reforms, growing economic and political engagement with the rest of the world, less repressive governance at home, and a more accommodating foreign policy.

Neither strategy worked. Neither, however, seemed doomed to fail when it was adopted. To the contrary, throughout the post-Cold War period regime change in North Korea appeared plausible, even imminent.[49] With the end of orthodox communism elsewhere in Asia and the collapse of communism entirely in Europe that brought with it the disappearance of Pyongyang's traditional patron the Soviet Union, the Kim regime found itself in dire economic straits. As a result of its dysfunctional economy, the end of Soviet patronage, and the commitment of a large part of the resources it did have to military purposes,[50] North Korea experienced, in the 1990s, something unique in the last third of the twentieth century: a severe famine. As many as 3.5 million people died of starvation. In such circumstances it was easy to believe that the end of the Pyongyang regime was fast approaching.

Its end did not, however, arrive. The government's repressive control of the population prevented popular uprisings, and its vigilant oversight of its armed forces forestalled a coup. The peculiar form of dynastic communism in North Korea survived for another reason: the support of its giant northern neighbor, China.

Presiding over a country that had achieved remarkable economic growth by forsaking central planning and economic autarky for free markets and membership in the international economy, the Chinese communists had little sympathy for their North Korean counterparts, who had done neither. The Chinese nonetheless supplied the food and fuel, in quantities far greater than other countries provided,[51] that the North Korean regime needed to maintain its hold on power. As unattractive as Beijing may have found the continuation of the Kim dynasty, the alternative—its collapse—held even less appeal.

The end of the North Korean regime, the Chinese government had good reason to fear, would create anarchy on its southern border, unleashing a flood of refugees into China. The ultimate outcome of such a scenario, it was reasonable to assume, would be a worse situation from the Chinese point of view: a Korean peninsula united under the auspices of the South, an American ally, in place of the post-World War II division with an anti-American buffer state on China's southern border.[52]

While they did not say so publicly, South Korean officials held similar views. They were not eager to assume the burden of supporting and integrating into their own society the impoverished people of North Korea, who had no experience with a free-market economy or a democratic political system. That burden promised to be even heavier than the very substantial one that the unification of Germany had imposed, after 1990, on the German Federal Republic, a richer country than South Korea. The government in Seoul also had to worry that in its death throes the North Korean leadership would lash out militarily, causing many casualties and extensive destruction of property in South Korea before expiring.[53] The United States could hardly attack the North against the wishes of a country that was both a neighbor and prospective target of North Korea and an American ally, and the South Koreans made it clear that they did not want another Korean war.[54]

Neither, of course, did the United States, but the Americans' priorities differed from those of China and South Korea. The supreme American goal was to prevent North Korea from acquiring nuclear weapons: the other two countries shared this goal but for them avoiding war and a North Korean collapse had greater importance. They were therefore willing to run the risk of allowing the North's nuclear program to proceed rather than take steps that would stop it—in the case of China cutting off all trade, for South Korea endorsing military action—that were likely to have results that were, for them, even worse than a nuclear-armed North Korea. China's and South Korea's order of preferences for North Korea differed from that of the United States in part, no doubt, because unlike the United States they would have to bear the direct consequences of a North Korean collapse.

The post-Cold War success of the North Korean nuclear program had a final cause: while the gains that it made were, from the point of view of virtually every other country, undesirable, the costs of these gains were, for all of them, at least bearable. The diversion of nuclear material, the underground nuclear explosions, and the test flights of ballistic missiles that North Korea had managed to stage by 2014 did not change the basic political or military conditions in East Asia. The United States, with its troop presence in South Korea and its formidable nuclear arsenal, could deter a major North Korean attack. It had, after all, been deterring a nonnuclear attack for more than half a century, since the end of the Korean War, and the requirements for deterring a nuclear-armed North Korea did not differ from what America was already doing.

The ongoing progress of the North Korean program threatened, however, to turn it into something that the United States could not accept. The more nuclear material Pyongyang generated, and the more bombs it was able to make,[55] the greater would become the likelihood that it would sell one to a terrorist group, thereby making real the nightmare about which George W. Bush had warned in 2002.[56] It already had a record of distributing bomb-relevant technology, although not a bomb itself, to other countries. Moreover, while in 2014 North Korea had not demonstrated its capacity either to fabricate a nuclear explosive compact enough to mount on a ballistic missile or to build a missile reliably capable of striking the United States,[57] given the advances in the relevant technologies it had made over the course of two decades it seemed only a matter of time before it accomplished both.

In 2006 William Perry, by then a former secretary of state, wrote an article arguing that a nuclear-armed North Korean missile targeted at North America would pose such a serious threat to the United States that if North Korea deployed such a missile the American military should attack and destroy it. Perry had a coauthor, his former Pentagon colleague Ashton Carter.[58] At the end of 2014, President Obama named Carter secretary of defense. As he took office, the development the two coauthors had designated a trigger for war no longer lay in the distant future.[59]

By 2014 the nuclear weapons program of another member of Bush's axis of evil—Iran—was also coming close to creating the kind of threat that had been normal historically but had all but disappeared after the end of the Cold War. The United States had a curious relationship with Iran's Islamist and virulently anti-American government during the post-Cold War era. On the one hand, the two countries remained adversaries, as they had been since the advent of the Islamic Republic in 1979. As in the case of North Korea, the United States led an international campaign to prevent Iran from acquiring nuclear weapons. On the other hand, however, American foreign policy strengthened, albeit unintentionally, the Iranian mullahs. The Afghan Taliban, Saddam Hussein, and the Islamic State of Iraq and Syria, each of them Sunni Muslim, were all bitterly opposed to Shia Iran. The American wars against these three therefore worked to Iran's advantage. American policy in the Middle East did not achieve what the United States wanted most—democracy and peace—but it did produce what American interests in the region needed least: a more powerful Iran.

That country's nuclear program began as an entirely legal nuclear-power-generating enterprise during the rule of America's ally, the shah. Under his rule, Iran signed the NPT and permitted IAEA inspections.[60] The mullahs who replaced him used the shah's program as the basis, and as a cover, for the pursuit of nuclear armaments. Iran's nuclear activities, combined with its aggressive anti-American policies in the Middle East and beyond, aroused enough suspicion in the United States in the 1990s that Congress and the executive branch imposed economic sanctions of various kinds on the Islamic

Republic. Then, in 2002, an Iranian opposition group revealed that the regime had built two secret weapons-related facilities with clandestine assistance from the Pakistani merchant of nuclear technology, A. Q. Khan:[61] a uranium enrichment plant at Natanz and a heavy water reactor generating plutonium near Arak. In September 2009, President Obama, French President Nicolas Sarkozy, and British Prime Minister Gordon Brown revealed that Iran had constructed an enrichment facility, placed underground—presumably to protect it from attack—at Fordow near Qom.

The international community registered its opposition: the IAEA issued 30 reports between 2003 and 2010 spelling out Iran's noncompliance with the NPT,[62] and the UN Security Council passed eight resolutions of disapproval, some of which authorized the imposition of economic sanctions.[63] The three largest Western European countries, Great Britain, France, and Germany undertook to negotiate an end to its nuclear program with the Iranian government. The EU3, as it was called, was succeeded as Iran's interlocutor by the five permanent members of the United Nations Security Council plus Germany, known as the P5 + 1.

The United States figured prominently in the anti-proliferation efforts against Iran. As with North Korea, while the Bush administration hoped for a change of regime in Tehran that would put an end to the country's nuclear program[64] (even as it was devoting its attention and resources to the occupation of neighboring Iraq), when Democrats were in charge of American foreign policy during the post-Cold War period they attempted conciliation. The Clinton administration sought political reconciliation even before the extent of the Iranian nuclear weapons program became known, going so far as to apologize for the American role in the 1953 overthrow of the elected government of Mohammed Mossadegh that had returned supreme power to the shah.[65] The Obama administration refrained from criticizing the regime's crackdown on the demonstrations in Tehran protesting the rigged presidential elections of 2009, sent warm public messages to the Iranian people, and conducted secret correspondence with the country's Islamist rulers. Obama sought, especially in his second term, to put an end to the long American estrangement from Iran and make a grand reconciliation with the Islamic Republic the hallmark foreign policy achievement of his presidency, his own version of the Nixon administration's rapprochement with China in the early 1970s.[66]

At the same time, the United States worked secretly to thwart Iran's pursuit of the bomb. It carried out a complicated cyber-attack, introducing, in concert with Israel, a computer virus into the centrifuges that were enriching uranium, which set back that crucial part of the bomb-making process. The "Stuxnet" virus retarded[67] but did not stop Iran's ongoing progress toward a full-fledged nuclear weapons capacity, which included advances in designing a warhead and building long-range missiles.[68]

The American government also rallied international support for increasingly comprehensive and strict economic sanctions, which had a significant impact on Iran. They were particularly effective because, in contrast to North Korea, Iran lacked the equivalent of China—a powerful neighbor prepared to violate the sanctions. Nor did the Islamic Republic, although an often-vicious dictatorship, have as powerful a capacity for repression to keep public discontent under control as did the North Korean regime. Sanctions on Iran had a political impact, finally, because the country had only one significant source of income, the sale of energy. By limiting energy exports the sanctions put considerable economic and therefore political pressure on the regime.[69]

In 2013 the Iranian presidential elections, conducted in deteriorating economic conditions, produced a winner committed, at least rhetorically, to a less confrontational relationship with the rest of the world. Secret negotiations yielded, in November of that year, an interim agreement on the Iranian nuclear program known as the Joint Plan of Action. Under its terms, Tehran agreed to freeze many of its nuclear activities for six months, the United States and others lifted some of the sanctions they had imposed, and talks began, to be concluded within six months, on a permanent settlement.[70]

The freeze left Iran, by most estimates, only a few months away from the capacity to make a nuclear weapon.[71] This meant that, as with North Korea, at the end of 2014 the Iranian nuclear program had come close to posing the kind of threat with which the United States had not had to deal since the collapse of the Soviet Union and the absence of which had cleared the way for the post-Cold War American preoccupation with missions of transformation around the world.

Like North Korea, Iran consistently got the better of the United States during the course of their nuclear negotiations. Not only did the Islamic Republic make progress in acquiring the bomb, the United States retreated from its initial goal. Whereas the American government, along with the United Nations, had originally demanded that Iran cease all its threatening activities, including enriching uranium (which the Tehran regime claimed, implausibly for an oil-rich country, to need for generating electricity), by 2014 the two sides were bargaining over how much enrichment capacity Iran would be permitted to retain: the United States had stopped insisting that the mullahs have none at all.

Its surrender on this crucial point reversed four decades of American and global nonproliferation policy. Since the mid-1970s the United States and other countries had taken the position that non-nuclear-weapon states should not be allowed to have uranium enrichment facilities, since these could be used to make nuclear weapons. Successive American administrations had insisted that even democratic, friendly governments forswear enrichment.[72] Yet in 2013 the Obama administration officially recognized the right to enrichment facilities of a government that was neither friendly nor democratic and had acquired its enrichment capacity secretly. In so doing, the administration abandoned one of the critical features of the ensemble of treaties, organizations, rules, and policies that the United States and the international community had built up over the decades since 1945 to prevent the spread of nuclear weapons. Having advocated, during the first year of his first term as president, the abolition of all the nuclear weapons on the planet,[73] Barack Obama proceeded, in the first year of his second term, to make a concession that made it all too likely that the world would have many more such weapons, not fewer, let alone none at all.

As with North Korea, working against the conciliatory approach to Iran was not only the high value both rogue regimes placed on getting nuclear weapons but also the fact that neither was eager for what the United States (and, in the case of North Korea, South Korea) was offering. The trade and investment promised in exchange for relinquishing or limiting their nuclear weapons programs would surely make the people of North Korea and Iran more prosperous. Greater contact between the societies they ruled and the West might well also, however, weaken the hold on power of the Kim dynasty and the Iranian clerics, which was far more important to them than any material benefits to the people they ruled. Not for nothing did the Iranian regime call the United States "the Great Satan." The term referred to the serpent in the biblical Garden of Eden who tempted Adam and Eve from the path of righteous conduct. The Iranian clerics wanted economic sanctions lifted so that they could sell their country's oil and use the proceeds to reinforce their grip on power and pursue their ambitions beyond their borders. They did not, however, want closer contact with the West, which, they feared, would make the Iranian public even more resistant to their rule than it already was.[74]

Unlike the North Korean case, the United States did have a military option against Iran. Whereas in Asia, America's chief local ally, South Korea, firmly opposed stopping its rogue neighbor's nuclear program by bombing it, in the Middle East the friends of the United States, especially Saudi Arabia and Israel, were willing to support such a course of action.[75] The Israelis, in fact, had the military resources to perform the task themselves, although not as thoroughly as the Americans could. The Obama administration lobbied Israel's government against an air strike on Iran's nuclear facilities,[76] which would, the administration assumed, make impossible its hoped-for rapprochement with the Islamic Republic and might also draw the United States, which already had troops in Afghanistan and Iraq, into another war.

America's Arab Middle Eastern allies also strongly favored the forcible elimination of Iran's nuclear program because the political and physical damage from the Iranian possession of a bomb promised to be greater than in the Korean case. Iran conducted a more aggressive foreign policy, which a nuclear capability was likely to shield and encourage, than did North Korea. The Islamic Republic aspired to dominate its own region,[77] a plausible ambition for Iran as it was not for North Korea because the Middle East was not populated by politically cohesive and economically dynamic countries as East Asia was. To the contrary, the oil-rich kingdoms of the Persian Gulf, especially, were vulnerable to attack and subversion.

They depended on the United States to protect them, but an Iranian bomb promised to complicate the task of protection. It would create a Middle Eastern version of the Cold-War problem of "extended deterrence" in Europe: to prevent a Soviet attack on Western Europe the United States had had to deter the Soviet Union by credibly threatening to respond to such an attack with a devastating salvo against the attacker. Working against the credibility of such a threat was the fact that, from the late 1950s onward, the Soviet Union could visit nuclear destruction on North America. French President Charles de Gaulle publicly doubted the credibility of American deterrence on the grounds that the Soviet authorities were unlikely to believe that the American government would risk New York to defend Paris.

To convince the Soviet leadership that America would indeed retaliate for an attack on its European allies, the United States stationed its own troops on the European continent. Their presence was meant to "couple" the United States to Europe, like two connected railroad cars that can only move together. American troops in South Korea similarly reinforced the credibility of Washington's commitment to defend that country against an attack from the North; but keeping troops in countries that Iranian nuclear weapons would threaten, such as Saudi Arabia, would be more difficult. South Korea and the NATO allies of the United States, were solidly democratic countries whose publics welcomed, or at least did not strongly oppose, an American military presence. Saudi Arabia, whose society and educational system had produced Osama bin Laden, had neither feature and was not a hospitable base for American troops in large numbers.

Charles de Gaulle used what he considered the shakiness of the American promise to defend France in the face of the Soviet capacity for nuclear strikes on the continental United States as a reason for the French to acquire nuclear weapons of their own. (De Gaulle had other reasons as well: he believed that his country belonged in the first rank of global powers, membership in which he deemed to require a nuclear capability.) The other members of the Atlantic alliance, however, notably West Germany, did not follow his example, remaining content to rely on the nuclear protection afforded by the United States: an epidemic of nuclear proliferation did not break out in Cold-War Europe. Similarly, North Korea's nuclear program did not, at least through 2014, provoke Japan, South Korea, or Taiwan, to arm themselves with nuclear weapons, as each was capable of doing.

Such restraint could not be taken for granted in the Middle East if Iran succeeded in crossing the nuclear threshold or even merely approached it. The countries opposed to Iran were unlikely to have as much confidence in the reliability of American guarantees as the Europeans did during the Cold War. Of these countries, certainly Saudi Arabia, possibly Turkey, and conceivably Egypt would have strong motives to obtain nuclear weapons of their own in order to deter the Islamic Republic militarily and to counterbalance it politically.[78]

Nuclear proliferation in the Middle East would increase the chances of nuclear war in the region because the condition that did most to prevent war between the United States and the Soviet Union would be absent. Both superpowers had large enough nuclear arsenals that even if the other launched a massive attack, enough of its weaponry would have survived to deal the attacker a devastating retaliatory blow: that is, each had, in the argot of nuclear strategy, the capacity for the "assured destruction" of the other. Since the capacity was mutual, giving rise to the grimly appropriate Cold-War acronym "MAD," an attack by either against the other would have amounted to an act of suicide: thus no such attack ever occurred.

Middle Eastern countries, by contrast, would not have nuclear stockpiles large enough and sufficiently well protected to guarantee the capacity for assured destruction of an adversary even after absorbing a nuclear attack.[79] Each country would therefore have an incentive, especially in a crisis, to be the first to strike at its adversary, in order to knock out the opposing nuclear forces and to avoid losing its own.[80] The widespread and potent incentive to strike first is a formula for war, which is what an Iranian bomb seemed all too likely to bring to the Middle East and the world.

A story about a man sentenced to death in a medieval court expresses a principal theme of American post-Cold War nonproliferation policy toward North Korea and Iran. The man promises that if the king spares his life he will teach the monarch's favorite horse to talk. The king grants him a year to do so. Asked why he has made such a promise the man replies that in a year anything may happen: he may die, the king may die, the horse may die—or the horse may learn to talk by itself. Like the man in the story, in its nonproliferation policies the United States was playing for time. By the end of 2014, however, time was running out.

The threat of an Iranian nuclear weapons capacity, and of a North Korean capacity to launch a nuclear attack on the United States, which had seemed distant for most of the post-Cold War period, were approaching fulfillment. This propelled traditional concerns about the national interest and national security, and considerations of whether and when to go to war to protect them, to the top of the agenda of American foreign policy, from which they had been absent since the end of the Cold War. They had been absent because the most trouble-some countries, those that aspired to overturn the existing international arrangements, were not dangerous. North Korean and Iranian nuclear progress ended that condition. They had been absent for a second rea-son as well: the most dangerous countries were not troublesome. Those with the means to undertake major initives contrary to American inter-ests chose not to do so. By the end of 2014, because of the foreign poli-cies of China and of Russia, that, too, was no longer the case.

The Rise of China

It became a truth almost universally acknowledged during the post-Cold War era that, in historical perspective, the rise of China would come to be seen as the most significant development of the last decades of the twentieth century. Once the wealthiest country on the planet, China had fallen far behind the West in the nineteenth century but staged a remarkable resurgence at the end of the twentieth and into the twenty-first. Beginning with its free-market reforms at the end of the 1970s, China achieved three decades of double-digit annual economic growth, a feat without precedent in any other place or time.[81]

Wealth begets power, and a rising power, as China had become when the Cold War ended, can disrupt international politics. Twenty-first-century China invited comparison to pre-World War I Germany, whose rapid economic growth fed the desire to control more territory—imperial control being the traditional prerogative of great powers. German geopolitical ambition in turn produced a great global conflict against a coalition, which the United States joined near the end of the war, led by the world leader of the day, Great Britain. It was not difficult, a hundred years later, to imagine China in the role of Wilhelmine Germany and the United States as pre-1914 Britain.

Yet for most of the post-Cold War period such a possibility had no visible effect on American foreign policy. To be sure, the United States had no easy way to stifle the source of China's rise—its remarkable economic growth. Nor did it wish to do so, since so many American firms and consumers benefitted from investing in, trading with, and buying from China. In addition, the United States was preoccupied with other, seemingly more urgent matters in Somalia, Haiti, the Balkans, Afghanistan, and Iraq.

The absence of official American alarm about China's dynamism had yet another cause, however: the confidence that as it became more powerful China, unlike Wilhelmine Germany, would maintain peaceful, cooperative relations with the rest of the world. Economic growth based on free markets, Americans believed, was making Chinese politics more open, less repressive, and more democratic; and the more democratic a country's political system becomes, they also believed, the more peaceful its foreign policies would be.[82]

On the basis of this view of the world, of the direction in which contemporary history was moving, and of China's future, the Clinton administration persuaded itself—and its successors, with varying degrees of conviction, concurred—that the failure of its efforts to compel the Chinese government to respect the human rights of those it governed by the threat of trade sanctions did not mean that China was destined to retain its authoritarian political system. To the contrary, what American policy had failed to achieve the powerful, impersonal forces of post-Cold War history would accomplish, and in so doing would put China's relations with other countries on a peaceful course.

Up to a point this optimistic assessment of China's future proved accurate. The country's remarkable economic growth continued, and as it did, Chinese citizens secured greater freedom. They could travel abroad, own property, start businesses, and engage in open public discussion of a wide range of subjects, all of which had been impossible during the Maoist era. China did not, however, become a democracy; and as it grew richer its foreign policies, contrary to American expectations, became more assertive.

The Chinese were conscious of their long history not only as a great civilization but also as the dominant power in East Asia. The aspiration to resume that role had deep roots in Chinese political culture, which inspired the desire among the Chinese to translate their country's economic success into wider political influence. Also pushing China toward an aggressive approach beyond its borders was a deeply embedded sense of grievance against the rest of the world. The Chinese communist authorities emphasized the "century of humiliation"—from British bullying in the first Opium War in 1839 to the communist consolidation of power 110 years later—that China had experienced at the hands of outside powers.[83] The Chinese saw themselves, not without reason, as victims of the West (and of Japan).* This colored their twenty-first-century view of the United States, which Chinese officials frequently accused of following the Western practice of working to reduce and contain China's power.[84]

The anti-Western and anti-American strain in Chinese official thinking and popular attitudes—which coexisted with extensive and mutually beneficial economic exchange and often-warm personal contacts—followed, as well, from the way China was governed. Having abandoned the utopian social and political goals and the murderous repression of the Maoist era, the Communist Party's rule had come to rest on two things: the provision of economic growth, from which most Chinese gained, and the Communist Party's identification with China's aspiration to assume what it deemed its rightful place in the world. The communists promised to make the country not only wealthy at home but also strong and respected abroad.

At the beginning of the economic reforms over which he presided the Chinese leader Deng Xiaoping laid down the rule that, in its relations with the rest of the world, China should keep a low profile: it

---

* The "century of humiliation" encompassed genuine assaults on China by outside powers: the two Opium Wars with Great Britain of 1839–1842 and 1856–1860; the British march on the Chinese capital and their burning of the Summer Palace in 1860; the suppression of the Boxer Rebellion in 1901; the defeat at the hands of Japan in 1895; the awarding of the German concessions on the China coast to Japan at the Paris Peace Conference in 1919; and the Japanese invasion and occupation of China from 1937 to 1945.

should "hide its brightness" as he put it.[85] As their country's economy continued its remarkable growth, Deng's successors began to stray from this principle. Instead, the Chinese people's sense of their proper place in the world, their version of their own history, and the political needs of the ruling autocracy combined, even in the face of the liberalizing impact of economic growth and wider liberty, to foster policies that put the world's most populous country increasingly at odds with the world's most powerful one.

Even their economic relationship, the source of considerable mutual benefit—American imports of inexpensive Chinese consumer goods raised Americans' standard of living while generating employment for hundreds of thousands of Chinese—became a cause of friction between the United States and China. American complaints included the theft of intellectual property through the unauthorized copying of American products,[86] the erection of barriers to foreign investment and the imposition of handicaps on foreign businesses in China,[87] and unfair trade practices, above all the artificial depression of the Chinese currency to enhance Chinese exports to, and reduce its imports from, the United States.[88] In the 2012 presidential election both major-party candidates, former governor Mitt Romney of Massachusetts and President Obama, promised to be "tough" on China in economic terms.[89]

The Chinese government converted many of the dollars its country's exports earned into United States treasury bills. The huge dollar holdings that resulted gave it, in theory, leverage over the United States because they made China, in effect, America's banker. The leverage would have been difficult to use by selling the American instruments on a large scale, however. While that would have inflicted hardship on the United States by driving down the value of the dollar (assuming that China could have found willing buyers for hundreds of billions of dollars), it would, by doing so, have lowered Chinese exports and reduced China's own wealth, much of which was tied up in treasury bills.[90]

In general, American officials came to believe, China designed its economic policies to enhance its own economic well-being—which is not, after all, a surprising goal for any country—but at the cost of protecting and strengthening the wider international economic order without which it could not have flourished as it did. Robert Zoellick, a deputy secretary of state in the George W. Bush administration and later president of the World Bank, expressed the hope that China would become an international "stakeholder" by assuming a measure of responsibility for preserving the open global trading and financial systems. The Chinese behaved, however, more like what economists call a "free rider," exploiting the system for their own gain without contributing to its upkeep.[91]

For their part, the Chinese accused the United States, and not without reason, of bearing responsibility for the financial disaster of 2008. China's financial system escaped the kind of infection from America's troubles that Europe experienced because it was not fully integrated into global finance; and the Chinese government prevented the steep decline in output that afflicted many other countries around the world by expanding the creation of credit and directing it to investment on a very large scale.[92]

The 2008 crisis persuaded the Chinese that the international economic institutions and practices established by the West after World War II, which the United States played the leading role in operating, needed substantial reform or even replacement. They proposed regional trade arrangements in Asia that excluded the United States.[93] They helped to establish a new development bank sponsored by the other major emerging-market countries, the BRICS (Brazil, Russia, India, China, and South Africa), with its headquarters in Shanghai. They suggested that the existing international monetary system, with the dollar at its center, give way to a new order based on an international currency. At the same time they took steps to give their own currency greater global prominence.[94]

These economic initiatives stemmed, as well, from a second conclusion that China drew from the events of 2008 and afterward. They saw the financial crisis and the global recession that followed as signs that American power, and American primacy in the world, were fading. American decline, they believed, created an opportunity for China to fulfill its ambition to enhance its own power and influence in East Asia and elsewhere.[95] The Chinese initiatives with the greatest potential for creating serious conflict with its neighbors and with the United States were not its economic proposals, however; they were China's post-Cold War military policies.

During the Cold War and into the first part of the post-Cold War period, China's armed forces posed little immediate threat to its maritime neighbors or to the United States. The People's Liberation Army was descended from Mao's guerrilla bands, which had formed the core of a mass army that won the Chinese civil war and played a major role in the politics of the People's Republic during the Maoist era. Large but ill-equipped, China's army did not intervene against American troops in Vietnam as it had in Korea; and its brief occupation of a slice of northern Vietnam in early 1979 demonstrated political determination rather than military virtuosity.

Chinese military preparations had Taiwan as their principal target. The communist regime deployed missiles on the coast across the Taiwan Strait from the island so as to be able to punish the Taiwanese if they declared formal independence and thus deter such a declaration. China also acquired nuclear weapons, beginning in 1964, but did not attempt to match the far larger American and Soviet arsenals. The Chinese practiced what came to be known as "minimum deterrence," relying on a small nuclear force to keep their more powerful adversaries at bay.[96] Deng Xiaoping did not accord high priority to enhancing his country's military might. He designated the improvement of China's armed forces the third of its "Four Modernizations," and therefore less important than the first two—agriculture and industry.[97] In its era of market reform China preferred butter to guns.

During the post-Cold War period, however, China began to invest an increasing share of its rapidly growing output in its military.[98] The Chinese investment in naval forces and the construction of a major naval base on Hainan Island off its south coast had disturbing implications for China's Asian neighbors and the United States. The maritime buildup broke with China's military tradition: the country had not had a formidable navy since the fifteenth century.[99] Moreover, the naval program aimed at more than intimidating and ultimately conquering Taiwan.[100] It was designed to give China the means to project power well into the East and South China Seas, and even farther. Because the American navy dominated the Western Pacific, as it had since World War II, the build-up of China's maritime force propelled it toward a direct conflict with the United States. The only plausible use for much of the weaponry that China was developing, particularly anti-ship missiles, was to push the American fleet out of East and Southeast Asia. The American navy termed this China's "anti-access/area denial" strategy.[101]

The Chinese did have a compelling motive for building a formidable navy. They depended heavily on transoceanic commerce: they shipped the products assembled in factories on the China coast all over the world and imported the oil they needed in increasing quantity to keep their economy operating, much of it from the Persian Gulf and virtually all of it in tankers. Since the American navy controlled the sea lanes from the Persian Gulf to the coast of Asia, and in particular the Strait of Malacca—the stretch of water between Malaysia and the Indonesian island of Sumatra—through which most of the oil bound for China had to pass, China's economic well-being depended on the good will of the United States. This state of affairs made the Chinese authorities uncomfortable, and supplied them with an incentive to acquire a military force that would give China's government ultimate control over China's economic destiny. The more powerful its navy, moreover, the easier it would be for China to avail itself of the large reserves of oil the South China Sea was believed to harbor.[102]

More generally, the Chinese identified naval power with the kind of global reach and global status to which they aspired and that they believed history as well as demography—the sheer size of their population—entitled them.[103] The American strategist Alfred Thayer Mahan, whose writing at the beginning of the twentieth century emphasized the central role of sea power in international politics, gained a twenty-first-century following in China.[104]

To accompany its growing naval force China adopted increasingly aggressive declaratory policies concerning the waters off its coast and to its south. It asserted that the vessels of other countries, including military vessels, need the permission of the country in question to operate in its 200-mile "Exclusive Economic Zone," an assertion disputed by the United States and most other countries, who favored free passage in all such zones.[105] China was at odds with Japan over the ownership of the five small, uninhabited Senkaku Islands in the East China Sea. To the south, the Chinese defined their own territorial waters in breathtakingly expansive fashion. The "nine-dashed line" or "cow's tongue" that China published to demarcate its claims reached as far south as Indonesia. It conflicted not only with the Indonesians' definition of their own territorial waters but with the claims of Vietnam, the Philippines, and Malaysia as well. Official Chinese statements designated this vast expanse of maritime acreage a "core interest" of China, putting it in the same category as Tibet and Taiwan, two places over which the regime had expressed its willingness to go to war.[106]

To the consternation, indeed alarm, of the other countries of the region, China went beyond rhetoric in asserting its maritime claims. It conducted naval maneuvers around the Senkakus. It took control of a reef also claimed by the Philippines. It installed an oil rig in waters the Vietnamese asserted belonged to them, drawing naval vessels from both countries to the spot and sparking anti-Chinese riots in Vietnam.[107] None of China's maritime initiatives constituted an unambiguous act of war, but all involved the use of force or the threat to use it; and together they made China considerably more threatening to its neighbors and to the United States than it had been before. A new chapter in the history of the region had begun, the other countries of Asia and the United States were pushed reluctantly to conclude, one whose principal theme seemed likely to be a twenty-first-century Chinese bid for mastery in Asia and beyond.

Seeing themselves as potential victims of such a bid, the other countries of Asia responded by seeking to strengthen themselves. Several increased defense spending.[108] The non-communist country perhaps best disposed to China, South Korea, was put off by Beijing's indulgence of the North Korean nuclear weapons program.[109] In Japan, Prime Minister Shinzo Abe suggested that his country modify its constitution, which dated from the post-World War II American occupation, to permit more robust military initiatives. In 2014, he compared the international relations of East Asia to the pre-World War I Anglo-German rivalry of a hundred years earlier, saying that China and Japan were in "a similar situation" to Germany and Great Britain.[110] Japan also expanded its ties with India, another Asian country wary of China. Vietnam purchased six submarines—a considerable expense for a country that was far from wealthy—presumably for the purposes of tracking and if necessary, countering Chinese naval activity along its coast.

The Asians also sought to reinvigorate their Cold-War security relationships with the United States, or in the case of Vietnam—a Cold-War adversary of the United States—to create such a relationship. The government of the Philippines, which had shut down the large American air and naval bases at Clark Field and Subic Bay in the early 1990s, invited the Americans to return, signing an agreement of Enhanced Defense Cooperation with the United States in 2014 that gave American forces the right to use Filipino military facilities.[111]

For its part the United States responded to China's heightened assertiveness and the resulting concern of its neighbors by announcing, during the Obama administration, a strategic "pivot" to Asia: America would devote greater attention and resources to Asia and, by implication, less of both to the Middle East. In addition, the American Department of Defense devised a new military doctrine for the Western Pacific, one designed to take into account the growth of Chinese naval capabilities, called Air Sea Battle.[112]

Wary as they had become of China's intentions, however, neither the Asians nor the Americans sought to form an overtly anti-Chinese coalition. Nor did they wish to revive the policy of deterrence, with an explicit threat to retaliate for Chinese aggression, that the United States had practiced toward the Soviet Union during the Cold War.

They did not want to make their relationships with China unambiguously hostile.[113] To the contrary, they wanted to preserve their access to China's dynamic economy. All of them depended, to one degree or another, upon such access for their own economic well-being. In response to China's expanding naval power and its assertive maritime maneuvers, therefore, the Asian countries and the West adopted a strategy not of firm and overt opposition but of hedging. Like an investor who makes an investment that will offset an adverse movement in the price of a particular asset, they took steps to prepare to defend themselves and their interests in the event that China posed a direct and serious challenge to either or both.[114]

Such a challenge seemed increasingly likely but was not certain. While Chinese power was rising, the basis of that power was starting to show cracks. By 2014 the country's economic growth rate had fallen well below double digits. The strategy for achieving growth that featured substantial investment and massive exports, which had enjoyed remarkable success for three decades, seemed to have run its course. The Chinese regime faced the difficult task of finding new sources and methods of economic expansion.[115]

Corruption continued to plague the country and in so doing, eroded the political standing, in the eyes of the public, of the organization responsible for it, the ruling Communist Party. The Chinese leader Xi Jinping, who assumed power in 2013, acknowledged the importance of the problem by launching an anti-corruption campaign that removed from power, and even sent to jail, a number of party officials (most of whom happened also to be Xi's political opponents). Residents of Hong Kong organized large demonstrations in 2014 demanding more democratic governance, which suggested that such demands, and demonstrations to press for them, could spread to the mainland. In addition, China was heading into a demographic headwind. Because of the communist regime's policy, begun in 1980, of imposing a one-child limit on families, the ratio of retirees to active workers was on course to begin to rise in the third decade of the twenty-first century. This would further depress economic growth, require increasing spending on support for the elderly, and leave fewer resources available for muscle-flexing abroad.

Far from being destined to gain ever more political, economic, and military strength, therefore, China in 2014 displayed signs of weakness. A weaker China would not necessarily conduct a more peaceful, less ambitious foreign policy, however. To the contrary, if it could not deliver the economic growth that the Chinese people had come to expect, the Communist Party might seek to maintain public support, or at least tolerance, for its rule by attempting to fulfill, perhaps forcibly, the country's aspirations to greater power and influence beyond its borders. That, in turn, could bring China into conflict with its Asian neighbors and with the United States.

China's future was unclear. What was clear by the end of 2014 was that the optimistic assumption that had underpinned American policy toward China after the end of the Cold War—the assumption that Chinese economic growth would render the country more democratic at home and more peaceful abroad—could no longer form the basis of American policy in the Asia-Pacific region.[116]

American policy toward China, which had gone through several twists and turns in the twentieth century,[117] experienced yet another one in the twenty-first. It traveled back to the future: once again the United States had to deal with China not as an unambiguously friendly commercial partner but as a potential threat. After what counts in historical terms as a brief absence, power politics returned to Asia. In this way, moreover, Asia was not unique. Security competition had, by the end of 2014, returned as well to Europe, its birthplace and the region where it had had, over the centuries, the bloodiest and most destructive consequences. Europe owed the restoration of the historically familiar pattern of international relations to the foreign policy of its largest country, Russia.

The Revenge of Russia

Like China, Russia abandoned orthodox communism in the latter part of the twentieth century, although later and more thoroughly than China did. The collapse of communism in Europe in fact marked the end of the period of international history, and American foreign policy, dominated by the Cold War. The dissolution of the Soviet Union served as the founding event of the post-Cold War era. More than any other development it made the world safe for the United States to devote itself to the mission of transforming the politics and economics of other societies rather than to the historically normal business of power politics.

As with China, but more intensively, the United States undertook to push Russia along the path toward democracy and free markets.[118] As with China, the United States failed in this enterprise, and after the Russian economic crash of 1998 the Russian government ceased to welcome either American economic assistance or American political advice. Still, American officials harbored the same hope for Russia as for China: that economic growth would make the country's foreign policy kinder and gentler than the Soviet Union's had been.

The United States was less concerned that post-communist Russia would carry out aggressive foreign policies than that China would do so because of a fundamental difference between the two countries: as the post-Cold War era began China's power was rising while Russia's was falling. The new Russia had only about two-thirds of the territory and half the population of the old Soviet Union. The formidable Soviet military machine, which the United States and its allies had invested trillions of dollars in counterbalancing, had shrunk to a fraction of its former size. While the Chinese economy grew by 10 percent or more each year in the 1990s, the Russian economy, staggered by the blows inflicted by the breakup of the Soviet Union, performed poorly. In American eyes, therefore, while Chinese power in the world loomed as a problem—perhaps *the* problem—for the future, the difficulties that Russian power could pose belonged to the past. Thanks largely to a steep rise in the price of oil, after 1998 Russia's economy began to grow rapidly,[119] although not as rapidly as China's. Like that of China, Russia's political trajectory after the beginning of the new millennium did not follow the course for which the United States hoped. Indeed, by American standards Russia went backward politically, becoming a less open, less tolerant, less democratic, more repressive place.

As the post-Cold War era proceeded, Russia, like China, replaced cooperation with rivalry in its relations with much of the rest of the world. Like their Chinese counterparts, the members of the Russian political elite harbored a grievance against the West, and especially the United States, which they held responsible for their country's steep decline in international status. The presumption of Russian weakness led the American government to ignore or override Russian preferences on a variety of international issues, beginning with the eastward expansion of NATO, which only increased Russian resentment and anger. Whereas China's most recent experience as a great power had occurred during the eighteenth century, for Russia the golden age of international power and prestige was the 1980s—within the living memories of the officials, and in particular the country's president, Vladimir Putin, who set themselves the task of reinstating it. It was Russia's foreign policy, and particularly its 2014 invasion of its neighbor, Ukraine, that, more than any other development, put an end to the unprecedentedly peaceful post-Cold War era and restored the old routines of rivalry, insecurity, and war to international relations and American foreign policy.

The Clinton administration's mission of transformation in Russia failed but its successor established what seemed to be friendly relations with the Russian government, at least at first. In July 2001, George W. Bush met Vladimir Putin, who had succeeded Boris Yeltsin as Russia's president at the beginning of 2000, and pronounced himself favorably impressed. "I looked the man in the eye," he said. "I found him very straightforward and trustworthy—I was able to get a sense of his soul."[120] Putin became the first foreign leader to call Bush to offer support after the attacks on New York and Washington on September 11, 2001. The next year the two countries managed to conclude a new agreement limiting strategic nuclear weapons, which their leaders signed in Moscow in May 2002.

Yet the relationship, which the Clinton administration had set on the path to acrimony with its expansion of NATO, deteriorated further during the Bush administration. The Russian government objected to the unilateral abrogation, under Bush, of the 1972 ABM Treaty and American plans to deploy missile defense systems in Poland and the Czech Republic. The Russian authorities joined their French and German counterparts in opposing the American attack on Iraq in the spring of 2003. The Russians took particular exception to the 2004 expansion of NATO beyond the initial group of new members, the central European countries of Poland, Hungary, and the Czech Republic, to the three Baltic countries, Estonia, Latvia, and Lithuania, which had been, until 1991, part of the Soviet Union.[121] This expansion brought the Western military alliance, from which the Clinton administration had excluded Russia,[122] to the Russian border.

Putin found further cause for distrust of the United States in the American (and Western European) approach to the former Soviet republics turned independent countries. The Russians assumed a proprietary attitude toward these countries, which they called their "Near Abroad." Dimitry Medvedev, who served as president between 2008 and 2012 while Putin exercised supreme power from the office of prime minister, referred to the Near Abroad as a zone of "privileged interests" for Russia.

In three of these countries spontaneous, nonviolent protest movements erupted against governments that were corrupt or autocratic or both and succeeded in removing them from power, just as similar movements had unseated the communist governments of central and eastern Europe in 1989. The uprisings adopted a particular color or flower as their symbol and so became known as the "color revolutions."

In November 2003 the Rose Revolution in Georgia in the Caucasus forced the resignation of President Eduard Shevardnadze, who had served as foreign minister of the Soviet Union. In the spring of 2005 the Tulip Revolution overthrew the autocratic rule of the leader of Kyrgyzstan, in Central Asia. The most important such event from Russia's point of view, the Orange Revolution in Ukraine, took place from November 2004 to January 2005. The runoff stage of the country's presidential election was marked by massive fraud. Large-scale protests forced a revote, which reversed the initial verdict and produced a majority for the candidate who had lost the tainted first round.

Ukraine mattered far more to Russia than either Georgia or Kyrgyzstan. It was larger, it was widely regarded as the cradle of Russian civilization, it had been part of a Russian-dominated state for much longer (since the seventeenth century), it was culturally and linguistically closer to Russia, and it contained the largest number of ethnic Russians outside Russia itself.[123] Indeed, some Russians had difficulty in thinking of Ukraine as properly independent. Their number apparently included Putin, who is reported to have said to George W. Bush in 2008, "You don't understand, George, that Ukraine is not even a country."[124]

The United States did nothing directly to instigate the color revolutions, although Russian officials more than once accused the American government of fomenting them; but because the movements proclaimed a commitment to democratic politics, fitting in with Bush's "Democracy Agenda," and because they appeared to command the allegiance of majorities in their countries, the American government accorded them political support. This put Washington at odds with Moscow. Russia had in fact exerted itself on behalf of Viktor Yanukovich, the candidate for president of Ukraine whose manipulated election the Orange Revolution reversed.[125]

The Putin regime opposed the color revolutions, especially the one in Ukraine, for the same reason that the United States supported them: their democratic aspirations. They threatened Putin because the political system he was building in Russia was not democratic. The conflict with the West and the United States that exploded in 2014 thus had its roots not only in Russians' anger at their treatment at the hands of the Cold War's winners but also in Russia's domestic politics.

The autocratic political system that took hold in Russia after 2000, the interests of Vladimir Putin and his associates who benefitted from that system, and their need to defend their dictatorship against anything that might weaken it—including nearby examples of democracy—combined, to toxic effect, with the anti-American sentiment created by NATO expansion and nurtured by the other episodes in which the United States ignored or brushed aside what the Russian government wanted. Together they produced the aggressive Russian policies that, by 2014, had restored power politics to Europe. Russian resentment, in concert with Russian autocracy, put an end to the peaceful post-Cold War era on the European continent.

From the moment he assumed the presidency Putin began to consolidate power in his own hands. He attacked the individuals, known as "oligarchs," who had grown wealthy and powerful in the Yeltsin years, dispossessing them or sending them to jail or into exile. He created his own small ruling elite, drawing on friends from his Leningrad days and members of the security services in which he himself had made his career, he had been a colonel in the Soviet secret police and intelligence service, the KGB—during the Soviet era who came to be called "siloviki," from the Russian word for strength. The Leningraders and secret police veterans formed the core of Putin's new, authoritarian, Russian political system.

In that system power was concentrated at the top,[126] and Putin intended to retain it permanently: Russia continued to hold elections but they were neither free nor fair. Serious opposition to the regime was not permitted and the government took control of the mass media to regulate the information that most Russians received. The new political system came to be called "managed democracy."[127] It had the form but not the substance of the kind of democratic government practiced in the West that the United States had hoped would flourish in post-communist Russia. Boris Yeltsin had seemed, for a time, committed in principle to building a Western-style democracy. Vladimir Putin was not. In a country with no tradition of democracy, he encountered relatively little effective resistance to his reinstitution of autocracy.

As well as the media, the government took control of Russia's substantial natural resources, including its oil and natural gas. This gave the regime its distinctive character: it became a kleptocracy. A handful of Russians in effect stole the country's wealth. The principal purpose of the Russian government became enriching the members of the ruling elite by channeling to them the lion's share of the income that the sale of the country's resources earned.[128] As the price of oil rose sharply during Putin's presidency, the available wealth expanded.[129] While the regime distributed some of this wealth beyond the small circle of the privileged elite in order to pacify the urban population of the country, Putin and his cronies amassed large fortunes. By one estimate, by 2014, 110 billionaires in a country of 150 million people controlled fully 35 percent of its wealth.[130] Post-Soviet Russia followed the pattern of other resource-rich countries in which a dictatorial elite wields political power for the purpose of enriching itself. It became a "petrostate."[131]

As in the societies where post-Cold War American missions of transformation had failed, Russia lacked the impersonal institutions, and especially the rule of law, that democracy requires. Instead, personal connections determined political outcomes, notably the distribution of wealth. Networks of cronies were the equivalents, for Russia, of the tribal structures of Somalia, Afghanistan, and Iraq.[132]

The character of its political system helped to shape Russia's foreign policy after 2000. The sense of grievance against the West and the perceived need to fend off Western encroachment on Russian interests justified the strong leadership that Putin presented himself as providing. International necessity, as the regime encouraged Russians to perceive it, gave the authorities a reason to stifle dissent, which, Russian officials argued, was unpatriotic because it weakened the country in its struggle against the predations of the West. The widely felt Russian resentment of the United States especially, in concert with the Russian regime's desire to monopolize political power, made the relationship between Russia and the West increasingly acrimonious during the eight years of Putin's first spell as the country's president, from 2000 to 2008. Then it got worse.

In February 2008, Kosovo declared independence and the United States and Western Europe decided to accord it diplomatic recognition, against Russia's wishes and despite the fact that NATO had conducted its 1999 war there without disputing its status as a province of Serb-dominated Yugoslavia.[133] The Western support, a decade after the war's end, for Kosovar independence demonstrated, as the Russian political elites saw it, the West's perfidy and hypocrisy as well as Russia's continuing political impotence in matters in what it defined as its own neighborhood.

At the beginning of April 2008, at a NATO summit meeting in Bucharest, the alliance declared that "NATO welcomes Ukraine's and Georgia's Euro-Atlantic aspirations for membership in NATO. We agreed today that these countries will join NATO."[134] In fact, the two countries had not been invited to join or given Membership Action Plans, the usual prelude to joining. The official statement papered over the division in the alliance between some countries, notably the United States, that wanted the two former Soviet republics admitted promptly and others, including Germany, that, in no small part out of sensitivity to Russian objections, did not.[135] At Bucharest, NATO deferred a decision rather than making one. It was not difficult for the Russians to persuade themselves, however, that the West was on the way to bringing Ukraine into what they saw as a hostile sphere of influence.

Indeed, the year before, at an annual conference on security held in Munich, Putin had made the most emphatic of the many statements over the years by Russian leaders opposing the eastward extension of the Atlantic alliance. "NATO expansion does not have any relation with the modernization of the Alliance itself or with ensuring security in Europe. On the contrary, it represents a serious provocation that reduces the level of mutual trust."[136] He used the occasion, as well, to launch a broader diatribe against American foreign policy: "Today we are witnessing an almost uncontained hyper use of force—military force—in international relations, force that is plunging the world into an abyss of permanent conflicts . . . the United States has overstepped its national borders in every way."[137] All this set the stage for an event that made the antipathy between Russia and the West even more acute: a war between Russia and Georgia.

Two parts of what had been the Soviet republic of Georgia, South Ossetia and Abkhazia, both of them populated mainly by people who were not ethnic Georgians, resisted inclusion in independent Georgia after 1991. Russia supported them. The Rose Revolution brought to power a new Georgian leader, Mikheil Saakashvili, with personal ties to the West,[138] enthusiasm for Georgian membership in NATO, and a determination to regain control of the areas that had broken away from Georgia's control. On the night of August 7–8, 2008, in response to artillery fire, according to the Georgian government Georgian troops moved into South Ossetia. Russian troops also entered the territory, defeated the Georgian forces, and went on to occupy part of Georgia itself.[139] Russia opened another front in Abkhazia as well. After a few weeks the Russian government removed its army from Georgia but recognized South Ossetia and Abkhazia as independent, sealing their status as protectorates of Russia.

The Bush administration strongly objected to what Russia had done but, with troops still in Iraq and Afghanistan, with its own popularity with the American public at a low ebb because of the costs of those interventions, and having entered the last months of its term in office, it did not make a stronger response. The Georgia war was nonetheless a milestone. It was the first time that the Russians had gone beyond rhetoric in their opposition to post-Cold War political arrangements and what they regarded as the provocations and infringements on their interests of other countries. It was also the first time since the Soviet invasion of Afghanistan, which had occurred three decades earlier and in different geopolitical circumstances, that Russian troops had crossed an internationally recognized border without permission, which is the basic definition of international aggression.

The financial crash of 2008 added to Russia's list of grievances against the United States. Unlike China, Russia suffered serious economic damage, connected as it was to the West both financially and through the sale of energy, revenues from which were reduced because of the subsequent European recession.[140] A few months later, however, Barack Obama replaced George W. Bush in the White House. As with the other countries with which the Bush administration had left office on bad terms, its successor sought to improve relations with Moscow. Obama announced a "reset" of the Russian-American relationship,[†] canceled the Bush plan to deploy ballistic missile defense systems in

---

[†] The new initiative got off to an awkward start when Secretary of State Hillary Clinton presented the Russian foreign minister with a yellow-and-red buzzer that was supposed to say "reset" on it. The Russian word that had been mistakenly chosen translated, instead, to "overcharge."

Poland and the Czech Republic, and negotiated a new set of limits on long-range nuclear-tipped missiles. In 2014, however, with Putin back in office as president and ruling in an increasingly repressive manner, and with defense spending on the rise,[141] Russia launched another cross-border assault, this time against Ukraine. The war in Ukraine not only dramatically worsened Russia's relations with the United States and the countries of Europe, it also inaugurated a new era in the international politics of Europe.

Viktor Yanukovich, whose fraudulent election the Orange Revolution had overturned, ran again for the Ukrainian presidency in 2010 and this time won an untarnished victory. He proceeded to govern in the manner of Vladimir Putin, making himself and a few favored people rich and jailing one of his principal political opponents. He also continued the negotiations his predecessor had begun for an Association Agreement with the European Union. This was designed to give Ukraine closer ties to Europe's economic powerhouse and to mark the first step on the long and, in the Ukrainian case, uncertain road to EU membership. At the same time, however, Yanukovich was discussing with Putin the possibility of Ukraine's being part of the Russian-dominated economic association of former Soviet republics, the Eurasian Customs Union, which Russia's president was organizing as a way of creating a Russian sphere of influence on the territory of the former Soviet Union.

In November 2013, having received the promise of a substantial payment from Russia to ease Ukraine's fiscal problems (and perhaps a generous stipend for himself as well), Yanukovich announced that he was abandoning his talks with the EU. The announcement outraged Ukrainians, especially in the western and central parts of the country, who believed, with good reason, that closer ties with the EU would mean brighter prospects for prosperity and liberty for them while the alternative, a closer association with Putin's Russia, would have the opposite consequences. In a reprise of the Orange Revolution they held large demonstrations in the heart of Kyiv, the Ukrainian capital, which grew in strength through the first weeks of 2014. On February 18 and 20 a number of demonstrators were killed by—it was widely believed—pro-government forces. A compromise between the demonstrators and the regime was arranged on February 21, but the following day Yanukovich fled the country, his government collapsed, and the opponents of his tilt toward Russia gained control of the government.[142]

Yanukovich's flight represented a serious defeat for his ally, Vladimir Putin: Ukraine, for Russia the most important former Soviet republic, was escaping his grasp; the West was encroaching further on what his regime had defined as Russia's sphere of privileged interests. In addition, a pro-Western Ukraine had the potential to develop along Western political and economic lines. This would provide, next door, an alternative model of governance to the one Putin had established, one that the Russian people might well find more attractive than the system he had imposed on them. A Western-oriented Ukraine thus threatened Putin's power in Russia.

Putin's response came first in the Crimean peninsula. A province of Ukraine jutting into the Black Sea, Crimea had been conquered and settled by imperial Russia in the eighteenth century and had become part of Ukraine through a 1954 administrative decree that at the time had seemed—and had been—meaningless because Ukraine was then firmly a part of the Soviet Union. Dominated by a naval base (which remained in Russian hands even after the Soviet collapse) and populated largely by ethnic Russians, Crimea could plausibly have joined Russia after 1991; the majority of its inhabitants might well have preferred this. Instead, following the principle of keeping intact the lines of demarcation of the Soviet republics when they became sovereign states, and because it had no common border with Russia, Crimea became part of independent Ukraine.

In the wake of Yanukovich's fall from power Putin sent paramilitary forces and, ultimately, uniformed soldiers to the peninsula, pushed aside the Ukrainian authorities there, staged—in effect at gunpoint—a referendum on accession to Russia that passed by what the Russian authorities reported as a wide margin, and declared that Crimea had become part of Russia. No comparable invasion, conquest, and annexation of part of another country had taken place in Europe since Nazi Germany's eastward thrust in the early years of World War II.

Putin's campaign against Ukraine did not end with the seizure of Crimea. Russian forces infiltrated the eastern, largely Russian-speaking Ukrainian provinces of Donestsk and Luhansk. They took over government buildings and proclaimed their independence from the Ukrainian government. That government fought back, sending part of its small, badly trained and poorly equipped army to oppose the rebels in the east. Russia responded by giving the rebels heavy weaponry, which the Ukrainians could not match, and by dispatching units of the Russian army, usually out of uniform, to fight in Ukraine. Over the course of 2014, as several thousand people died and hundreds of thousands more were displaced, the Moscow-supported side gained the upper hand.

The West had no commitment to defend Ukraine's territorial integrity—the country did not, after all, belong to NATO—and no appetite for a military conflict with Russia, with its large stockpile of nuclear weapons. Shocked and appalled at the Russian aggression, however, the Western countries regarded doing nothing as an entirely inappropriate response.[143] They therefore imposed economic sanctions on individuals close to the Putin regime and on certain sectors of the Russian economy. On July 17, as fighting raged in eastern Ukraine, a surface-to-air missile almost certainly fired by Russian-sponsored insurgents, and presumably intended to strike a Ukrainian government aircraft, brought down instead Malaysian Airlines Flight 17, which had originated in Amsterdam and was bound for Kuala Lumpur, killing all 298 people aboard, 193 of them from the Netherlands. The atrocity shook public opinion in the countries of Europe, which proceeded to expand and tighten the sanctions they had already levied on Russia.

Those sanctions took a toll on the Russian economy, which, by the end of 2014 was also reeling from a sharp decline in the global price of oil.[144] The combination weakened Russia; but, as in the case of China, it was far from clear that a weaker Russia would conduct a more peaceful foreign policy.

The United States played only a marginal role in the Ukrainian drama.[145] The Association Agreement that sparked the events that led to the Russian invasion involved the Europeans, not the Americans. The American government sympathized with the protests against Yanukovich but did not instigate them or take a leading part in the efforts to broker a compromise between Yanukovich and the protesters. Because the EU had more extensive economic relations with the Russians than did the United States,[146] the European participation in the post-invasion sanctions had a greater impact than theAmerican actions on Russia's economic well-being.

Still, in justifying the annexation of Crimea and the assault on eastern Ukraine to the world and, most importantly, to the Russian public, Putin accorded a major share of responsibility for what had happened to the United States. Through his own speeches and especially by means of an intensive propaganda campaign in the Russian media he portrayed the uprising against Yanukovich as the work of anti-Russian Ukrainian "fascists" that was part, the propaganda hinted, of an American-led plot.[147] He depicted what had happened, as well, as part of an ongoing Western campaign to encircle Russia and reduce its power and influence.[148] After having been repeatedly provoked by the West, he gave the world to understand, Russia had finally struck back.[149]

Its attack on Ukraine reflected the kind of country post-Soviet Russia had, over two decades, become: autocratically governed, with unchecked power vested in a single person to whom portraying himself as the defender of the national interest and honor had a powerful appeal because it reinforced his grip on power. The Russian political system that made possible the invasion of Ukraine in turn had two major sources: first, a centuries-old authoritarian political tradition that carried over into the post-Soviet period, a tradition that, like the political histories of the places where more active American missions of transformation had failed, did not include regular elections or the protection of liberty; and second, the gusher of oil money that enabled Putin to recruit a loyal cadre of beneficiaries while paying the public to remain politically quiescent and launching a military buildup, all without the normal underpinnings of economic success.

The assault on Ukraine also stemmed, however, from the Russian resentment of the West, based on its perception of its mistreatment by the United States and Europe since the end of the Cold War. Putin appealed to that sentiment, which was widely felt not only among the country's political elite but in the Russian public as well, to justify his Ukrainian policy. Without that long-building resentment he could not have rallied as much domestic support for the war that he started as he did; and to that sentiment the United States had made, unintentionally, a major contribution, beginning with the Clinton administration's ill-considered and ill-fated decision to expand NATO eastward.[150]

In this sense the war in Ukraine had something in common with a story with which George Bernard Shaw, the Anglo-Irish playwright of the first half of the twentieth century, is sometimes associated. At a dinner party, the story goes, Shaw was seated next to a very elegant lady and asked her whether she would be willing to accompany him to bed for a million pounds. She blushed, stammered, and gave him an equivocal answer. He then asked her whether she would do this for sixpence. Indignantly the lady responded, "Sir, what kind of woman do you think I am?" "Oh, we've already established that," Shaw replied, "now we're just haggling over the price." For the Russian regime and much of the Russian public, the United States had already decided, with its policy of NATO expansion, that Europe would be divided, with Russia on the other side of the dividing line. The war in Ukraine was part of the struggle to determine where, precisely, that line would be drawn.

The Russian invasion of Ukraine violated the fundamental principle of international law, the inviolability of sovereign borders. It violated the 1975 Helsinki Accords that reaffirmed that principle for Europe. It violated the 1994 agreement by which Ukraine relinquished the nuclear weapons it had inherited from the Soviet Union in return for guarantees, in which Russian joined, of its security.[151] In doing all this, the invasion ended the historical period in which American policy in Europe could be based on the presumption that peaceful international conduct had become the unchallengeable norm there.

The United States, the mainstay of Europe's principal security organization, NATO, and therefore itself a European power, could no longer afford to ignore Russia. Given its willingness to invade Georgia and Ukraine, two former Soviet republics that had become independent countries, Russian aggression against others, including countries such as Estonia, Latvia, and Lithuania that had explicit American security guarantees through their membership in NATO, could not be ruled out.[152] Nor could the Americans continue to assume that exposure to the West and economic growth would dissolve any aggressive impulses the Russian government might harbor. Russia had become once again, as it had been for the United States during the Cold War and for the great powers of Europe for three centuries before that, a military problem.

The invasion of Ukraine did not bring back the Cold War. Russia, unlike the Soviet Union, did not have a global military reach or an anti-democratic ideology or an alternative form of economic organization to free markets that it aspired to spread throughout the world. What had returned to Europe was not the ideological rivalry of the second half of the twentieth century but rather the kind of security competition that had been the norm in the centuries before.

The return of security competition to Europe, along with China's increasingly assertive foreign policy and the growing danger to American interests posed by the nuclear weapons programs of North Korea and Iraq, changed the world in which the United States had to operate and thus reconfigured the agenda of American foreign policy. The eclipse of power politics after the end of the Cold War had given the world's strongest and wealthiest country the opportunity to concentrate on missions of transformation in places not previously important enough to attract American attention: Somalia, Haiti, the Balkans, Afghanistan, and Iraq. The restoration of power politics in the regions that were important to the United States—Europe, East Asia, and the Middle East—turned such missions into a luxury that America could no longer afford.

Conclusion

THE POST-COLD WAR ERA from 1993 to 2014 qualifies as the fourth distinct period in the history of American foreign policy. In the first one, between the beginning of George Washington's initial presidential term in 1789 and the Spanish-American war of 1898, the nation's focus was largely inward. The United States settled the North American continent, decided, through the Civil War of 1861 to 1865, that one rather than two countries would occupy the territory stretching from the Atlantic to the Pacific Ocean between Canada and Mexico, and developed, in the wake of the Civil War, the world's largest economy.

Between 1898 and 1945 the United States turned outward, functioning as one among several great powers. Like the others, it acquired imperial possessions. With the others it took part in two great wars of global scope, joining the winning coalition part of the way through World War I and serving as a mainstay of the victorious alliance in World War II. From 1945 to the end of the Cold War America was one of two great nuclear superpowers and the chief organizer and protector of the security and economic orders of the Western world. The United States and its allies prevailed in their four-decades-long struggle with the other superpower, the Soviet Union, ushering in American foreign policy's post-Cold War era.

In each of the first three periods America's power increased. That power gave it unusually broad latitude, in the wake of the Cold War, to choose what it would do in the world. It chose to embark on missions of transformation in China, Russia, Somalia, Haiti, Bosnia, Kosovo,

Afghanistan, Iraq, and the wider Arab world. None of these missions achieved its goals. Paradoxically, therefore, between 1993 and 2014 the United States had more power but, in its foreign policy, experienced less success than ever before.

Historically, where their foreign policies are concerned sovereign states inhabit the realm of necessity: they do what they must do to survive. The United States after the Cold War, by contrast, dwelled in the difficult-to-reach kingdom of choice. It was not obliged by the imperative of self-preservation to engage in what became widely known as nation-building. Why did the American government so frequently choose such missions?

To be sure, in none of them did the United States deliberately embark on a protracted nation-building exercise. The Clinton administration threatened economic sanctions if the Chinese government did not change its political system to protect human rights but quickly backed down when the Chinese refused. The same administration provided technical assistance to the Russian economy at the request of the Russian government, but after its financial crash of 1998, Russia discontinued this cooperative enterprise.

The Clinton humanitarian interventions did involve, as its China and Russia policies did not, occupying other countries and trying directly to remake their political and economic institutions; but at the outset of its interventions in Somalia, Haiti, Bosnia, and Kosovo, the administration saw itself as acting as a good Samaritan—or, to use a more contemporary metaphor, an emergency medical service—rescuing distressed peoples, not rebuilding defective governments. The Bush administration went to Afghanistan and Iraq not for the purpose of nation-building, which its senior officials, notably Secretary of Defense Donald Rumsfeld, initially eschewed, but instead out of the most familiar of all foreign-policy motives: to defend the United States against threats to its safety.

As for Barack Obama, he came to office determined to end what he (and by that time most Americans) considered the ill-advised interventions of the Bush years as well as to avoid the kind the Clinton administration had undertaken. He did authorize attacks on Libya for ostensibly humanitarian purposes but, unlike his two predecessors, declined to send American troops there after removing its government.

Like Clinton and Bush, Obama aspired to make the world a better place for Americans and others. As his instrument for doing so, however, he relied not on the use of American military force but rather on the force of his own personality, which, he believed upon entering office, could improve relations between the United States and other countries.[1] This strategy proved less costly than the policies of his two immediate predecessors but no more successful.

Still, when the various interventions immersed the United States in nation-building the American government did not flee from the task. The American public as a whole had no particular desire to use American power to transform other countries but the foreign policy establishment, whose views counted most, was, if anything, enthusiastic about the project. It was rare to hear it said about a humanitarian intervention—in the Balkans, for example—that what was happening was regrettable, indeed tragic, but not any business of the United States: that would have been considered, at best, unfeeling. Nor, about nation-building, was it common to encounter the idea that while bringing democracy to Iraq, for instance, was surely a worthy aim, the United States did not have the power to achieve it: that would have been deemed defeatist and even un-American. Nor was it acceptable to venture the opinion that the inhabitants of Haiti, or the Balkans, or Afghanistan, or Iraq were incapable, under existing conditions, of building and sustaining Western-style institutions and practices, even though that proved to be true. Such sentiments would have been treated as ethnocentric bordering on racist. Instead, the recent historical experience of the United States, America's own political culture, and the circumstances of the post-Cold War world combined to make the missions the country undertook seem initially plausible in the eyes of those responsible for them.

During the Cold War the United States became accustomed to a leading international role, developing a sense of responsibility for events all over the world that carried over into the post-Cold War period. Moreover, the end of the Cold War coincided with—and was in no small part caused by—the rapid diffusion of precisely the Western institutions and practices it was the purpose of America's nation-building efforts to establish.[2] The number of democracies in the world increased from 35 in 1970 to 120 in 2010.[3] The free-market system of economic organization gained still greater popularity, spreading even to countries that spurned democratic politics and becoming all but universal. The proponents and agents of the missions of transformation that the United States undertook had reason to see themselves as supplying institutions and practices for which there was a widespread and powerful global demand.

This recent history combined with ideas that dated back to the founding of the republic to produce, at first, support for the American missions. The post-Cold War managers of American foreign policy believed, as had their predecessors, that American values had universal applicability, that American institutions had universal utility, and that it was the role of the United States to spread both as widely as possible.

They also partook of what is sometimes called the national "can-do" spirit, the conviction that, with enough time, patience, resources, determination, and ingenuity, Americans are capable of accomplishing any task. Secretary of State Hillary Clinton, a reliable expositor of the conventional wisdom, as public officials tend to be, expressed this widely shared belief: "Americans have always risen to the challenges we have faced. It is in our DNA. We do believe there are no limits on what is possible or what can be achieved."[4] Finally, the enormous power of the United States after the collapse of communism in Europe and the absence of serious challenges to the country's security in the post-Cold War world created the opportunity to put these long-held ideas into practice.

Had the missions that the United States undertook in the wake of the Cold War achieved their goals they would surely have made the world a better place. If America had managed to install Western-style political and economic institutions in Somalia, in Haiti, in the Balkans, in Afghanistan, in Iraq, and throughout the Arab Middle East, the people living in these places would have been safer and more prosperous. If such institutions had come to the rogue states of North Korea and Iran, where the United States did not in fact try to establish them, or to China and Russia, where it did, people everywhere would have been safer. The danger to other countries that all four posed had roots in their domestic politics. The governing ideologies of communist North Korea and the Islamic Republic of Iran provided the basis for their aggressive foreign policies. The need they felt to bolster their standing with their publics by appearing to defend, vigorously, an expansive version of the national interest underlay the initiatives that the governments of China and Russia pursued in their regions—China at sea, Russia on land—that helped to put an end to the post-Cold War era. A democratic China and a democratic Russia would likely have had more peaceful relations with their neighbors.[5] The missions of transformation that dominated American foreign policy in the post-Cold War era would, that is, have redounded, if they had succeeded, to the benefit of the United States and the rest of the world. They did not, however, succeed. Americans overestimated not the benefits but the feasibility of making other countries over in their own image. Admirable in theory, the missions failed in practice. Why did they fail?

THE MISSIONS FAILED IN some countries because the governments of those countries were able to resist the kinds of changes the United States was trying to introduce. The ruling Communist Party maintained its authoritarian grip on China. Vladimir Putin steadily eroded the democratic institutions and practices that his predecessor Boris Yeltsin had tried, unsteadily, to establish in Russia. In the rogue states, the North Korean regime kept suffocatingly tight control of the country's population and Iran's ruling mullahs suppressed the demonstrations protesting the country's stolen presidential election in 2009. The attempted—or, in the case of the rogues, hoped-for—transformations of these four countries set the United States at odds with their governments. Those governments, being firmly entrenched in power with the instruments of coercion under their control, easily prevailed.

In Somalia, Haiti, Bosnia, Kosovo, Afghanistan, and Iraq, the United States did not have to contend with recalcitrant governments. American military power removed the governments and occupied the countries. In these places mission failure stemmed from the absence of the social conditions necessary to support the public institutions the United States hoped to install. Such institutions required patterns of behavior alien or unacceptable to the people who had, in the end, the responsibility for making them work. In each case the United States led the horse to water but could not make it drink.

In particular, the societies involved were dominated by social and political loyalties too narrow to support the institutions based on impersonal norms that Americans sought to implant in them. Where allegiances based on kinship predominated, as they did, for example, in Haiti and Afghanistan, the rule of law, under the terms of which decisions are made and resources distributed on the basis of abstract principles rather than personal relationships, seemed bizarre and objectionable and thus had no chance of being adopted. This means that where kinship ties predominate, the institutions of a modern state, all of which rely on the rule of law, cannot operate effectively. Similarly, where loyalty to a particular ethnic group or religion or sect is powerful, political units that include two or more them, as did Bosnia, Kosovo, and Iraq, will be unstable and prone to internal conflict. Where different groups do not form a single nation it is difficult to establish and maintain a cohesive state. The United States attempted its post-Cold War domestic transformations in places where these narrow allegiances were potent. The attempts, accordingly, did not succeed.

While America failed in its mission of state- and nation-building in the post-Cold War era, states and nations do get built. None of the places where America intervened acquired a modern government—none managed to "get to Denmark"—but many countries, not least Denmark itself, have arrived there. All of the countries that have made this journey, moreover, at one time had societies dominated by kinship ties. All managed to transcend their parochial allegiances, to "escape from kinship."[6]

In almost every case, however, the processes of state- and nation-building were protracted and complicated and followed no single, simple pattern.[7] In almost none was a modern state designed and built deliberately and rapidly.[8] What Americans came to call nation-building, that is, does occur; it goes on all the time in the modern world. It cannot, however, be *made* to happen, especially by an outside power, which was precisely what the United States attempted to do. The goal that the strongest power on the planet pursued around the world in the wake of the Cold War can therefore be seen in retrospect as either unnecessary or impossible.

The foreign policy of the United States proceeded on the assumption that this project was not impossible. That assumption turned out to be incorrect but it was not entirely fanciful. In support of it, American officials and members of the country's foreign policy establishment could and sometimes did cite what seemed to be examples from history of the successful creation, from the outside, of working, effective, modern political and economic institutions: the record of Great Britain, which preceded the United States as the world's strongest country; the American role in the political evolution, after 1945, of its two major adversaries in World War II, Germany and Japan; and the cascade of conversions to democracy and free markets in the latter stages of the Cold War.

In all three cases the kind of nation- and state-building that the United States attempted after the Cold War did occur. Upon inspection, however, none offers a useful precedent for the American attempts. History, properly understood, does not provide good reasons to believe that the American missions could have succeeded.

Through its far-flung empire Britain did more to spread modern institutions around the world than any other country. The United States in the wake of the Cold War had some similarities to—although also major differences from—imperial Britain. The similarities gave rise to the idea that the British imperial experience in the nineteenth and twentieth centuries held lessons for post-Cold War American foreign policy.[9] Britain's imperial heyday ended, however, well before the post-Cold War era, and by the time the United States embarked on its missions of transformation the conditions that had made the British and other empires possible had vanished. It was no longer possible for one people to govern another, against the wishes of the governed, for decades on end without significant resistance. The British presence in India spanned two centuries; the American presence in Iraq lasted less than a single decade.

While the British did leave behind modern institutions in some parts of their empire, moreover, for most of their tenure as imperial masters throughout most of their empire this is not what they were attempting to accomplish. The chief goal of empire for the British was economic gain, not the dissemination of British institutions.[10] In much of that empire, in fact, the British deliberately avoided trying to implant their institutions. The widely practiced system of indirect rule kept in place local customs and (under British supervision) local rulers.[11]

Finally, while in some of its formerly imperial possessions modern institutions remained long after the British had left, in others, including Afghanistan (which Britain twice occupied but did not make part of its empire) and Iraq, they did not. India, the jewel in the imperial crown, did adopt and keep a democratic government, with free, fair, regular elections and the protection of religious, economic, and political liberty.[12] Indian democracy owed as much to the country's initial post-independence leadership, however, notably its first prime minister, Jawaharlal Nehru, who was deeply committed to it, as to British imperial tutelage. Other countries, such as India's fraternal twin Pakistan, were not as fortunate as India in their leaders and have had histories of mainly autocratic rule. Democracy lasted in India as well because the country is so diverse that only democratic rules and procedures, with their provision for peaceful accommodation and compromise, could have held it together. The British imperial experience, therefore, had little if any relevance to America's post-Cold War missions of transformation.

The histories of Germany and Japan after World War II seem to resemble those missions more closely. American military power removed the governments of both countries and American forces occupied the two, which became model democracies with flourishing free-market economies. Unlike Somalia, Haiti, Bosnia, Kosovo, Afghanistan, and Iraq, however, Germany and Japan had each developed a strong national identity and an effective modern state well before American troops set foot on their territories. They did not have to create from scratch the institutions of liberty-protecting governance and free markets. The ongoing American military presence in both countries was no doubt helpful, but Germans and Japanese welcomed the American forces, as Afghans and Iraqis did not, because the Americans were protecting them against the Soviet Union. During the Cold War Germans and Japanese regarded the United States as an ally, rather than an occupying power.

In the final years of the Cold War and afterward, many countries that, unlike America's two World War II adversaries, lacked histories of strong nationalism or effective modern institutions nonetheless managed to adopt democratic politics and free-market economic institutions. The role that the United States was thought to have played in these developments, and therefore could play elsewhere—including in the countries where it intervened after the Cold War—was expressed by a term that came into usage in foreign policy circles in the 1990s: "soft power."

Distinct from "hard power"—the use of or threat to use force—with soft power a country gets its way in the international arena through its culture: its institutions, customs, values, beliefs, ideas, and reputation.[13] Soft power is the power of example. The concept came to have considerable appeal because it promised influence without exertion. It appealed in particular to the Western Europeans, who had ceased to field formidable military forces but believed—not without reason— that the peaceful, prosperous, cooperative community they had built since World War II inspired others to emulate them.

The term soft power contains an important truth. Culture *is* powerful. If war is, as the ancient Greek philosopher Heraclitus said, the father of all things, then culture is the mother. People change their ways and adopt new patterns of behavior because of what they observe others doing.[14] Conversion more often comes from persuasion through compelling examples than by coercion. The Cold War ended in just this way. The communist side was not defeated in battle: it decided, through complicated historical twists and turns, to abandon its political and economic institutions and practices in favor of those of the West.[15] Democracy and free markets spread rapidly at the end of the twentieth century through the power of example—that is, by means of soft power.

The term soft power, however, and the implications drawn from it, are misleading in an important way. Culture is powerful but it is not a form of power in the sense that it can be wielded to achieve a specific goal. American efforts to bring soft power directly to bear in Somalia, Haiti, Bosnia, Kosovo, Afghanistan, and Iraq all failed. Culture operates like the forces of nature: it is mighty but not controllable. The proper post-Cold War contribution of the United States to the task of nation-building was not, therefore, to do the building itself; it was to help create and maintain the conditions in which nation-building would occur if local circumstances made this possible, as they did not where the United States conducted its missions of transformation.

The lesson of the British imperial experience, and of the flowering of Germany and Japan after 1945, and of the failure of the American missions after the Cold War, is that the appropriate metaphor for the contribution the United States can make to nation-building in other countries is not architecture; it is gardening. America did not have the power, hard or soft, to do the nation-building itself. It did have the power to foster the conditions in which large impersonal forces—in the case of gardening the forces of nature, for nation-building the forces of culture—can do this work. How well did the United States play this role?

IN THE OPENING SCENE of his 1977 film *Annie Hall,* a classic romantic comedy, Woody Allen tells a joke about two women in a restaurant. The food here is terrible, the first one observes. Yes, the second one replies, and the portions are so small. The joke captures the principal features of post-Cold War American foreign policy. The missions in other countries to which the American government devoted the bulk of its efforts between 1993 and 2014 failed; but the failures did not matter much because they did not affect the world beyond the places where the United States intervened.[16]

That does not mean, however, that these missions had no importance. While in the greater historical scheme of things they themselves did not much matter, they were significant for their effects on what did matter. What did matter in the post-Cold War period was the preservation of its defining conditions: a robust global economy contributing to widespread economic growth; and above all the absence of security competition—the need of the strongest countries to prepare for and occasionally fight major wars—that had shaped international politics for most of recorded history. Whereas the tasks that seemed urgent to American policymakers, the missions of transformation that they undertook, were, for the societies they sought to change, revolutionary in intent, the most important post-Cold War interest of the United States was a profoundly conservative one: maintaining the deep peace that had freed America to launch those missions in the first place. Even the world's strongest power could not make democracy and free markets bloom where they were absent; but it could, like a gardener, help to create an environment that maximized the chances that modern institutions would bloom through the efforts of those who would benefit most from them.[17]

The pervasive peace did not hold. By the end of 2014 power politics had returned: in eastern Ukraine it had returned with a vengeance. The restoration of the old regime in international politics did not, to be sure, arise exclusively from what the United States did or failed to do beyond its borders. American foreign policy could no more exercise complete control over the international system than it could make Somalia, Haiti, Bosnia, Kosovo, Afghanistan, or Iraq into modern countries with Western institutions.

China's challenge to the American-dominated political and economic order in East Asia emerged from a combination of surging economic growth and deeply rooted nationalist sentiment. As their country became richer, the conviction of the Chinese that it should be powerful as well came increasingly to inform its policies toward its neighbors. Occasional Chinese claims to the contrary notwithstanding, the United States did not attempt to block China's post-Cold War rise. Instead, American trade with and investment in China assisted its remarkable economic advance. While China's growth led to a more aggressive foreign policy, the United States was never in a position to arrest, much less prevent it. Other countries, in Europe and in Asia, would not have taken part in a campaign to set back the Chinese economy. In the United States businesses and consumers, both of whom gained from China's growth, would not have been happy with such a policy had the American government proposed it—which it never did.

The 2008 financial crisis severely wounded the global economy and here the United States did play a major role. The crisis originated, after all, in the American housing market because of errors of omission and commission in American public policy. These were not, however, errors of American *foreign* policy. Although they had a global impact, the initiatives and oversights that produced the events of September 15, 2008, and afterward came from the country's regulators, investors, and central bankers, not from its foreign policy officials.

Three American foreign policies, on the other hand—the Iraq war, the Arab-Israeli peace process, and the expansion of NATO—did contribute to the erosion of the international conditions that defined the post-Cold War era and were extraordinarily advantageous for the United States. Each of the three counted, moreover, not only as a failure but also as a mistake, a measure the United States should have known better than to carry out.

The central mistake of the Iraq war lay not in the belief that removing Saddam Hussein from power was desirable, even important. The mistake was, rather, to assume, contrary to virtually all informed opinion, that his removal would lead readily—indeed almost automatically—to the creation of a stable, decent government in Baghdad. The direct costs of the war exceeded those of all the other post-Cold War American missions in lives lost and damaged, in money spent (and spent in ways that brought no benefit to Americans and precious little to Iraqis), and in the depth of the political divisions the conflict produced in the United States—the sharpest since the Vietnam War a generation earlier.

The intervention exacted another kind of toll: its "opportunity costs"—a term economists use to refer to the value of the alternative uses of resources that are foregone, in this case in favor of attacking and occupying Iraq. The attack and occupation diverted the attention of the American government from, and consumed military and economic resources and political capital that might have been used to oppose, the nuclear weapons programs of the two rogue states, North Korea and Iran. When the North Korean program crossed a crucial threshold in 2003, the Bush administration was preoccupied with Iraq.[18] As Iran expanded its bomb-making capacity, the Bush and Obama administrations did not credibly threaten to stop its programs by force. The political trauma of the Iraq experience made them loath to risk initiating armed conflict with another regime in the region, no matter how dangerous that regime was. In the fullness of time, and depending on how the Iranian drive for nuclear weapons and for regional hegemony turns out, Americans may conclude that in the first decade of the twenty-first century they invaded the wrong Middle Eastern country. Whether, without the war in Iraq, the United States would have adopted more forceful and successful measures against the rogue nuclear proliferators cannot be known; but the Iraq mission, with its unexpectedly and dismayingly high costs, at the very least made such responses less likely.

The mistake the United States made in the Arab-Israeli peace process, which all three post-Cold War administrations pursued, was the failure to recognize the basic cause of the Arab-Israeli conflict: the Arab, and specifically the Palestinian, refusal to accept Jewish sovereignty in the Middle East. A proper American appreciation of the basis of the conflict could not, by itself, have ended it. This would have required the kind of change of political culture among the Palestinians that the United States had been unable to bring about in Somalia, Haiti, Bosnia, Kosovo, Afghanistan, or Iraq. An understanding of the roots of the conflict might, however, have yielded an American policy toward it that would have reduced its costs. Having seen the conflict clearly, the American government might even have refrained from the futile efforts to settle it that consumed so much of its high-level attention. It was, more than anything else, the American devotion to the peace process that made it the oldest established permanent floating con game in the world.

The United States had only a modest incentive to reduce the costs of the Arab-Israeli conflict because it was Israel that had to pay these costs. The peace process coincided with—and if it did not help to cause, it certainly did nothing to prevent—a series of wars waged against Israeli civilians by neighboring terrorist groups. In addition, while the various rounds of negotiation failed due to Palestinian recalcitrance, much of the world, especially in Europe, blamed the Israelis. This in turn bolstered the Palestinians' pursuit of their principal goal, which was not to create their own state but rather to destroy the political legitimacy of the Jewish state in the eyes of other countries in the hope that this would ultimately lead to its demise. Still, while Israel was small, because the Israelis were a cohesive, resourceful, and resilient people, the costs that the American-sponsored peace process either inflicted or failed to prevent proved to be bearable for them.

In expanding NATO eastward to Russia's border while deliberately excluding Russia, the United States made a double-edged mistake. On the one hand, the initiative brought no gain: it was hardly necessary to assure democracy in the new members, which was the benefit the Clinton administration claimed for expansion. Indeed if belonging to the alliance had in fact been a recipe for democratic government, Russia should have been the first country included.[19] On the other hand, and as was widely predicted when it was proposed, expansion alienated Russia, pushing Europe's largest country, and one armed with thousands of nuclear weapons, on to the path that led to the 2014 invasion of Ukraine.

To be sure, Russia invaded Ukraine at least in part because an auto-cratic government had taken root in Moscow, whose dictator opted for foreign conquests as a way of enhancing his own popularity; and Russian autocracy had its roots in the country's long and entirely undemocratic political tradition as well as in the gusher of oil money that gave Vladimir Putin both the incentive and the means to monop-olize power. The shaky, imperfect democratic political system that governed Russia in the 1990s might not have survived under any cir-cumstances; but without NATO expansion (or with Russia's inclusion in the Atlantic alliance) an undemocratic Russia would not necessar-ily have opposed the West and the United States in the international arena.[20] It might have become a post-Cold War version of the Cold-War-era "friendly tyrants," undemocratic at home but cooperative, or at least not hostile, abroad. Certainly, without expansion a Russian leader would not have been able to mobilize popular resentment and fear of the West in support of wars against Georgia and Ukraine. Putin would not have found it as easy as he did to present these conflicts to the Russian public as defensively motivated rather than what at least the Ukraine incursion certainly was: a war of aggression.

By making opposition to the United States the default position of Russian foreign policy everywhere, moreover, NATO expansion and the other American policies—the Balkan interventions and the with-drawal from the ABM treaty in particular—that the Russians believed violated their interests and betrayed the spirit in which the Cold War had ended[21] had adverse consequences for the United States beyond the territory of the former Soviet Union. Despite deep suspicion of China's geopolitical goals and genuine fear of China's rising power, Russia aligned itself with the Chinese in the Shanghai Cooperation Organization, a loose regional security grouping that China domi-nated.[22] In the Middle East it adopted a less firm position on the Iranian nuclear program than did the United States despite being within closer range of Iranian missiles than is North America, and staunchly sup-ported Bashar Assad's bloody repression of the rebellion against him in Syria.[23]

Unlike the Iraq war, NATO expansion had negligible costs for the United States when it began: that was the reason the Clinton adminis-tration felt free to undertake it. As Russian resentment grew, however, and Russian power expanded, like a slow-acting virus in the human body the damage to American interests increased. As the post-Cold War era ended, it seemed all too likely to continue to increase. On the list of challenges confronting the United States after the golden interval without power politics that followed the collapse of communism in Europe, an angry, dangerous Russia was certain to remain high. In that case, the expansion of NATO would have a claim to being, in historical perspective, the most consequential American foreign policy of the post-Cold War years: its malign effects would be felt long after the failed missions in Somalia, Haiti, Bosnia, Kosovo, and even Afghanistan and Iraq had faded from memory.

NOTES

───◦◦◦◦───

Introduction

1. The role of the foreign policy community in the making of foreign policy is discussed on pp. 81–82.
2. On the Kurdish rescue operation see Lawrence Freedman and Ephraim Karsh, *The Gulf Conflict, 1990–1991: Diplomacy and War in the New World Order*, Princeton, New Jersey: Princeton University Press, 1993, pp. 420–425.
3. The phrase is from Richard K. Betts, *American Force: Dangers, Delusions, and Dilemmas in National Security*, New York: Columbia University Press, 2012, p. 20.
4. American rule was interrupted by the Japanese occupation of 1942–1945.
5. For a comparison between the post-Cold War United States and the British Empire see pp. 373–374.
6. Quoted in George Herring, *From Colony to Superpower: U.S. Foreign Relations Since 1776*, New York: Oxford University Press, 2008, p. 1.
7. The distinction comes from Richard Haass's study of the American wars in Iraq of 1991 and 2003, *War of Necessity, War of Choice*, New York: Simon and Schuster, 2009.
8. Francis Fukuyama, *Political Order and Political Decay: From the Industrial Revolution to the Globalization of Democracy*, New York: Farrar, Straus, and Giroux, 2014, p. 399.
9. This is a major theme of Francis Fukuyama, *The Origins of Political Order: From Prehuman Times to the French Revolution*, New York: Farrar Straus, and Giroux, 2011. See especially chapters 3–5.

Chapter 1

1. Quoted in Geoff Dyer, *Contest of the Century: The New Era of Competition With China—and How America Can Win*, New York: Alfred A. Knopf, 2014, p. 6.

2. George F. Kennan, "A Fateful Error," *The New York Times*, February 5, 1997.

3. Kennedy: "Let the word go forth from this time and place, that the torch has been passed to a new generation of Americans—born in this century, tempered by war, disciplined by a hard and bitter peace, proud of our ancient heritage." Clinton: "Today a generation raised in the shadows of the Cold War assumes new responsibilities in a world warmed by the sunshine of freedom but troubled still by ancient hatreds and new plagues."

4. Roosevelt himself had served as Assistant Secretary of the Navy during World War I.

5. The Cold War ended during the presidency of George H. W. Bush, but most of his term was devoted to the events that brought that conflict to a conclusion.

6. This pattern is expressed in the title of James Mann's excellent book about Sino-American relations from Nixon to Clinton, *About Face*, New York: Knopf, 1999.

7. Jonathan Spence, *The China Helpers: Western Advisors in China, 1620–1960*, London: The Bodley Head, 1969, chapters 2 and 6.

8. Andrew J. Nathan, "Preface to the Paperback Edition: The Tiananmen Papers—An Editor's Reflections," in *The Tiananmen Papers: The Chinese Leadership's Decision to Use Force Against Their Own People—In Their Own Words*, Compiled by Zhang Liang, Edited by Andrew J. Nathan and Perry Link, New York: PublicAffairs, 2002, p. viii.

9. Mann, *op. cit.*, p. 187.

10. "The number of dead has been variously estimated as between 700 and 2700." *Ibid.*, p. 192.

11. David M. Lampton, *Same Bed Different Dreams: Managing U.S.-China Relations, 1989–2000*, Berkeley, California: University of California Press, 2002, p. 258.

12. A total of 11,000 more Chinese had become permanent residents of the United States. Mann, *op. cit.*, p. 105.

13. Bush vetoed the bill, but issued an Executive Order giving the students the same rights that the bill had provided. *Ibid.*, p. 215

14. The Senate failed to override his veto and the bill did not become law. *Ibid.*, p. 263.

15. *Ibid.*, pp. 101–103.

16. Such an audience "had existed on a few rare occasions before, for such events as the Americans' landing on the moon in 1969." Harvard study quoted in Lampton, *op. cit.*, p. 265.

17. Mann, *op. cit.*, p. 236.

18. *Ibid.*, pp. 241–245.

19. George Stephanopoulos, an aide to the Democratic majority leader in the House of Representatives, Richard Gephardt, who had become a champion of the Chinese students in the United States in promoting linkage, assumed an important role in the Clinton campaign.

20. Quoted in Lampton, *op. cit.*, p. 32.

21. Quoted in *Ibid.*, p. 33.

22. Mann, *op. cit.*, p. 280.

23. In 1980 Vance resigned the position and was succeeded by Maine Senator Edmund Muskie, not Christopher.

24. Quoted in Elizabeth Drew, *On the Edge: The Clinton Presidency*, New York: Simon & Schuster, 1994, p. 27.

25. Mann, *op. cit.*, p. 301.

26. *Ibid.*, p. 303.

27. On the general track record of economic sanctions as a tool of diplomacy see Daniel Drezner, *The Sanctions Paradox*, New York: Cambridge University Press, 1999.

28. Mann, *op. cit.*, p. 308.

29. Lampton, *op. cit.*, pp. 137–138.

30. Mann, *op. cit.*, pp. 247, 293; David Shambaugh, *China Goes Global: The Partial Power*, New York: Oxford University Press, 2013, p. 50.

31. I. M. Destler, *American Trade Politics, Fourth Edition*, Washington, DC: The Brookings Institution, 2005, pp. 211–213; Mann, *op. cit.*, pp. 283–287. By 1994 the economic officials of the Clinton administration had come to oppose the policy of linkage. *Ibid*, p. 294.

32. The war between the communists and the Kuomintang actually began in 1927, was more or less suspended during the Japanese occupation and World War II, and resumed after the Japanese defeat in 1945.

33. Andrew Nathan and Robert Ross, *The Great Wall and the Empty Fortress: China's Search for Security*, New York: W.W. Norton, 1997, p. 204.

34. This is a major theme of Alan Wachman, *Why Taiwan? Geostrategic Rationales for China's Territorial Integrity*, Stanford, California: Stanford University Press, 2007. On China's post-Cold War maritime policies see pp. 348–350.

35. ". . . for Beijing, preventing the de jure separation of Taiwan from the mainland is inextricably linked to regime legitimacy and, therefore, survival." Lampton, *op. cit.*, p. 99.

36. Nancy Bernkopf Tucker, *Strait Talk: United States-Taiwan Relations and the Crisis With China*, Cambridge, Massachusetts: Harvard University Press, 2009, p. 200.

37. It would have had no strategic value at all if the United States had concluded that China would never pose a military threat of any kind. Even in the 1990s American officials were not so convinced, and subsequent events proved them correct. See pp. 348–349.

38. Mann, *op. cit.*, pp. 316–318.

39. *Ibid.*, pp. 337–338.

40. Quoted in Mann, *op. cit.*, p. 337.

41. China could not have captured Taiwan, but it could have inflicted physical damage on the island and sharply reduced trade and investment there through missile attacks.

42. Lampton, *op. cit.*, p. 138.

43. Quoted in Lampton, *ibid.*, p. 111.

44. Mann, *op. cit.*, p. 294. "It was commonplace in the 1990s for Washington to defend the maintenance of a good relationship with Beijing by making either or both of two arguments: One claim was that democracy will inexorably come to China someday. The other argument was that conciliatory U.S. policies toward Beijing—such as trade, education, and cultural contacts—would in the long run help serve the causes of liberty and democracy in China." *Ibid.*, p. 376. See also *Ibid.* pp. 236 and 357, and Lampton, *op. cit.*, p. 276.

45. On the democratizing impact of free markets see Michael Mandelbaum, *Democracy's Good Name: The Rise and Risks of the World's Most Popular Form of Government*, New York: Public Affairs, 2007, chapter 3. On the economic incentives for political liberalization in China see Mandelbaum, *The Road to Global Prosperity, op cit.*, pp. 156–166.

46. "Deng Xiaoping and his reform-minded colleagues saw their regime's legitimacy after the decade of the Cultural Revolution residing in their ability to put goods on the shelves." Lampton, *op. cit.*, p. 113.

47. Mann, *op. cit.*, p. 304; Lampton, *op. cit.*, p. 44.

48. Paul Blustein, *The Chastening: Inside the Crisis that Rocked the Global Financial System and Humbled the IMF*, New York: PublicAffairs, 2001, p. 229. " 'They thought we were a bunch of ignoramuses poaching on their turf,' said [an economic official]. 'And we thought they were willing to give any amount of money to anyone under the naive assumption that it would actually stabilize the country.' " *Ibid.*, p. 229.

49. The changes that made for greater difficulty are discussed in Destler, *op. cit.*, chapter 7.

50. Drew, *op. cit.*, p. 288.

51. On the side agreements see Gary Clyde Hufbauer and Jeffrey J. Schott, *NAFTA Revisited: Achievements and Challenges*, Washington, DC: Institute for International Economics, 2005, p. 7.

52. Drew, *op. cit.*, pp. 338–342.

53. "In the twelve years from 1982 to 1994, private capital flows to emerging markets had increased more than six times, from $24 billion to $148 billion." Robert E. Rubin and Jacob Weisberg, *In An Uncertain World: Tough Choices from Wall Street to Washington*, New York: Random House, 2003, p. 17. "For emerging markets alone, the amount of private capital flowing into them from abroad rose from $188 billion in 1984–1990 to $1.043 trillion in 1991–1997." Blustein, *op. cit.*, p. 17.

54. "'We pushed full steam ahead on all areas of liberalization, including financial,' recalled Jeffrey E. Garten, a former senior Commerce Department official . . . 'I never went on a trip when my brief didn't include either advice or congratulations on liberalization.'" Quoted in Nicholas D. Kristoff with David E. Sanger, "How U.S. Wooed Asia to Let Cash Flow In," *The New York Times*, February 16, 1999, http://www.nytimes.com/library/world/global/021699global-econ.html.

55. This was also a way of addressing the problem of moral hazard. If countries could escape financial crises without penalty they would have no incentive to avoid the policies and practices that brought on these crises.

56. The administration's reasons for the rescue effort are set out in Rubin and Weisberg, *op. cit.*, chapter 1.

57. *Ibid.*, p. 24. Rubin noted a paradox inherent in the situation. In order to persuade Congress to vote money for Mexico the administration had to emphasize the danger of an economic collapse there. But that would make investors less likely to keep their money in the country. *Ibid.*, p. 19

58. Blustein, *op. cit.*, pp. 87, 207–210.

59. The loan was worth $55 billion, the largest offered in such circumstances until then. A total of $35 billion came from the IMF and the World Bank and another $20 billion came in bilateral loans pledged by individual countries should they be necessary. *Ibid.*, p. 178.

60. Rubin and Weisberg, *op. cit.*, pp. 232–241.

61. Blustein, *op. cit.*, pp. 313–314. On LTCM see Roger Lowenstein, *When Genius Failed: The Rise and Fall of Long-Term Capital Management*, New York: Random House, 2001.

62. That reputation was fragile because Brazil had a history of very high inflation.

63. One economic measure for which the IMF lobbied, which did not have political implications, was a commitment to flexible rather than to fixed exchange rates. Blustein, *op. cit.*, p. 368

64. Strobe Talbott, *The Russia Hand: A Memoir of Presidential Diplomacy*, New York: Random House, 2002, p. 8.

65. ". . . Clinton and his foreign policy team made Russia a top priority . . . aides estimated that he spent 'about 50 percent of his foreign policy day cramming to understand the place.'" James Goldgeier and Michael McFaul, *Power and Purpose: U.S. Policy toward Russia after the Cold War*, Washington, DC: The Brookings Institution, 2003, p. 89.

66. *Ibid.*, p. 94.

67. *Ibid.*, pp. 157, 160.

68. *Ibid.*, pp. 126–130.

69. *Ibid.*, pp. 136–144.

70. Talbott, *op. cit.*, p. 195.

71. On the 1996 Russian presidential election and American policy see Goldgeier and McFaul, *op. cit.*, pp. 144–156.

72. On American influence on the 1996 election Goldgeier and McFaul weigh in as follows: "Did any of these American initiatives help Yeltsin win re-election? Probably not. Russian voters did not cast their ballots in these elections based on recommendations from Clinton. At its core, the 1996 presidential vote was a choice between two opposite political and socioeconomic systems. It was a referendum about Russia's future, not a vote about specific issues, foreign or domestic." *Ibid.*, p. 155.

73. Russia paid the Soviet debt in full, with the final payment coming in 2006.

74. On the Bush policy toward the Russian economy, see Goldgeier and McFaul, *op.cit.*, chapter 4. The Bush administration ultimately offered $24 billion to Russia, but emphasized that it included no new money: all of it came from programs already authorized. *Ibid.*, p. 82.

75. The high point of direct American grants came in 2004, when the total was $1.6 billion. Thereafter, until the end of the Clinton administration, the annual amount averaged around $150 million. *Ibid.*, p. 94.

76. Advisors not affiliated with any government had, perhaps, even more influence overall. "Oddly, the most notable Western presence in Russia in 1991 and 1992 was independent economic advisors, the most prominent of whom was Harvard University Professor Jeffrey Sachs. Yeltsin and Gaidar invited foreign advisors and they listened to them to a surprising degree." Anders Aslund, *Russia's Capitalist Revolution: Why Market Reform Succeeded and Democracy Failed*, Washington, DC: Peterson Institute for International Economics, 2007, p. 119.

77. Daniel Treisman, *The Return: Russia's Journey from Gorbachev to Medvedev*, New York: The Free Press, 2010, p. 208.

78. The initials stood for "Gosudartsvennye Kratkosrochney Obligatsii"—in English, "state short-term obligations." Blustein, *op. cit.*, p. 238.

79. On this episode see Goldgeier and McFaul, *op. cit.*, chapter 9.

80. *Ibid.*, pp. 37, 88.

81. Aslund, *op. cit.,* p. 118; Goldgeier and McFaul, *op. cit.*, chapter 4, especially pp. 84–86.

82. Treisman, *op. cit.*, pp. 231–232.

83. According to Andrei Ilarionov, a staunchly pro-free-market Russian economist, "The most serious *ideological* consequence of the crisis [of August 17, 1998] was a powerful shift in public opinion. The words 'democracy,' 'reforms,' and 'liberal' and the concepts and the people associated with them have been discredited. The ideas of the market economy, liberalism, and friendship with the West have been seriously undermined." Quoted in Goldgeier and McFaul, *op. cit.*, p. 233

84. Aslund, *op. cit.*, pp. 288–292; Anders Aslund, "Building Capitalism: Lessons of the Postcommunist Experience," Washington, DC: Carnegie Endowment for International Peace, Policy Brief 10, December 2001.

85. Some countries have gone through several episodes of failed democratic experiments before this form of government has taken root. See Samuel P. Huntington, *The Third Wave: Democratization in the Late Twentieth Century*, Norman, Oklahoma: University of Oklahoma Press, 1991, pp. 41–43.

86. Mandelbaum, *The Road to Global Prosperity*, pp. 140–145.

87. Lenin and his colleagues put communism in place far more quickly, by using the simple expedient of force to eliminate—through intimidation, expulsion, or murder—all opposition. A democrat could not, and Boris Yeltsin did not, employ that tactic. As a consequence, many Russians with vested interests in or simply nostalgia for the old ways of doing things actively resisted the new ones Yeltsin was trying to establish. Managers of factories and collective farms lobbied for resources to sustain their enterprises, which were not viable under free-market conditions. Inflation was one result of their efforts. Another was what came to be known as Russia's "virtual economy," in which unprofitable enterprises kept themselves afloat by engaging in barter with one another, outside the country's money economy. Clifford G. Gaddy and Barry W. Ickes, "Russia's Virtual Economy," *Foreign Affairs,* 77:5 (September/October 1998).

88. This is a major theme of Francis Fukuyama, *The Origins of Political Order: From Prehuman Times to the French Revolution*, New York: Farrar, Straus, and Giroux, 2011. See, for example, p. 453. Fukuyama argues that modern, Western-style institutes require the "exit from kinship." p. 81. See also Lawrence Rosen "Understanding Corruption," *The American Interest*, Spring (March/April 2010).

89. See Konstantin Simis, *USSR: The Corrupt Society*, New York: Simon & Schuster, 1982. On the patrimonial tradition in pre-Soviet Russia see Richard Pipes, *Russia Under the Old Regime*, New York: Charles Scribner's Sons, 1974.

90. Fukuyama, *The Origins of Political Order*, p. 400.

91. Goldgeier and McFaul, *op. cit.*, p. 214.

92. This is a theme of Treisman, *op. cit.* See, for example, p. 242 and pp. 340–343.

93. "Opinion polls . . . show that anti-Americanism has permeated the whole society and is now probably deeper than at any time in Russian history. A substantial majority believes that the United States and the West have weakened Russia deliberately in order to exploit and humiliate it." Russia specialist Peter Reddaway, quoted in Jonathan G. Clarke, "A Foreign Policy Report Card on the Clinton-Gore Administration," Washington, DC: The Cato Institute, Policy Analysis No. 382, October 3, 2000, p.8.

94. The short-range, "tactical" nuclear weapons remaining in the countries of Western and Eastern Europe were removed through parallel unilateral policies of withdrawing them adopted by the United States and the Soviet Union. Goldgeier and McFaul, *op. cit.*, pp. 44–45.

95. Formally the agreement was a Protocol to the START Treaty. Ukraine dragged its feet at carrying out the agreement. More negotiations over several years were required for the nuclear-tipped missiles that Ukraine had inherited from the Soviet Union to be sent to Russia. *Ibid.*, pp. 55–56.

96. The idea emerged from a meeting to discuss the nuclear weapons remaining in the former Soviet Union organized by David Hamburg, President of the Carnegie Corporation of New York.

97. This is the subject of Michael Mandelbaum, *The Dawn of Peace in Europe*, New York: The Twentieth Century Fund, 1996.

98. Jack F. Matlock, *Superpower Illusions: How Myths and False Ideologies Led America Astray—and How to Return to Reality*, New Haven: Yale University Press, 2010, pp. xi, 319 note 9; Treisman, *op. cit.*, p. 316; Jonathan Power, "Breaking a Promise to Russia," *Jordan Times*, June 4, 2015, www.jordantimes.com/opinion/jonathan-power/breaking-promise-russia.

99. The decision to expand NATO was made "in characteristic Clinton administration style, without a structured evaluation of competing viewpoints, without political debate, and over the initial objections of senior military officers." R. W. Apple Jr., "Road to Approval Is Rocky, And the Gamble Is Perilous," *The New York Times*, May 15, 1997, p. A1.

100. Goldgeier and McFaul, *op. cit.*, p. 195. Clinton "appears to have decided sometime in the spring or summer of 1994 to push to enlarge NATO at some point . . ." *Ibid.*, p. 201. The meeting at which Perry was informed of the decision took place in December of that year. See also James M. Goldgeier, *Not Whether but When: The U.S. Decision to Enlarge NATO*, Washington, DC: The Brookings Institution, 1999, p. 163.

101. J. L. Black, *Russia Faces NATO Expansion: Bearing Gifts or Bearing Arms?* Lanham, MD: Rowman and Littlefield, 2000, p. 2. For Russians, NATO became "a four-letter word." Talbott, *op. cit.*, p. 85.

102. Goldgeier and McFaul, *op. cit.*, p. 191.

103. *Ibid.*, *op. cit.*, pp. 208–209, 173–174.

104. See pp. 354–366.

105. Goldgeier and McFaul, *op. cit.*, p. 184.

106. According to Russia's Ambassador to the United States, Yuli Vorontsov, "When the decision [to expand NATO] was originally floated, I came to the State Department and had a long talk with the then assistant secretary of state, Mr. [Richard] Holbrooke. I said, 'have you thought about Russia while you were putting forward this idea of enlargement of NATO?' And his answer was very honest. He said, 'No, not at all; you have nothing to do with that.' 'Aha,' I said, 'that's very interesting, and what about invitation for Russia to join enlarged NATO?' He said, 'Anybody but Russia; no.' . . . And from all the quarters I received that kind of answer: 'Anyone but Russia; not you.'" Transcript of Panel II,

"The Emerging NATO-Russia Charter and Relationship," Conference on Russia and NATO, Washington, DC, George Washington University, February 4, 1997.

107. See pp. TKK–TKK.

108. See Michael Mandelbaum, *NATO Expansion: A Bridge to the Nineteenth Century*, Washington, DC: Center for Political and Strategic Studies, June 1997, Part II. Steven Sestanovich, who worked on Russia-related issues in the Clinton administration, retrospectively justified the policy of NATO expansion on the grounds that the United States had a supreme interest in preserving NATO and that Russia did not qualify for membership. Steven Sestanovich, "Could It Have Been Otherwise?" *The American Interest*, Vol. X, No. 5 (May/June) 2015. That is not what American officials said in promoting the policy, however. Moreover, this justification confuses ends and means. The purpose of NATO was to enhance the security of America's allies in Europe. NATO expansion made them less secure.

109. Treisman, *op. cit.*, p. 317; Goldgeier, *op. cit.*, pp. 143, 167; Goldgeier and McFaul, *op. cit.*, pp. 197, 202.

110. Goldgeier, *op. cit.*, p. 4.

111. Goldgeier and McFaul, *op. cit.*, p. 195. Eight former ambassadors and State Department officials urged this course. Treisman, *op. cit.*, p. 317.

112. Of the next seven countries admitted, the three Baltic countries had borders with Russia.

113. American officials "joked among themselves about how hard it was to get the Russians to 'eat their spinach.' They were the patient parents, their interlocutors the difficult children." Treisman, *op. cit.*, p. 328.

114. Mandelbaum, *NATO Expansion*, Part IV.

Chapter 2

1. Quoted in Doug Bandow, "America's Balkan Quagmire," http://cato.org/publications/commentary/americas-balkan-quagmire.

2. In his description of the Melian dialogue Thucydides depicts such interventions as something very close to a law of international relations. He records the Athenians as saying to the less powerful Melians that the strong do what they will, the weak do what they must: " . . . the standard of justice depends on the power to compel and . . . in fact the strong do what they have the power to do and the weak accept what they have to accept." Thucydides, *The Peloponnesian War*, Translated by Rex Warner, Harmondsworth, England: Penguin Books, 1954, p. 402.

3. The "Roosevelt Corollary" of 1904 to the Monroe Doctrine proclaimed a similar intent: " . . . brutal wrongdoing, or an impotence which results in a general loosening of the ties of civilized society, may finally require intervention by some civilized society, and in the Western Hemisphere the United States cannot ignore this duty." Quoted in George

C. Herring, *From Colony to Superpower: U.S. Foreign Relations Since 1776*, New York: Oxford University Press, 2008, p. 371. Theodore Roosevelt applied the corollary to the Dominican Republic, imposing a treaty giving the United States control over Dominican finances. The initiative was not, however, entirely disinterested: holders of Dominican bonds, including Americans, did benefit economically. *Ibid.*, pp. 371–372. The brief American intervention in Mexico in 1914, during which American troops occupied the city of Veracruz for seven months, was also undertaken, according to the man who authorized it, President Woodrow Wilson, for purely selfless reasons. *Ibid.*, pp. 391–394.

4. Quoted in Robert Merry, "America's Default Foreign Policy," *The National Interest* (September-October 2013), http:/nationalinterest.org/print/article/americas-default-foreign-policy.

5. Its formal origins are customarily traced to the Treaty of Westphalia of 1648.

6. Section 4: "All Members shall refrain . . . from the threat or use of force against the territorial integrity or political independence of any state." Section 7: "Nothing in the present Charter shall authorize the United Nations to intervene in matters which are essentially within the domestic jurisdiction of any state."

7. The supremacy of sovereignty came in for occasional challenge in the nineteenth century as well. In 1876 the British political leader William E. Gladstone denounced the Ottoman Empire's treatment of its Christian subjects in the then-Ottoman province of Bulgaria. He made his objections a part of his party's campaign in the British general election of 1880. Britain did not, however, intervene in Bulgaria.

8. Ultimately there came to be "more than twenty United Nations human rights agreements." Stephen D. Krasner, *Sovereignty: Organized Hypocrisy*, Princeton, New Jersey: Princeton University Press, 1999, p. 105.

9. Samuel Moyn's *The Lost Utopia: Human Rights in History*, Cambridge, Massachusetts: Harvard University Press, 2010, describes the rise in international attention to human rights during that decade and explains it as stemming from "the collapse of prior universalistic schemes and the construction of human rights as a persuasive alternative to them." p. 7.

10. The exception was Iraq's invasion of Kuwait in 1990 and the war that followed in 1991.

11. "Secretary-General's Address at University of Bordeaux," United Nations Press Release, SG/SM/4560, April 26, 1991,

12. The exception to this rule is when the United States is at war.

13. Powell wrote in his memoirs that he "thought I would have an aneurysm" in response. Colin Powell, *My American Journey*, New York: Ballantine Books, 1995, p. 561.

14. Justin Vaisse, *Neoconservatism: The Biography of a Movement*, Translated by Arthur Goldhammer, Cambridge, Massachusetts: Harvard University Press, 2010, pp. 11–12, 223–236.

15. Johanna Neuman, *Lights, Camera, War: Is Media Technology Driving International Politics?* New York: St. Martin's Press, 1996, pp. 14–15, describes the CNN effect, of which the author is skeptical.

16. John Mueller, "American foreign policy and public opinion in a new era: eleven propositions," in Mueller, *War and Ideas: Selected Essays*, London and New York: Routledge, 2011, p. 171.

17. "With respect to foreign interventions, the public seems to apply a fairly reasonable cost-benefit calculus. A substantial loss of American lives may have been tolerable if the enemy was international Communism or the country that had attacked Pearl Harbor, but risking lives for a goal as ungraspable and vaporous as policing a small, distant, unthreatening, and seemingly perennially-troubled place like Somalia or Bosnia has proved difficult to manage." John Mueller, "Public Opinion as a Constraint on U.S. Foreign Policy: Assessing the Perceived Value of American and Foreign Lives," Paper prepared for presentation at the National Convention of the International Studies Association, Los Angeles, California, March 14–18, 2000, p. 9.

18. NATO expansion was the other. See pp. 68–74.

19. See pp. 3–4.

20. Derek Chollet and James Goldgeier, *America Between the Wars: From 11/9 to 9/11—the Misunderstood Years Between the Fall of the Berlin Wall and the Start of the War on Terror*, New York: PublicAffairs, 2008, pp. 4–5.

21. South Somalia was a United Nations protectorate from 1949 to 1960.

22. David Halberstam, *War in a Time of Peace: Bush, Clinton, and the Generals,* New York: Scribners, 2001, p. 249.

23. Mueller, "11 Propositions," p. 177. "Perhaps never has so much been done for so many at so little cost." *Ibid.*

24. Halberstam, *op. cit.*, p. 252. In an address announcing the mission Bush said, "Our mission has a limited objective, to open the supply routes, to get the food moving, and to prepare the way for a U.N. peacekeeping force to keep it moving . . . We will not stay one day longer than absolutely necessary." Quoted in Chollet and Goldgeier, *op.cit.*, p. 54.

25. Bush may also have felt, the year before, that the United States, having triggered the Kurdish uprising by defeating the Iraqi army, bore some responsibility for its fate.

26. On the "CNN Effect" on American policy in Somalia see Neuman, *op. cit.*, pp. 227–230.

27. Quoted in Halberstam, *op. cit.*, p. 256.

28. *Ibid.* p. 256.

29. *Ibid.*, p. 257. In an op-ed essay in *The New York Times* Madeleine Albright defended the new policy: "Failure to take action (against Aidid) would have signaled to other clan leaders that the UN is not serious . . . The decision we must make is whether to pull up stakes and allow Somalia to fall back into the abyss or to stay the course and help lift the country and its people from the category of a failed state into that of an emerging

democracy. For Somalia's sake, and for our own, we must persevere." *Ibid.*, p. 258.

30. The events are described in detail in Mark Bowden, *Black Hawk Down: A Story of Modern War*, New York: Penguin, 2000. The book became the basis for a 2000 Hollywood film with the same title that won two Academy Awards. The Somali casualty estimates are on p. 333. A brief description of the events is in Halberstam, *op. cit.*, pp. 261–262.

31. Cited in Chollet and Goldgeier, *op. cit.*, p. 77.

32. Halberstam, *op. cit.*, pp. 262–263; Chollet and Goldgeier, *op. cit.*, p. 75.

33. Elizabeth Drew, *On the Edge: The Clinton Presidency*, New York: Simon & Schuster, 1994, p. 330.

34. He incurred criticism for refusing a request to send tanks, armored personnel carriers, and AC-130 gunships to Somalia, which might have made a difference on October 3. He had in fact had reservations about the entire American and UN mission in the country, but had been denied the opportunity to express them directly to Clinton, and even to the National Security Advisor, W. Anthony Lake. Aspin had also, however, in a year on the job, proven to be a disorganized administrator of the Defense Department. Halberstam, *op. cit.*, pp. 259, 265; Bowden, *op. cit.*, p. 335.

35. John Mueller, "Public Opinion as a Constraint on U.S. Foreign Policy: Assessing the Perceived Value of American and Foreign Lives," Paper prepared for presentation at the National Convention of the International Studies Association, Los Angeles, California, March 14–18, 2000, p. 28.

36. Halberstam, *op. cit.*, p. 264.

37. The events are described in *Ibid.*, p. 269–272.

38. See pp. 127–129.

39. Some estimates of the death toll range as a high as a million, including Tutsis and Hutus. Halberstam, *op. cit.*, p. 277.

40. The evacuation force was not equipped to stop the slaughter. Alan J. Kuperman, *The Limits of Humanitarian Intervention: Genocide in Rwanda*, Washington, DC: The Brookings Institution Press, 2001, p. 94.

41. Kofi Annan, "Secretary-General Reflects on 'Intervention' in Thirty-fifth annual Ditchley Foundation Lecture," New York: United Nations Press Release SG/SM/6613, June 26, 1998, p. 8.

42. Kuperman, *op. cit.*, pp. 40, 78. The United States was instrumental in blocking the UN from sending a more robust force. *Ibid.*, pp. 110, 116.

43. This is Kuperman's thesis. *Ibid.*

44. Chollet and Goldgeier, *op. cit.*, p. 92; Halberstam, *op. cit.*, pp. 277–278.

45. In her 1995 book *Balkan Tragedy: Chaos and Dissolution After the End of the Cold War*, Washington, DC: The Brookings Institution, Susan Woodward argued, to the contrary, that the dissolution of the country and ensuing conflicts had economic roots. "The conflict is not a result of historical animosities and it is not a return to the precommunist past: it

is the result of the politics of transforming a socialist society to a market economy and democracy. A critical element of this failure was economic decline, caused largely by a program intended to resolve a foreign debt crisis." p. 15.

46. Steven L. Burg and Paul S. Shoup, *The War in Bosnia-Herzegovina: Ethnic Conflict and International Intervention*, Armonk, New York: M.E. Sharpe, 1999, p. 70. This is the authoritative book in English on the war in Bosnia.

47. *Ibid.*, p. 26.

48. *Ibid.*, p. 20.

49. *Ibid.*, pp. 16–17, 25.

50. "The [World War II] massacres of Serbs in Bosnia-Herzegovina, in which hundreds of thousands perished, were largely the work of the Croatian Ustashe. But it appears that Muslims also participated in the Ustashe atrocities, notably in eastern Herzegovina, where the Croats depended on locally recruited Muslims to carry out their work." *Ibid.*, p. 38.

51. *Ibid.*, pp. 29–32. The term "Bosniak" came to refer to Bosnian Muslims only.

52. In 1993 the European Community renamed itself the European Union (EU).

53. Burg and Shoup, *op. cit.*, p. 123.

54. *Ibid.*, pp. 137–138.

55. *Ibid.*, pp. 169–171.

56. *Ibid.*, p. 133.

57. "In the last analysis, given the number of Muslims expelled from Serb-controlled territory and the brutality that accompanied the expulsions, the sum total of atrocities committed by the Serbs was in a category by itself." *Ibid.*, p. 173.

58. Samantha Power, *"A Problem from Hell": America in the Age of Genocide*, New York: HarperCollins Perennial, 2003, pp. 276–277.

59. Burg and Shoup, *op. cit.*, p. 149. The Muslims sometimes launched attacks on the Serbs from these safe areas. *Ibid.*, p. 287; Power, *op. cit.*, p. 398.

60. Burg and Shoup, *op. cit.*, p. 340.

61. The American military leadership also did not want to get involved in Bosnia. *Ibid.*, p. 200.

62. *Ibid.*, p. 33, 42.

63. *Ibid.*, pp. 11, 13, 46–47, 60, 195–196.

64. Power, *op. cit.*, p. 57.

65. Burg and Shoup, *op. cit.*, pp. 81–85.

66. Kuperman, *op. cit.*, pp., 1–2; Moyn, *op. cit.*, p. 220.

67. His stance attracted the support of some neoconservatives, for whom the use of foreign policy to defend and promote American values around the world was important.

68. Burg and Shoup, *op. cit.*, p. 210. Shortly after the beginning of the Clinton administration, on February 3, 1993, Secretary of State

Christopher said of the ongoing violence, "Our conscience revolts at the idea of passively accepting such brutality." Drew, *op. cit.*, p. 147.

69. "The Clinton administration's early opposition to the Vance-Owen plan appeared to be based on a belief that the plan ratified ethnic partition. It may also have been based on domestic political considerations on the part of the Clinton advisors, who, according to Owen, viewed Vance as 'an 'old-style Democrat' and just what Clinton's 'new Democrats' wanted to put behind them.'" Burg and Shoup, *op. cit.*, p. 233.

70. Later in the war the administration looked the other way as Islamic countries shipped arms to the Bosnian Muslims. It also encouraged retired American military officers to help train the armed forces of Croatia. *Ibid.*, pp. 197, 307, 339.

71. Clinton's statements on Bosnia in the first year of his presidency betrayed considerable ambivalence about the use of force there. Richard K. Betts, *American Force: Dangers, Delusions, and Dilemmas in National Security*, New York: Columbia University Press, 2012, p. 53.

72. Burg and Shoup, *op. cit.*, p. 253.

73. The United States was committed to furnishing 25,000 of the 60,000 troops planned for the NATO extrication force. Power, *op. cit.*, p. 424. By some accounts Clinton did not realize the implications of this commitment—the dispatch of a substantial American military force to a war zone in Europe—until the middle of 1995. Burg and Shoup, *op. cit.*, p. 323. At the same time, seeing an opportunity to diminish Clinton politically, Congressional Republicans, who had won control of both the House and the Senate in the 1994 elections, were criticizing him for the weakness of his Balkan policy. The Senate voted, in July 1995, to stop enforcing the arms embargo. About half the body's Democrats supported the resolution. Power, *op. cit.*, p. 429.

74. "The deniability of direct U.S. government involvement in the effort to build up the Muslim and Croatian militaries was preserved through the use of ostensibly private military contractors to provide the necessary training and advice." Burg and Shoup, *op. cit.*, p. 339.

75. Ivo Daalder, *Getting to Dayton*, Washington, DC: Brookings, 2000, pp. 122–123.

76. Burg and Shoup, *op. cit.*, pp. 206, 248.

77. *Ibid.*, p. 82. They had also met in December, 1993, to modify the Vance-Owen Plan. *Ibid.*, p. 284.

78. On relations between the Clinton administration and the Bosnian Muslims see *Ibid.*, pp. 315, 317, 318, 336, 360, and 383, and Daalder, *op. cit.*, pp. 136–137.

79. Among these powers was the sole right to raise and maintain armed forces, depriving the central Bosnian government of the core function of sovereignty. Daalder, *op. cit.*, p. 180

80. By dividing Bosnia into three more or less ethnically homogeneous parts, ethnic cleansing made possible a settlement of the war based on de facto partition.

81. Ivo H. Daalder and Michael E. O'Hanlon, *Winning Ugly: NATO's War to Save Kosovo*, Washington, DC: The Brookings Institution, 2000, p. 9.

82. As with Bosnia, none of the parties favored partition although, as in Bosnia, after the war a de facto partition was established. Among the reasons for their opposition was the fact that, as in Bosnia, the Serbs and Muslims were not neatly separated geographically. As a result of the postwar ethnic cleansing of the Serbs in southern Kosovo, the Serb population did come to be concentrated in the north, on the border with Serbia proper, making partition easier. On the prospects for partition see *Ibid., op. cit.*, pp. 15, 27, 66–67.

83. Tim Judah, *Kosovo: War and Revenge*, New Haven: Yale University Press, 2000, p. 124; Halberstam, *op. cit.*, pp. 366, 397; Daalder and O'Hanlon, *op. cit.*, p. 10. "The [initial] KLA attacks took place five months after the signature of the Dayton Agreement. The Kosovo Albanians looked northwards to Croatia and Bosnia with envy. They observed that with the help of the international community, the Serbs had been defeated completely in the former and partially in the latter. In Bosnia-Hercegovina, the international community had pledged $5 billion to aid reconstruction. Despite being Milosevic's first victims, the Albanians had received nothing. As long as they remained passive, the more radical Albanians reasoned, the outside world would ignore them ..." Misha Glenny, *The Balkans: Nationalism, War and the Great Powers, 1804–1999*, New York: Penguin, 1999, pp. 653–654.

84. Judah, *op. cit.*, p. 191.

85. *Ibid.*, pp. xix–xx. William Cohen, the secretary of defense in Clinton's second term, said that before the war, "my concern was that if there was going to be any kind of action taken, it must be consistent with making sure that we were entirely neutral, that the KLA was not going to use NATO to serve its own purposes. And for many months, I made the statement that we will not be the air force for the KLA." Daalder and O'Hanlon, *op. cit.*, p. 35.

86. "[Albright] was passionate about one issue and one man, the Balkans and Milosevic. The reference point she used again and again when the subject came up, was Munich. He must not be appeased; only force would stop him." Halberstam, *op. cit.*, p. 386.

87. During the Cold War, when the United States did confront an adversary, the Soviet Union, as powerful as Nazi Germany, Albright had had a different view of the world. She had "supported the nuclear freeze ... opposed aid to the Nicaraguan contras and opposed the [1991] Persian Gulf War." Charles Krauthammer, "Empty Threats, Useless Gestures," *The Washington Post*, March 5, 1999, p. A33.

88. Halberstam, *op. cit.*, p. 370.

89. *Ibid.*, pp. 376, 387.

90. Ivo Daalder and Michael O'Hanlon, *Winning Ugly: NATO's War to Save Kosovo*, p. 41.

91. *Ibid.*, pp. 41–42.

92. *Ibid.*, p. 44.

93. Milosevic had been promised that the monitors would control the Kosovars and that if they failed to do so the Muslims would be blamed for the ensuing violence. The Americans and Europeans kept neither of these promises. *Ibid.*, pp. 57–58; Judah, *op. cit.*, p. 230.

94. Daalder and O"Hanlon, *op. cit.*, p. 64.

95. *Ibid.*, pp. 75–77.

96. Judah, *op. cit.*, p. 214.

97. The terms of the plan also called for NATO to have unimpeded access to all of Yugoslavia, that is to Serbia proper, as well. *Ibid.*, p. 210.

98. *Ibid.*

99. Daalder and O'Hanlon, *op. cit.*, p. 89.

100. *Ibid.*, p. 221. Madeleine Albright said "I don't see this as a long-term operation. I think that this is something . . . that is achievable within a relatively short period of time." *Ibid.*, p. 91.

101. *Ibid.*, p. 90.

102. *Ibid.*, p. 109.

103. The administration may have mistakenly believed that the Bosnia war, in which NATO did bomb and Milosevic did cooperate in reaching a settlement, offered a useful precedent. To the contrary, "the bombing in Bosnia commenced *after* Milosevic was committed to finding a diplomatic solution to the Bosnian war." *Ibid.*, p. 93. Some in the West believed that Milosevic would in fact welcome light bombing because it would give him a pretext to comply with the Contact Group's plan, protecting him against the anger of the Serbs for making sweeping concessions in Kosovo. This belief also proved mistaken. Halberstam, *op. cit.*, p. 450; Judah, *op. cit.*, p. 311.

104. Daalder and O'Hanlon, *op. cit.*, pp. 111–112. An estimated 5,000 to 10,000 Kosovars were killed during the war, and approximately 500 Serbs. *Ibid.*, p. 110.

105. Glenny, *op. cit.*, p. 658.

106. Daalder and O'Hanlon, *op. cit.*, p. 97.

107. *Ibid.*, p. 53. The American military did not favor the use of ground troops in Kosovo. Halberstam, *op. cit.*, pp. 464–465.

108. Daalder and O'Hanlon, *op. cit.*, p. 100.

109. *Ibid.*, pp. 152–153.

110. *Ibid.*, p. 142; Judah, *op. cit.*, p. 258.

111. Daalder and O'Hanlon, *op. cit.*, p. 106.

112. Halberstam, *op. cit.*, pp. 461–462.

113. Daalder and O'Hanlon, *op. cit.*, p. 19; Halberstam, *op. cit.*, p. 452; Judah, *op. cit.*, p. 251.

114. Daalder and O'Hanlon, *op. cit.*, p. 157.

115. *Ibid.*, pp. 157–158.

116. Chollet and Goldgeier, *op. cit.*, p. 220. See also Daalder and O'Hanlon, *op. cit.*, pp. 161–162.

117. Both he and his then-national security advisor, Samuel Berger, said, after Milosevic had capitulated, that without that capitaluation Clinton would indeed have ordered one. Daalder and O'Hanlon, *op. cit.*, p. 160. When they made these statements, however, the point had become moot.

118. Russia had also sympathized with and given political support to Milosevic during the war in Bosnia. See Burg and Shoup, *op. cit.*, pp. 301, 330, 343, 350.

119. Daalder and O'Hanlon, *op. cit.*, p. 167.

120. Judah, *op. cit.*, p. 274; James Goldgeier and Michael McFaul, *Power and Purpose: U.S. Policy toward Russia after the Cold War*, Washington, DC: Brookings Institution, 2003, pp. 253–254.

121. Daalder and O'Hanlon, *op. cit.*, p. 142.

122. *Ibid.*, pp. 160, 171, 205.

123. On May 27, 1999, Milosevic and four other Serbs were indicted for "Crimes Against Humanity" by the International Criminal Tribunal for the Former Yugoslavia in The Hague. Milosevic died in prison in The Hague in March, 2006. Judah, *op. cit.*, p. 280.

124. Judah, *op. cit.*, pp. 286–287. In the wake of the war, the United Nations High Commission on Refugees and the Organization for Security and Cooperation in Europe published a report stating that non-Albanians in Kosovo faced "a climate of violence and impunity, as well as widespread discrimination, harassment and intimidation directed at non-Albanians." *Ibid.*, p. 292. See also Daalder and O'Hanlon, *op. cit.*, p. 177.

125. Daalder and O'Hanlon, *op. cit.*, p. 150.

126. See pp. 35–37.

127. Daalder and O'Hanlon, *op. cit.*, p. 147.

128. David M. Lampton, *Same Bed, Different Dreams: Managing US-China Relations, 1989–2000*, Berkeley, California: The University of California Press, 2001, pp. 59–60.

129. Subsequent conversations convinced Ahtisaari that Milosevic had agreed to the Contact Group plan with the understanding that Russia would establish its own zone in the northern part of Kosovo in order to protect the Serbs, a zone that could have been annexed to Yugoslavia in the event of independence for Kosovo. Goldgeier and McFaul, *op. cit.*, pp. 265–266.

130. *Ibid.*, p. 253. At the same time, "public opinion polls in Russia showed anti-American sentiment doubling from 23 to 49 percent of the population and the favorable rating of the United States declining from 67 to 39 percent." Daalder and O'Hanlon, *op. cit.*, p. 127.

131. On the Russian reaction see J. L. Black, *Russia Faces NATO Expansion*. Lanham, Maryland: Rowman and Littlefield, 2000, p. 149.

132. " . . . the principle of non-interference must be qualified in important respects. Acts of genocide can never be a purely internal matter. When oppression produces massive flows of refugees which unsettle neighbouring countries then they can properly be described as 'threats to international peace and security.' When regimes are based in minority rule they lose legitimacy—look at South Africa. . . . So how do we decide when and whether to intervene. I think we need to bear in mind five major considerations. First, are we sure of our case? . . . Second, have we exhausted all diplomatic options? . . . Third, on the basis of a practical assessment of the situation, are there military operations we can sensibly and prudently undertake? . . . Fourth, are we prepared for the long term? . . . And finally, do we have national interests involved?" "The Blair Doctrine," http//www.pbs.org/newshour/bb/international-jan-june99-blair_doctrine. Kosovo did not qualify as a minority regime since it was legally part of Yugoslavia, in which Serbs constituted the majority. Nor was any American national interest at stake there.

133. Chollet and Goldgeier, *op. cit.*, p. 221. Clinton also said, in his last year in office, "If the world community has the power to stop it, we ought to stop genocide and ethnic cleansing." Quoted in Kuperman, *op. cit.*, p. 2.

134. Chollet and Goldgeier, *op. cit.*, pp. 218–219.

135. See, for example, Gareth Evans, *The Responsibility to Protect: Ending Mass Atrocies Once and for All*, Washington, DC: Brookings Institution, 2008, p. 6.

136. Gary J. Bass, *Freedom's Battle: The Origins of Humanitarian Intervention*, New York: Knopf, 2008, p. 277.

137. The United States did not disengage entirely from Somalia in the following two decades. From 2007 to 2013 it spent more than $500 million to train a force of the African Union attempting to bring order to the country. In October 2013, a small number of American trainers and advisors were secretly dispatched to Somalia. Craig Whitlock, "U.S. advisers are first to be sent to Somalia since 1993," *The Washington Post*, January 11, 2014, p. A1.

138. James Fergusson, *The World's Most Dangerous Place*, Boston: Da Capo Press, 2013, p. 50.

139. refugeesinternational.org/where-we-work/africa/somalia.

140. Jonathan M. Katz, *The Big Train That Went By: How the World Came to Save Haiti and Left Behind a Disaster*, New York: Palgrave Macmillan, 2013, p. 50.

141. Laurent Dubois, *Haiti: The Aftershocks of History*, New York: Metropolitan Books Henry Holt, 2012, p. 360.

142. Katz, *op. cit., p.* 2.

143. Daalder, *op. cit.*, pp. 175–176.

144. Rajan Menon, "Breaking the State," *The National Interest* (May/June 2011), p. 34.

145. " . . . both the country's elections and its institutions mirror, and in fact have deepened, the ethno-religious divide." Menon, *op. cit..* p. 34. "In a country smaller than West Virginia and with a population the size of Oregon's, there exist 142 municipalities, two highly autonomous entities, 10 cantons, a special district, a national government and an internationally appointed high representative to oversee them all. It amounts to approximately 180 ministers, 600 legislators and an army of about 70,000 bureaucrats . . . Between 1997 and 2007, of 529 proposed laws, 156 were vetoed outright, and another 113 failed to reach parliamentary majority." Aleksandar Hemon and Jasmin Mujanovic, "Stray Dogs and Stateless Babies," *The New York Times*, February 21, 2014, www.nytimes.com/2014/02/22/opinion/sunday/stray-dogs-and-stateless-babies. On the dysfunction of the Dayton Accords in practice see also Milada Vachudova, "Thieves of Bosnia: The complicated Legacy of the Dayton Peace Accords," *Foreign Affairs*, March 3, 2014, www.foreignaffairs.com/print/38079.

146. Post-Dayton, Bosnia received more than $15 billion in economic assistance. "On a per capita basis, the reconstruction of Bosnia, with less than four million citizens, made the post-World War II rebuilding of Germany and Japan look modest." Patrice C. McMahan and Jon Western, "The Death of Dayton," *Foreign Affairs* 88, no. 5, (2009), www.foreignaffairs.com/articles/bosnia-herzegovina/2009-08-17/death-of-dayton.

147. Alison Smale, "Roots of Bosnian Protests Lie in Peace Accords of 1995," *The New York Times*, February 15, 2014, p. A4. "It is not surprising that Bosnians are angry. Eighteen years after the end of the war the people are poor, the politicians are rich and corruption is rife." "On fire," *The Economist*, February 15, 2014, p. 48.

148. In April 2013, Serbia and Kosovo reached an agreement whereby the Serbs would not obstruct Kosovo's efforts to integrate more closely with Europe and, in return, the government of Kosovo promised considerable autonomy for the Serb community in the northern part of the country. Serbia itself was rewarded with the start of negotiations for membership in the EU. Naftali Bendavid and Gordon Fairclough, "Serbia, Kosovo Reach Tentative Deal," *The Wall Street Journal*, April 20–21, 2013, p. A11.

149. In the words of one European, America cooked the meal and the Europeans washed the dishes.

150. See pp. 63–64. "Creating new national armies, police forces, and state and local civilian bureaucracies requires a substantial supply of literate individuals with basic skills, the very things that are often in short supply in poor, conflict-ridden nations." Menon, *op. cit.*, p. 31.

151. Francis Fukuyama, *The Origins of Political Order: From Prehuman Times to the French Revolution*, New York: Farrar, Straus, and Giroux, 2011. See, for example, pp. 438, 453.

Chapter 3

1. Quoted in Peter Baker, *Days of Fire: Bush and Cheney in the White House*, New York: Doubleday, 2013, p. 130.
2. Sherard Cowper-Coles, *Cables from Kabul: The Inside Story of the West's Afghanistan Campaign*, London: HarperPress, 2011, reprinted on the inside cover.
3. Nigel Hamilton, *Bill Clinton: Mastering the Presidency*, New York: PublicAffairs, 2007, p. 637.
4. George Washington was commander-in-chief during the Revolutionary War and Abraham Lincoln during the Civil War; Thomas Jefferson was a major political figure during the first of these conflicts as the wartime governor of Virginia (as well as the author of the Declaration of Independence); and Theodore Roosevelt resigned as Assistant Secretary of the Navy in 1898, raised a battalion of soldiers, and led it into battle in Cuba in the Spanish-American War.
5. Bush, July 6; Clinton, August 19.
6. It is arguable but not, of course, provable that Clinton's preoccupation with the scandal throughout 1998 prevented the kind of high-level attention to the escalating violence in Kosovo that could have avoided the American bombing campaign there in 1999.
7. Baker, *op. cit.*, pp. 17, 85.
8. See pp. 200–202.
9. Quoted in James Mann, *Rise of the Vulcans: The History of Bush's War Cabinet*, New York: Viking, 2004, p. 256. Writing about the prospective Bush foreign policy in the journal *Foreign Affairs* in early 2000, Condoleezza Rice, his chief foreign policy advisor who would become first his national security advisor and then his second secretary of state, cast doubt on the wisdom of engaging in humanitarian intervention. "Promoting the National Interest," *Foreign Affairs* (January/February 2000) pp. 53–54.
10. On this issue see chapter 6, pp. 250–287.
11. The Chinese interpreted the American message as an apology; the Americans did not.
12. A total of 2,744 people were killed there. Lawrence Wright, *The Looming Tower: Al-Qaeda and the Road to 9/11*, New York: Alfred A. Knopf, 2006, p. 361.
13. Baker, *op. cit.*, p. 128. Al Qaeda means "the base" in Arabic.
14. Wright, *op. cit.*, p. 127.
15. *Ibid.*, p. 234.

16. Peter L. Bergen, *The Longest War: The Enduring Conflict between America and al-Qaeda*, New York: Free Press, 2011, p. 24.

17. At the time, Bin Laden wrote to a member of the Saudi royal family that he personally could raise a hundred-thousand-man army to defend the kingdom. Wright, *op. cit.*, p. 157.

18. On this subject see Bernard Lewis, *What Went Wrong? Western Impact and Middle Eastern Response*, New York: Oxford University Press, 2002.

19. Max Boot, *Invisible Armies: An Epic History of Guerrilla Warfare from Ancient Times to the Present*, New York: Liveright, 20013, pp. 522–523. Bin Laden boasted that al Qaeda personnel had assisted the Somali tribesmen who ambushed American forces in Mogadishu in October, 1993. See pp. 88–89. The perpetrators of the first attack on the World Trade Center in Manhattan on February 26, 1993, which did far less damage than the two attacks of September 11, 2001, apparently had no direct connection to bin Laden's organization.

20. *9/11 Commission Report: Final Report of the National Commission on Terrorist Attacks upon the United States*, New York: W.W. Norton, 2004, p. 277; Wright, *op. cit.*, p. 350.

21. *9/11 Commission Report*, p. 344.

22. Subsequent investigation suggested that the explosion may well have been the result of an accident, not Spanish sabotage.

23. "In November 2011 . . . Rumsfeld said in one television interview that it was 'reasonable to assume' Osama bin Laden had some access to chemical and biological weapons." Mann, *op. cit.*, p. 317. " [Vice President] Cheney had long nursed dark views about the world's dangers, views that seemed ratified on September 11. He spent the rest of his time in office consumed not with another September 11 but with a much worse scenario where terrorists would be armed with nuclear or chemical weapons instead of box cutters." Baker, *op. cit.*, p. 9

24. "Officials who worked in the White House and other sensitive posts with access to raw intelligence files during the fall of 2001 say it is nearly impossible to exaggerate the sense of mortal and existential danger that dominated the thinking of the upper rungs of the Bush Administration during those months." Jane Mayer, *The Dark Side: The Inside Story of How the War on Terror Turned into a War on American Ideals*, New York: Doubleday, 2008, p. 4.

25. In this terminology the Cold War counted as World War III.

26. John Mueller and Mark G. Stewart, "The Terrorism Delusion: America's Overwrought Response to September 11," *International Security*, 37:1 (Summer 2012) p. 81.

27. On September 12 "the White House was brimming with guns, and military units were in the streets of the capital." ". . . the West Wing following the attacks was almost unrecognizable. Large, menacing men swathed in black and armed with assault rifles and shotguns suddenly

showed up everywhere. Tours were cut off. Access to the West Wing was restricted." Baker, *op. cit.*, pp. 133, 156–157.

28. Often this meant that he was working at home, in the vice presidential residence a few miles from the White House. *Ibid.*, p. 155. For the same reason the president and vice president by tradition never travel on the same airplane.

29. "Each morning greeted Bush and Cheney with a new Threat Matrix, a compendium of potential horrors, as many as a hundred threats a day culled from a broad array of intelligence sources . . . almost nothing, it seemed was left out, no matter how far-fetched." *Ibid.*, p. 157.

30. The war in Iraq is the subject of chapter 4.

31. Quoted in Jack Goldsmith, *The Terror Presidency: Law and Judgment Inside the Bush Administration*, New York: W. W. Norton, 2007, p. 104.

32. Baker, *op. cit.*, p. 134; Goldsmith, *op. cit.*, p. 106; Mark Mazzetti, *The Way of the Knife: The CIA, a Secret Army, and a War at the Ends of the Earth*, New York: Penguin Press, 2013, p. 88. Bin Laden had been indicted in an American federal court for plotting to kill American soldiers in Yemen. The indictment had no effect on his activities or on American policy. Stephen Sestanovich, *Maximal: America in the World from Truman to Obama*, New York: Alfred A. Knopf, 2014, p. 265.

33. Walter Laqueur, *The New Terrorism: Fanaticism and the Arms of Mass Destruction*, New York: Oxford University Press, 1999, pp. 110–111.

34. The cost to al Qaeda of the September 11 attacks was estimated at between $400,000 and $500,000. Bin Laden could have financed it out of his own pocket—and perhaps did. *9/11 Commission Report*, p. 172.

35. Boot, *op. cit.*, p. 231.

36. The distinguished British historian Michael Howard expressed the European view. Terrorism, he wrote, was "a dangerous, antisocial activity, one that can never be entirely eliminated but can be reduced to, and kept at, a level that does not threaten social stability." Michael Howard, "What's in a Name? How to Fight Terrorism," *Foreign Affairs* (January/February 2002), p. 8.

37. At first the Bush administration rejected the idea of creating such a "super-agency," fearing, no doubt with reason, that it would become a bureaucratic monstrosity. In response to Congressional pressure, however, the president decided to establish it. Baker, *op. cit.*, p. 201.

38. Bergen, *op. cit.*, p. 245.

39. John Mueller and Mark G. Stewart, *Terror, Security, and Money: Balancing the Risks, Benefits, and Costs of Homeland Security*, New York: Oxford University Press, 2011, pp. 1–3.

40. *Ibid.*, pp. 160, 167.

41. On November 6, 2006, Major Nidal Hassan, an army psychiatrist inspired by Islamic radicalism, went on a shooting spree at Fort Hood,

Texas, that killed 13 people and wounded many others. Bergen, *op. cit.*, p. 239.

42. A list and brief description of the 50 attempted or suspected attacks is in Mueller and Stewart, "The Terrorism Delusion," pp. 83–87. Two efforts to blow up passenger airlines in mid-flight did come close to success, one undertaken by the "shoe bomber" on a flight from Rome to Miami on December 22, 2001, the other by the "underwear bomber" on a flight from Amsterdam to Detroit on Christmas Day 2009.

43. This is a principal theme of Mueller and Stewart, *Terror, Security, and Money.*

44. " . . . American policy makers usually concluded that a large response was the only way to turn back the threat at hand—and the still larger ones probably lurking behind it." Sestanovich, *op. cit.*, p. 8.

45. The would-be terrorists were described by those who observed and studied them as "incompetent, ineffective, unintelligent, idiotic, ignorant, inadequate, unorganized, misguided, muddled, amateurish" among other adjectives. Mueller and Stewart, "The Terrorism Delusion," p. 88.

46. For a history of the CIA with an emphasis on its covert operations see Tim Weiner, *Legacy of Ashes,* New York: Anchor Books, 2006.

47. Baker, *op. cit.*, p. 148.

48. Mark Bowden, *The Finish: The Killing of Osama bin Laden,* New York: Atlantic Monthly Press, 2012, p. 148; Mazzetti, *op. cit.*, p. 129; Jack Goldsmith, "The Trust Destroyer," *The New Republic*, May 13, 2013, p. 32.

49. The military personnel who carried out the raid were part of the JSOC, and were, for legal reasons, temporarily transferred to the control of the civilian CIA for this operation.

50. During the operation one helicopter landed awkwardly and had to be destroyed at the villa. Dropping bin Laden's body into the ocean avoided creating a burial site that followers and sympathizers could transform into a shrine.

51. Colin Dueck, *The Obama Doctrine: American Grand Strategy Today,* New York: Oxford University Press, 2015, p. 133.

52. Quoted in David Sanger, *Confront and Conceal: Obama's Secret Wars and Surprising Use of American Power,* New York: Crown Publishers, 2012, p. 102. See also Hussein Ibish, "The monster that won't die," *Now*, December 24, 2013, now.mmedia.me/lb/en/commentaryanalysis/ 527155-the-monster-that-wont-die

53. Mazzetti, *op. cit.*, p. 90; Sanger, *op. cit.*, pp. 248–249.

54. In 1976 President Gerald Ford imposed a ban on assassinations by the American government. In the wake of September 11, government lawyers wrote memos justifying targeted killings by the CIA and JSOC. Mazzetti, *op. cit.*, pp. 300–301.

55. *Ibid.*, p. 87.
56. Goldsmith, "The Trust Destroyer," p. 33.
57. Guidelines issued in May 2013 appeared to end signature strikes. Geoff Dyer, "Obama recasts rules on drone strikes in terror campaign," *Financial Times*, May 24, 2013, p. 4.
58. "Last summer Pew Research reported 'considerable opposition' in 'nearly all countries,' and especially in predominantly Muslim countries, to Obama's drone program." Goldsmith, "The Trust Destroyer," p. 34.
59. By one estimate 13 percent of the casualties from American drone attacks were civilians. Micah Zenko, *Reforming U.S. Drone Strike Policies*, New York: Council on Foreign Relations Center for Preventive Action, Council Special Report No. 65, January 2013, p. 13.
60. Quoted in Mayer, *op. cit.*, p. 11.
61. The internment of Japanese-Americans was found to be constitutionally permissible by the Supreme Court in 1944. In 1974, however, President Gerald Ford said that policy had been wrong, and in 1988 and 1992 Congress passed legislation awarding financial compensation to those who had been interned.
62. "Renditions were not invented for the war on terror. The U.S. government had carried out renditions at least since the Reagan Era. But they were originally used on an extremely limited basis and for a different purpose." Mayer, *op. cit.*, p. 108. "The most common destinations for rendered suspects were Egypt, Morocco, Syria, Jordan, Uzbekistan, and Afghanistan, all of which have long been cited for human rights violations by the State Department . . . " *Ibid.*, p. 110.
63. Among the countries in which these "ghost prisons" were located were reported to be Poland, Romania, and Thailand. *Ibid.*, p. 148.
64. *Ibid.*, pp. 299–300.
65. This is the subject of Jess Bravin, *The Terror Courts: Rough Justice at Guantanamo Bay*, New Haven: Yale University Press, 2013.
66. Mayer, *op. cit.*, p. 150.
67. *Ibid.*, pp. 151–152.
68. Mazzetti, *op. cit.*, p. 118.
69. Mayer, *op. cit.*, pp. 172–177; Bergen, *op. cit.*, p. 119.
70. See, for example, Alan M. Dershowitz, *Why Terrorism Works: Understanding the Threat, Responding to the Challenge*, New Haven: Yale University Press, 2002.
71. The NSA's mission is to collect signals intelligence of all kinds from around the world.
72. By 2013 the companies said that they were no longer cooperating. Luke Harding, *The Snowden Files: The Inside Story of the World's Most Wanted Man*, New York: Vintage Books, 2014, p. 208.
73. The justification used for bypassing FISA was the president's power as commander-in-chief under Article II of the Constitution. Baker, *op. cit.*, pp. 163–164.

74. "Metadata is data about data. For telephone records, it can include numbers dialed, the date, time, and length of calls, and the unique identification of a cell phone. Internet metadata can include e-mail and IP addresses, along with location information, Web sites visited, and many other electronic traces left when a person goes online." Ryan Lizza, "State of Deception," *The New Yorker*, December 16, 2013, http://www. newyorker.com/reprting/2013/12/16131216fa_fact_lizza.

75. Tapping telephones abroad is not illegal in the United States, and seeking information about foreign leaders, even friendly ones, is not something that only the American government does.

76. Goldsmith, *The Terror Presidency*, p. 208; Harding, *op. cit.*, p. 96.

77. Jerry Markon, "Long-delayed headquarters for DHS in doubt," *The Washington Post*, May 21, 2014, p. A1. Another indicator of the change of national attitude was a July 2013 poll that found that 39 percent of Americans believed it was more important to preserve privacy than to investigate terrorism. In 2002 the comparable figure had been only 18 percent. Harding, *op. cit.*, p. 293.

78. The area of Texas is 696,000 square kilometers, of Afghanistan 652,000.

79. In 1973 a cousin ousted the reigning king, Zahir Shah, and proclaimed a republic, but Durrani political primacy continued. The standard history of the development of the modern Afghan state is Vartan Gregorian, *The Emergence of Modern Afghanistan: Politics of Reform and Modernization, 1880–1946*, Stanford, California: Stanford University Press, 1969.

80. "[The members of the PDPA] were not just interested in ruling Afghanistan but also in transforming the country through revolutionary policies of land reform, education, and changes in family law. They moved to destroy all who opposed them ... " Thomas Barfield, *Afghanistan: A Cultural and Political History*, Princeton, New Jersey: Princeton University Press, 2010, p. 225.

81. *Ibid.*, pp. 226–233.

82. The Afghans experienced invasion by the British twice in the nineteenth century, the first time between 1839 and 1842, the second between 1878 and 1880. On both occasions, the British eventually withdrew.

83. Barfield, *op. cit.*, pp. 171, 254.

84. The Soviets had deployed 110,000 troops to the country. An estimated 15,000 had died. *Ibid.*, p. 242.

85. It was more destructive in Kabul. "Kabul, which had been spared any fighting during the war because of its many lines of defenses, was devastated over the next three years [after 1992], and large parts of the city were reduced to rubble. Many of its residents fled the city, seeking safety elsewhere, and twenty-five thousand people were believed to have died as a result of the fighting." *Ibid.*, p. 250.

86. Even then, however, "No Afghan leader saw the collapse of central power in Kabul as an opportunity to seek independence." *Ibid.*, p. 252.

87. Wright, *op. cit.*, p. 230.

88. Baker, *op. cit.*, p. 152.

89. To a Pakistani general sent to persuade him to give up al Qaeda, the Taliban leader, Mullah Omar, said "You want to please the Americans and I want to please God." Mazzetti, *op. cit.*, p. 32. " . . . in October 2001 the Taliban convened in Kandahar a great *jirga* to decide how to respond to American demands that Osama bin Laden and those responsible for the 9/11 attacks be handed over. Some of those present believe that, given a bit more patience and pressure, the majority would gradually have swung in favour of expelling those Arabs and other foreigners who had abused Pashtun hospitality by orchestrating the 9/11 attacks from Afghan territory." Cowper-Coles, *op. cit.*, p. 290.

90. On September 10, 2001, an al Qaeda operative posing as a journalist had assassinated the Northern Alliance leader and former Afghan defense minister Ahmad Shah Massoud by blowing himself up in Massoud's presence.

91. "The U.S. campaign against the Taliban was conducted with massive American airpower, tens of thousands of northern Alliance forces, allied with some three hundred U.S. Special Forces soldiers working with 110 CIA officers." Bergen, *op. cit.*, p. 59.

92. "The war did not have any decisive battles. Just as the Taliban had come to power by persuading people that they were winners without fighting and buying the defection of wavering commanders with suitcases full of hundred dollar bills, they lost the war in a reverse process. After the fall of Mazar they were seen as losers, and their nominal allies deserted them." Barfield, *op. cit.*, p. 270.

93. Bergen, *op. cit.*, p. 60.

94. Barfield, *op. cit.*, p. 283. The Taliban were excluded.

95. Steve Coll, *Ghost Wars: The Secret History of the CIA, Afghanistan, and Bin Laden from the Soviet Invasion to September 10, 2001*, New York: Penguin Press, 2004, p. 286.

96. The meeting was called a "loya jirga." The term had occasionally been used to describe royally summoned conclaves and was employed to connect the twenty-first-century proceedings with the Afghan past. Meetings in Afghan history were retrospectively termed loya jirgas, an example of what historians call "the invention of tradition." Barnett Rubin, *Afghanistan from the Cold War to the War on Terror*, New York: Oxford University Press, 2013, pp. 467–468. On this pattern see Eric Hobsbawm and Terence Ranger, *The Invention of Tradition*, London: Canto, 1992.

97. Barfield, *op. cit.*, p. 270.

98. *Ibid.*, p. 275.

99. "Trapped in Afghanistan," *The New York Times*, May 28, 2014, p. A20.

100. "Banyan: A gesture of defiance," *The Economist*, April 12, 2014, p. 33; Seth Jones, *In the Graveyard of Empires: America's War in Afghanistan*, New York: W. W. Norton, 2009, p. 206.

101.   Bergen, *op. cit.*, p. 176. The same poll showed that 80 percent of Afghans approved of the presence of international military forces and only 8 percent approved of the Taliban.

102.   Barfield, *op. cit.*, p. 318.

103.   The left-leaning Parisian newspaper *Le Monde*'s front-page headline on September 12 read, "We are all Americans."

104.   The two principal additional groups were the Haqqani network and Hezb-i-Islami, led by Gulbuddin Hekmatyar, a warlord who had twice been prime minister of Afghanistan between the fall of Najibullah and the ascendance of the Taliban. Jones, *op. cit.*, p. xxiii.

105.   Jones, *op. cit.*, pp. 228 ff.

106.   Bergen, *op. cit.*, p. 185.

107.   Jones, *op. cit.*, pp. 210, 218.

108.   Bergen, *op. cit.*, pp. 310, 320.

109.   "Afghan's insurgency was caused by a supply of disgruntled villagers unhappy with their government, and a demand for recruits by ideologically motivated leaders." Jones, *op. cit.*, p. 315.

110.   Bergen, *op. cit.*, p. 189; Jones, *op. cit.*, p. 64.

111.   James Joyner, "Was Afghanistan Worth It?" *The National Interest*, March 6, 2013, http://nationalinterest.org/print/commentary/was-afghanistan-worth-it.

112.   "The U.S. government did not engage, anywhere in any of its various departments and agencies, in extensive planning for a post-Taliban Afghanistan. There was no time, and not much incentive, to do so. Policy was focused on obviating the threat of another attack on the American homeland from al Qaeda's sanctuary in Afghanistan. The assumption was that the international community would pick up the pieces after the Taliban regime was displaced." Dov Zakheim, *A Vulcan's Tale: How the Bush Administration Mismanaged the Reconstruction of Afghanistan*, Washington, DC: Brookings Institution Press, 2011, p. 3.

113.   Two years after the defeat of the Taliban the Afghan army had only 6,000 men. Bergen, *op. cit.*, p. 317.

114.   Jones, *op. cit.*, p. 115.

115.   Bergen, *op. cit.*, p. 179; Jones, *op. cit.*, p. 112.

116.   Jones, *op. cit.*, p. 116.

117.   *Ibid.*, pp. 118–120. "In terms of historical troop levels, the Afghan mission ranks with some of the international community's most notable failures." p. 119.

118.   This is a major theme of Zakheim, *op. cit.* "Afghanistan required three specific types of international assistance to restore stability after the expulsion of the Taliban. The first was the deployment of international troops to all the country's major regions . . . The second was a large-scale investment in agriculture for rural Afghans . . . The third was the rapid restoration and expansion of the country's infrastructure . . .

Unfortunately for Afghanistan this assistance was not provided at the levels needed." Barfield, *op. cit.*, pp. 312–313.

119. Western ignorance of Afghanistan is a major theme of Rory Stewart, "The Plane to Kabul," in Rory Stewart and Gerald Knaus, *Can Intervention Work?* New York: W. W. Norton, 2012.

120. In 2008, for example, the United States had 35,000 troops in Afghanistan and 160,000 in Iraq. Carlotta Gall, *The Wrong Enemy: America in Afghanistan, 2001–2014*, Boston: Houghton Mifflin Harcourt, 2014, p. 195. See also Bergen, *op. cit.*, p. 181.

121. Jones, *op. cit.*, pp. 139–142.

122. *Ibid.*, pp. 248–253; Sanger, *op. cit.*, p. 47.

123. Much of the money ostensibly devoted to state-building in Afghanistan went to pay the salaries of Westerners, not all of them resident in the country full time. Stewart, *op. cit.*, p. 10; Bergen, *op. cit.*, p. 183.

124. Jones, *op. cit.*, pp. 201–202.

125. Rubin, *op. cit.*, p. 462.

126. "As [onetime American ambassador to Afghanistan Karl] Eikenberry puts it: It's 'like trying to do development on an outpost on the moon. They're still stuck in the fourteenth century.'" "The US tried to install anesthesia, X-ray, ventilator, and defibrillator devices worth $1.75 billion in Afghan military hospitals, but . . . Afghan staffers were completely incapable of maintaining the equipment because they did not have 'the requisite technical expertise.'" Joel Brinkley, "Money Pit: The Monstrous Failure of US Aid to Afghanistan," *World Affairs Journal*, http://worldaffairsjournal.org/print/6132?utm_source=World.

127. In traditional societies women have a distinctly premodern status. In Afghanistan they were often secluded and seldom educated.

128. Barfield, *op. cit.*, p. 18.

129. "For almost a century, attempts to bring about social change in Afghanistan have been led by governments in Kabul determined to modernize the country. For an equal period of time, they have been resisted by the inhabitants in rural Afghanistan as well as conservative Islamic clerics who distrusted such changes and saw them as a threat to their traditional way of life. The most contentious policies concerned women's rights, secular education, the primacy of state law (including family law) over customary law, and reducing the autonomy of Islamic clerics." *Ibid.*, p. 339.

130. "In 2002, at a UN meeting in Kabul, I was told that the goal emerged from an Afghan consensus to create a 'gender-sensitive, multi-ethnic centralized state, based on democracy, human rights, and the rule of law.'" Stewart, *op. cit.*, p. 34. These goals had no constituency in rural Afghanistan, and rural Afghanistan lacked the prerequisites for them.

131. Barfield, *op. cit.*, pp. 298, 302, 337.

132. *Ibid.*, pp. 303–305; Jones, *op. cit.*, p. 130; Rubin, *op. cit.*, p. 354.

133. Gall, *op. cit.*, pp. 211–212.

134. Vanda Felbab-Brown, *Aspiration and Ambivalence: Strategies and Realities of Counterinsurgency and State Building in Afghanistan*, Washington, DC: Brookings Institution Press, 2013, p. 265.

135. See, for example, *Ibid.*, p. 245.

136. Bob Woodward, *Obama's Wars*, New York: Simon and Schuster, 2010, pp. 65–66.

137. Barfield, *op. cit.*, pp. 7, 237, 310, 341–342. Anti-foreign sentiment was not confined to rural Afghanistan. " 'The Taliban are the people who are defending this country,' said Hamad, a leader of the self-appointed Nangarhar University student council that organizes regular demonstrations against the U.S. and President Hamid Karzai's government. 'The foreign troops are invaders.' " Nathan Hodge and Habib Khan Totakhil, "U.S. Funds Buy No Love at Afghan College," *The Wall Street Journal*, July 30, 2013, p. A1.

138. Tim Craig, "Afghan workers fear loss of aid," *The Washington Post*, June 10, 2014, p. A9. By other estimates it was even higher. " . . . the World Bank estimates that 97 percent of Afghanistan's $28 billion gross domestic product depends on development aid and in-country spending for foreign troops." Sanger, *op. cit.*, p. 139.

139. Francis Fukuyama, *The Origins of Political Order: From Prehuman Times to the French Revolution*, New York: Farrar, Straus, and Giroux, 2011, p. 14.

140. "With a great deal of investment and luck and many years of effort, they [foreign state-builders] might have hoped to turn Afghanistan into a poorer version of its neighbors." Stewart, *op. cit.*, p. 39.

141. Wright, *op. cit.*, p. 225.

142. Jones, *op. cit.*, pp. 98–99.

143. In 1971 the United States sent an aircraft carrier into the Bay of Bengal as a signal to India of American opposition to the complete dismemberment of Pakistan. As a result of that war, however, Pakistan was partly dismembered, losing its eastern, Bengali wing, which became the independent country of Bangladesh.

144. India's alignment with the Soviet Union between 1971 and 1991, a period in which India bought arms from Moscow, shadowed Indo-American relations but never made the two countries adversaries.

145. For Pakistan's generals, strategic depth "meant they wanted to ensure that they had a pliant, pro-Pakistani Afghan state on their western border in the event that India attacked over their eastern border." Bergen, *op. cit.*, p. 248.

146. Barfield, *op. cit.*, p. 48. The line was named after the British foreign secretary of the time, Sir Mortimer Durand.

147. There were about 29 million Pashtuns in Pakistan and about 12 million in Afghanistan. Pashtuns made up, however, a much

larger proportion of the total population of the much smaller Afghanistan.

148. Rubin, *op. cit.*, p. 367.

149. Mann, *op. cit.*, p. 299; Jones, *op. cit.*, pp. 88–89.

150. Daniel Markey, *No Exit from Pakistan: America's Tortured Relationship with Islamabad*, New York: Cambridge University Press, 2013, p. 128–129.

151. Jones, *op. cit.*, pp. 271–273.

152. "Pakistan needs Afghanistan to be run by Pashtuns so the country holds together but can't allow those Pashtuns to become too strong for fear that a Pashtun-led Afghan government might become powerful enough to assert its objections to the Durand Line more forcefully. Pakistan's strategic dilemma is that it needs to have Pashtuns run Afghanistan but also needs to have them run it badly." John Ford, "In Afghanistan, It's Deja Vu All Over Again," *The American Interest*, February 13, 2015, www.the-american-interest.com/2015/02/13/in-afghanistan-its-deja-vu-all-over-again.

153. Sanger, *op. cit.*, p. 7.

154. Markey, *op. cit.*, pp. 16–18.

155. American drone strikes in Pakistan occasionally targeted militants who were attacking the Pakistani, not the Afghan government. Mazzetti, *op. cit.*, pp. 227–228; Sanger, *op. cit.*, p. 250.

156. That convention nominated Senator John F. Kerry of Massachusetts for president and Senator John Edwards of North Carolina for vice president. They lost the general election to the incumbents, President George W. Bush and Vice President Dick Cheney.

157. Jackson had been a member of the entourage of the most important civil rights leader, Reverend Martin Luther King Jr., and had capitalized on that association after King's death in 1968. He had competed in the Democratic primaries in 1984 and 1988 and on the second occasion received the second-highest vote total after the eventual winner, Governor Michael Dukakis of Massachusetts. Jackson had never looked likely to be the Democratic nominee, however, let alone the president.

158. James Mann, *The Obamians: The Struggle Inside the White House to Redefine American Power*, New York: Viking, 2012, p. 85.

159. *Ibid.*, pp. 63–64.

160. In 2004 his principal Democratic opponent dropped out of the contest for personal reasons, as, subsequently, did his Republican opponent in the general election, who was replaced by a far less formidable candidate whom Obama easily defeated.

161. "In Pew's latest national survey, conducted Feb. 20–24 among 1,508 adults, a 54% majority said the U.S. made the wrong decision in using military force in Iraq, while 38% said it was the right decision." "Public Attitudes Toward the War in Iraq: 2003–2008," Pew Research Center,

March 19, 2008. http://pewresearch.org/2008/03/19/public-attitudes-toward-the-war-in-iraq.20032008/.

162. Mann, *The Obamians*, pp. 86, 130.

163. *Ibid.*, p. 64.

164. "By the spring of 2009, inside the Kabul office of the Afghan interior minister, Hanif Atmar, a map showed that nearly half the country was a danger zone for his officials. Ten of Afghanistan's 364 districts were colored black, meaning they were wholly under Taliban control, and 156 were colored red or amber to indicate high-risk areas for officials or anyone associated with the government." Gall, *op. cit.*, p. 196.

165. Mann, *The Obamians*, p. 130.

166. For a critical account of the Obama Afghanistan policy see Vali Nasr, *The Dispensable Nation: American Foreign Policy in Retreat*, New York: Doubleday, 2013, chapters 1 and 2.

167. Bergen, *op. cit.*, p. 309.

168. Sanger, *op. cit.*, pp. 19–20; Stewart, *op. cit.*, pp. 28, 39.

169. Sanger, *op. cit.*, p. 22.

170. Barfield, *op. cit.*, p. 332; Sanger, *op. cit.*, pp. 24–25.

171. The leader of the review was Bruce Riedel, a former CIA analyst specializing in South Asia who had taken part in the Obama campaign and worked in a Washington think tank.

172. See chapter 5, pp. 234–237.

173. Sestanovich, *op. cit.*, p. 304; Mann, *The Obamians*, p. 126.

174. Sanger, *op. cit.*, p. 31.

175. Mann, *The Obamians*, p. 31.

176. *Ibid.*, p. 135.

177. "House Speaker Nancy Pelosi warned there was 'serious unrest' among House Democrats about paying for a wider war in Afghanistan." Mann, *The Obamians*, p. 134. See also Woodward, *op. cit.*, p. 307.

178. Sanger, *op. cit.*, p. 23.

179. Woodward, *op. cit.*, pp. 159–160.

180. *Ibid.*, pp. 167–168, 251; Mann, *The Obamians,* p. 128.

181. "Remarks by the President in Address to the Nation on the Way Forward in Afghanistan and Pakistan," http://www.whitehouse.gov/the-press-office/remarks-president-address-nation-way-forward-afghanistan-and-pakistan.

182. One official described the trajectory of Obama's Afghanistan policy in this way: "We started with what everyone thought was a pragmatic vision, but, at its core, was a plan for changing the way Afghanistan is wired. We ended up thinking about how to do as little wiring as possible." Quoted in Sanger, *op. cit.*, p. 51.

183. Several read *Lessons in Disaster* by Gordon Goldstein (New York: Times Books, 2008), based on the recollections of McGeorge Bundy, the National Security Advisor for all of John Kennedy's presidency and

part of Lyndon Johnson's. Woodward, *op. cit.*, pp. 129, 377; Mann, *The Obamians*, p. 131; Sanger, *op. cit.*, pp. 26–27.

184. Mann, *op. cit.*, p. 318.

185. Sestanovich, *op. cit.*, p. 309.

186. Policy for Afghanistan was a source of ongoing tension between the military leadership and the White House, dating from the beginning of Obama's term, when administration officials felt that the military was exerting undue political pressure on them—"jamming" was the term they used—to increase the number of troops committed to that country. Robert Gates, *Duty: Memoirs of a Secretary at War*, New York: Random House, 2014, pp. 338–339; Woodward, *op. cit.*, p. 313; Sanger, *op. cit.*, p. 30; Mann, *The Obamians*, p. 135.

187. In fact, some American combat operations—air strikes and special operations raids—did continue after 2014. Matthew Rosenberg and Mark Mazzetti, "More U.S. Troops Seen Staying in Afghanistan," *The New York Times*, March 20, 2015, p. A4.

188. At the end of September 2014 the United States signed a security agreement with the new Afghan government headed by Ashraf Ghani, who had succeeded Karzai as president. Its terms exempted American troops from prosecution under Afghan law, making it possible to keep them in the country even beyond 2016 if the American government chose to do so. Sudarsan Raghavan and Karen DeYoung, "U.S., Afghanistan sign security agreement," *The Washington Post*, October 1, 2014, p. A6. In October 2015 Obama decided to retain an American troop presence beyond 2016.

189. The American military declared an end to its formal combat role in Afghanistan at the end of 2014. Margherita Stancati, "U.S.-Led Forces End Afghan Combat Mission," *The Wall Street Journal*, December 29, 2014, p. A8.

190. " . . . the Afghan forces suffered from such high rates of illiteracy, corruption, and drug addiction that maintaining a cohesive force was a huge challenge. The Americans would build checkpoints; the Afghan troops would man them sporadically. About 14 percent walked away from their posts every year." Sanger, *op. cit.*, p. 45.

191. Gall, *op. cit.*, p. 286. "The conflict has killed more than 3,484 allied forces, including 2,356 Americans and 453 Britons, cost an estimated $1tn and become the US's longest war . . . " May Jeong, Geoff Dyer, and Victor Mallet, "'This is not over yet,'" *Financial Times*, December 15, 2014, p. 7.

192. A December 2013 poll found that only 30 percent of Americans considered the Afghan war to have been worth fighting. By contrast, 66 percent said that it had not been worth fighting. Scott Clement, "Most in U.S. now oppose Afghan war," *The Washington Post*, December 20, 2013, p. A19.

Chapter 4

1. Toby Dodge, *Inventing Iraq: The Failure of Nation-Building and a History Denied*, New York: Columbia University Press, 2003, pp. 169–170.

2. David Fromkin, *A Peace to End All Peace: Creating the Modern Middle East, 1914–1922*, New York: Henry Holt and Company, 1989, p. 450. "Gertrude Bell, working on her own plans for a unified Iraq, was cautioned by an American missionary that she was ignoring rooted historical realities in doing so. 'You are flying in the face of four millenniums of history if you try to draw a line around Iraq and call it a political entity! Assyria always looked to the west and east and north and Babylonia to the south. They have never been an independent unit.'" *Ibid.*, pp. 450–451.

3. "The Shi'a-Sunni split in Islam did not occur, as is often claimed, upon the death of the Prophet Muhammad on 8 June, 632. It evolved over centuries before doctrinal positions hardened and the religious and community distinctiveness of the two groups crystallised. What is indisputable, though, is that the succession to the Prophet formed the basis for this schism." Ali A. Allawi, *The Occupation of Iraq: Winning the War, Losing the Peace*, New Haven: Yale University Press, 2007, p. 23.

4. "Those three provinces of the Ottoman empire that had been forced into this most peculiar of states were three distinctly different worlds: in the north, Mosul's ties and commerce were with Turkey and Syria, whereas Baghdad and the Shia shrine cities of Najaf and Karbala on the Euphrates were oriented toward Persia, and Basra looked to the Gulf and to the commerce with India." Fouad Ajami, *The Foreigner's Gift: The Americans, the Arabs, and the Iraqis in Iraq*, New York: Free Press, 2006, p. 158; see also p. 312.

5. On the role of the state in creating the nation see Ernest Gellner, *Nations and Nationalism*, Oxford, England: Blackwell, 1983, and Eric Hobsbawm, editor, *Nations and Nationalism Since 1780: Programme, Myth, Reality*, Cambridge, England: Cambridge University Press, 1990.

6. "[Iraqi sociologist] Ali al-Wardi invented a new type of sociology, which was that of a fragmented social order interacting within the framework of a tumultuous historic legacy. It emphasised the disjointed nature of Iraqi society, held together by geographic imperatives of coexistence in the same space rather than a common sense of shared history or purpose." Allawi, *op. cit.*, p. 15.

7. The assistance included economic aid, the sale of dual-use technology, and sharing militarily relevant intelligence. The United States was motivated by the alarm of friendly governments in the region, in particular that of Saudi Arabia, at the prospect of an Iranian victory.

8. Kuwait also produced oil, although on a smaller scale than Saudi Arabia. It was noted at the time that if the country's principal export had been turnips nobody would have been interested in rescuing it.

9. See pp. 3–4.

10. "As Clarke remembered it, Bush grabbed him and a few others and closed the door. 'Look, I know you have a lot to do and all,' Bush said, 'but I want you, as soon as you can, to go back over everything, everything. See if Saddam did this. See if he's linked in any way.' Clarke was incredulous. 'But, Mr. President, al-Qaeda did this.' 'I know, I know, but see if Saddam was involved. Just look. I want to know any shred.'" Peter Baker, *Days of Fire: Bush and Cheney in the White House*, New York: Doubleday, 2013, p. 135.

11. From contemporaneous notes by Rumsfeld: "Then he [Bush] said I want you to develop a plan to invade Ir[aq]. Do it outside the normal channels. Do it creatively so we don't have to take so much cover." Quoted in Mark Danner, "Rumsfeld's War and Its Consequences Now," *The New York Review of Books*, December 19, 2003, p. 87.

12. Michael R. Gordon and Bernard E. Trainor, *Cobra II: The Inside Story of the Invasion and Occupation of Iraq*, New York: Pantheon Books, 2004, pp. 88–89.

13. A grand total of 240,000 personnel were in the region. Peter Baker, *Days of Fire: Bush and Cheney in the White House*, New York: Doubleday, 2013, p. 252.

14. The phrase evoked, presumably deliberately, a similar one familiar to Americans as denoting a serious emergency. The Supreme Court of the United States used the phrase "clear and present danger" to describe circumstances in which limits on the First Amendment freedoms of speech, press, and assembly are permissible. Bush's words conveyed a less urgent peril; and indeed the United States only attacked Iraq a full 15 months after he spoke them.

15. Derek Chollet and James Goldgeier, *America Between the Wars*, New York: PublicAffairs, 2008, p. 15; Baker, *op. cit.*, pp. 42, 6.

16. Baker, *op. cit.*, pp. 5, 6–7.

17. *Ibid.*, p. 211.

18. *Ibid.*, p. 226.

19. John Mueller, *War and Ideas: Selected Essays*, London: Routledge, 2001, pp. 194–196.

20. James Mann, *The Rise of the Vulcans: The History of Bush's War Cabinet*, New York: Viking, 2004, p. 247; Philip H. Gordon and Jeremy Shapiro, *Allies at War: America, Europe, and the Crisis Over Iraq*, New York: McGraw-Hill, 2004, p. 70.

21. The Turkish parliament voted in favor of such cooperation with the United States but because of abstentions the measure did not win a majority of all parliamentarians and so did not pass. Gordon and Trainor, *Cobra II*, p. 115.

22. The lack of a northern front did not noticeably assist the defense that Saddam's regime mounted, but it meant that virtually no American

troops were present in the areas of the country north and west of Baghdad
where the anti-American insurgency became most virulent.

23. Among them was the German Foreign Minister Joschka Fischer.
    See Thomas Ricks, *Fiasco: The American Military Adventure in Iraq*,
    New York: Penguin Press, 2006, p. 93. See also Gordon and Shapiro, *op.
    cit.*, p. 8.

24. Gordon and Shapiro, *op. cit.*, p. 144.

25. Michael Mandelbaum, *The Case for Goliath: How America Acts as the
    World's Government in the 21st Century*, New York: PublicAffairs, 2006,
    p. 153.

26. Chirac explained French opposition to war in Iraq "in terms of its desire
    to 'live in a multipolar world . . . ' " Gordon and Shapiro, *op. cit.*, p. 152.
    The sentiment was very much in keeping with the spirit of Gaullism.

27. Powell's memoir, *My American Story* (New York: Random House, 1995),
    written and published after he had retired from the army but before his
    appointment as secretary of state, sold 1.35 million copies. By contrast,
    President George H. W. Bush's memoir of his administration's major
    foreign policy challenges, *A World Transformed* (New York: Knopf , 1998),
    written with his national security advisor Brent Scowcroft, sold 49,500
    copies. David Halberstam, *War in a Time of Peace: Bush, Clinton, and the
    Generals*, New York: Scribner's, 2001, p. 238.

28. Like Eisenhower, Powell was mentioned as a possible presidential
    candidate after leaving the army. Unlike Eisenhower, Powell declined
    to run.

29. George Herring, *From Colony to Superpower: U.S. Foreign Relations Since
    1776*, New York: Oxford University Press, 2008, p. 875.

30. Like George W. Bush, Tony Blair became closely identified with the
    war and, like Bush, suffered politically for it. As the occupation of Iraq
    declined in popularity, so did Blair's personal ratings in Great Britain.

31. The chapter in Bush's memoir dealing with Iraq does not settle the
    question. George W. Bush, *Decision Points*, New York: Crown Publishers,
    2010, Chapter 8. In general the administration lacked an orderly approach
    to decision-making, at least for foreign and security policy, which
    frustrated Secretary of State Powell. Baker, *op. cit.*, pp. 331, 363. See also
    Richard Haass, *War of Necessity, War of Choice: A Memoir of Two Iraq
    Wars*, New York: Simon and Schuster, 2009, p. 272.

32. Baker, *op. cit.*, p. 226.

33. *Ibid.*, p. 206.

34. Gordon and Trainor, *Cobra II*, p. 72.

35. Haass, *op. cit.*, p. 5.

36. Baker, *op. cit.*, pp. 215–216.

37. "The Iraq Invasion Ten Years Later: A Wrong War," Interview of Richard
    Haass by Bernard Gwertzman, New York: Council on Foreign Relations,

March 14, 2013, www.cfr.org/iraq/iraq-invasion-ten-years-later-wrong-war/
p3. The case against war was made publicly by Brent Scowcroft, national
security advisor in the administration of George H. W. Bush (father
of George W. Bush), in an August 15, 2002 *Wall Street Journal* article
published under the headline "Don't Attack Saddam." Baker, *op. cit.*,
pp. 208–209.

38. Baker, *op. cit.*, p. 92.

39. "In a closed meeting with eighteen lawmakers . . . Bush also embraced
     another unfounded assertion. 'Saddam Hussein is a terrible guy who is
     teaming up with al-Qaeda,' he told the lawmakers . . . " Baker, *op cit.*,
     p. 221. See also *Ibid.*, p. 245. On December 9, 2001, Vice President Cheney
     said "[9/11 hijacker Mohamed Atta] did go to Prague and he did meet
     with a senior official of the Iraqi intelligence service in Czechoslovakia
     last April, several months before the attack." Dylan Matthews, "17 reasons
     not to trust Dick Cheney on Iraq," *Vox*, June 19, 2014, www.vox.com/
     2014/6/19/5822482/17-reasons-not-to-trust-dick-cheney.

40. Matthews, *op. cit.*; Ricks, *op. cit.*, p. 51.

41. "A poll taken [in January 2002] showed that 77 percent of Americans
     supported military action in Iraq and just 17 percent opposed it. In a
     separate poll, almost an identical number, 76 percent, thought Hussein
     provided help to al-Qaeda, and another poll released around then found
     that 72 percent said it was very or somewhat likely that Hussein was
     'personally involved in the September 11 attacks.'" Baker, *op. cit.*, p. 191.

42. The 9/11 Commission found that "while there had been contacts between
     al Qaeda and Saddam Hussein's Iraq, it had seen no evidence of 'a
     collaborative operational relationship.'" Ricks, *op. cit.*, p. 377.

43. Baker, *op. cit.*, p. 348.

44. Baker, *op. cit.*, p. 308; Stephen F. Knott, "When Everyone Agreed About
     Iraq," *The Wall Street Journal*, March 16/17, 2013, p. A13; Laurence
     H. Silberman, "The Dangerous Lie that 'Bush Lied,'" *The Wall Street
     Journal*, February 9, 2015, p. A13. "Not once in all my meetings in my
     years in government did an intelligence analyst or anyone else for that
     matter argue openly or take me aside and say privately that Iraq possessed
     nothing in the way of weapons of mass destruction." Haass, *op. cit.*,
     p. 230.

45. Ricks, *op. cit.*, p. 22; Baker, *op. cit.*, p. 195; Gordon and Trainor, *Cobra II*,
     pp. 125, 126.

46. Baker, *op. cit.*, p. 308; Gordon and Trainor, *Cobra II*, pp. 55–56, 64–65,
     119, 121, 135.

47. See Michael Mandelbaum, *The Nuclear Revolution: International Politics
     Before and after Hiroshima*, New York: Cambridge University Press, 1981,
     Chapter 2.

48. "As [Deputy Secretary of Defense Paul] Wolfowitz told an
     interviewer after the fall of Baghdad, WMD was the least common

denominator: 'The truth is that for reasons that have a lot to do with the U.S. government bureaucracy, we settled on the one issue that everyone could agree on, which was weapons of mass destruction.'" George Packer, *The Assassins' Gate: America in Iraq*, New York: Farrar, Straus, and Giroux, 2005, p. 60.

49. "'The only reason we went into Iraq, I tell people now, is we were looking for somebody's ass to kick,' said the administration official who worked on Iraq. 'Afghanistan was too easy.'" Baker, *op. cit.*, p. 191.

50. Douglas J. Feith, *War and Decision: Inside the Pentagon at the Dawn of the War on Terrorism*, New York: Harper, 2008, p. 56.

51. *Ibid.*, pp. 19, 81; Gordon and Trainor, *Cobra II*, pp. 18–19, 73–74. "According to those attending National Security Council meetings in the days after September 11, 'The primary impetus for invading Iraq . . . was to make an example of [Saddam] Hussein, to create a demonstration model to guide the behavior of anyone with the temerity to acquire destructive weapons or, in any way, flout the authority of the United States.'" Mark Danner, "In the Darkness of Dick Cheney," *The New York Review of Books*, March 6, 2014, p. 49.

52. According to Douglas Feith, under secretary of defense for policy, "Dangers that had seemed remote or manageable now looked closer and more distressing. President Bush's national security team had to reconsider how willing the United States should be to abide threats—or how active it should be to end them." Feith, *op. cit.*, p. 214; see also p. 216.

53. *Ibid.*, p. 181. "In the light of September 11 [Condoleezza] Rice said, the United States had to reassess threats. Tolerating someone as dangerous as Hussein no longer seemed tenable." Baker, *op. cit.*, pp. 213–214.

54. Gordon and Shapiro, *op. cit.*, p. 40.

55. Ricks, *op. cit.*, p. 54; Baker, *op. cit.*, p. 348; Feith, *op. cit.*, p. 203.

56. Mandelbaum, *The Case for Goliath*, pp. 56–57.

57. Quoted in Feith, *op. cit.*, p. 391.

58. "A democracy can not of course engage in an explicit preventive war. But military leadership can heighten crises to the point where war becomes unavoidable." Reinhold Niebuhr, *The Irony of American History*, New York: Charles Scribner's Sons, 1952, p. 146.

59. Mandelbaum, *The Case for Goliath*, pp. 60–61.

60. Gordon and Trainor, *Cobra II*, p. 138; Thomas E. Ricks, "Army Historian Cites Lack of Postwar Plan," *The Washington Post*, December 25, 2004, p. A1.

61. In his book *The Marines Take Anbar,* Richard H. Shultz Jr. cites an American diplomat as describing the plan for regime change "as based on 'The Wizard of Oz'—'We go in, we kill the wicked witch, the munchkins jump up, they're grateful, and then we get in the hot-air balloon and we're out of there." Quoted in John Nagl, "Admiration of the Nation," *The Wall Street Journal*, May 11, 2013, p. A13.

62. Ricks, *op. cit.*, p. 96; Baker, *op. cit.*, pp. 207, 253.
63. According to Barbara Bodine, a former American ambassador to Yemen who served briefly in Iraq after the end of the war, "One of the operating assumptions . . . is that we would go in, and there would be a fully functioning Iraqi bureaucracy. They would all be in their offices, at their desk, pen and paper at the ready. And we would come in and essentially, you know, take them off the pause button. And the Iraqi bureaucracy would continue to function, and they would run Iraq and the city and everything else." Quoted in Charles Ferguson, *No End in Sight: Iraq's Descent Into Chaos*, New York: PublicAffairs, 2008, p. 88. See also Gordon and Trainor, *Cobra II*, pp. 73, 105.
64. Robert Hormats, *The Price of Liberty: Paying for America's Wars*, New York: Times Books Henry Holt and Company, 2007, p. 264.
65. Gordon and Trainor, *Cobra II*, p. 169; Michael R. Gordon and Bernard E. Trainor, *The Endgame: The Inside Story of the Struggle for Iraq from George W. Bush to Barack Obama*, New York: Pantheon Books, 2012, p. 10.
66. "Eventually, not just the Council on Foreign Relations and the Center for Strategic and International Studies, but a who's who of foreign policy and military think tanks—the Rand Corporation, the Army War College, the United States Institute of Peace, the National Defense University's Institute for National Strategic Studies—produced reports that were striking for their unanimity of opinion. Security and reconstruction in postwar Iraq would require large numbers of troops for an extended period, and international cooperation would be essential." Packer, *op. cit.*, p. 113. See also Larry Diamond, *Squandered Victory: The American Occupation and the Bungled Effort to Bring Democracy to Iraq*, New York: Times Books; 2005, pp. 282–285, Haass, *op. cit.*, p. 278; Ricks, *op. cit.*, pp. 72–73, 101–102; Baker, *op. cit.*, pp. 226–227; Gordon and Trainor, *Cobra II*, p. 158.
67. Baker, *op. cit.*, p. 208; Ricks, *op. cit.*, p. 48; Gordon and Trainor, *Cobra II*, p. 71. In fact the Pottery Barn chain did not have such a rule. The phrase was first used by the *New York Times* foreign affairs columnist Thomas L. Friedman.
68. Ricks, *op. cit.*, p. 97.
69. See Richard K. Betts, *American Force: Dangers, Delusions, and Dilemmas in National Security*, New York: Columbia University Press, 2012, p. 156.
70. Ricks, *op. cit.*, p. 98. Wolfowitz also dismissed the importance of ethnic differences in Iraq, which were to become the defining feature of the country after the fall of Saddam. *Ibid.*, p. 96. Bush himself said the same thing to Tony Blair. Baker, *op. cit.*, p. 244.
71. A good summary of the American war in Iraq is in Gideon Rose, *How Wars End*, New York: Simon & Schuster, 2010, chapter 8.
72. Gordon and Trainor, *Cobra II*, chapter 9.

73. The most notable military failure involved an operation using Apache attack helicopters, which demonstrated their unsuitability for the mission they had been given. *Ibid.*, chapter 14.
74. *Ibid.*, pp. 374–375.
75. Battle deaths were fewer than 150, a lower total than that of the 1991 war. Mueller, *op. cit.*, p. 198.
76. Gordon and Trainor, *Cobra II*, pp. 185–186.
77. *Ibid.*, p. 51.
78. American commanders had also worried that Iraq would fire Scud missiles at Israel, as in the first Gulf War. In the second, it did not. *Ibid.*, p. 91. They feared as well a massive wave of refugees, which similarly did not materialize. *Ibid.*, p. 139.
79. *Ibid.*, p. 304.
80. *Ibid.*, pp. 61–62, 122, 205–206, 366; Baker, *op. cit.*, p. 262.
81. Gordon and Trainor, *Cobra II*, p. 314.
82. *Ibid.*, p. 428.
83. Baker, *op. cit.*, p. 268.
84. Gordon and Trainor, *Cobra II*, p. 428.
85. Toby Dodge, *Iraq: From War to a New Authoritarianism*, London: The International Institute for Strategic Studies, 2012, p. 132. The looting included power-generating facilities. According to an official of the United States Agency for International Development, "They just started at one end of the transmission line and worked their way up, taking down the towers, taking away the valuable metals, smelting it down, selling it into Iran and Kuwait . . . The price of metal in the Middle East dropped dramatically during this period of time." Quoted in Gordon and Trainor, *Cobra II*, p. 468.
86. Rajiv Chandrasekaran, *Imperial Life in the Emerald City: Inside Iraq's Green Zone*, New York: Alfred A. Knopf, 2006, p. 46.
87. The State Department had led postwar efforts in the Balkans and Afghanistan. Gordon and Trainor, *Cobra II*, p. 141.
88. Ricks, *op. cit.*, p. 136.
89. According to Ambassador Barbara Bodine, "the initial looting was merely the first symptom of a far more serious security vacuum that generated street violence, organized crime, and militias." Ferguson, *op. cit.*, p. 132.
90. See p. 3.
91. Gordon and Trainor, *The Endgame*, p. 11.
92. He was asked to stay on and work under the man who replaced him, former Ambassador L. Paul Bremer, but declined.
93. Diamond, *op. cit.*, p. 37.
94. Shortly after arriving in Baghdad, Bremer said that his top priority was economic reform, for which "[h]e had a three-step plan. The first was to restore electricity, water, and other basic services. The second was to put 'liquidity in the hands of people'—reopening banks, offering loans,

paying salaries. The third was to 'corporatize and privatize state-owned enterprises,' and to 'wean people from the idea the state supports everything.'" Chandrasekaran, *op. cit.*, p. 61; see also p. 115.

95. As brief as the CPA's life span was, many of its employees stayed in Iraq only for a fraction of it. Ricks, *op. cit.*, p. 204.

96. In September 2003, the Congress passed a supplementary spending bill authorizing an additional $18.4 billion for reconstruction in Iraq. A year later, only $1 billion of it had been spent. Joseph E. Stiglitz and Linda J. Bilmes, *The Three Trillion Dollar War: The True Cost of the Iraq Conflict*, New York: W. W. Norton, 2008, p. 14.

97. Chandrasekaran, *op. cit.*, p. 91.

98. "Virtually nobody in the CPA . . . spoke Arabic. Maybe five or six among the top forty, fifty, seventy officials had Arabic knowledge . . . " Yaroslav Trofimov, a reporter, quoted in Ferguson, *op. cit.*, p. 284; Chandrasekaran, *op. cit.*, p. 11.

99. Chandrasekaran, *op. cit.*, pp. 14–19.

100. According to Ali Allawi, an Iraqi exile well acquainted with the West who served for a time in the post-Saddam Iraqi government, the Americans who came to Iraq "were of three types: 'wet-behind-the-ears' young people who were given vast responsibilities and power; there were 'worn-out bureaucrats' having a second runs at things. Finally there were the 'half-baked ideologues' who had their own wild notions of Iraq and who quit in a hurry when the country disappointed them." Ajami, *op. cit.*, p. 324.

101. Packer, *op. cit.*, p. 385. " . . . very early, in the weeks after the invasion and occupation, I was told by a very senior official that we were going to fix the Middle East the same way we fixed Europe after World War II." Chairman of the National Intelligence Council Robert Hutchings, quoted in Ferguson, *op. cit.*, p. 556. See also Ajami, *op. cit.*, p. 136.

102. Chandrasekaran, *op. cit.*, p. 119.

103. Allawi, *op. cit.*, p. 13.

104. Dodge, *Inventing Iraq*, p. 161.

105. "In Iraq, from 2003 until the end of 2006 the United States pursued a strategy grounded in the assumption that political solutions would drive security benefits." Meghan L. O'Sullivan, "The Iraq War at Ten," *The American Interest,* March 19, 2013, www.the-american-interest.com/article.cfm?piece=1398.

106. Of the 25, 13 were Shia, 11 were Sunni—of whom 5 were Kurds, 5 Arabs, and 1 Turkomen—and 1 was a Christian. Nine had been exiles prior to April 2003. Chandrasekaran, *op. cit.*, p. 79.

107. "Council members looked good on paper and in pictures, but their on-the-job performance exasperated the CPA. The council had taken weeks to select a president, and then had opted for a rotating presidency among nine members, eight of whom were former exiles. Once the leadership

was settled, many members stopped attending meetings. They used their new status to stake claim to riverfront villas and to travel overseas at government expense." *Ibid.*, p. 163.

108. Baker, *op. cit.*, p. 284.
109. Gordon and Trainor, *The Endgame*, p. 66.
110. Chandrasekaran, *op. cit.*, p. 164.
111. The transfer of power was moved up for fear of an outburst of violence on the date that had been announced. The transfer on the new date was kept secret until it had occurred. Baker, *op. cit.*, p. 338.
112. Chandrasekaran, *op. cit.*, p. 297.
113. Dawa provided the country's prime ministers because unlike two larger Shia parties it did not have its own militia, and so was acceptable to each of them as the other was not. Dodge, *Iraq: From War to a New Authoritarianism*, p. 158.
114. On Maliki's background see Ned Parker and Raheem Salman, "Notes from the Underground: The Rise of Nouri al-Maliki and the New Islamists," *World Policy Journal* (Spring 2013).
115. After several months as a member of the CPA, Larry Diamond wrote a memo to his former Stanford colleague Condoleezza Rice that said in part " . . . in my weeks in Iraq, I did not meet a single military officer who felt, privately, that we had enough troops. Many felt we needed (and need) tens of thousands more soldiers, and at this point . . . at least another division or two." Diamond, *op. cit.*, p. 241.
116. Ricks, *op. cit.*, p. 96.
117. "By autumn [2003] Abu Ghraib contained some ten thousand prisoners." *Ibid.*, p. 238.
118. *Ibid.*, pp. 291–293.
119. The two were General Instrument and Gilead Sciences.
120. "Here, with the benefits of the doubling of the defense budget following the September 11 attacks, he managed to achieve a good deal: he enormously expanded the Special Forces; he created a more flexible army based on brigades not divisions; he implanted small 'lily pad' bases in scores of countries around the world; he created the Africa Command and the North American Command." Mark Danner, "Rumsfeld: Why We Live in His Ruins," *The New York Review of Books*, February 6, 2014, p. 40.
121. "[Rumsfeld] had so emphasized the need to transform the military to a lighter, more agile force that when he asked commanders if they needed more troops in Iraq—and he had asked on numerous occasions—the answer came back no, perhaps because the generals had come to internalize his transformation goals or because they assumed they knew the answer he wanted." Baker, *op. cit.*, p. 479. Bremer did on at least one occasion request more troops. He received no reply. *Ibid.* p. 332–333. Bush repeatedly said that the troop levels would be decided by the commanders on the ground. *Ibid.*, p. 467.

122. Bush had the same view. Gordon and Trainor, *Cobra II*, p. 458.
123. Ricks, *op. cit.*, p. 98.
124. The failure to obtain UN approval for the attack on Iraq damaged the chances of eliciting contributions of troops, which is not to say that other countries would have provided substantially more soldiers if the Bush administration had secured the backing of the Security Council.
125. Ricks, *op. cit.*, p. 163; Chandrasekaran, *op. cit.*, p. 74.
126. Allawi, *op. cit.*, p. 157.
127. In disbanding the army Bremer "was trying to reassure the Kurds and the Shiites who had long suffered at the hands of Hussein's party and security organs. Restoring the army might have touched off a sectarian backlash. 'We would have had a civil war on our hands right away,' Bremer said later." Baker, *op. cit.*, p. 272. See also Feith, *op. cit.*, p. 432.
128. Allawi, *op. cit.*, p. 150; Chandrasekaran, *op. cit.*, pp. 69–71.
129. This is a theme of Feith, *op. cit.*
130. *Ibid.*, pp. 494–496.
131. The secretary of the army said later that the working assumption "was that ninety days after completion of the operation, we would withdraw the first fifty thousand and then every thirty days we'd take out another fifty thousand until everybody was back. The view was that whatever was left in Iraq would be de minimis." Quoted in Gordon and Trainor, *Cobra II*, p. 461.
132. Shortly before the war Deputy Defense Secretary Wolfowitz said that postwar Iraq was "not going to be handed over to some junior Saddam Hussein. We're not interested in replacing one dictator with another dictator." Quoted in Ricks, *op. cit.*, p. 96.
133. One Middle East expert, Daniel Pipes, did warn, shortly after the American military victory, of the problems an extended American occupation would bring and did suggest an alternative course for American policy in Iraq. Daniel Pipes, "A Strongman for Iraq?" *The New York Post*, April 28, 2003, www.danielpipes.org/1068/a-strongman-for-iraq. See also Pipes, "Let Iraqis Run Iraq," *Jerusalem Post*, October 15, 2003, www.danielpipes.org/1281/let-iraqis-run-iraq.
134. Chandrasekaran, *op. cit.*, p. 152; Allawi, *op. cit.*, p. 114; Gordon and Trainor, *Cobra II*, p. 193.
135. " . . . the United States had committed itself to an unparalleled reconstruction effort in an unstable and dangerous environment. In sector after sector—oil, electricity, water and sanitation—targets were consistently missed, ignored, or changed. Iraqis continued to suffer from increasing blackouts and untreated sewage." Allawi, *op. cit.*, p. 252. See also Dodge, *Iraq: From War to a New Authoritarianism*, p. 202.
136. See pp. TKK–TKK.
137. Gordon and Trainor, *The Endgame*, p. 114.
138. *Ibid.*, p. 21; Allawi, *op. cit.*, p. 175.

139. "There was a general sense [among the Sunnis] that an unnatural, alien force had overthrown an entire system of power and authority. It had no connection to Iraq's history or experience and could not therefore be considered a legitimate arbiter of the country's destiny. There was also the underlying unease that was felt about the loss of privileges and advantages with which the previous regime had disproportionately favoured the Sunni Arabs." Allawi, *op. cit.*, p. 136.

140. In a meeting with soldiers in Iraq in 2004 one of them asked Secretary of Defense Rumsfeld for more armored vehicles. In response he said "you go to war with the army you have, not the army you might want or wish to have at a later time."

141. Two months after the bombing the number had been reduced from 650 to 40, none of them in Baghdad. Packer, *op. cit.*, p. 218.

142. Other major American operations took place in the western city of Ramadi in April 2004 and again during the summer of 2006. Gordon and Trainor, *The Endgame*, pp. 64, 246.

143. The killings briefly called attention to an unusual feature of the American effort in Iraq: the heavy use of private contractors. "When the U.S. troop level was about 150,000, and the allied troop contributions totaled 25,000, there were about 60,000 additional civilian contractors supporting the effort. Of those, perhaps 15,000 to 20,000 were shooters—that is, people hired as bodyguards or for other security roles ... " Ricks, *op. cit.*, p. 371. "In 2008, at the height of the war, the Congressional Budget Office estimated that one of every five dollars spent on the Iraq war had gone to contractors; at that point, the contracts were worth about $85 billion. That year, contractors employed about 180,000 people in Iraq—often from third-world countries—who worked as bodyguards, translators, construction workers, launderers, cooks, and drivers. They amounted to a second private army that was larger than the U.S. military force in Iraq." Trudy Rubin, "Worldview: The Real Winners in the War," *The Philadelphia Inquirer*, March 31, 2013, philly.com/2013-03-31/news/38165576.

144. A leading Sunni member of the Governing Council, the UN representative Lakhdar Brahimi, and the British government all complained about it. Gordon and Trainor, *The Endgame*, pp. 61–62, 66.

145. Gordon and Trainor, *The Endgame,* p. 120.

146. "The speed and extent of the Islamist wave that swept over Shi'a Iraq was as if a tsunami had silently and very rapidly spread to cover the South. No one had predicted the strength of this wave and the depth of support that it engendered amongst the poor and deprived population of the area." Allawi, *op. cit.*, p. 91. See also p. 237.

147. The Mahdi is an apocalyptic figure in Shia theology.

148. "By 2004, the Mahdi Army controlled Sadr City, the huge Shiite slum in Baghdad. Nobody could enter Sadr City without gaining permission

and passing through Mahdi Army checkpoints." Ferguson, *op. cit.*, p. 328.

149. Gordon and Trainor, *The Endgame*, pp. 67–69.

150. *Ibid.*, pp. 100–105.

151. Allawi, *op. cit.*, pp. 233–234.

152. Gordon and Trainor, *The Endgame*, p. 192.

153. Dodge, *Iraq: From War to a New Authoritarianism*, pp. 64–65, 68–69; Gordon and Trainor, *The Endgame*, p. 272.

154. "By the end of 2006, Baghdad had been transformed into a series of fortified ghettos, where rising violence had reorganised the city's population along sectarian lines." Dodge, *Iraq: From War to a New Authoritarianism,* p. 59.

155. Ajami, *op. cit.*, p. 275; Gordon and Trainor, *The Endgame*, p. 83; Chandrasekaran, *op. cit.*, pp. 130–131; Ricks, *op. cit.*, p. 209.

156. Ajami, *op. cit.*, pp. 106–107.

157. Allawi, *op. cit.*, p. 305.

158. Dodge, *Iraq: From War to a New Authoritarianism*, p. 187; Gordon and Trainor, *The Endgame*, pp. 315–316. One of the deadliest explosives used against American forces in Iraq was the explosively formed penetrator, which the military abbreviated as "EFP." Its component parts were manufactured in Iran and smuggled into Iraq. *Ibid.*, pp. 151–153.

159. Gordon and Trainor, *The Endgame*, pp. 424, 534.

160. *Ibid.*, p. 230; Ricks, *op. cit.*, p. 409.

161. In 2011 Sunnis in Syria, an oppressed majority in that country just as the Shia had been in Saddam's Iraq, rose up against the regime, touching off a bloody civil war. See pp. 305–306.

162. "The barrage of anti-Shi'a literature emanating from Saudi-sponsored schools, universities and seminaries became required reading for the recently energised Sunni Muslims of Iraq. The bookstalls outside Baghdad's main Sunni mosques . . . displayed mainly Salafist or Wahhabi-inspired literature, mostly imported from Saudi Arabia." Allawi, *op. cit.*, p. 236.

163. Gordon and Trainor, *The Endgame*, p. 231.

164. Allawi, *op. cit.*, p. 178.

165. Ricks, *op. cit.*, p. 170.

166. Baker, *op. cit.*, p. 277.

167. *Ibid.*, p. 292. The first public acknowledgment by a high-ranking official of what the United States was facing in Iraq came on July 16, 2003, when General John Abizaid, the head of CENTCOM, the regional American military command that covered the Middle East, called what was happening "a classic guerrilla-type campaign." Gordon and Trainor, *Cobra II*, p. 489.

168. Allawi, *op. cit.*, p. 242.

169. Dodge, *Iraq: From War to a New Authoritarianism*, p. 77.

170. Baker, *op. cit.*, p. 480.
171. Dodge, *Iraq: From War to a New Authoritarianism*, p. 77.
172. Iraqi units took part in the second battle for Fallujah, for example, but did not acquit themselves particularly well. Ricks, *op. cit.*, p. 406. See also Dodge, *Iraq: From War to a New Authoritarianism*, pp. 78.
173. Ricks, *op. cit.*, p. 131.
174. Gordon and Trainor, *The Endgame*, pp. 98, 285.
175. Gordon and Shapiro, *op. cit.*, p. 2. Support had been high since the attacks of September 11, 2001. See p. 190.
176. See p. 190.
177. Baker, *op. cit.*, p. 344.
178. *Ibid.*, pp. 341, 358.
179. Stiglitz and Bilmes, *op. cit.*, p. 7; Chandrasekaran, *op. cit.*, p. 151.
180. Baker, *op. cit.*, p. 219.
181. Stiglitz and Bilmes, *op. cit.*, pp. 21–24.
182. Robert D. Hormats, *The Price of Liberty: Paying for America's Wars*, New York: Times Books, 2007, p. xix.
183. *Ibid.*, p. 271; Baker, *op. cit.*, p. 293.
184. Baker, *op. cit.*, p. 149; Betts, *op. cit.*, p. 276.
185. That is of course true of spending on every war, and indeed of every government expenditure of any kind. But few government programs become as unpopular as the war in Iraq ultimately did. By June 2014, 71 percent of Americans said that it had not been worth fighting. Carrie Dann, "Not Worth It: Huge Majority Regret Iraq War, Exclusive Poll Shows," www.nbcnews.com/storyline/iraq-turmoil/not-worth-it.
186. Hormats, *op. cit.*, p. 262. See also Michael Mandelbaum, *The Frugal Superpower: America's Global Leadership in a Cash-Strapped Era*, New York: PublicAffairs, 2010, pp. 19–29, 156–165.
187. This is the subject of Stiglitz and Bilmes, *op. cit.* One of the coauthors of that study later revised her estimate upward (while including the costs of Afghanistan in the total). "The Iraq and Afghanistan conflicts, taken together, will be the most expensive wars in US history—totaling somewhere between $4 to $6 trillion." Linda J. Bilmes, "The Financial Legacy of Iraq and Afghanistan: How Wartime Spending Decisions Will Constrain Future National Security Budgets," Cambridge, Massachusetts: Harvard Kennedy School Faculty Research Working Paper Series RWP13–006, March 2013, p. 1. Bush also might have used the political windfall to undertake more robust opposition to the nuclear weapons programs of North Korea and Iran. See pp. 325–343.
188. "While military appropriations in 2003, in inflation-adjusted terms, were roughly the same as during the high defense spending years of the Korean and Vietnam Wars, the exponential growth of the U.S. economy over the previous half century meant the figure amounted to a far smaller portion of the nation's GDP than in the 1950s or 1960s. Military

outlays were roughly 15 percent of GDP during the peak of the Korean War and 10 percent during the most intense years of the Vietnam War, but only 4 percent at the outset of the Iraq War." Hormats, *op. cit.*, p. 253. On the other hand, the total costs of the Iraq War will outstrip those of all previous conflicts except World War II. " . . . even in the best case scenario, these costs [of the Iraq War] are projected to be almost ten times the cost of the first Gulf War, almost a third more than the cost of the Vietnam War, and twice that of World War I. The only war in our history which cost more was World War II . . . " Stiglitz and Bilmes, *op. cit.*, pp. 5–6.

189. Mueller, *op. cit.*, pp. 199–200.

190. Nor did the fact that Vietnam spawned a larger, noisier antiwar movement than did Iraq affect the trajectory of the war. Mueller, *op. cit.*, pp. 203–204. For Iraq, antiwar sentiment had as its vehicle the Democratic Party, which was not available for this purpose during much of the Vietnam War because it was a Democratic president who was conducting the war.

191. " . . . the public places a far lower value on the stakes in Iraq than it did in the earlier wars [in Korea and Vietnam] . . . after two years of war, support for war on this measure had slumped to around 50 percent. However, at that point around 20,000 Americans had been killed in Vietnam and Korea, but only about 1,500 in Iraq. Korea and Vietnam were seen, initially at least, to be important necessary components in dealing with international Communism . . . Although Americans ultimately soured on the war [in Vietnam], it took far more American deaths to accomplish this than in Iraq. That is, casualty for casualty, support dropped off far more quickly in the Iraq war than in either of the earlier two wars." Mueller, *op. cit.*, pp. 200–201.

192. *Ibid.*, pp. 197, 205. "In the fall of 2003, 78 percent of Republicans still supported the war in Iraq, but 78 percent of Democrats did not support it." Gordon and Shapiro, *op. cit.*, pp. 192–193.

193. Joseph C. Wilson 4th, "What I Didn't Find in Africa," *The New York Times, July 6, 2003*, http://www.nytimes.com/2003/07/06/opinion/what-i-didn-t-find-in-africa.

194. To make the whole affair even more legally and morally suspect, the prosecution in the case used legally dubious tactics against Libby. See Arthur Herman, "The Smearing of Scooter Libby," *Commentary*, June, 2015; Peter Berkowitz, "The False Evidence Against Scooter Libby," *The Wall Street Journal*, April 7, 2015, p. A13; Peter Berkowitz, "Judith Miller Recants: Where's the Media?" Real Clear Politics, April 18, 2015, www.realclearpolitics.com/articles/2015/04/18/judith-miller-recants.

195. Mueller, *op. cit.*, p. 204. The Senate Republican majority whip, Mitch McConnell of Kentucky, met with the president shortly before the election. " 'Mr. President, your unpopularity is going to cost us control

of the Congress,' McConnell told Bush. 'Well, Mitch, what do you want me to do about it?' Bush asked. 'Mr. President, bring some troops home from Iraq,' McConnell urged." Bush refused. Baker, *op. cit.*, p. 487.

196. It became known as the Baker-Hamilton Commission.

197. Baker, *op. cit.*, p. 513; Gordon and Trainor, *The Endgame*, p. 278.

198. The year 2006 had been the worst one yet for the United States in Iraq, despite the installation of Nouri al-Maliki as prime minster in May and the killing of Abu Musab al-Zarqawi, the leader of al Qaeda in Iraq, in June. Baker, *op. cit*, pp. 456, 474.

199. Gordon and Trainor, *The Endgame*, p. 370.

200. *Ibid.*, p. 418.

201. Ricks, *op. cit.*, p. 133.

202. This is a major theme of Max Boot, *Invisible Armies: An Epic History of Guerrilla Warfare from Ancient Times to the Present*, New York: Liveright Publishing Corporation, 2013.

203. Mark Danner, "Warrior Petraeus," *The New York Review of Books*, March 7, 2013, p. 42.

204. Gordon and Trainor, *The Endgame*, p. 331; Fred Kaplan, *The Insurgents: David Petraeus and the Plot to Change the American Way of War*, New York: Simon & Schuster, 2013, p. 363.

205. Bush's change of strategy encountered opposition within his government as well. Condoleezza Rice, who had become secretary of state, opposed it as did General George Casey, the commander in Iraq, and General John Abizaid, the head of Central Command. Gordon and Trainor, *The Endgame*, pp. 301, 307, 410. Of the plan to add troops in Iraq, General Peter Schoomaker, the Army chief of staff, said to Bush "We're concerned we're going to break the army." Baker, *op. cit.*, p. 520.

206. Gates had also served on the Iraq Study Group but proved to be amenable to the new policy.

207. Gordon and Trainor, *The Endgame*, p. 366.

208. *Ibid.*, p. 205; Boot, *op. cit.*, pp. 542–543; Kaplan, *op. cit.*, p. 266. The establishment of mobile phone networks in Iraq made tracking insurgent leaders much easier. Dodge, *Iraq: From War to a New Authoritarianism*, p. 106.

209. Cooperating with the Sunnis "was possible in large part because Sunni Iraq is still a tribal society. Make a deal with the sheik—promise him security, hand him a bag of money—and he can plausibly deliver the rest of his tribe, even if, as was often the case, many members of that tribe had spent the past few years killing Americans." Dexter Filkins, "Surging and Awakening," *The New Republic*, May 20, 2009, p. 30. See also Francis Fukuyama, *The Origins of Political Order: From Prehuman Times to the French Revolution*, New York: Farrar, Straus, and Giroux, 2011, p. 196.

210. Gordon and Trainor, *The Endgame*, pp. 35, 37, 96.

211. *Ibid.*, pp. 347, 382–384.
212. The Americans called their new Sunni allies "The Sons of Iraq." Kaplan, *op. cit.*, p. 262. By one account they numbered more than 100,000. Boot, *op. cit.*, p. 533.
213. "Violence fell by more than 90% between 2007 and 2009." Max Boot, "Doubling Down on Iraq," *The Wall Street Journal*, November 2–3, 2013, p. C6. For other estimates of the decrease in violence see Dodge, *Iraq: From War to a New Authoritarianism*, p. 21; Gordon and Trainor, *The Endgame*, p. 338; Kaplan, *op. cit.*, p. 267.
214. The British had occupied Basra but had withdrawn at the end of 2007. Gordon and Trainor, *The Endgame*, pp. 465–468. On the British performance in Iraq see *Ibid.*, p. 481.
215. *Ibid.*, chapter 25.
216. *Ibid.*, chapter 26.
217. " . . . by late 2008, the percentage of people who thought US efforts were making things better had risen from 30 to 46 while those believing they were having no impact had dropped from 51 to 32. And the percentage holding that the US was making significant progress rose from 36 to 46 while the percentage concluding that it was winning the war rose from 21 to 37. Despite this change, however . . . support for the war did not increase—nor did it do so on measures tapping those who favored the war, those who felt it had been worth the effort or the right decision, or those who favored staying as long as it takes." Mueller, *op. cit.*, p. 214.
218. Gordon and Trainor, *The Endgame*, pp. 331–332, 437.
219. *Ibid.*, pp. 529–532, 539–541, 556–558; Baker, *op. cit.*, pp. 601, 619.
220. On December 14, 2011, at a ceremony marking the withdrawal of American forces, President Obama said, "Everything that American troops have done in Iraq—all the fighting and all the dying, the bleeding and the building, and the training and the partnering—all of it has led to this moment of success." Quoted in Adam Taylor, "WorldViews," *The Washington Post*, June 14, 2014, p. A10.
221. Gordon and Trainor, *The Endgame*, pp. 632, 638–639. Dodge, *Iraq: From War to a New Authoritarianism*, p. 152. According to the American ambassador to Iraq in 2010, "Many allege that the Obama administration then threw its weight behind Maliki. Not so. The Shia parties, supported by Iran and the new religious establishment, were adamant that one of theirs would be the new prime minister. The Shia held half of the seats in parliament, and with Kurdish parties, with almost 20 percent additional seats, also tilting towards the Shia, Maliki was the all-but-inevitable choice." James Jeffrey, "How Maliki Broke Iraq," *Politico*, August 13, 2014, http://www.politico.com/magazine/story/2014/08/how-maliki-broke-iraq-109996.
222. Kaplan, *op. cit.*, pp. 265, 269, 289; Gordon and Trainor, *The Endgame*, pp. 406, 506; Dodge, *Iraq: From War to a New Authoritarianism*, p. 81; Boot, *op. cit.*, p. 544.

223. "Iraqi and U.S. officials, both current and former, tell tales of extortion, bribery, kickbacks and theft. Many involve the siphoning of Iraq's oil revenues . . . " Dexter Filkins, "What We Left Behind," *The New Yorker*, April 28, 2014, www.newyorker.com/reporting/2014/04/28/140428fa.

224. *Ibid.*

225. "Initially hostile to the idea of arming and funding Sunni fighters, Maliki eventually relented after intense lobbying from [U.S. Ambassador Ryan] Crocker and Petraeus, but only on the condition that Washington foot the bill. He later agreed to hire and fund some of the tribal fighters, but many of his promises to them went unmet—leaving them unemployed, bitter, and again susceptible to radicalization." Ali Khedery, "Why we stuck with Maliki—and lost Iraq," *The Washington Post*, July 3, 2014, *www.washingtonpost.com/opinion/why-we-stuck-with-maliki*. See also Dodge, *Iraq: From War to a New Authoritarianism*, pp. 98–100.

226. Gordon and Trainor, *The Endgame*, p. 4.

227. "The slow road back," *The Economist*, March 2, 2013, p. 24.

228. Dodge, *Iraq: From War to a New Authoritarianism*, pp. 129,159, 174, 182, 206, 208.

229. See pp. 298–310.

230. In Mosul " 'the number of Isis fighters that came in were in the hundreds, but they were joined by many more people in black masks,' said Mohammed, a sweet vendor. 'Many people were just happy to take up arms. This was the beginning of a Sunni revolution.' " Erika Solomon, "Mosul residents tell of army flight," *Financial Times*, June 14/June 15, 2014, p. 4. In Fallujah, "locals interviewed say the strongest occupying force in the Sunni-majority city isn't al Qaeda but tribal fighters whose impatience with Mr. Maliki has finally boiled over into violence." Mark Bradley and Ali A. Nabhan, "Iraqi Officer Takes Dark Turn to al Qaeda," *The Wall Street Journal*, March 17, 2014, p. A12.

231. The ISIS conquests raised the question of whether a continuing American military presence in Iraq could have prevented them. A former American ambassador to the country thought not. James Franklin Jeffrey, "Behind the U.S. Withdrawal from Iraq," *The Wall Street Journal*, November 3, 2014, p. A15.

232. Chandrasekaran, *op. cit.*, pp. 242–243.

233. "The semiautonomous [Kurdish] area has an economy growing 12 percent a year and a per capita GDP that is 50 percent higher than the rest of the country. In a clear sign of its growing importance, the region now hosts 25 consulates and foreign representations, seven universities, and two international airports." David DeVoss, "The Other Iraq," *The Weekly Standard*, March 4, 2013, p. 27.

234. " 'In Kurdistan, the leaders steal about twenty per cent, but eighty per cent makes it to the people,' a Kurdish friend told me in Erbil. 'In Baghdad, the percentages are reversed.' " Filkins, *op. cit.*

235. The United States did, on occasion, play an important role in calming relations between the Kurds and the government of neighboring Turkey. Gordon and Trainor, *The Endgame*, pp. 450–455.

236. As an example of American opposition to Kurdish independence, when, in 2014, the Kurds attempted to sell oil on the world market against the wishes of the central government in Baghdad, the Americans sided with Baghdad. See Steven Mufson, "How the U.S. got mixed up in a fight over Kurdish oil," *The Washington Post*, August 5, 2014, p. A1; Emre Peker, Sarah Kent, and Joe Parkinson, "In Challenge to Iraq, Kurds Pin Future on Stealth Oil Sales," *The Wall Street Journal*, July 22, 2014, p. A1. On earlier American clashes with the Kurds see Gordon and Trainor, *Cobra II*, pp. 448–450.

237. Gordon and Trainor, *The Endgame*, p. 291.

238. "We are likely to have debates for years and years between those who say it [the Iraq enterprise] was a fool's errand and those who say it was a matter of faulty execution . . . I think one of the implications of the sorts of assessments that the intelligence community made before the war about the awesome challenges to be faced afterwards . . . is that no matter how expertly the policy had been executed, the challenges and problems would have been immense . . . I think, on balance, that tilts the argument in favor of the fool's-errand position." American intelligence official Paul Pillar, quoted in Ferguson, *op. cit.*, p. 532.

239. Ajami, *op. cit.*, p. 343.

Chapter 5

1. Quoted in Elliott Abrams, *Tested by Zion: The Bush Administration and the Israeli-Palestinian Conflict*, New York: Cambridge University Press, 2013, p. 130.

2. "Remarks by President George W. Bush at the 20th Anniversary of the National Endowment for Democracy," November 6, 2003, www.ned. org/george-w-bush/remarks-by-president-george-w-bush.

3. Martin Kramer, "How Not to Fix the Middle East," Middle East Paper Number 7, Middle East Strategy at Harvard, December 2009, p. 1.

4. Neither had been entirely absent from the Middle East prior to World War I. The British had dominated Egypt since the 1880s. The French had made parts of North Africa colonial possessions as early as the 1830s.

5. On these see Michael Oren, *Power, Faith, and Fantasy: America in the Middle East, 1776 to the Present*, New York: W.W. Norton and Company, 2007.

6. Joel S. Migdal, *Shifting Sands: The United States in the Middle East*, New York: Columbia University Press, 2014, p. 3.

7. Nadav Safran, *Saudi Arabia: The Ceaseless Quest for Security*, Cambridge, Massachusetts: Harvard University Press, 1985, p. 110.

8. " . . . in practice . . . dual containment was more defensive than offensive, more declaratory than operational." Lawrence Freedman, *A Choice of Enemies: America Confronts the Middle East*, New York: PublicAffairs,

2008, p. 301, citing Kenneth Pollack, *The Persian Puzzle: The Conflict Between Iran and America*, New York: Random House, 2004, p. 263. On dual containment see also Freedman, *op. cit.*, p. 284.

9. In 1958 the United States briefly sent troops to Lebanon. The president at the time, Dwight D. Eisenhower, "wanted to send a message to Nasser and the Soviets." Stephen Sestanovich, *Maximalist: America and the World from Truman to Obama*, New York: Knopf, 2014, p. 82.

10. The British expected their continental allies to do whatever fighting was needed in Europe and, for the most part—until the two wars of the twentieth century—that is what happened. The United States, by contrast, did not expect its chief Middle Eastern client, Saudi Arabia, to be able to defend itself, and when Iraq threatened the Saudi regime in 1990, 400,000 American troops came to its rescue.

11. Israel was the exception. Its democratic political system was one of the several reasons the American public supported it. See pp. 260–261.

12. The phrase and the concept are from Daniel Pipes and Adam Garfinkle, editors, *Friendly Tyrants: An American Dilemma*, New York: St. Martin's Press, 1991.

13. Greece, Spain, and Portugal were governed autocratically for parts of the Cold War period.

14. On the Madrid conference see Dennis Ross, *The Missing Peace: The Inside Story of the Fight for Middle East Peace,* New York: Farrar, Straus, and Giroux, 2004, pp. 80–81.

15. The line in the song is "the oldest established permanent floating crap game in New York."

16. "Jews, under Koranic doctrine, are inherently inferior by virtue of their false religion, and must not be allowed to be equal to Muslims. For Muslim Arabs, the conceit of Jews establishing their own state, Israel, and on territory conquered by Muslims and since Muhammad under the control of Muslims, can only be considered outrageous and intolerable." Philip Carl Salzman, *Culture and Conflict in the Middle East*, Amherst, New York: Humanity Books, 2008, pp. 165–166.

17. *Ibid.*, pp. 160–170.

18. The attacks came from the armies of Egypt, Jordan, and Syria, together with an expeditionary force from Iraq.

19. The British were furious at Egyptian president Nasser's move to nationalize the Canal, which Great Britain had built and operated. The French were retaliating against Nasser for his support of the rebellion against French rule in Algeria.

20. The definitive account of this conflict is Michael B. Oren, *Six Days of War: June 1967 and the Making of the Modern Middle East*, New York: Oxford University Press, 2002.

21. On American policy toward Israeli independence see Allis Radosh and Ronald Radosh, *A Safe Haven: Harry S. Truman and the Founding of Israel*, New York: Harper, 2009.

22. "Before President Johnson met [Israeli Foreign Minister Abba] Eban at the White House, his top foreign policy adviser, Walt Rostow, was forced to visit Eisenhower's home in Gettysburg, Pennsylvania. Eisenhower issued Rostow an affidavit stating that in 1957 the United States had indeed pledged to open the waterway if Egypt closed it again." Oren, *Six Days of War,* p. 112.

23. The agreements are listed in Michael Mandelbaum, *The Fate of Nations: The Search for National Security in the Nineteenth and Twentieth Centuries,* New York: Cambridge University Press, 1988, p. 288.

24. Ironically, Sadat decided to go to Jerusalem because he was alarmed at the direction in which the Carter administration was taking American Middle East diplomacy. He opposed the administration's plan to convene an international conference and give the Soviet Union a major part in it and went to Israel to put a stop to this initiative.

25. It turned out to be a "cold peace." In 2013, "Israeli journalists cannot obtain visas to Egypt and Egyptian reporters do not come to Israel because of a ban by their union. The Israeli airline El Al has stopped flying to Cairo due to business and security concerns. The Israeli Academic Center in Cairo is still open but mainly serves local students studying Hebrew. And the Egyptian government discourages citizens from seeking the required permit to visit Israel . . . " Ehud Yaari, "Israeli-Egyptian Peace: 40 years and Holding," Washington, DC: The Washington Institute for Near East Policy, Policy Watch 2149, October 2, 2013, p. 3.

26. The United States also supplied the military personnel stationed in the Sinai to assure that it remained demilitarized, which was one of the terms of the treaty.

27. Their basic grievance remained Israel's existence, which the United States did not address in the way the Arab world would have preferred.

28. On linkage see Dennis Ross and David Makovsky, *Myths, Illusions, and Peace: Finding a New Direction for America in the Middle East,* New York: Viking, 2009, chapters 2 and 3.

29. British Prime Minister Tony Blair had a particularly strong belief in the reality of linkage. See Abrams, *op. cit.,* pp. 39, 57. The idea also had a powerful grip on the imaginations of senior officials in the Obama administration. "The notion of 'linkage'—all Middle Eastern disputes are tied to that between Israel and the Palestinians—became doctrine in the Obama administration and [National Security Advisor James] Jones's belief in it bordered on the religious. As he once confessed to an Israeli audience, 'If God had appeared in front of the president and said he could do one thing on the planet it would be the two-state solution.'" Michael B. Oren, *Ally: My Journey Across the American-Israeli Divide,* New York: Random House, 2015, p. 109.

30. "Note the words of Egyptian president Hosni Mubarak in early 2008 when, standing next to President George W. Bush at a joint press

conference . . . he recounted their conversation: 'I emphasized that the Palestinian question, of course, is the core of problems and conflict in the Middle East, and it is the entry to contain the crisis and tension in the region . . . ' " Ross and Makovsky, *op. cit.*, p. 12. Mubarak was practicing deflection. His remarks came after the Bush administration had publicly pressed him to do something that it considered the best way to address the problems of the region but that he emphatically did not wish to do (and in the end did not do): make the Egyptian political system more democratic. On this issue see pp. 288–289.

31. President George W. Bush "was well aware that, despite their endless speeches about Palestinian rights, most Arab leaders treated resident Palestinian populations badly and placed their own interests far above those of the 'Palestine' they claimed to protect." Abrams, *op. cit.*, p. 2. Vice President Cheney shared this view. *Ibid.*, p. 88. "In reality, Arab states tend to pursue their own national interests, and inter-Arab dynamics are their own variable, independent of the Arab-Israeli conflict." Ross and Makovsky, *op. cit.*, p. 88.

32. The December 2006 report of the Iraq Study Group, co-chaired by former Secretary of State James Baker and former Congressman Lee Hamilton, which recommended the withdrawal of American forces from Iraq, included these words: "To put it simply, all key issues in the Middle East—the Arab-Israeli conflict, Iraq, Iran, the need for political and economic reforms, and extremism and terrorism—are inextricably linked." Quoted in Ross and Makovsky, *op. cit.*, p. 13.

33. Mandelbaum, *op. cit.*, p. 281. Egypt was large and important enough, moreover, that its president could make a separate peace with Israel, as the leaders of the other Arab countries and movements could not, or at least would not.

34. According to one of the leading academic anti-Zionists in the United States, Tony Judt, "The solution to the crisis in the Middle East lies in Washington. On this there is widespread agreement." "An Alternative Future: An Exchange," *The New York Review of Books*, December 4, 2003, www.nybooks, com/articles/archives/2003/dec/04/an-alternative-future.

35. This is the thesis of John J. Mearsheimer and Stephen Walt, *The Israel Lobby and U.S. Foreign Policy*, New York: Farrar, Straus, and Giroux, 2007. On the distortions and errors of this book see, inter alia, Robert C. Lieberman, "The 'Israel Lobby' and American Politics," *Perspectives on Politics*, 7:2 (June 2009); Itamar Rabinovich, "Testing the 'Israel Lobby' Thesis," *TheAmerican Interest*, March/April 2008; and Jeffrey Goldberg, "The Usual Suspect," *The New Republic*, October 8, 2007. As Goldberg notes, while Mearsheimer and Walt accuse the Israeli government and its Washington lobby of pushing the United States into war in 2003, the Israelis actually *opposed* that war, believing Iran to present the greater threat. See pp. 49–50.

36. Yair Rosenberg, "U.S. Policy Is Pro-Israel Because Americans Are Pro-Israel, Not Because of AIPAC," *Tablet*, February 27, 2014, www.tabletmag.com/jewish-news-and-politics/164223.

37. "The fact that there has not been a general Arab-Israeli war since 1973 is proof that this pax Americana, based on the United States-Israel alliance, has been a success. From a realist point of view, supporting Israel has been a low-cost way of keeping order in part of the Middle East, managed by the United States, from offshore and without the commitment of any force." Martin Kramer, "The American Interest," *Azure*, No. 26 (Fall 2006), pp. 21–33, www.martinkramer.org/sandbox/2006/12/the-american-interest.

38. Migdal, *op. cit.*, pp. 81–83.

39. On the Israeli and American negotiations with Syria see Itamar Rabinovich, *The Brink of Peace: The Israeli-Syrian Negotiations*, Princeton, New Jersey: Princeton University Press, 1998. Despite the book's title the author, an academic expert on Syria who negotiated extensively with the Syrians during his time, from 1992 to 1995, as Israel's ambassador to the United States, writes "At no time during this period (August 1992–March 1996) were Israel and Syria on the brink of a breakthrough." p. 235. On these negotiations see also Ross, *The Missing Peace*, especially chapters 5, 9, and 20–22, and Martin Indyk, *Innocent Abroad: An Intimate Account of American Peace Diplomacy in the Middle East*, New York: Simon and Schuster, 2009, especially chapters 1, 6, 12–14.

40. Freedman, *op. cit.*, p. 325.

41. Ross, *op. cit.*, p. 142; Indyk, *op. cit.*, p. 284.

42. "There was an old script in Damascus written by Hafez al-Assad: the struggle against Israel took precedence over all other concerns . . . Tell the young that their desire for bread, freedom, and opportunities, and their taste for the world beyond the walls of the big prison that the regime had erected would have to wait until the Syrian banners are raised over the Golan Heights." Fouad Ajami, *The Syrian Rebellion*, Stanford, California: Hoover Institution Press, 2012, p. 70. See also Barry Rubin, *The Tragedy of the Middle East*, New York: Cambridge University Press, 2002, p. 207.

43. Indyk, *op. cit.*, p. 280.

44. Freedman, *op. cit.*, p. 311.

45. In Jordan, a Bedouin minority governed a Palestinian majority. The ruling Bedouins feared, not without reason, that the PLO was interested in taking over not only the West Bank but the Kingdom of Jordan as well.

46. Netanyahu became even less popular with the American peace processers in his second term as prime minister beginning in 2009, as events proved his skepticism about the Palestinians to be more firmly grounded in reality than the American faith in their good intentions.

47. Arafat in 1983: "The fate of all mankind today is being subjected to a real test as a result of the insane plans of American imperialism, which is striving to escalate further the worldwide arms race . . . we are witnessing how foreign imperialist wars are again being unleashed by America." Quoted in Daniel Pipes, "Breaking All the Rules: The Middle East in U.S. Policy," *International Security* (Fall 1984) www.danielpipes.org/169/breaking-all-the-rules-the-middle-east-in-us-policy. See also Barry Rubin and Judith Colp Rubin, *Yasir Arafat: A Political Biography*, New York: Oxford University Press, 2003, p. 23.

48. "Arafat went to Oslo after the first Gulf War not because he made a choice but because he had no choice. He chose wrong in siding with Saddam Hussein, and his leadership was being challenged from within and without. Hundreds of thousands of Palestinians were expelled from the Gulf. The PLO was in deep financial crisis, having lost its financial base in the Gulf. Many in the Arab world were prepared to marginalize him, particularly as he seemed to have no answers. Oslo was his salvation." Ross, *op. cit.*, p. 766.

49. "Never throughout the Oslo process did [Arafat] declare that those carrying out terror and violence against Israelis were wrong, were illegitimate, were enemies of the Palestinian cause." *Ibid.*, p. 776.

50. Freedman, *op. cit.*, p. 318. In 2000, when the peace process broke down, he sponsored and helped organize such violence on a large scale. See pp. 275–276.

51. "[Arafat] continued to promote hostility toward Israel. Thousands of Palestinian children went to summer camps where they were taught how to kidnap Israelis. Suicide bombers were called martyrs . . . " Ross, *op. cit.*, p. 766. See also Rubin, *The Tragedy of the Middle East*, p. 221, and Rubin and Rubin, *op. cit.*, p. 164.

52. Freedman, *op. cit.*, p. 338.

53. "In 1998 Arafat's men kidnapped the Editor of the *Al Kuds* newspaper (published in East Jerusalem) after he had failed to print on the front page an article that compared Arafat to Saladin, the great conqueror who took Jerusalem from the Crusaders. Written by one of Arafat's lackeys, the article was printed on page three, for which offense the Editor was held for a week and physically assaulted." Edward Luttwak, "An Insufficient War," *Times Literary Supplement*, December 22, 2000, p. 12. See also Rubin and Rubin, *op. cit.*, p. 19.

54. Rubin and Rubin, *op. cit.*, p. 225.

55. *Ibid.*, p. 233.

56. *Ibid.*, p. 144.

57. Abrams, *op. cit.*, p. 24.

58. Clinton was absent for three days, attending a Group of Eight meeting on Okinawa.

59. The text is reprinted in Indyk, *op. cit.*, pp. 441–447.

60. *Ibid.*, pp. 367–370.
61. "For all sorts of reasons, ethnic groups were either forcibly or voluntarily moved during that troubled period [the mid-1940s to early 1950s] and usually in far worse circumstances and for far longer distances than the Palestinians. There were no fewer than 20 different groups—including the Sikhs, Muslims and Hindus of the Punjab, the Crimean Tatars, the Japanese and Korean Kuril and Sakhalin Islanders, the Soviet Chechens, Ingush, and Balkars . . . Yet all of these refugee groups, except one, chose to try to make the best of their new environments. Most have succeeded . . . The sole exception has been the Palestinians . . . " Andrew Roberts, "From an Era of Refugee Millions, Only Palestinians Remain," *The Wall Street Journal*, November 22–23, 2014, p. A13.
62. The "right of return" was also popular among Jordan's ruling Bedouins, who hoped against hope that it would result in Palestinians leaving their country in large numbers. "A kingdom of two halves," *The Economist*, March 8, 2014, p. 51.
63. Clinton told Arafat that, "No other Israeli prime minister would have ever contemplated going as far as Barak. Yet in return he heard nothing meaningful from Arafat." Indyk, *op. cit.*, p. 313.
64. "Arafat had been seeking an escape route from the moment he arrived at Camp David." *Ibid.*, p. 326.
65. According to Shlomo Ben-Ami, the Israeli foreign minister at Camp David and a passionate advocate of a compromise peace with the Palestinians, "Arafat is not an earthly leader. He sees himself as a mythological figure. He has always represented himself as a kind of modern Salah a-Din. Therefore, even the concrete real-estate issues don't interest him so much. At Camp David, it was clear that he wasn't looking for practical solutions, but was focused on mythological subjects . . . He floats on the heights of the Islamic ethos and the refugee ethos and the Palestinian ethos. Arafat's discourse is never practical, either . . . At the end of the process, you suddenly understand that you are not moving ahead in the negotiations because you are in fact negotiating with a myth." Ari Shavit, "End of a Journey," *Haaretz.com*, English edition, March 8, 2003.
66. " . . . whereas Israelis traditionally want peace, the Palestinians always demand justice." Oren, *Ally*, p. 323.
67. Israel's post-1967 circumstances corresponded to what students of international relations call "the security dilemma." See Mandelbaum, *op. cit.*, pp. 254–266.
68. Rubin, *The Tragedy of the Middle East*, p. 196.
69. "Hamas's strategy is to provoke a response from Israel by attacking from behind the cover of Palestinian civilians, thus drawing Israeli strikes that kill those civilians, and then to have the casualties filmed by one of the world's largest press contingents, with the understanding that the

resulting outrage abroad will blunt Israel's response. This is a ruthless strategy, and an effective one. It is predicated on the cooperation of journalists." Matti Friedman, "What the Media Gets Wrong About Israel," *The Atlantic*, November 30, 2014, www.theatlantic.com/ international/archive/2014/14/11/how-the-media-gets-israel-wrong.

70. According to Arafat, "The [Israelis] suffer because of casualties. I don't. My people are glorified as martyrs." Indyk, *op. cit.*, p. 352.

71. "'Imad Falouji, a Palestinian cabinet minister, declared that the Intifada 'had been planned since Chairman Arafat's return from Camp David, when he turned the tables in the face of the former U.S. President and rejected the American conditions.'" Quoted in Ross, *op. cit.*, p. 730. See also Rubin and Rubin, *op. cit.*, p. 258; Indyk, *op. cit.*, p. 354; and Edward Luttwak, "The Facts about Palestine," *Times Literary Supplement*, January 19, 2001, p. 17.

72. Abrams, *op. cit.*, p. 31.

73. "During 2002, 451 Israelis died as a result of terrorist attacks, many in the first months of the year. The next year saw 214 die, and in 2004 the numbers halved again to 117. They halved once more in 2005." Freedman, *op. cit.*, p. 460. In 2006 the number was 15, Abrams, *op. cit.*, p. 122.

74. Ross and Makovsky, *op. cit.*, p. 21.

75. Abrams, *op. cit.*, p. 186–191.

76. "After the war [Nasrallah] admitted that he had not thought 'even one percent, that the capture would lead to a war at this time and of this magnitude.' If he had known he would not have done it. 'Absolutely not.'" Freedman, *op. cit.*, p. 481.

77. By some accounts he intended to withdraw from much of the West Bank as well, but was unable to do so because of the stroke that ended his career. Abrams, *op. cit.*, p. 154.

78. On the Hamas Charter see Freedman, *op. cit.*, p. 260. Representative of Hamas's public rhetoric are the words of one of its leaders, Khaled Mashal, during the Second Intifada: "Tomorrow we will lead the world, Allah willing. Apologize today [you infidels] before remorse will do you no good. Our nation is moving forward, and it is in your interest to respect a victorious nation . . . Before Israel dies, it must be humiliated and degraded. Allah willing, before they die, they will experience humiliation and degradation every day." Quoted in Richard Landes, "Why the Arab World Is Lost in an Emotional Nakba, and How We Keep It There," *Tablet*, June 24, 2014, www.tabletmag.com/jewish-news-and-politics/176673.

79. Abrams, *op. cit.*, pp. 144–146. The American State Department believed, wrongly, that Fatah would win the elections.

80. " . . . Clinton used the brief and usually ceremonial meeting with his successor to vent his frustration. He told Bush and Vice President-elect Cheney that Arafat had torpedoed the peace process; Cheney often

repeated later how bitter Clinton had been and how strongly he had warned the new team against trusting Arafat." Abrams, *op. cit.*, p. 5.

81. Abrams, *op. cit.*, pp. 25–27; Freedman, *op. cit.*, p. 454.

82. United Nations Resolution 181 of November, 1947, which recommended the creation of a Jewish state in Mandatory Palestine and for which the United States voted, also called for an Arab Palestinian state to come into being beside it.

83. Two of the changes, on borders and refugees, were outlined in a letter dated April 14, 2005, that Bush sent to Sharon. Abrams, *op. cit.*, pp. 104–109.

84. *Ibid.*, p. 75.

85. Jordan had ruled the territory but only two countries had officially recognized Jordanian sovereignty there.

86. The settlements also created divisions within Israel, with some Israelis strongly favoring, and others just as strongly opposing, keeping and expanding them. See Gadi Taub, *The Settlers: And the Struggle Over the Meaning of Zionism*, New Haven, Connecticut: Yale University Press, 2010.

87. Abrams, *op. cit.*, pp. 67, 260, 311. See also Condoleezza Rice, *No Higher Honor: A Memoir of My Years in Washington*, New York: Crown Publishers, 2011, pp. 281–283.

88. Several Israeli proposals offered to compensate the Palestinians with land from within the Green Line for the territory outside that Line that would become part of Israel.

89. Abrams, *op. cit.*, pp. 41–42.

90. *Ibid.*, p. 52.

91. "[Abbas] was always pleasant to work with, possessed a good sense of humor, and was fond of Americans . . . But from the president on down, we doubted that day and ever after whether he could deliver on his pledges. He seemed better suited by nature to be a prime minister in some small and peaceful state in northern Europe than to lead the Palestinians." Abrams, *op. cit.*, p. 75.

92. Efraim Karsh, "Palestinian Leaders Don't Want an Independent State," *Middle East Quarterly* (Summer 2014), www.meforum.org/3831/palestinians-reject-statehood.

93. "Another theme of recent official Palestinian incitement is the demonisation of Israelis and Jews, often as animals. For example, on 9 January 2012 PA television broadcast a speech by a Palestinian Imam, in the presence of the PA Minister of Religious Affairs, referring to the Jews as 'apes and pigs' and repeating the gharqad hadith, a traditional Muslim text about Muslims killing Jews hiding behind trees and rocks, because 'Judgement day will not come before you fight the Jews.'" David Pollock, "Time to End Palestinian Incitement," *Fathom* (Autumn 2013), http://fathomjournal.org/time-to-end-palestinian-incitement/.

94. Dov Zakheim, *A Vulcan's Tale: How the Bush Administration Mismanaged the Reconstruction of Afghanistan*, Washington, DC: Brookings Institution Press, 2011, p. 283.
95. George Packer, *The Assassins' Gate: America in Iraq*, New York: Farrar, Straus, and Giroux, 2005, p. 111.
96. Rice, *op. cit.*, p. 293.
97. *Ibid.*, p. 603.
98. Abrams, *op. cit.*, pp. 196, 202, 216.
99. "The weaker he became politically, the more Olmert seemed willing to risk. This was perhaps logical as a matter of individual psychology, but where would it lead Israel? How far would he go—and, more to the point, would anyone go there with him?" *Ibid.*, p. 233.
100. *Ibid.*, pp. 288, 293.
101. Migdal, *op. cit.*, p. 255.
102. Elliott Abrams, "Hillary Is Wrong About the Settlements," *The Wall Street Journal*, June 6, 2009, www.wsj.com/articles/SB124588743827438279950599.
103. Israel did, as per a Palestinian demand endorsed by the United States, release Palestinian prisoners, including some found guilty of murdering Israeli civilians.
104. Salzman, *op. cit.*, chapter 7.
105. "Can anyone in the Palestinian territories or the Arab world form a party that advocates peace, coexistence, and harmony with Israel? On the contrary, the only voices that are being heard among Palestinians and other Arabs are those who seek to boycott and delegitimize Israel. Any Palestinian or Arab who dares to talk to Israelis or visit Israel is accused of being a traitor for promoting 'normalization' with the 'Zionist enemy.'" Khaled Abu Toameh, "Where Are the Moderate Arabs and Palestinians?" Gatestone Insitute, online article, June 4, 2012, www.gatestoneinstitute.org/3091/moderate-arabs-palestinians
106. "Accepting reconciliation [with Israel] would transform the Palestinians in one fell swoop from the world's ultimate victim into an ordinary (and most likely failing) nation-state. It would force Palestinian leaders into responsibility, accountability, and the daunting task of state building." Efraim Karsh, "The Myth of Palestinian Centrality," *Mideast Security and Policy Studies* No. 108, Begin-Sadat Center for Strategic Studies, 2014, p. 3.
107. Ross, *op. cit.*, p. 105; Abrams, *Tested by Zion*, p. 258.
108. Joshua Muravchik, *Making David into Goliath: How the World Turned Against Israel*, New York: Encounter Books, 2014, especially chapter 6.
109. See pp. 8–9.
110. That speech built on others Bush had given at the American Enterprise Institute in Washington in February 2003, at the National Endowment for Democracy in Washington in November 2003, and later that month at Whitehall Palace in London.

111.   Peter Baker, *Days of Fire: Bush and Cheney in the White House*, New York: Doubleday, 2013, p. 373.

112.   These programs are discussed in Tamara Coffman Wittes, *Freedom's Unsteady March: America's Role in Building Arab Democracy*, Washington, DC: Brookings Institution Press, 2008, pp. 85–97.

113.   Steven A. Cook, *The Struggle for Egypt: From Nasser to Tahrir Square*, New York: Oxford University Press, 2012, p. 264.

114.   Rice, *op. cit.*, p. 337.

115.   *Ibid.*, p. 337.

116.   *Ibid.*, p. 379.

117.   Wittes, *op. cit.*, p. 85.

118.   James Mann, *The Rise of the Vulcans: The History of Bush's War Cabinet*, New York: Viking, 2004, p. 367.

119.   Rice, *op. cit.*, p. 376.

120.   Cook, *op. cit.*, p. 252.

121.   Wittes, *op. cit.*, p. 74. "By quietly allowing the rise of a conservative, anti-Western religious movement, Arab autocrats have been able to portray themselves to the West as bulwarks against Islamist bogeymen." Larry Diamond, Marc F. Plattner, and Nate Grubman, "Introduction," in Diamond and Plattner, editors, *Democratization and Authoritarianism in the Arab World*, Baltimore: Johns Hopkins University Press, 2014, p. xviii.

122.   " . . . over the course of [George W. Bush's] administration, too, America's bold intentions with respect to Arab democracy were blunted repeatedly by the real and perceived risks of fundamental change in the region . . . in the end his administration's actions came nowhere near matching his soaring rhetoric, either in implementation or in effects." Wittes, *op. cit.*, p. 77.

123.   Cook, *op. cit.*, p. 260.

124.   Historically, liberty and elections—popular sovereignty—were considered incompatible. Only in the second half of the nineteenth century did it become clear that both could be part of a single political system. Michael Mandelbaum, *Democracy's Good Name: The Rise and Risks of The World's Most Popular Form of Government*, New York: PublicAffairs, 2007, chapter 1.

125.   " . . . just as a fish is the last to discover water, the American political class generally seems to think that democracy is mainly a technical exercise concerned with forming political parties, ensuring press freedoms, and voting, rather than the attitudinal embodiment of a specific historical experience that, for any practical purpose, falls far short of being universal." Adam Garfinkle, "Reflections on the 9/11 Decade," *The American Interest*, September 22, 2011, www.the-american-interest.com.

126.   In the Middle East "some of the norms critical to a democratic society—trust, political interest, and involvement in political and civil society

organizations—enjoy comparatively tepid support." Diamond, Plattner, and Grubman, *op. cit.*, p. xvii.

127. Wittes, *op. cit.*, p. 2.
128. "Westerners have become accustomed to think of good and bad government in terms of tyranny versus liberty. In Middle-Eastern usage, liberty or freedom was a legal not a political term. It meant one who was not a slave and unlike the West, Muslims did not use slavery and freedom as political metaphors. For traditional Muslims, the converse of tyranny was not liberty but justice." Bernard Lewis, *What Went Wrong? Western Impact and Middle Eastern Response*, New York: Oxford University Press, p. 54.
129. Salzman, *op. cit.*, pp. 176–187. "I against my brothers, my brothers and I against my cousins, my brothers, my cousins and I against strangers" is an often-cited Bedouin saying that describes the predominant outlook in the countries of the region.
130. The relationship between free markets and democracy is the subject of Mandelbaum, *Democracy's Good Name*, chapter 3.
131. Wittes, *op. cit.*, p. 60; Dalibor Rohac, "The Dead Hand of Socialism: State Ownership in the Arab World," Washington, DC: Cato Institute Policy Analysis Number 753, August 25, 2014. A broader discussion of the Arab economies is in Marcus Noland and Howard Pack, *The Arab Economies in a Changing World*, Washington, DC: Peterson Institute for International Economics, 2007.
132. Lewis, *op. cit.*, "Introduction."
133. "It is difficult for the United States to have any influence in promoting democracy or anything else when there is a knee-jerk reaction against whatever it does by the mainstream Arab nationalists and Islamists. This response is inevitably based not just on an honest misunderstanding or an independent examination of facts but on the anti-American card's usefulness for stirring up nationalist and religious anger." Rubin, *The Long War for Freedom*, p. 128.
134. Lewis, *op. cit.*, pp. 100–101; Daniel Pipes, *In the Path of God: Islam and Political Power*, New York: Basic Books, 1983, p. 11.
135. On the elements of Arab Islam that are incompatible with democracy see Adam Garfinkle, "Missionary Creep in Egypt," *The American Interest*, July 11, 2013, www.the-american-interest.com/garfinkle/2013/07/11.
136. " . . . the relative success of democracy in Albania, India, Indonesia, Senegal, and Turkey—together home to half a billion Muslims— provides strong evidence against Muslim exceptionalism." Diamond, Plattner, and Grubman, *op. cit.*, p. xix.
137. Pipes, *op. cit.*, p. 92.
138. This is one of the principal themes of *Ibid.*
139. *Ibid.*, p. 304.

140. "What Went Wrong: Bernard Lewis Discusses the Past, Present, and Future of the Middle East," *Princeton Alumni Weekly,* September 11, 2002, www.princeton.edu/paw/archive. He preceded those remarks with the following observation: "The Wahhabi branch of Islam is very fanatical, to the extent of being totally intolerant, very oppressive of women, and so on. Two things happened in the 20th century that gave Wahhabis enormous importance. One of them was that the sheikhs of the House of Saud, who were Wahhabis, and their followers obtained control of the holy places of Islam—Mecca and Medina—which gave them enormous prestige in the Muslim world. And second, probably more important, they controlled the oil wells and the immense resources those gave them."

141. James Mann, *The Obamians: The Struggle Inside the White House to Redefine American Power,* New York: Viking, 2012, p. 159.

142. *Ibid.,* p. 161.

143. Before being elected president Obama said, "The day I raise my hand to take that oath of office as president of the United States, the world will look at us differently . . . " Quoted in Joseph Lelyveld, "Obama: Confessions of the Consultant," *The New York Review of Books,* April 23, 2015, p. 10.

144. On the speech see Mann, *op. cit.,* pp. 143–147.

145. "I have come here to seek a new beginning between the United States and Muslims around the world . . . " "Text: Obama's Cairo Speech," www.nytimes.com/2009/06/04/us/politics/04obama.text.html?.

146. *Ibid.*

147. Mann, *op. cit.,* pp. 83–84.

148. Obama did initiate secret negotiations with the Islamic Republic of Iran over its nuclear program in 2013.

149. Colin Dueck, *The Obama Doctrine: American Grand Strategy Today,* New York, Oxford University Press, 2015, p. 53.

150. "Besides Tunisia, the regimes in Egypt, Yemen, Libya, Syria, Bahrain and Morocco all were roiled by large-scale protests . . . Other countries, Jordan, Iraq, and Saudi Arabia, felt the sting of smaller protests." Migdal, *op. cit.,* p. 330.

151. Demographers call such a cohort a "youth bulge." On the potential of youth bulges for creating instability see Richard Jackson and Neil Howe, *The Graying of the Great Powers: Demography and Geopolitics in the 21st Century,* Washington, DC: Center for Strategic and International Studies, 2008, pp. 141–150. When rebellion broke out in Syria, its "population was perilously young: 50 percent were under 19 years of age, and 57 percent of people under 25 were unemployed." Ajami, *op. cit.,* p. 71.

152. Mann, *op. cit.,* pp. 266–267.

153. " . . . I heard the news of Mubarak's overthrow while discussing the Egyptian situation with senior National Security Council officials.

They appeared delighted by the events in Cairo—high-fives were exchanged—and credited themselves for remaining 'on the right side of history.'" Oren, *Ally*, p. 200.

154. Diamond, Plattner, and Grubman, *op. cit.*, pp. xxiii, xxv.

155. Dueck, *op. cit.*, p. 78.

156. On the Muslim Brotherhood's year in power see Samuel Tadros, "Victory or Death: The Muslim Brotherhood in the Trenches," *Current Trends in Islamist Ideology*, Vol. 15, Washington, DC: The Hudson Institute, Center on Islam, Democracy, and the Future of the Muslim World, August 2, 2013, pp. 5–24, http://www.hudson.org/research/9687-victory-or-death-the-muslim-brotherhood-in-the-trenches.

157. Cook, *op. cit.*, p. 302.

158. *Ibid.*, p. 304. "The Obama Administration . . . somehow managed to persuade the military (and not only the military) that it was pro-Brotherhood, and then to persuade the Brotherhood that it was pro-military. It was neither; it was just trying to avoid being denuded of all influence once the dust settled . . . " Adam Garfinkle, "Our Storyteller in Chief," *The American Interest*, May 13, 2014, www.the-american-interest.com/garfinkle/2014/05/13/our-storyteller-in-chief/

159. Details of Egypt's financial problems are in Steven A. Cook, "Egypt's Solvency Crisis," New York: Council on Foreign Relations, Center for Preventive Action Contingency Planning Memorandum No. 20, April, 2014.

160. Although both officially embraced Islamist principles, the Brotherhood regarded the al-Saud tribe as illegitimate rulers of the Arabian peninsula, making it the Saudi government's mortal enemy.

161. "Obama and Clinton made calls to Bahrain's leaders to express concern, but they also expressed considerably less support for the Bahraini protesters than they had for those in Egypt's Tahrir Square . . . As Bahrain crushed the protests, American appeals for restraint by the police and security forces went unheeded. To go further and push for democracy in Bahrain, the Obama administration would have had to be willing to risk a rupture in the relationship the United States had built up with Saudi Arabia over the previous seven decades." Mann, *op. cit.*, p. 272.

162. The date usually designated as the beginning of the uprising is February 17. Christopher Chivvis, *Toppling Qaddafi: Libya and the Limits of Liberal Intervention*, New York: Cambridge University Press, 2014, p. 25.

163. Freedman, *op. cit.*, pp. 485–486; Baker, *op. cit.*, pp. 620–621.

164. Mann, *op. cit.*, pp. 286–289; Chivvis, *op. cit.*, p. 38.

165. Mann, *op. cit.*, pp. 284–286. The book was *"A Problem from Hell:" America and the Age of Genocide*, New York: Harper Perennial, 2003; first published in 2002.

166. Mann, *op. cit.*, p. 290.

167. In 2005 Doris Kearns Goodwin published a book entitled *Team of Rivals: The Political Genius of Abraham Lincoln* (Simon & Schuster).

168.   Quoted in Chivvis, *op. cit.*, p. 92.

169.   *Ibid.*, p. 93.

170.   At the end of 2014 "Libya has two rival governments, two parliaments, two sets of competing claims to run the central bank and the national oil company, no functioning national police force or army, and an array of militias that terrorise the country's 6m citizens, plunder what remains of the country's wealth, ruin what little is left of its infrastructure, and torture and kill wherever they are in the ascendancy." "The next failed state," *The Economist*, January 10, 2015, p. 10.

171.   Alan J. Kuperman, "A Model Humanitarian Intervention? Reassessing NATO's Libya Campaign," *International Security*, 38:1 (Summer 2013) pp. 128–129; Joshua Hammer, "When the Jihad Came to Mali," *The New York Review of Books,* March 21, 2013.

172.   This is a principal argument of Kuperman, *op. cit.* See especially pp. 108–113. "The government did attempt to intimidate the rebels by promising to be relentless in pursuing them. For example, on February 20, Qaddafi's son Saif al-Islam declared that 'we will fight to the last man and woman and bullet.' Two days later, Qaddafi warned that he would deploy forces to tribal regions to 'sanitize Libya an inch at a time' and 'clear them of these rats,' as he referred to the rebels. This rhetoric, however, never translated into reprisal targeting of civilians." *Ibid.*, p. 112.

173.   *Ibid.*, pp. 116–123. Estimates of the death toll range from 8,000 to 11,500. *Ibid.*, p. 123.

174.   In July 2014 Tripoli became so dangerous that the United States evacuated its diplomatic personnel from the city.

175.   Emile Hokayem, *Syria's Uprising and the Fracturing of the Levant,* London: Routledge for the International Institute for Strategic Studies, 2013, pp. 28, 43. The drought may have been aggravated by human-induced climate change. "With Malthus sending broad smiles in the direction of Syria from his grave, the climate change that has hit the region has wrecked Syria's countryside. Shifts in rain patterns have led to prolonged droughts all around the Middle East in recent years. But their impact was particularly devastating in Syria . . . With water shortages reported in many parts of the country, some rural areas have become impoverished disaster zones. Whole villages and fields have been abandoned, while slums around Syrian cities have been swelling with hundreds of thousands of climate refugees." Aymenn Jawad Al-Tamimi and Oskar Svadkovsky, "Demography Is Destiny in Syria," *The American Spectator*, February 6, 2012, www.meforum.org/3170/syria-demography.

176.   Hokayem, *op. cit.*, p. 39.

177.   Ajami, *op. cit.*, p. 154.

178.   David A. Graham, "Attacking Syria Is the Least Popular Intervention Idea since Kosovo," *The Atlantic*, September 6, 2013.

www.theatlantic.com/politics/archive/2013/09/
attacking-syria-is-the-least-popular-intervention-idea-since-kosovo.

179. The Syrian government did give up some, but not, as far as could be determined, all of its chemical armaments.

180. It also came to be known as simply the Islamic State (IS) and the Islamic State of Iraq and the Levant (ISIL), the term the Obama administration used.

181. See pp. 240–241.

182. Rumania was the one country where violence occurred. The communist dictator, Nicolae Ceausescu, was executed.

183. Ukraine and Russia west of the Ural Mountains are now Eastern Europe.

Chapter 6

1. Geoff Dyer, *Contest of the Century: The New Era of Competition with China—and How America Can Win*, New York: Alfred A. Knopf, 2014, p. 47.

2. "How the west lost Putin," *Financial Times*, February 3, 2015, p. 6.

3. On this general subject see Walter Russell Mead, "The Return of Geopolitics: The Revenge of the Revisionist Powers," *Foreign Affairs* (May/June 2014).

4. Michael Mandelbaum, "Foreign Policy As Social Work," *Foreign Affairs*, 75:1 (January/February 1996), pp. 16–32.

5. On the decline of war see Michael Mandelbaum, "Is Major War Obsolete?" *Survival*, 10:4 (Winter 1998/1999), pp. 20–38.

6. Michael Mandelbaum, *The Case for Goliath: How America Acts as the World's Government in the Twenty-first Century*, New York: PublicAffairs, 2006, chapter 3.

7. On the changes in Russian and Chinese conduct see Gideon Rachman, *Zero-Sum Future: American Power in an Age of Anxiety*, New York: Simon and Schuster, 2011, pp. 233–240.

8. Michael Mandelbaum, *The Road to Global Prosperity*, New York: Simon and Schuster, 2014, pp. xiii-xxi.

9. Mandelbaum, *The Case for Goliath*, chapter 3.

10. Mandelbaum, *The Road to Global Prosperity*, pp. 87, 90–91.

11. Alan Blinder, *After the Music Stopped: The Financial Crisis, the Response, and the World Ahead*, New York: Penguin Press, 2013, p. 29; Mandelbaum, *The Road to Global Prosperity*, pp. 84–86.

12. For an overview of the 2008 financial crisis and its causes see Blinder, *op. cit.*, Part II.

13. See p. 142.

14. Martin Wolf, *The Shifts and the Shocks: What We've Learned—and Have Still to Learn—from the Financial Crisis*, New York: Penguin Press, 2014, pp. xvi, 194–196.

15. On arguably excessive government measures after September 11, 2001, see pp. 153–158. On similarly dubious, or at least unprecedented, measures during the financial crisis see, for example, Blinder, *op. cit.*, p. 136.

16. See pp. 45–49.

17. On international cooperation to limit the damage to the global economy see Daniel Drezner, *The System Worked: How the World Stopped Another Great Depression*, New York: Oxford University Press, 2014, chapter 2.

18. Wolf, *op. cit.*, p. 9.

19. *Ibid.*, p. 4; Mandelbaum, *The Road to Global Prosperity*, pp. 103–108.

20. Blinder, *op. cit.*, p. 35.

21. Wolf, *op. cit.*, p. 125, 136–138.

22. On the impact of the 2008 economic crisis on American global power see Rachman, *op. cit.*, pp. 179–185.

23. "How big the costs of these crises will end up being is still unknowable. But, in the cases of the US and the UK, the fiscal costs are of roughly the same scale as a world war, while the present value of the economic costs could be even greater, since economies often recover more strongly after wars than after financial crises . . ." Wolf, *op. cit.*, p. 325.

24. The post-2008 domestic focus did not, however, include addressing the nation's major long-term problem and chief threat to its capacity, over time, to support trade, investment, and peace around the world: its large fiscal imbalance, the consequence of the soaring costs of medical care in the United States and the large prospective increases in outlays for pensions and health care for the elderly due to the aging of the 75-million-person strong "baby boom" generation born between 1946 and 1964. On these issues see Michael Mandelbaum, *The Frugal Superpower: America's Global Leadership in a Cash-Strapped Era*, New York: PublicAffairs, 2010, chapter 1.

25. For an overview of the euro crisis see Wolf, *op. cit.*, chapter 2, and Mandelbaum, *The Road to Global Prosperity*, pp. 108–118.

26. Wolf, *op. cit.*, pp. 289–291, 309; Mandelbaum, *The Road to Global Prosperity*, pp. 109–110.

27. The Clinton administration discarded the term "rogue state" in favor of "states of concern." The new name did not catch on. Robert S. Litwak, *Regime Change: U.S. Strategy through the Prism of 9/11*, Baltimore: The Johns Hopkins University Press, 2007, p. 213.

28. Mandelbaum, *The Case for Goliath*, p. 41.

29. The array of anti-proliferation institutions also included the Nuclear Suppliers Group and the Missile Technology Control Regime. *Ibid.*, p. 47.

30. Of the two atomic bombs used in combat, the first, which was dropped on the Japanese city of Hiroshima on August 6, 1945, used uranium while the second, which struck another city in Japan, Nagasaki, on August 9 of that year, employed plutonium.

31. This was called the Cooperative Threat Reduction initiative, or the Nunn-Lugar program after Senators Sam Nunn, a Georgia Democrat, and Richard Lugar, an Indiana Republican, who conceived of it and cosponsored the legislation that authorized it. See pp. 65–66.

32. To be sure, the Pakistani nuclear program was scarcely benign from the American point of view. One of its architects, A. Q. Kahn, transferred sensitive technology to several rogue states. American officials worried about the overthrow of the Pakistani government, or its disintegration, giving Islamic terrorists the opportunity to take control of the country's nuclear weapons. See pp. 174–175.

33. "States like these and their terrorist allies constitute an axis of evil, arming to threaten the peace of the world. By seeking weapons of mass destruction, these regimes pose a grave and growing danger. They could provide these arms to terrorists, giving them the means to match their hatred. They could attack our allies or attempt to blackmail the United States." Quoted in Peter Baker, *Days of Fire: Bush and Cheney in the White House*, New York: Doubleday, 2013, p. 186.

34. Litwak, *Regime Change*, pp. 247–249.

35. The reactor had been shut down previously, in 1989, when, it was estimated, enough plutonium to make two bombs could have been withdrawn from it. Robert S. Litwak, *Outlier States: American Strategies to Change, Contain, or Engage Regimes*, Baltimore: The Johns Hopkins University Press, 2012, p. 141.

36. Don Oberdorfer, *The Two Koreas: A Contemporary History*, Reading, Massachusetts: Addison-Wesley, 1997, pp. 305–306.

37. See pp. 90–92.

38. Litwak, *Regime Change*, p. 256.

39. " . . . the Clinton administration, even while pressing ahead for a ballistic-missile deal in 1999–2000, had received sketchy reports of a covert North Korean uranium enrichment program in contravention of the nuclear agreement." *Ibid*, p. 260–261.

40. *Ibid.*, p. 260. The Clinton administration's commitment to protect people oppressed by their governments did not survive contact with the North Korean nuclear program. When Secretary of State Madeleine Albright, who had made the vilification of the (certainly villainous) Serbian leader Slobodan Milosevic the hallmark of her public career, visited Pyongyang in 2000, she complimented the far worse North Korean leader Kim Jong-il, who had succeeded to power upon his father's death in 1994 and whose regime had caused the deaths of many more innocent people than had Milosevic, for his "exceptional hospitality." Quoted in Michael Rubin, *Dancing with the Devil: The Perils of Engaging Rogue Regimes*, New York: Encounter Books, 2014, p. 118.

41. Of such negotiations Vice President Cheney said, "We don't negotiate with evil; we defeat it." Quoted in Litwak, *Regime Change*, p. 246.

42. Rubin, *op. cit.*, p. 120; Baker, *op. cit.*, p. 227.

43. Litwak, *Outlier States*, pp. 145–146.

44. David Sanger, *Confront and Conceal: Obama's Secret Wars and Surprising Use of American Power*, New York: Crown Publishers, 2012, p. 403–404.

45. By one estimate North Korea had sufficient material for six to eight bombs by the end of 2014. "Nuclear Weapons: Who Has What At a Glance," Fact Sheets and Briefs, The Arms Control Association, www.armscontrol.org/factsheets/Nuclearweaponswhohaswhat.

46. Rubin, *op. cit.*, p. 132. South Korea and Japan also furnished aid worth hundreds of millions of dollars.

47. The phrase is from Sanger, *op. cit.*, p. 406. See also Rubin, *op. cit.*, p. 133. The almost invariable failure of negotiations with rogue states is the theme of *Dancing with the Devil*.

48. "General Gary Luck, then [in 1994] commander of U.S. forces in South Korea, warned that [a general war on the Korean peninsula] could result in 1 million casualties and entail economic costs of $1 trillion." Litwak, *Outlier States*, p. 142.

49. Rubin, *op. cit.*, pp. 108–109. By some estimates the North Korean economy contracted by 50 percent during the 1990s. Litwak, *Regime Change*, p. 275.

50. North Korea devoted an estimated one-third of its GDP to military purposes, far more than any other country not actively at war. www.wisegeek.com/what-percent-of-gdp-do-countries-spend-on-military.

51. "Beijing provides what is in effect a massive subsidy as North Korea imports far more from China, possibly as much as $1 billion annually, than it exports to China." Richard N. Haass, "Time to End the North Korean Threat," *The Wall Street Journal*, December 24, 2014, p. A15.

52. Sanger, *op. cit.*, p. 384.

53. " . . . South Korean officials spoke of the need to 'gradually bring the North back to the world community.' This shorthand phrase was a political remedy to their nightmare scenario—the violent implosion of the DPRK, [North Korea] with profound social and economic consequences for the ROK [South Korea]." Litwak, *Regime Change*, pp. 252–253.

54. "South Korean president Roh Moo Hyun . . . visited Washington in May 2003 (a few weeks after the toppling of Saddam) and told the White House that Seoul would not support military action of any kind against Pyongyang." *Ibid.*, pp. 281–282.

55. The American intelligence community estimated that North Korea had a dozen by 2012. Litwak, *Outlier States*, p. 138.

56. Officials of the Bush administration said that the United States would act against such a transfer of nuclear weapons. Litwak, *Regime Change*, pp. 272–273. President Bush himself made a somewhat less categorical statement. Baker, *op. cit.*, p. 493.

57. On these issues, which involve the "operationality" of North Korea's nuclear weapon capacity, see Gregory J. Moore, editor, *North Korea's Nuclear Operationality*, Baltimore: Johns Hopkins University Press, 2014.

58. Ashton B. Carter and William J. Perry, "If Necessary, Strike and Destroy," *The Washington Post*, June 22, 2006.

59. In 2011, Secretary of Defense Robert Gates had told the Chinese leader Hu Jintao that North Korea was no longer simply a regional East Asian problem and was "becoming a direct threat to the United States." Litwak, *Outlier States*, p. 153. On the North Korean threat to South Korea see Robert E. Kelly, "Will South Korea Have to Bomb the North, Eventually?" *The Diplomat*, March 6, 2015, http://thediplomat.com/2015/5/03/will-south-korea-have-to-bomb-the-north-eventually.

60. Matthew Kroenig, *A Time to Attack: The Looming Iranian Nuclear Threat*, New York: Palgrave Macmillan, 2014, pp. 10–12.

61. *Ibid.*, pp. 15–16.

62. Litwak, *Outlier States*, p. 167.

63. Kroenig, *op. cit.*, p. 208.

64. Litwak, *Regime Change*, p. 225.

65. *Ibid.*, pp. 213–214, 215.

66. Michael Doran, "Obama's Secret Iran Strategy," *Mosaic*, February 2, 2015, http:/mosaicmagaine.com/essay/2015/15/02/obamas-secret-iran-strategy.

67. "Thanks to a mix of incompetence, sabotage, and sanctions [Iran's nuclear weapons program] has already taken a decade longer than it should have." Sanger, *op. cit.*, p. 141.

68. Kroenig, *op. cit.*, p. 118.

69. "By the summer of 2013, Iran's oil exports had been slashed by two thirds . . . Iran's currency, the rial, also collapsed, losing roughly half its value." Kroenig, *op. cit.*, p. 76. See also Robert Litwak, "Iran's Nuclear Chess: Calculating America's Moves," Washington, DC: The Woodrow Wilson Center Middle East Program, July, 2014, pp. 44–45 and Sanger, *op. cit.*, p. 148.

70. The Joint Plan of Action is summarized in Litwak, "Iran's Nuclear Chess," p. 31. In July 2015, the United States, along with the other four permanent members of the United Nations Security Council and Germany (the P5+1) arrived at an agreement with the Iranian government on Iran's nuclear program.

71. Kroenig, *op. cit.*, pp. 20–22, 28.

72. The American government also opposed facilities for reprocessing plutonium, another route to the bomb. "When U.S. allies Taiwan and South Korea began reprocessing programs in the late 1970s, the United States threatened to withdraw America's security guarantee if the programs continued and the countries relented. As one Taiwanese scientist said, 'After the Americans got through with us, we wouldn't have been able to teach physics here on Taiwan.'" Matthew Kroenig, "Why Is

Obama Abandoning 70 Years of U.S. Nonproliferation Policy?" *Tablet*, June 15, 2015, www.tabletmag.com/jewish-news-and-politics-191479.

73. See p. 297.

74. Kroenig, *A Time to Attack,* pp. 99–100; Litwak, "Iran's Nuclear Chess," p. 81.

75. Sanger, *op. cit.*, p. 160. The United States Senate expressed tacit, indirect support as well. "In May 2013, by a 99–0 vote, the US Senate passed a resolution declaring that 'the policy of the United States is to prevent Iran from acquiring a nuclear weapon capability and to take such action as may be necessary to implement this policy.'" Kroenig, *A Time to Attack,* p. 108.

76. Michael B. Oren, *Ally: My Journey Across the American-Israeli Divide,* New York: Random House, 2015, p. 187.

77. Kroenig, *A Time to Attack,* pp. 133–134.

78. *Ibid.*, p. 119; Sanger, *op. cit.*, p. 119.

79. Israel was thought to have nuclear-armed submarines, giving it the capacity to retaliate for an Iranian nuclear attack even after suffering an attack itself.

80. Kroenig, *A Time to Attack,* pp. 141–143.

81. In 1980 China's GDP was $202 billion. By 2014 it had grown to over $7 trillion. Nina Hachigian, "Introduction" to Hachigian, editor, *Debating China: U.S.-China Relations in Ten Conversations*, New York: Oxford University Press, 2014, p. xiv.

82. On this set of ideas, widely held among Americans if not always systematically expressed by their leaders, see Michael Mandelbaum, *The Ideas That Conquered the World*, New York: PublicAffairs, 2001, Part III and Michael Mandelbaum, *Democracy's Good Name: The Rise and Risks of the World's Most Popular Form of Government*, New York: PublicAffairs, 2007, chapters 3 and 4.

83. Dyer, *op. cit.*, pp. 150–154.

84. Aaron Friedberg, *A Contest for Supremacy: China, America, and the Struggle for Mastery in Asia*, New York: W. W. Norton, 2011, pp. 134, 142.

85. Dyer, *op. cit.*, p. 6.

86. Barry Naughton, "The Economic Relationship," in Hachigian, editor, *op. cit.*, pp. 23–24.

87. *Ibid.*, p. 24; Dyer, *op. cit.*, p. 264.

88. Naughton, *op. cit.*, pp. 25–26.

89. Robert Sutter, "China and America: The Great Divergence?" *Orbis*, 58:3 (Summer 2014) pp. 360–361.

90. The very large Chinese store of dollars, estimated at one point at more than $2 trillion, made the economic relationship between the United States and China a financial version of the even more uncomfortable but, in the end, relatively stable Cold-War nuclear relationship between the United States and the Soviet Union. Dyer, *op. cit.*, pp. 232–235.

91. "[China] wants to have as little involvement abroad as it can get away with, except for engagements that enhance its image as a great power. It will act abroad when its own interests are at stake, but not for the greater or general good." "What China wants," *The Economist*, August 23, 2014, p. 46.

92. Dyer, *op. cit.*, pp. 244–245.

93. Sutter, *op. cit.*, p. 361.

94. Dyer, *op. cit.*, p. 236.

95. *Ibid.*, p. 12.

96. Michael Mandelbaum, *The Fate of Nations: The Search for National Security in the Nineteenth and Twentieth Centuries*, New York: Cambridge University Press, 1988, pp. 243–248.

97. The four modernizations were first set forth in 1963 by Prime Minister Zhou Enlai but Deng made them central to the Communist Party's program in 1978. The fourth modernization was science and technology.

98. "Even adjusting for inflation, official Chinese military spending has risen by about 11% per year for the last two decades. I believe, as do most analysts outside of China, that the official budget figures are incomplete. Detailed non-governmental analysis suggests that true spending is 40 to 70% higher than China's official figures." Christopher P. Twomey, "Military Developments," in Hachigian, editor, *op. cit.*, p. 153.

99. The far-flung voyages of China's "treasure fleet" in that century were brought to an end by a decision of the Ming court and never resumed. Dyer, *op. cit.*, pp. 75–76.

100. Relations between Taiwan and the mainland, in fact, improved during the latter stages of the post-Cold War period, due to the election in 2008 of a Taiwanese president, Ma Ying-jeou, friendlier to the communist regime than his predecessor. Ma was reelected in 2012.

101. Twomey, *op. cit.*, p. 156. The Chinese were, perhaps not surprisingly, sensitive about American military operations near their borders. On March 31, 2001, an American reconnaissance plane collided with a Chinese aircraft, presumably as a result of an error by the Chinese pilot, and had to make an emergency landing on Hainan Island. After some diplomatic exchanges about the Chinese demand for an American statement of apology the crew was allowed to return to the United States. Baker, *op. cit.*, pp. 99–100. See p. 198.

102. Robert D. Kaplan, *Asia's Cauldron: The South China Sea and the End of a Stable Pacific*, New York: Random House, 2014, p. 10.

103. In response to complaints from Southeast Asian countries in 2010 about his country's international conduct, the Chinese foreign minister Yang Jiechi said, "China is a big country and other countries are small countries and that is just a fact." Twomey, *op. cit.*, p. 168.

104. Dyer, *op. cit.*, pp. 27–29.

105. Ian Johnson, "The China Challenge," *The New York Review of Books*, May 8, 2014, p. 34.
106. Arthur Waldron, "China's 'Peaceful Rise' Enters Turbulence," *Orbis*, Spring, 2014, p. 165.
107. On other such incidents involving Chinese naval power see Sanger, *op. cit.*, p. 392, Waldron, *op. cit.*, p. 177, and Dyer, *op. cit.*, p. 91.
108. "At the double," *The Economist*, March 15, 2014, p. 42.
109. Dyer, *op. cit.*, pp. 84–85.
110. "The centenary delusion," *The Economist*, January 3, 2015, p. 30.
111. David Pilling, "China is stealing a strategic march on Washington," *Financial Times*, May 29, 2014, p. 9.
112. Dyer, *op. cit.*, pp. 117–119.
113. The commander-in-chief of the Indonesian armed forces wrote in *The Wall Street Journal*, in an article generally critical of China, that "Indonesia certainly does not wish to see the evolution of an American policy that gives China reason to suspect the surreptitious creation of a coalition of countries aimed at encircling it militarily." Moeldoko, "China's Dismaying New Claims in the South China Sea," *The Wall Street Journal*, April 25, 2014, p. A13.
114. According to Australian Prime Minister Kevin Rudd, "the goal should be to integrate China into the international community 'while also preparing to deploy force if everything goes wrong.'" Dyer, *op. cit.*, p. 100.
115. See Mandelbaum, *The Road to Global Prosperity*, pp. 156–168.
116. ". . . the optimistic scenario of a peaceful China, closely cooperating with the United States, which has sustained Washington since the 1970s, looks effectively to be dead." Waldron, *op. cit.*, p. 178.
117. See pp. 18–23.
118. See pp. 56–60.
119. "In 1998 a barrel of oil sold for $15. By 2000 the price had climbed to $32, and after three years of stability it began, in 2004, a very steep ascent, exceeding $100 by . . . 2008 and reaching a peak of almost $150 per barrel in August of that year." Mandelbaum, *The Road to Global Prosperity*, pp. 140–141.
120. Quoted in Angela Stent, *The Limits of Partnership: U.S.-Russian Relations in the Twenty-first Century*, Princeton, New Jersey: Princeton University Press, 2014, p. 62.
121. The decision in favor of such an expansion was made in 2002. Bulgaria, Romania, Slovakia, and Slovenia also joined.
122. Early in his presidency Putin expressed interest in Russia's joining NATO, an interest that the Bush administration, like its predecessor, did not reciprocate. Stent, *op. cit.*, pp. 75–76.
123. Of Ukraine Putin said, "We have common traditions, common mentality, common history, common culture. We . . . are one people."

Quoted in "Playing East against West," *The Economist*, November 23, 2013, p. 57.

124. Rajan Menon and Eugene Rumer, *Conflict in Ukraine: The Unwinding of the Post-Cold War Order*, Cambridge, Massachusetts: MIT Press, 2015, p. 1.

125. Putin himself made seven trips to Ukraine to support Yanukovich. Stent, *op. cit.*, p. 113.

126. The Russians called the defining feature of the Putin-era political system the "vertical of power." Fiona Hill and Clifford Gaddy, *Mr. Putin: Operative in the Kremlin*, Washington, DC: Brookings Institution Press, 2013, p. 232.

127. The Putin regime called it "sovereign democracy." Stent, *op. cit.*, pp. 142–143.

128. This is the subject of Karen Dawisha, *Putin's Kleptocracy: Who Owns Russia?* New York: Simon and Schuster, 2014.

129. "Russia in Putin's years experienced a massive windfall in petrodollars: $33.5 billion more per year on average in 2001–2004 than it did in 1999; $223.6 billion more per year in 2005–2008; and $394.0 billion more per year in 2011–13." Vladislav Inozemtsev, "The Ruble's Wild Ride," *The American Interest*, December 19, 2014, www.the-american-interest.com/2014/12/19/the-rubles-wild-ride.

130. Dawisha, *op. cit.*, p. 1.

131. On petrostates see Terry Lynn Karl, *The Paradox of Plenty: Oil Booms and Petrostates*, Berkeley, California: University of California Press, 1997 and Michael Ross, *The Oil Curse: How Petroleum Wealth Shapes the Development of States*, Princeton, New Jersey: Princeton University Press, 2013.

132. The political and economic dominance of networks of patrons and clients made Russia what political scientists call a "neopatrimonial" state. Francis Fukuyama, *Political Order and Political Decay: From the Industrial Revolution to the Globalization of Democracy*, New York: Farrar, Straus, and Giroux, 2014, pp. 287–289.

133. Stent, *op. cit.*, p. 161. See also chapter 3, p. 122.

134. Quoted in Menon and Rumer, *op. cit.*, p. 118.

135. Ukrainians themselves were divided over the desirability of belonging to NATO. *Ibid.*, p. 152.

136. *Ibid.*, p. 72.

137. Quoted in Stent, *op. cit.*, p. 147.

138. He had studied in the United States, and the Russians saw him as being close to the Americans.

139. "In September 2009 the European Union issued a three-volume, fifteen-hundred-page report, *Independent International Fact-Finding Mission on the Conflict in Georgia*. It apportioned blame for the conflict equally to both sides." Stent, *op. cit.*, p. 172.

140.   " . . . Russia was very badly affected by the 2008 global financial crisis. Oil prices fell to $35 per barrel in six months, the stock market suffered a 75 percent fall in value over the same period, and its hard currency reserve fell from $600 billion to less than $400 billion. Growth rates fell from 7 percent to 2–3 percent in one year. Unemployment rose to 9 percent . . ." *Ibid.*, p. 183.

141.   "According to IHS Jane's Russia's defence spending has nearly doubled in nominal terms since 2007. This year alone it will rise by 18.4%." "Putin's new model army," *The Economist*, May 24, 2014, p. 47.

142.   These events are described in Menon and Rumer, *op. cit.*, pp. 53–81.

143.   In the words of German Chancellor Angela Merkel in November, 2014: "We are suddenly confronted with a conflict that goes, so to speak, to the core of our values. Old thinking in terms of spheres of influence, in which international law is trampled upon, cannot be allowed to assert itself." Quoted in Gregory L. White and Anton Troianovski, "Putin's Year of Defiance, Miscalculation," *The Wall Street Journal*, December 18, 2014, p. A16.

144.   "The end of the line," *The Economist*, November 23, 2014.

145.   Menon and Rumer, *op. cit.*, pp. 65–67.

146.   *Ibid.*, p. 122.

147.   *Ibid.*, pp. 82, 84; Dawisha, *op. cit.*, p. *318*.

148.   Menon and Rumer, *op. cit.*, p. 118.

149.   In December 2014, Putin said, "The issue is not Crimea. We are protecting our sovereignty and our right to exist." Quoted in Ambrose Evans-Pritchard, "The week the dam broke in Russia and ended Putin's dreams," *The Daily Telegraph* (London), December 20, 2014, www.telegraph.co.uk/finance/economics/11305146/ The-week-the-dam-broke-in-russia-and-ended-putins-dreams.

150.   Menon and Rumer, *op. cit.*, pp. 133–134.

151.   *Ibid.*, p. 25.

152.   See Richard Milne, "Frontline Latvia starts to feel heat as Putin probes resolve of Baltic states," *Financial Times*, October 9, 2014, p. 7, and Richard Milne and Neil Buckley, "Tensions on the frontier," *Financial Times*, October 21, 2014, p. 8.

Conclusion

1.   "Obama, and those closest to him, believed that his voice, his (non-white) face, his story, could help usher the people of the world to a higher plane." James Traub, "When Did Obama Give Up: Reading Between the Lines?" *Foreign Policy*, February 26, 2015, http:// foreignpolicy.com/2015/02/26/when-did-obama-give-up-speeches/.

2.   This is a major theme of Michael Mandelbaum, *The Ideas That Conquered the World: Peace, Democracy and Free Markets in the Twenty-first Century*, New York: PublicAffairs, 2002.

3. Francis Fukuyama, *Political Order and Political Decay: From the Industrial Revolution to the Globalization of Democracy*, New York: Farrar, Straus, and Giroux, 2014, p. 399.

4. "A Conversation with Secretary of State Hillary Rodham Clinton," The Council on Foreign Relations, September 8, 2010, http://www.cfr.org/world/conversation-us-secretary-state-hillary-rodham-clinton/p34808.

5. See Michael Mandelbaum, *Democracy's Good Name: The Rise and Risks of the World's Most Popular Form of Government*, New York: PublicAffairs, 2007, chapter 4 and pp. 190–218.

6. This is the major theme of Francis Fukuyama, *The Origins of Political Order: From Prehuman Times to the French Revolution*, New York: Farrar, Straus, and Giroux, 2011.

7. Perhaps the most common feature on the road to Denmark is war, a practice that, whatever its contribution to consolidating modern institutions, invariably comes with costs, sometimes very steep ones. *Ibid.*, p. 330.

8. Modern Japan, which acquired a modern state in the final decades of the nineteenth century during the Meiji Restoration, is the exception to this rule; but by that time the Japanese had long since formed a cohesive nation.

9. Comparisons between Britain in the earlier period and the United States in the later one are a major theme of Niall Ferguson, *Colossus: The Price of America's Empire*, New York: Penguin Press, 2004; see especially pp. 9–10, 14–15, 25–26, and 222–226. See also "Manifest destiny warmed up?" *The Economist*, September 16, 2003.

10. John Darwin, *Unfinished Empire: The Global Expansion of Britain*, New York: Bloomsbury Press, 2012, pp. xi, 20, 389.

11. Fukuyama, *Political Development and Political Decay*, pp. 299–308.

12. India did experience a 21-month period of undemocratic governance, a period known as "the Emergency," between 1975 and 1977.

13. The term was coined by the political scientist Joseph Nye in *Bound to Lead: The Changing Nature of American Power*, New York: HarperCollins, 1990. See also Nye, *Soft Power: The Means to Success in World Politics*, New York: PublicAffairs, 2004.

14. "Through the larger part of recorded history the main drive wheel of historical change was contacts among strangers, causing men on both sides of such encounters to reconsider and in some cases alter their familiar ways of behaving." William McNeill, *The Shape of European History*, New York: Oxford University Press, 1974, pp. 42–43.

15. Mandelbaum, *The Ideas*, chapter 2.

16. In the film Allen explains the meaning of the joke for him in this way: "Well, that's essentially how I feel about life. Full of misery, loneliness, and suffering and unhappiness—and it's all over much too quickly."

17. This is a theme of Michael Mandelbaum, *The Case for Goliath: How America Acts as the World's Government in the Twenty-first Century*, New York: PublicAffairs, 2006.

18. See pp. 331–332.

19. One of the new NATO members, Hungary, became less democratic despite its membership. See "Orban the Unstoppable," *The Economist*, September 27, 2014, and Rick Lyman and Alison Smale, "Defying Soviets, Then Pulling Hungary to Putin," *The New York Times*, November 8, 2014.

20. "If Russia had been embraced as part of Europe immediately after the collapse of the Soviet Union, NATO might have expanded to include Russia, a prospect that Putin saw as a distinct possibility back in 2000. All the conflicts that have occurred in Eastern Europe since then have been the result of the fateful decision to exclude Russia from the European alliance system and set up a separate track for dealing with Russia, instead of bringing her into the consultative process. Had Russia been included as part of Europe, the entire political and cultural conflict in Ukraine would also have been avoided, since there would be no 'civilizational choice' to make." Nicolai Petro, "How We Won the Cold War, but Lost the Peace," *National Interest*, September 4, 2014, http:// nationalinterest.org/feature/how-we-won-the-cold-war-but-lost-the-peace.

21. "President Bill Clinton supported NATO's bombing of Serbia without U.N. Security Council approval and the expansion of NATO to include former Warsaw Pact countries. Those moves seemed to violate the understanding that the United States would not take advantage of the Soviet retreat from Eastern Europe. In 1991, polls indicated that about 80 percent of Russians had a favorable view of the United States. In 1999 nearly the same percentage had an unfavorable view." Jack F. Matlock Jr., "Who won the Cold War? And who will win now?" *The Washington Post*, March 16, 2014, p. B4.

22. Besides Russia and China, in 2014 the other members were Central Asian countries that had been part of the Soviet Union: Kazakhstan, Kyrgyzstan, Tajikistan, and Uzbekistan.

23. "They [Russians] are not much interested in Syria, certainly not in the dismal humanitarian situation. But a major defeat of the rebels [against Assad] is seen as a sweet victory over the west. You can hear them now: 'Do you still think we are not important?'" Andrei Nekrasov, "Russia's motives in Syria are not all geopolitical," *Financial Times*, June 19, 2013, p. 9.

INDEX

———

Abbas, Mahmoud, 280–81, 282,
  283, 440*n*91
Abizaid, John, 226, 426*n*167
ABM (Anti-Ballistic Missile) Treaty
  of 1972, 329, 355, 380
Abu Ghraib prison, 213, 423*n*117
Adams, John, 153
Afghanistan, 158–84. *See also* Taliban
  anti-foreign sentiment in, 411*n*137
  Bush (G.W.) administration policies
    on, 8, 161–62, 164, 166–71
  corruption in, 169–70
  counterinsurgency efforts in,
    179–81, 184
  democratic transformation
    initiatives in, 163, 164
  demographic characteristics
    of, 158–59
  elections in, 163, 179
  financial assistance for, 166, 170,
    411*n*138
  foreign policy failures in, 10, 165–66,
    168, 371
  geographical location of, 158
  humanitarian interventions in, 166

kinship networks in, 159, 168
military operations in, 12, 161–62,
  164, 408*n*91
nation-building efforts in,
  178, 181–82
Obama administration policies on,
  177–82, 183–84, 413*n*182
Pakistan and, 172, 173–75, 411*n*145,
  412*n*152
public support for war in, 414*n*192
resistance to modernization,
  410*nn*129–30
restoration of stability in,
  409–10*n*118
Soviet occupation of, 159–60
state-building efforts in, 12, 165–71,
  410*n*123
Taliban in, 160–62, 165–66, 171, 181,
  413*n*164
violence in, 165
women in, 161, 410*n*127
Africa. *See specific countries*
Agreed Framework, 330–31
Ahtisaari, Martti, 121, 399*n*129
Aidid, Mohammed Farah, 88–89

MFN (Most Favored Nation) status,
    21, 22, 23, 26
Middle East, 245–310. *See also*
    Arab Spring; Arab-Israeli
    conflict; peace process; *specific
    countries*
  Bush (G.W.) administration
    policies on, 245, 287–92, 295
  Carter administration policies
    on, 255
  Cold War policy on, 247–49
  containment initiatives in,
    248, 432n8
  democratic transformation
    initiatives in, 163, 164, 207–8,
    246, 287–94
  economies of, 293
  European governance of,
    246–47
  importance of, 245
  kinship networks in, 159,
    168, 292–93
  nuclear proliferation in, 342
  Obama administration policies
    on, 295–97
  oil, influence on foreign policy of,
    4, 225, 247–48
Middle East Free Trade
    Area, 288
Middle East Partnership
    Initiative, 288
Milosevic, Slobodan
  Albright on, 113, 114, 397n86
  in Bosnian war negotiations, 108
  death of, 399n123
  indictment for crimes against
    humanity of, 399n123
  in Kosovo negotiations, 115, 117, 121,
    399n129
  rise to power by, 95, 111–12
  support for, 119, 399n118
Missile Technology Control
    Regime, 448n29
mission creep, 77, 88, 126

missionaries, 9, 19, 26
Mitchell, George, 283
Mogadishu, Battle of (1993), 89, 91,
    125, 403n19
money
  cross-border flow of, 45
  currencies, conditions necessary
    for successful functioning
    of, 324
  in market economies, 44–45,
    386–87nn53–54
moral hazard, 58, 124, 387n55
Morris, Dick, 85
Morsi, Mohammed, 299–300
Most Favored Nation (MFN) status,
    21, 22, 23, 26
Mubarak, Hosni, 288, 289, 290, 299,
    434–35n30
Mueller, John, 149, 393n17
mukhabarat states, 293
Mullen, Mike, 174, 179
Muskie, Edmund, 385n23
Muslim Brotherhood, 262, 277, 290,
    299–300, 445n160
Muslims. *See also* Arab Muslims; Shia
    Muslims; Sunni Muslims
  in Bosnia, 96–97, 99–106, 107–8,
    109, 129
  in Kosovo, 111–12, 117
mutual assured destruction
    (MAD), 342

NAFTA (North American Free Trade
    Agreement), 41–43, 47
Najibullah (Afghan ruler), 160
Nakba Day, 270
Nasrallah, Hassan, 276–77, 439n76
Nasser, Gamal Abdel, 248, 253,
    254, 433n19
National Counterterrorism
    Center, 147
National Security Agency (NSA),
    156–57, 406n71
national self-determination, 97, 98